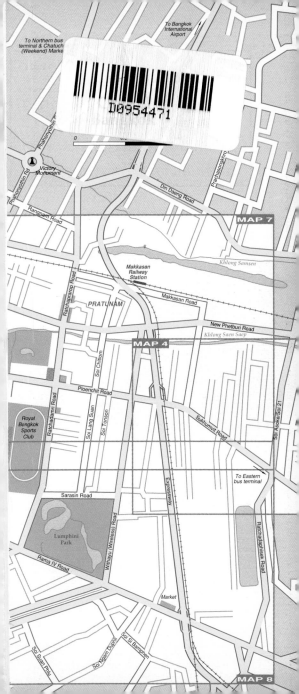

To Northern bus
terminal & Chatuch
(Weekend) Marke

To Bangkok
International
Airport

D0954471

0

Phahonyothin Rd

Victory
Monument

Rangnam Road

Din Daeng Road

Prachasongkhro

MAP 7

Ratchaprarop Road

Khlong Samsen

Makkasan
Railway
Station

PRATUNAM

Makkasan Road

New Phetburi Road

MAP 4

Khlong Saen Saep

Soi Chitlom

Ploenchit Road

Ratchadamri Road

Soi Lang Suan

Soi Tonson

Sukhumvit Road

Soi Asoke/Soi 21

Royal
Bangkok
Sports
Club

To Eastern
bus terminal

Sarasin Road

Expressway

Lumphini
Park

Withayu (Wireless) Road

Ratchadaphisek Road

Rama IV Road

Market

Soi Suan Phlu

Soi Ngam Duphli

Soi Si Bamphen

MAP 8

Bangkok

a Lonely Planet
city guide

Joe Cummings

Bangkok
3rd edition

Published by
Lonely Planet Publications
Head Office: PO Box 617, Hawthorn, Vic 3122, Australia
Branches: 155 Filbert St, Suite 251, Oakland, CA 94607, USA
10 Barley Mow Passage, Chiswick,
London W4 4PH, UK
71 bis rue du Cardinal Lemoine, 75005 Paris, France

Printed by
SNP Printing Pte Ltd, Singapore

Photographs by
Glenn Beanland, Michael Clark, Sara-Jane Cleland, Joe Cummings,
Paul Beinssen, Richard I'Anson, Mark Kirby, Bernard Napthine,
Richard Nebesky, Joanna O'Brien, Tom Smallman, Tourist Authority of
Thailand (TAT), Paul Wentford.

Front cover: Wat Arun (The Temple of Dawn)
(G.V. Faint, The Image Bank)

First Published
September 1992

This Edition
September 1997

**Although the authors and publisher have tried to make
the information as accurate as possible, they accept no
responsibility for any loss, injury or inconvenience sus-
tained by any person using this book.**

National Library of Australia Cataloguing in Publication Data

Cummings, Joe
Bangkok.

3rd. ed.
Includes index.
ISBN 0 86442 406 X.

1. Bangkok (Thailand) – Guide-books. I. Title.

915.93

text & maps © Lonely Planet 1997
photos © photographers as indicated 1997

Joe Cummings

Joe has travelled extensively in Thailand for over 20 years. Before his travel writing became a full-time job, Joe was a Peace Corps volunteer in Thailand, an extra in the Indochina War film *The Deer Hunter*, a translator/interpreter of Thai, a graduate in Thai language and Asian art history at the University of California at Berkeley, a columnist for *The Asia Record*, an East-West Center Scholar in Hawaii, a university lecturer in Malaysia and a bilingual studies consultant in the USA and Taiwan.

Able to speak, read and write Thai fluently, Joe has travelled through all 76 of the kingdom's provinces. Joe is also the author of Lonely Planet's *Thai phrasebook* and guides to *Bangkok*, *Laos* and *Myanmar*, and a contributor to LP guides to *South-East Asia*, *China*, *Malaysia*, *Singapore & Brunei* and *Indonesia*. He occasionally writes for *Geographical*, *World & I*, *Outside*, *Worldview*, *Earth Journal*, *BBC Holidays*, *The Independent*, *Bangkok Post*, *The Nation*, *Sawasdee*, *Asia Magazine* and other periodicals.

From the Author

Thanks very much to Nicole Altclass, Jennifer Bartlett, Lynne Cummings, John Demodena, Rachel Foord, Sarah Lynch and Phra Sujato for logistical and moral support.

Author's Note to Readers

When using the information contained in this guide to find your way around Thailand, keep in mind the Buddhist concept of *anicca*, or 'impermanence'. All things in the world, especially the world of travel, are in a constant state of flux and Thailand is no exception. What you read here are conceptual snapshots of single moments in time, filtered through one person's perceptions. They represent the very best of my research efforts at the time of writing, but were bound to change the second I turned my attention away from research and began writing it all down, a necessary part of the process in getting this book to you. Don't expect to find things to be exactly as described in the text – stay flexible and you'll enjoy yourself more.

From the Publisher

This 3rd edition of *Bangkok* was edited in LP's Melbourne office by Emma Miller and Greg Alford. Verity Campbell took care of the design and layout, and Bethune Carmichael did the proofing and editorial layout. Maps were drawn and coordinated by Paul Piaia, Dan Levin designed the special Thai fonts and made sure the script behaved properly, and Adam McCrow designed the cover.

Thanks to all the travellers who took the time to write to us about their experiences. They were:

Donna Acord, Roger Bayliss, Markus Borner, G Breels, J Bregman, Kate Gibbs, Jean & Tony Gimmell, L Hurley, Julia Keller, Heikki Lehikoinen, Teresa Johnson, Dean Moore, John P O'Sullivan, Karen Oushman, Josep M Suelves, L Thus.

Warning & Request

Things change – prices go up, schedules change, good places go bad and bad places go bankrupt – nothing stays the same. So, if you find things better or worse, recently opened or long since closed, please tell us and help make the next edition even more accurate and useful.

We value all of the feedback we receive from travellers. Julie Young coordinates a small team who read and acknowledge every letter, postcard and email, and ensure that every morsel of information finds its way to the appropriate authors, editors and publishers.

Everyone who writes to us will find their name in the next edition of the appropriate guide and will also receive a free subscription to our quarterly newsletter, *Planet Talk*. The very best contributions will be rewarded with a free Lonely Planet guide.

Excerpts from your correspondence may appear in updates (which we add to the end pages of reprints); new editions of this guide; in our newsletter, *Planet Talk*; or in the Postcards section of our Web site – so please let us know if you don't want your letter published or your name acknowledged.

Contents

Introduction

Bangkok – the name explodes with images of the quint-essential steamy Asian metropolis. While squeaky clean Singapore has become the Switzerland of Asia and Hong Kong has begun its new life under the socialist bureau-cracy of China, Bangkok remains one of South-East Asia's most intriguing and perpetually surprising desti-nations. The booming economy has brought air-conditioned shopping malls and many other accou-trements of civilisation, yet the city is as far from being 'tamed' by international ideas and technology as when it was founded over 200 years ago.

Although the city is incredibly urbanised, beneath its modern veneer lies an uncompromised Thai-ness. Glass-and-steel buildings shaped like cartoon robots stand next to glittering temple spires; wreaths of jasmine dangle from the rear-view mirrors of buses and taxis; shaven-headed, orange-robed monks walk barefoot along the street beneath a bank of television screens carrying synchronised images of the latest world dance craze.

At times Bangkok seems like it's hurtling toward disaster. The city is reportedly sinking at a rate of 90 cm per year as wells suck the water table dry beneath the spongy Chao Phraya flood plains upon which the city was laid out in the 18th century. During the dry season, a thick traffic-induced haze fills busy intersections – in a city where an estimated 400 new vehicles are registered every day. Over 10% of Thailand's population lives in the capital and every bus from the provinces brings in yet more fortune-seekers.

Maddening? Definitely. But the amazing thing is how well the city works. Public transport may be excruciat-ingly slow at times, but it is plentiful; try flagging a taxi on the street anywhere else in Asia at 3 am. You can buy a bowl of mouth-watering noodles from a street vendor while standing outside a US$200-a-night hotel; or have your muscles gently kneaded for an hour and a half at the oldest temple in the city for less than the price of a cinema ticket in most Western capitals. Hitch a ride aboard a canal taxi on the Thonburi side and you can disappear down shaded waterways where modern Bangkok is soon left behind. Unlike many cities, the longer you stay in Bangkok, the more exotic it seems to become.

Facts about Bangkok

HISTORY

Before it became the capital of Thailand in 1782, the settlement known as Bang Makok, meaning 'Place of Olives' (not the European variety), was only a very small part of what is today called Bangkok by foreigners. Bang Makok was, in fact, only an outlying district of Thonburi Si Mahasamut (now Thonburi) on the east bank of the Chao Phraya River.

Thonburi was founded on the west bank by a group of wealthy Thais during the reign of King Chakkaphat (1548-68). It became an important trading city during the 17th and 18th centuries, when Siam's capital was in Ayuthaya to the north. Constantine Phaulkon, a Greek minister to Ayuthaya's King Narai, convinced the monarch to build a fortress on the banks of the Chao Phraya at the mouth of the Bangkok Yai Canal; a great iron chain was suspended across the river from the fortress to guard against the entry of unauthorised ships.

Following the Burmese defeat of Ayuthaya in 1765, the Thai general Phaya Taksin made himself king in 1769 and established a new capital at Thonburi. Taksin eventually came to regard himself as the next Buddha, but his ministers, who did not approve of his religious fantasies, deposed and then executed him in the custom reserved for royalty – by beating him to death in a velvet sack so that no royal blood touched the ground.

Chao Phraya Chakri replaced Taksin and, as King Rama I, became the first king of the Chakri dynasty (the current monarch, King Bhumibol, is the ninth). In 1782 Rama I moved the capital to the Bangkok district on the east bank of the river, believing the area to be more easily defended against naval attack.

The site chosen for the new royal palace and government buildings was occupied by a Chinese settlement; the Chinese were relocated to the Sampeng district, Bangkok's Chinatown today. Using thousands of Khmer prisoners of war, Chakri built 10 km of city walls and expanded Bangkok's canal system to create a royal 'island' – Ko Ratanakosin. Sections of the 4.5-metre-thick walls are still standing in the area of Wat Saket and the Golden Mount, and water still flows, albeit sluggishly, around the canals of the original royal district.

Artisans from Ayuthaya contributed several new temples to the city. Upon completion of the new capital in 1785, at a three day consecration ceremony the city was given a new name:

Krungthep mahanakhon bowon rattanakosin mahintara ayuthaya mahadilok popnopparat ratchathani buriromudomratchaniwet mahasathan-amonpiman-avatansathirsakkathatitya-visnukamprasit

Quite a tongue-twister. Fortunately, it is shortened to Krung Thep, meaning 'City of Angels', in everyday usage. The name Bangkok persisted among foreign traders, the capital of Thailand is still known by its old name to most outside the kingdom.

Temple construction remained the highlight of most early development in Bangkok through the reign of Rama III. Until King Mongkut's rule (Rama IV, 1851-68), Bangkok residents made their way around the city via the vast river and canal system established under the first three kings of the Chakri dynasty. These waterways were supplemented by a network of meagre footpaths. Responding to appeals from foreign residents for a road system on which they could stroll and employ horsedrawn carriages, an 1861 royal decree initiated the construction of the 10 km, cobbled Charoen Krung Rd (also known as 'New Rd') from Wat Pho along the river to Thanon Tok, a project that took four years to complete.

In 1863 two more roads, Bamrung Meuang and Feuang Nakhon, were built to provide access to royal temples in the Ko Ratanakosin area. Rama V (1868-1910) ordered the construction of Ratchadamnoen Klang (Royal Walk) Rd to link the Grand Palace with the growing city centre. Horse-drawn carriage and rickshaw (called *rót chék*, or 'Chinese vehicle') became the main road conveyances through the end of the 19th century.

After motorised transport arrived in the early 20th century, roadways connecting these original four streets were steadily added as the city expanded in all directions. When Thailand established a constitutional government in 1932, Bangkok became the nerve centre of a vast civil service, which, coupled with its growing success as a world port, transformed the city into a mecca for Thais seeking economic opportunity and contemporary culture. Following a period of stagnancy during WWII, when the Japanese briefly occupied parts of the city, Bangkok quickened its pace toward 20th-century development. Bridges were built over the Chao Phraya River, canals were filled in to provide space for new roads, and multistorey buildings began crowding out traditional teak structures.

During the 1962-75 Indochina War, Bangkok (along with nearby Pattaya Beach) gained notoriety as a 'rest and recreation' (R&R) spot for foreign troops stationed in South-East Asia. Although the troops are long gone, the city's promiscuous image lingers on in the massage parlours, coffee shops and nightclubs sprinkled throughout the capital. Except for a couple of highly visible strips that cater to Westerners, the vast majority of such places are operated by and for Thai nationals.

Since the recent opening up of Vietnam, Cambodia, Laos and Myanmar to foreign investment, Bangkok has become the financial hub for mainland South-East Asia. Although today it's a city groaning under the weight of an overtaxed infrastructure, Bangkok continues to lure rural and working-class Thais, Asian and Western investors, and curious visitors from around the world with its a phantasmagoric blend of the carnal, spiritual and entrepreneurial.

CLIMATE

Rainfall

Bangkok and central Thailand are well within tropical latitudes, and experience a dry and wet monsoon climate, in which periods of dry weather alternate with periods of wet. The south-west monsoon arrives between May and July and lasts into October. This is followed by a dry period from November to May, a period that begins with lower relative temperatures until mid-February (because of the influences of the north-east monsoon, which bypasses this part of Thailand, but results in cool breezes), followed by much higher relative temperatures from March to May.

According to the official Thai agricultural calendar, the rains begin in July; however, the arrival of the monsoon can vary from one year to the next. Occasional rains in the dry season are known as 'mango showers'. In Bangkok it usually rains most during August and September, though there may be floods in October since the ground has reached full saturation by then. If you are in Bangkok in early October, don't be surprised to find yourself in hip-deep water in certain parts of the city. In 1983, when the floods were reputed to be the worst in 30 years, it was that deep in every part of the city! An umbrella is a very useful accessory during the rainy season; because of the heat, a raincoat usually causes more discomfort than it prevents.

Temperatures

During the cool/dry season (November to February), night-time temperatures may dip as low as 12°C, with normal daytime temperatures averaging around 28°C. During the rainy months (June to October), the temperature averages 32°C in the daytime, and 26°C to 28°C at night. Add four or five degrees to the latter temperatures for the hot season (March to May) average.

As the city climate is very humid for most of the year, perceived temperatures are often higher than what the thermometer reads; 34°C may feel more like 39°C. During the hot season the humidity is compounded by air pollution – the high level of particulate keeps the moisture in the air from evaporating. The lowest humidity occurs between November and May, especially when the occasional upland breeze arrives from the Khorat Plateau to the north-east and pushes back the humid delta air.

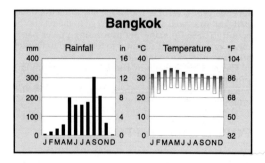

GOVERNMENT & POLITICS

The Bangkok Metropolitan Authority administers the capital, and the city boasts the only elected governorship in the nation (provincial governors are appointed). In the most recent election (June 1996) 29 candidates were fielded. The winner was 50-year-old Bhichit Rattakul, an academic with a PhD in industrial microbiology.

Nationally, September 1996 saw the collapse of a seven-part coalition government led by the Chart Thai (Thai Nationality) Party and headed by Banham Silapa-archa, a 63 year old billionaire who the Thai press called a 'walking ATM (automatic teller machine)'. Banharn wasn't very popular with the Thai media, who immediately attacked his tendency to appoint from a pool of rural politicians known to be heavily involved in money politics. His government fell apart amidst a spate of corruption scandals and a crisis of confidence, and the national election held two months later was marked by electoral violence and accusations of vote buying. Former deputy prime minister as well as armed forces chief, Chavalit Yongchaiyudh, of the New Aspiration Party, secured the premiership with a dubious mix of coalition partners.

ECONOMY

Although only about 10% of the national population resides in Bangkok, roughly 60% of the country's wealth is concentrated here. Banking, finance, wholesale and retail trade, transportation, tourism and energy dominate the immediate municipality, while the surrounding metropolitan area adds manufacturing, shipping, food processing and intensive farming to the list of top revenue producers. Per capita income in metropolitan Bangkok runs well above the average in the rest of the country (US$6870 using the purchasing power parity measure), although it's second to that found in Phuket, an island province in the south.

The minimum wage in Bangkok and surrounding provinces is 145B (US$5.80) per day; it can be as low as 95B a day in the outer provinces. Current inflation runs around 7.5% per annum.

POPULATION & PEOPLE

Official estimates place Metropolitan Bangkok's population at 6.5 million, though some sources claim this figure may be as much as a million short. The city's population density averages an astonishing 3600 persons per sq km.

The majority of the city's inhabitants are ethnic Thais, ie they were born of Thai parentage and speak Thai as their first language. Up to 25% of the city's population may be of Chinese or mixed Thai and Chinese descent. The Chinese influence is strong throughout central Thailand's Chao Phraya Delta and Bangkok is no exception; even the Bangkok dialect shows Chinese influence in the common substitution of 'l' for 'r' in spoken Thai, even among non-Chinese. Many Bangkok Chinese-Thais speak both Thai and a Chinese dialect, such as Cantonese, Hokkien or Chiu Chau (Chao Zhou). Bangkok's second largest Asian minority is of Indian descent.

Bangkok Primacy
Bangkok has dominated Thailand's urban hierarchy since the late 18th century and is today considered Asia's quintessential 'primate city' by sociologists. A primate city is one that is demographically, politically, economically and culturally dominant over all other cities in the country. Approximately 70% of Thailand's urban population (and 10% of the total population) lives in Bangkok, as compared with 30% in Manila and 27% in Kuala Lumpur (the second and third most primate in the region). More statistics: 79% of the country's university graduates, 78% of its pharmacists and 45% of its physicians live in the capital; 80% of the nation's telephones and 72% of all passenger cars registered in the country (30% of all motor vehicles) are found in Bangkok. ■

Most Indian Thais can trace their heritage to northern India; many are Sikhs who immigrated during the 1947 Partition of India. Many other South Asians in Bangkok – especially Nepalese, Bangladeshis and Pakistanis – are illegal immigrants who have overstayed their visitor visas in the hope of finding employment and permanent residence.

Caucasian residents number around 15,000, but since many of them live in Bangkok on non-immigrant visas, which they renew every three or six months in Malaysia or Laos, it's difficult to pin their number down with any accuracy.

ARTS

Sculpture & Architecture

Traditional The table which follows is the latest one used by Thai art historians to categorise historical styles of Thai art, principally sculpture and architecture (since very little painting prior to the 19th century has survived).

In Bangkok you'll have the opportunity to view art from these eras in the excellent National Museum as well as other smaller museums. Post-17th-century Thai art and architecture can also be seen in several of the city's older temples and, to a lesser extent, Thai art can be seen in top-end antique shops.

Thai Art Styles

Style	Duration	Centred in	Characteristics
Mon Art (formerly Dvaravati)	6th to 13th C	Central Thailand, also North and North-east	adaptation of Indian styles, principally Gupta
Khmer Art	7th to 13th C	Central and North-east Thailand	post-classic Khmer styles accompanying spread of Khmer empires
Peninsula Art (formerly Srivijaya period)		Chaiya and Nakhon Si Thammarat	Indian influence 3rd to 5th C, Mon and local influence 5th to 13th C, Khmer influence 11th to 14th C
Lan Na (formerly Chiang Saen)	13th to 14th C	Chiang Mai; Chiang Rai, Phayao, Lamphun, Lampang	Shan/Burmese and Lao traditions mixed with local styles
Sukhothai	13th to 15th C	Sukhothai, Si Satchanalai, Kamphaeng Phet, Phitsanulok	unique to Thailand
Lopburi	13th to 15th C	Central Thailand	mix of Khmer, Pala and local styles
Suphanburi–Sangkhlaburi (formerly U Thong)	13th to 15th C	Central Thailand	mix of Mon, Khmer and local styles; prototype for Ayuthaya style
Ayuthaya A	1350-1488	Central Thailand	Khmer influences gradually replaced by revived Sukhothai influences
Ayuthaya B	1488-1630	Central Thailand	ornamentation distinctive of Ayuthaya style – eg crowns and jewels on buddhas – begins
Ayuthaya C	1630-1767	Central Thailand	baroque stage and decline
Ratanakosin	19th C to present	Bangkok	return to simpler designs, beginning of European influences

Modern Modern Thai architects are among the most daring in South-East Asia, as even a short visit to Bangkok will confirm. Thais began mixing traditional Thai with European forms in the late 19th and early 20th centuries, as exemplified by Bangkok's Vimanmek Mansion, the Author's Wing of the Oriental Hotel, the Chakri Mahaprasat next to Wat Phra Kaew, the Thai-Chinese Chamber of Commerce on Sathon Tai Rd, and any number of older residences and shophouses in Bangkok or provincial capitals throughout Thailand. This style is usually referred to as 'old Bangkok' or 'Ratanakosin'. The recently completed Old Siam Plaza shopping centre, adjacent to Bangkok's Chalermkrung Royal Theatre, is an attempt to revive the old Bangkok school.

In the 1920s and 30s a simple Thai Deco style emerged, blending European Art Deco with functionalist restraint. Surviving examples include the restored Chalermkrung Royal Theatre, the Royal Hotel, Ratchadamnoen Boxing Stadium, Hualamphong train station, the General Post Office and several buildings along Ratchadamnoen Klang Rd. According to world Art Deco expert Carol Rosenstein, Bangkok possesses the richest trove of Art Deco in South-East Asia, even surpassing former colonial capitals such as Jakarta, Kuala Lumpur, Singapore, Hanoi and Yangon (Rangoon).

JOE CUMMINGS

Bangkok's glossy World Trade Centre, a relatively new office and shopping complex containing the city's trendiest food centre.

Buildings of mixed heritage in the north and north-east exhibit French and English influences, while those in the south typically show Portuguese influence. Shophouses throughout the country, whether 100 years or 100 days old, share the basic Chinese shophouse (hâwng tháew) design in which the ground floor is used for trading and the upper floors contain offices or residences. During most of the post-WWII era the trend in modern Thai architecture – inspired by the European Bauhaus movement – was towards a boring functionalism in which the average building looked like a giant egg carton turned on its side. The Thai aesthetic, so vibrant in prewar eras, almost disappeared in this characterless style of architecture.

When Thai architects finally began experimenting again during the building boom of the mid-80s, it was to provide high-tech designs like Sumet Jumsai's famous robot-shaped Bank of Asia on Sathon Tai Rd. Few people seemed to find the space-age look endearing, but at least it was different. Another trend affixed gaudy Roman and Greek-style columns to rectangular Art Deco boxes in what was almost a parody of Western classical architecture. One of the outcomes of the latter fashion has been the widespread use of curvilinear banisters on the balconies of almost every new shophouse, apartment or condominium throughout Thailand, often with visually disturbing results.

More recently a handful of rebellious architects have begun reincorporating traditional Thai motifs – mixed with updated Western classics – in new buildings. Rangsan Torsuwan, a graduate of Massachusetts Institute of Technology, introduced the neoclassic (or neo-Thai) style, the best example of which is the new Grand Hyatt Erawan in Bangkok. Another architect using traditional Thai architecture in modern functions is Pinyo Suwankiri, who has designed a number of government buildings in Bangkok as well as the Cittaphawan Buddhist School in Chonburi.

A good book for anyone with a general interest in Thai residential design, both interior and exterior, is William Warren's *Thai Style* (Asia Books), a coffee-table tome with excellent photography by Luca Invernizzi Tettoni.

Painting

Traditional Except for a few prehistoric cave or rock-wall murals found in Ratburi, Ubon and Udon provinces, not much painting exists in Thailand predating the 18th century. Presumably there were a great number of temple murals in Ayuthaya that were destroyed by the Burmese invasion of 1767. The earliest surviving temples are found at Ayuthaya's Wat Ratburana (1424), Bangkok's Wat Chong Nonsii (1657-1707) and Phetburi's Wat Yai Suwannaram (late 17th century).

Nineteenth-century religious painting has fared better; Ratanakosin-style temples are in fact more highly esteemed for their painting than their sculpture or architecture. Typical temple murals feature rich colours and lively detail. Some of the finest are found in Wat Phra Kaew's Wihaan Phutthaisawan (Buddhaisawan Chapel) in Bangkok and at Wat Suwannaram in Thonburi.

Modern The beginnings of Thailand's modern art movement are usually attributed to Italian artist Corrado Feroci, who was invited to Thailand by King Rama VI in 1924. Feroci founded the country's first fine arts institute in 1933, which eventually developed into Silpakorn University, Thailand's premier training ground for artists and art historians. In gratitude for his contributions, the government gave Feroci the Thai name Silpa Bhirasri.

Modern painting and sculpture are exhibited at a number of Bangkok and Chiang Mai venues. One of the most important modern movements in Thai art was an updating of Buddhist themes, begun in the 1970s by painters Pichai Nirand, Thawan Duchanee and Prateung Emjaroen. The movement's early efforts combined modern Western schemata with Thai motifs. One Bangkok gallery, the Visual Dhamma Gallery (off Soi Asoke), specialises in the display of modern Thai Buddhist art by a number of artists.

Another important venue and source of support for modern art is Bangkok's luxury hotels. The largest collection of modern Thai painting anywhere in the world is found in the lobbies and public areas of the Grand Hyatt Erawan; the displays are changed regularly.

Music

Traditional From a Western perspective, traditional Thai musical forms are some of the most bizarre on the planet, but acquiring a taste for them is well worth the effort. The classical, central Thai music is spicy, like Thai food, and features an incredible array of textures and subtleties, hair-raising tempos and pastoral melodies.

The classical orchestra is called the *pìi-phâat* and can include as few as five players or more than 20. Among the more common instruments is the *pìi*, a woodwind instrument that has a reed mouthpiece and is heard prominently at Thai boxing matches. The pìi is a relative of a similar Indian instrument, as is the *phin*, a banjo-like stringed instrument descended from the Indian *vina*. A bowed instrument similar to ones played in China and Japan is aptly called the *saw*. The *ranâat èk* is the bamboo-keyed percussion instrument resembling the Western xylophone, while the *khlui* is a wooden flute.

One of the more amazing Thai instruments is the *kháwng wong yài*, tuned gongs arranged in a semicircle. There are also several different kinds of drums, some played with the hands, some with sticks. The most important Thai percussion instrument is the *tà-phon* (or *thon*), a double-headed hand drum, which sets the tempo for the ensemble. Prior to a performance, the players make offerings of incense and flowers to the tà-phon, which is considered to be the 'conductor' of the music's spiritual content.

MARK KIRBY

Tà-phon players setting the tempo in a street procession.

The pìi-phâat ensemble was originally developed to accompany classical dance-drama and shadow theatre, but can be heard in straightforward performance these days in temple fairs as well as concerts. One reason classical Thai music may sound strange to the Western ear is that it does not use the tempered scale we have been accustomed to hearing since Bach's time. The standard scale does feature an eight note octave, but it is arranged in seven full intervals, with no 'semi-tones'. Thai scales were first transcribed by a Thai-German called Peter Feit (Phra Chen Duriyanga), who also composed Thailand's national anthem in 1932.

In the north and north-east there are several popular types of reed instruments with multiple bamboo pipes, which basically function like a mouth organ. Chief among these is the *khaen*, which originated in Laos and when played by an adept musician sounds like a rhythmic, churning calliope (steam organ). The funky *lûuk thûng*, or 'country' style, which originated in the north-east, has become a favourite throughout Thailand.

If you're interested in learning how to play traditional Thai instruments, contact the Bangkok YMCA (☎ 286-1542/2580) to inquire about its weekly classes.

Recommended books on the subject are *The Traditional Music of Thailand* by David Morton, and *Thai Music* by Peter Feit (Phra Chen Duriyanga).

Modern Popular Thai music has borrowed much from Western music, particularly its instruments, but still retains a distinct flavour of its own. Although Bangkok bar bands can play fair imitations of everything from Hank Williams to Madonna, there is a growing preference among Thais for a blend of Thai and international styles.

The best example of this is Thailand's famous rock group Carabao. Recording and performing for nearly 20 years, Carabao is by far the most popular musical group in Thailand, and has even scored hits in Malaysia, Singapore, Indonesia and the Philippines with songs like 'Made in Thailand' (the chorus is in English). This band and others have crafted an exciting fusion of Thai classical and lûuk thûng forms with heavy metal. These days almost every other Thai pop group sounds like a Carabao clone, and individual members of the original band are putting out their own albums using the now classic Carabao sound.

Another major influence on Thai pop was a 70s group called Caravan, which created a modern Thai folk style known as *phleng phêua chii-wít*, or songs for life. Songs of this nature have political and environmental topics rather than the usual moonstruck love themes; during the authoritarian dictatorships of the 70s many of Caravan's songs were banned by the government. Though the band dissolved in the early 80s, they re-form for the occasional live concert. The group's most gifted songwriter, Surachai, continues to record and release solo efforts.

Yet another inspiring movement in modern Thai music is the fusion of international jazz with Thai classical and folk motifs. The leading exponent of this newer genre is the composer and instrumentalist Tewan Sapsanyakorn (also known as Tong Tewan), whose performances mix Western and Thai instruments. The melodies of his compositions are often Thai-based, but the improvisations and rhythms are drawn from such heady sources as Sonny Rollins and Jean-Luc Ponty. Tewan himself plays soprano and alto sax, violin and khlui with equal virtuosity. When Tewan isn't touring internationally you may catch him and his extremely capable band Tewan Noveljazz at the Cool Tango and other Bangkok clubs (see the Entertainment chapter later in this book for details).

Other notable groups fusing international jazz and indigenous Thai music include Kangsadarn and Boy Thai; the latter adds Brazilian *samba* to the mix. Thai instrumentation in world music settings are specialities of Todd Lavelle and Nupap Savantrachas, each of whom has scored huge hits in Thailand and look set to be hot for the next few years. Fong Nam, a Thai orchestra led by American composer Bruce Gaston, performs an inspiring blend of Western and Thai classical motifs.

Cassette tapes of Thai music are readily available throughout the country in department stores, cassette shops and street vendors. The average price for a Thai music cassette is 55 to 75B. Western bootlegged tapes are cheaper (about 30B each), but the days of pirate tapes in Thailand are numbered now that the US music industry is enforcing international copyright laws. Licensed Western music tapes cost 90 to 110B, still a good deal by the pricing standards of most Western nations.

Theatre & Dance

Traditionally, Thailand has six kinds of theatre: *khŏn*, formal masked dance-drama depicting scenes from the *Ramakian* (the Thai version of India's *Ramayana)* and originally performed only for the royal court; *lákhon*, a general term covering several types of dance-dramas (usually for non-royal occasions) as well as Western theatre; *lí-khe* (likay), a partly improvised, often bawdy folk play with dancing and music; *mánohra*, the southern Thai equivalent of *lí-khe*, but based on a 2000-year-old Indian story; *nãng*, or shadow plays, limited to southern Thailand; and *hùn lũang* or *lákhon lék* – puppet theatre.

Khõn In all khõn performances, four types of characters are represented – male humans, female humans, monkeys and demons. Monkey and demon figures are always masked with the elaborate head coverings often seen in tourist promo material. Behind the masks and make-up, all actors are male. Traditional khõn is very expensive to produce – Ravana's retinue alone (Ravana is the story's principal villain) consists of over a hundred demons, each with a distinctive mask. Perhaps because it was once limited to royal venues and hence never gained a popular following, the khõn or Ramakian dance-drama tradition has all but died out in Thailand. Until recently Bangkok's National Theatre was one of the few places where khõn was still performed for the public. Now the renovated Chalermkrung Royal Theatre hosts weekly khõn performances enhanced by laser graphics and high-tech audio.

Scenes performed in traditional khõn (and lákhon performances) come from the *Ramayana*, India's classic 'epic journey' tale with obvious archetypal parallels in the Greek epic the *Odyssey* and the Greek myth Jason and the Argonauts. The central story revolves around Prince Rama's search for his beloved Princess Sita, who has been abducted by the evil 10-headed demon Ravana and taken to the island of Lanka. Rama is assisted in his search, and in the final battle against Ravana, by a host of mythical half-animal, half-human characters, including the monkey-god Hanuman.

Lákhon The more formal *lákhon nai* (inner lákhon) was originally performed for lower nobility by all-female ensembles; like royal khõn it's a dying art. In addition to scenes from the *Ramakian*, lákhon nai performances may include traditional Thai folk tales; whatever the story, text is always sung.

Lákhon nâwk (outer lákhon) deals exclusively with folk tales and features a mix of sung and spoken text, sometimes with improvisation. Both male and female performers are permitted. Like khõn and lákhon nai, performances are increasingly rare. More common these days is the less-refined *lákhon chaa-trii*, a fast-paced, costumed dance-drama usually performed at temple festivals or shrines (commissioned by a shrine devotee whose wish was granted by the shrine deity).

JOE CUMMINGS

Performers participating in a traditional dance.

TAT

The costuming for Thai classical dancers – heavily
embroidered silks, silver jewellery and the chadok
or royal headdress – can weigh several kilos.

Lákhon phûut (spoken lákhon) is the equivalent of Western theatre based on the Greek model – all dialogue is spoken rather than sung. This is the most modern of Thailand's theatre traditions, as well as the most popular in cities and larger towns.

SOCIETY & CONDUCT

When outsiders speak of 'Thai culture' they're referring to a complex of behavioural modes rooted in the history of Thai migration throughout South-East Asia, with many commonalities shared by the Lao of neighbouring Laos, the Shan of north-eastern Myanmar (Burma) and the numerous tribal Thais found in isolated pockets stretching from Dien Bien Phu, Vietnam, all the way to Assam, India. Nowhere are such norms more generalised than in Thailand, the largest of the Thai homelands.

Practically every ethnicity represented in Thailand, whether of Thai ancestry or not, has to a greater or lesser degree been assimilated into the Thai mainstream. Although Thailand is the most 'modernised' of the existing Thai (more precisely, Austro-Thai) societies, the traditional cultural underpinnings are evident in virtually every facet of everyday life. Those aspects that might be deemed 'Westernisation' – eg the wearing of trousers instead of *phâakhamāa* (short sarong) and the presence of automobiles, cinema and 7-Eleven convenience stores – show how Thailand has adopted and adapted tools invented elsewhere.

But such adaptations do not necessarily represent cultural loss. Ekawit Na Talang, a scholar of Thai culture and head of the government's National Culture Commission, defines culture as 'the system of thought and behaviour of a particular society – something which is dynamic and never static'. Talang and other world culture experts agree that it's paradoxical to try to protect a culture from foreign influences, because cultures cannot exist in a vacuum. Culture evolves naturally as outside influences undergo processes of naturalisation. From this perspective, trying to maintain a 'pure' culture is like breeding pedigree dogs; it eventually leads to a weakening of the species. As Talang has said: 'Anything obsolete, people will reject and anything that has a relevant role in life, people will adopt and make it part of their culture'.

Nevertheless, there are features of Thai society that virtually everyone recognises as 'Thai' cultural markers. The Thais themselves don't really have a word that corresponds to the English term 'culture'. The nearest

equivalent, *wátánátham*, emphasises fine arts and ceremonies over other aspects usually covered by the
concept. So if you ask Thais to define their culture, they'll
often talk about architecture, food, dance, festivals and
the like. Religion – a big influence on culture as defined
in the West – is considered more or less separate from
wátánátham.

Sanùk

The Thai word *sanùk* means 'fun'. In Thailand anything
worth doing – even work – should have an element of
sanùk, otherwise it automatically becomes drudgery.
This doesn't mean Thais don't want to work or strive,
it's just that they tend to approach tasks with a sense of
playfulness. Nothing condemns an activity more than
the description *mâi sanùk* (not fun). Sit down beside a rice
field and watch workers planting, transplanting or har-
vesting rice while you're in Thailand. The work is
obviously back-breaking, but workers generally inject
the activity with lots of sanùk – flirtation between the
sexes, singing, trading insults and cracking jokes. The
same goes in an office or a bank, or other 'white-collar'
work – at least when the office is predominantly Thai
(businesses run by non-Thais don't necessarily exhibit
sanùk). The famous Thai smile comes partially out of
this desire to make sanùk.

Saving Face

Thais strongly believe in the concept of 'saving face', that
is avoiding confrontation and endeavouring not to
embarrass themselves or other people (except when it's
sanùk to do so!). The ideal face saver doesn't bring up
negative topics in everyday conversation. When the face
saver notices stress in another's life, he or she usually
won't say anything unless that person complains or asks
for help. Laughing at minor accidents – like when
someone trips and falls down – may seem callous to
outsiders, but it's really just an attempt to save face on
behalf of the person undergoing the mishap. This is
another source of the Thai smile – it's the best possible
face to put on in almost any situation.

Traditional Relationships

All relationships in traditional Thai society – and virtually all relationships in the modern Thai milieu as well
– are governed by connections between *phûu yài* (literally big person) and *phûu náwy* (little person). Phûu

náwy are supposed to defer to phûu yài following
simple lines of social rank defined by age, wealth, status,
and personal and political power. Examples of
'automatic' phûu yài status include adults (vs children),
bosses (vs employees), elder classmates (vs younger
classmates), elder siblings (vs younger siblings), teachers (vs pupils), military (vs civilian), Thai (vs non-Thai)
and so on.

While this tendency toward social ranking is to some
degree shared by many societies around the world, the
Thai twist lies in the set of mutual obligations linking
phûu yài to phûu náwy. Sociologists have referred to this
phenomenon as the 'patron-client relationship'. Phûu
náwy are supposed to show a degree of obedience and
respect (together these concepts are covered by the
single Thai term *kreng jai*) toward phûu yài, but in return
phûu yài are obligated to care for or 'sponsor' the phûu
náwy they have frequent contact with. In such relationships phûu náwy can, for example, ask phûu yài for
favours involving money or job access. Phûu yài re-
affirm their rank by granting such requests when
possible; to refuse would be to risk loss of face and
status.

Age is a large determinant where other factors are
absent or weak. In such cases the terms *phîi* (elder
sibling) and *náwng* (younger sibling) apply more than
phûu yài/phûu náwy although the intertwined obligations remain the same. Even people unrelated by blood
quickly establish who's phîi and who's náwng; this
partly explains why one of the first questions Thais ask
new acquaintances is 'How old are you?'.

When dining, touring or entertaining, the phûu yài
always picks up the tab; if a group is involved, the
person with most social rank pays for everyone, even if
it empties his or her wallet. For a phûu náwy to try and
pay would risk loss of face. Money plays a large role in
defining phûu yài status in most situations. A person
who turned out to be successful in his or her post-school
career would never think of allowing an ex-classmate of
lesser success – even if they were once on equal social
footing – to pay the bill. Likewise a young, successful
executive will pay an older person's way in spite of the
age difference.

The implication is that whatever wealth you come
into is to be shared – at least partially – with those who
have been less fortunate. This doesn't apply to strangers
– the average Thai isn't big on charity – but always comes
into play with friends and relatives.

Foreigners often feel offended when they encounter
such phenomena as two-tiered pricing for hotels or

sightseeing attractions – one price for Thais, a higher price for foreigners. But this is simply another expression of the traditional patron-client relationship. On the one hand, foreigners who can afford to travel to Thailand from abroad are seen to have more wealth than Thai citizens (on average this is self-evident), hence they're expected to help subsidise Thai enjoyment of these commodities; and at the same time, paradoxically, the Thais feel they are due certain special privileges as home-landers – what might be termed the 'home-town discount'. Another example: in a post office line, Thais get served first as part of their national privilege.

Comportment

Personal power (*baará-mii*, sometimes mistranslated as 'charisma') also has a bearing on one's social status, and can be gained by cleaving as close as possible to the ideal 'Thai' behaviour. Thai-ness is first and foremost defined, as might be expected, by the ability to speak Thai. It doesn't matter which dialect, although southern Thai – with its Malay/Yawi influences – is slightly more suspect, mainly due to the south's association with the 'foreign' religion of Islam.

Other hallmarks of the Thai ideal – heavily influenced by Thai Buddhism – include discretion in behaviour toward the opposite sex; modest dress; a neat and clean appearance; and modes of expression and comportment that value the quiet, subtle and indirect rather than the loud, obvious and direct.

The degree to which Thais can conform to these ideals matches the degree of respect they receive from most of their associates. Although high rank – age related, civil, military or clerical – will exempt certain individuals from chastisement by their social 'inferiors', it doesn't exempt them from the way they are perceived by other Thais. This goes for foreigners as well, even though most first-time visitors can hardly be expected to speak idiomatic Thai. But if you do learn some Thai, and you do make an effort to respect Thai social ideals, you'll come closer to enjoying some of the perks awarded for Thai-ness.

Dos & Don'ts

Monarchy and religion are the two sacred cows in Thailand. Thais are tolerant of most kinds of behaviour as long as it doesn't insult one of the following:

King & Country The monarchy is held in considerable respect in Thailand and visitors should be respectful, too – avoid disparaging remarks about the king, queen or anyone in the royal family. One of Thailand's leading intellectuals, Sulak Sivaraksa, was arrested in the early 80s for treason because of a passing reference to the king's fondness for yachting (Sulak referred to His Majesty as 'the skipper'), and again in 1991 when he referred to the royal family as 'ordinary people'. Although on that occasion he received a royal pardon, in 1992 Sulak had to flee the country to avoid prosecution again for alleged remarks delivered at Thammasat University about the ruling military junta, with reference to the king (Sulak has since returned under a suspended sentence). The penalty for treason is seven years' imprisonment.

While it's OK to criticise the Thai government and even Thai culture openly, it's considered a grave insult to Thai nationhood, as well as to the monarchy, not to stand when you hear the national or royal anthems. Radio and TV stations in Thailand broadcast the national anthem daily at 8 am and 6 pm; in towns and villages (even in some Bangkok neighbourhoods) this can be heard over public loudspeakers in the streets. The Thais stop whatever they're doing to stand during the anthem (except in Bangkok where nobody can hear anything above the street noise) and visitors are expected to do likewise. The royal anthem is played just before films are shown in public cinemas; again, the audience always stands until it's over.

Religion Correct behaviour in temples entails following several guidelines, the most important of which is to dress neatly and to take your shoes off when you enter any building that contains a Buddha image. Buddha images are sacred objects, so don't pose in front of them for pictures and definitely do not clamber upon them.

Shorts or sleeveless shirts are considered improper dress for both men and women when visiting temples. Thai citizens wearing either would be turned away by monastic authorities, but except for the most sacred temples in the country (eg Wat Phra Kaew), Thais are often too polite to refuse entry to improperly clad foreigners. Some wats will offer trousers or long sarongs for rent so that shorts-wearing tourists may enter the compound.

Monks are not supposed to touch or be touched by women. If a woman wants to hand something to a monk, the object should be placed within reach of the monk, not handed directly to him.

When sitting in a religious building, keep your feet pointed away from any Buddha images. The usual way to do this is to sit in the 'mermaid' pose, with your legs folded to the side and your feet pointing backwards.

Social Gestures Traditionally, Thais greet each other not with a handshake but with a prayer-like palms-together gesture known as a *wâi*. If someone wâis you, you should wâi back (unless wâi-ed by a child). Most urban Thais are familiar with the Western-style handshake and will offer the same to a foreigner, although a wâi is always appreciated.

The feet are the lowest part of the body (spiritually as well as physically), so don't point your feet at people or point at things with your feet. In the same context, the head is regarded as the highest part of the body, so don't touch Thais on the head either.

Don't sit on pillows meant for sleeping, as this represents a variant of the taboo against head touching. I recently watched a young woman on Ko Samet bring a bed pillow from her bungalow to sit on while watching TV; the Thai staff got very upset and she didn't understand why.

When handing things to other people you should use both hands or your right hand only, never the left hand (reserved for toilet ablutions). Books and other written material are given a special status over other secular objects. Hence you shouldn't slide books or documents across a table or counter-top, and never place them on the floor – use a chair instead if table space isn't available.

Terms of Address

Thais are often addressed by their first name with the honorific *khun* or other title preceding it. Other formal terms of address include *Nai* (Mr) and *Naang* (Miss or Mrs). Friends often use nicknames or kinship terms like phîi (elder sibling), náwng (younger sibling), *mâe* (mother) or *lung* (uncle) depending on the age difference.

Dress & Attitude

Shorts – except knee-length walking shorts – sleeveless shirts, tank tops (singlets) and other beach-style attire are not considered appropriate dress in Thailand for anything other than sporting events. Such dress is especially counter-productive if worn to government offices (eg when applying for a visa extension). The attitude of 'This is how I dress at home and no-one is going to stop me' gains nothing but contempt/disrespect from the Thais.

Sandals or slip-on shoes are OK for almost any but the most formal occasions. Short-sleeved shirts and blouses with capped sleeves likewise are quite acceptable.

When things go wrong, don't be quick to anger – it won't help matters, since losing one's temper means loss of face for everyone present. Remember that this is Asia, where keeping your cool is paramount. Talking loudly is perceived as rude behaviour by cultured Thais, whatever the situation. See the previous entries in this section on Saving Face and Comportment regarding the rewards for 'Thai-ness' – the pushy foreigner often gets served last.

A smile and *sawàt-dii khráp\khâ* (the all-purpose Thai greeting) goes a long way toward calming the initial trepidation that locals may feel upon seeing a foreigner, whether in the city or the countryside.

RELIGION

Buddhism

About 95% of the Thai citizenry are Theravada Buddhists. The Thais themselves frequently call their religion Lankavamsa (Sinhalese lineage) Buddhism because Siam originally received Buddhism during the Sukhothai period from Sri Lanka. Strictly speaking, Theravada refers to only the earliest forms of Buddhism practised during the Ashokan and immediate post-Ashokan periods in South Asia. The early Dvaravati and pre-Dvaravati forms of Buddhism are not the same as that which has existed in Siamese territories since the 13th century.

Since the Sukhothai period, Thailand has maintained an unbroken canonical tradition and 'pure' ordination lineage, the only country among the Theravadin (using Theravada in its doctrinal sense) countries to do so. Ironically, when the ordination lineage in Sri Lanka broke down during the 18th century under Dutch persecution, it was Siam that restored the Sangha (Buddhist brotherhood) there. To this day the major sect in Sri Lanka is called Siamopalivamsa (Siam-Upali lineage, Upali being the name of the Siamese monk who led the expedition to Ceylon), or simply Siam Nikaya (the Siamese sect).

Basically, the Theravada school of Buddhism is an earlier and, according to its followers, less corrupted form of Buddhism than the Mahayana schools found in East Asia or in the Himalayan lands. The Theravada (literally Teaching of the Elders) school is also called the 'southern' school since it took the southern route from

India, its place of origin, through South-East Asia (Myanmar/Burma, Thailand, Laos and Cambodia in this case), while the 'northern' school proceeded north into Nepal, Tibet, China, Korea, Mongolia, Vietnam and Japan. Because the Theravada school tried to preserve or limit the Buddhist doctrines to only those canons codified in the early Buddhist era, the Mahayana school gave Theravada Buddhism the name Hinayana, or the 'lesser vehicle'. The Mahayana school was the 'great vehicle', because it built upon the earlier teachings, 'expanding' the doctrine in such a way as to respond more to the needs of lay people, or so it is claimed.

Theravada or Hinayana doctrine stresses the three principal aspects of existence: *dukkha* (suffering, unsatisfactoriness, disease); *anicca* (impermanence, transience of all things); and *anatta* (non-substantiality or non-essentiality of reality – no permanent 'soul'). The truth of anicca reveals that no experience, no state of mind, no physical object lasts; trying to hold onto experience, states of mind and objects that are constantly changing creates dukkha; anatta is the understanding that there's no part of the changing world we can point to and say 'This is me', 'This is God' or 'This is the soul'. These concepts, when 'discovered' by Siddhartha Gautama in the 6th century BC, were in direct contrast to the Hindu belief in an eternal, blissful self *(paramatman)*, hence Buddhism was originally a 'heresy' against India's Brahmanic religion.

JOE CUMMINGS

Chinese Temple, Chinatown

JOE CUMMINGS

The wheel is a common motif in Buddhist iconography.

JOE CUMMINGS

The 15m reclining Buddha at Wat Pho is one of
the largest such images in the world.

Gautama, an Indian prince-turned-ascetic, subjected himself to many years of severe austerity before he realised that this was not the way to reach the end of suffering. He then turned his attention to investigating the arising and passing away of the mind and body in the present moment. Seeing that even the most blissful and refined states of mind were subject to decay, he abandoned all desire for what he now saw as unreliable and unsatisfying. He then became known as Buddha, 'the enlightened' or 'the awakened'. Gautama Buddha spoke of four noble truths that had the power to liberate any human being who could realise them. These four noble truths are:

1) the truth of dukkha – 'All forms of existence are subject to dukkha (disease, unsatisfactoriness, imperfection)'
2) the truth of the cause of dukkha – 'Dukkha is caused by tanha (desire)'
3) the truth of the cessation of dukkha – 'Eliminate the cause of dukkha (ie desire) and dukkha will cease to arise'
4) the truth of the path – 'The Eightfold Path is the way to eliminate desire/extinguish dukkha'

The Eightfold Path (Atthangika-Magga), which if followed will put an end to suffering, consists of (1) right understanding, (2) right mindedness (right thought), (3) right speech, (4) right bodily conduct, (5) right livelihood, (6) right effort, (7) right attentiveness and (8) right concentration. These eight limbs belong to three different 'pillars' of practice: morality or *sila* (3 to 5); concentration or *samadhi* (6 to 8); and wisdom or *pañña* (1 and 2). The path is also called the Middle Way, since ideally it avoids both extreme austerity and extreme sensuality. Some Buddhists believe it is to be taken in successive stages, while others say the pillars and/or limbs are interdependent. Another key point is that the word 'right' can also be translated as 'complete' or 'full'.

The ultimate end of Theravada Buddhism is *nibbana* (Sanskrit: nirvana), which literally means the extinction of all desire and thus of all suffering (dukkha). Effectively it is also an end to the cycle of rebirths that is existence. In reality, most Thai Buddhists aim for rebirth in a 'better' existence rather than the supramundane goal of nibbana, which is highly misunderstood by Asians as well as Westerners.

Many Thais express the feeling that they are somehow unworthy of nibbana. By feeding monks, giving donations to temples and performing regular worship at the local *wat* (temple), they hope to improve their lot, acquiring enough merit (Pali (derived from Sanskrit and a significant influence on Thai): *puñña*; Thai: *bun*) to prevent or at least lessen the number of rebirths. The making of merit *(tham bun)* is an important social and religious activity in Thailand. The concept of reincarnation is almost universally accepted in Thailand, even by non-Buddhists, and the Buddhist theory of karma is well expressed in the Thai proverb *tham dii, dâi dii; tham chûa, dâi chûa* – 'do good and receive good; do evil and receive evil'.

The Triratna, or Triple Gems, highly respected by Thai Buddhists, include the Buddha, Dhamma (teachings) and Sangha (Buddhist brotherhood). Each is quite visible in Thailand. The Buddha, in his myriad and omnipresent sculptural forms, is found on a high shelf in the lowliest roadside restaurants as well as in the lounges of expensive Bangkok hotels. The Dhamma is chanted morning and evening in every wat and taught to every Thai citizen in primary school. The Sangha is seen everywhere in the form of orange-robed monks, especially in the early morning hours when they perform their alms rounds, in what has almost become a travel-guide cliché in motion.

Socially, every Thai male is expected to become a monk for a short period in his life, optimally between the time he finishes school and the time he starts a career or marries. Men or boys under 20 years of age may enter the Sangha as novices – this is not unusual since a family earns great merit when one of its sons takes robe and bowl. Traditionally, the length of time spent in the wat is three months, during the Buddhist lent (phansāa), which begins in July and coincides with the rainy season. However, nowadays men may spend as little as a week or 15 days to accrue merit as monks. There are about 32,000 monasteries in Thailand and 200,000 monks; many of these monks ordain for life. Of these a large percentage become scholars and teachers, while some specialise in healing and/or folk magic.

The Sangha is divided into two sects, the Mahanikai and the Thammayut. The latter is a minority sect (there is one Thammayut to every 35 Mahanikai) begun by King Mongkut and patterned after an early Mon form of monastic discipline that he had practised as a monk (bhikkhu). Generally, discipline for Thammayut monks is stricter. For example, they eat only once a day, before noon, and must eat only what is in their alms bowl, whereas Mahanikais eat twice before noon and may accept side dishes. Thammayut monks are expected to attain proficiency in meditation as well as Buddhist scholarship or scripture study; the Mahanikai monks typically 'specialise' in one or the other.

An increasing number of foreigners come to Thailand to be ordained as Buddhist monks, especially to study with the famed meditation masters of the forest wats in north-east Thailand (see the Meditation Study section under Courses in the Things to See & Do chapter).

There is a Buddhist bookshop across the street from the north entrance to Wat Bovornives (Bowonniwet) that sells English-language books.

If you wish to find out more about Buddhism you can contact the World Fellowship of Buddhists (☎ 251-1188), 33 Sukhumvit Rd (Map 4, between Sois 1 and 3). There's an English meditation class here on the first Sunday of each month; all are welcome.

JOE CUMMINGS

Buddhist monk caught in festival traffic.

LANGUAGE

Learning some Thai is indispensable for travelling in the kingdom; naturally, the more language you pick up, the closer you get to Thailand's culture and people. Foreigners who speak Thai are so rare that it doesn't take many Thai words to impress most Thais.

Your first attempts to speak the language will probably meet with mixed success, but keep trying. When learning new words or phrases, listen closely to the way the Thais themselves use the various tones – you'll catch on quickly. Don't let laughter at your linguistic attempts discourage you; this amusement is an expression of their appreciation.

Many people also report modest success with *Robertson's Practical English-Thai Dictionary* (Charles E Tuttle Co, Tokyo), which has a phonetic guide to pronunciation with tones and is compact in size. It may be difficult to find, so write to the publisher, Suido 1-chome, 2-6, Bun-kyo-ku, Tokyo.

For more serious language-learners there is Mary Haas' *Thai-English Student's Dictionary* (Stanford University Press, Stanford, California) and George McFarland's *Thai-English Dictionary* (also Stanford University Press), which is the cream of the crop.

For a more complete selection of phrases and basic vocabulary and grammar for travel in Thailand, see Lonely Planet's *Thai phrasebook*.

Script

The Thai script, a fairly recent development in comparison with the spoken language, consists of 44 consonants (but only 21 separate sounds) and 48 vowel and diphthong possibilities (32 separate signs). Experts disagree as to the exact origins of the script, but it was apparently developed around 800 years ago from Mon and possibly Khmer models. Like these language models, written Thai proceeds from left to right, though vowel signs may be written before, above, below, 'around' (before, above *and* after), *or* after consonants, depending on the sign.

Though learning the alphabet is not difficult, the writing system itself is fairly complex, so unless you are planning a lengthy stay in Thailand it should perhaps be foregone in favour of learning to actually speak the language. Where possible, place names occurring in headings are given in Thai script as well as in Roman script, so that you can at least 'read' the names of destinations at a pinch, or point to them if necessary.

Tones

In standard central Thai the meaning of a single syllable may be altered by means of five different tones: level or mid tone, low tone, falling tone, high tone and rising tone. Consequently, the syllable *mai*, for example, can mean, depending on the tone, 'new', 'burn', 'wood', 'not?' or 'not'. This makes it rather tricky to learn at first, especially for those of us who come from non-tonal-language traditions. Even when we 'know' what the correct tone in Thai should be, our tendency to denote emotion, verbal stress, the interrogative, etc, through tone modulation, often interferes with speaking the correct tone. So the first rule in learning to speak Thai is to divorce emotions from your speech, at least until you have learned the Thai way to express them without changing essential tone value.

The following is a brief attempt to explain the tones. The only way to really understand the differences is by listening to a native or fluent non-native speaker. The range of all five tones is relative to each speaker's vocal range so there is no fixed 'pitch' intrinsic to the language.

The level or mid tone is pronounced 'flat', at the relative middle of the speaker's vocal range. Example: *dii* means good. (No tone mark used.)

The low tone is 'flat' like the mid tone, but pronounced at the relative *bottom* of one's vocal range. It is low, level and with no inflection. Example: *bàat* means baht (the Thai currency).

The falling tone is pronounced as if you were emphasising a word, or calling someone's name from afar. Example: *mâi* means 'no' or 'not'.

The high tone is usually the most difficult for Westerners. It is pronounced near the relative top of the vocal range, as level as possible. Example: *níi* means 'this'.

The rising tone sounds like the inflection English speakers generally give to a question – 'Yes?' Example: *sǎam* means 'three'.

On a visual curve the tones might look like this:

Mid   Low   Falling   High   Rising

Words in Thai that appear to have more than one syllable are usually compounds made up of two or more word units, each with its own tone. They may be words taken directly from Sanskrit or Pali or English, in which case each syllable must still have its own tone. Sometimes the tone of the first syllable is not as important as that of the last, so for these I am omitting the tone mark.

Here is a guide to the phonetic system that has been used in the Language, Food and Drink sections, as well as throughout the book when transcribing directly from Thai. It is based on the Royal Thai General System of transcription (RTGS), except that it distinguishes between vowels of short and long duration (eg 'i' and 'ii'; 'a' and 'aa'; 'e' and 'eh', 'o' and 'oh'), between 'o' and 'aw' (both would be 'o' in the RTGS); between 'u' and 'eu' (both 'u' in the RTGS); and between 'ch' and 'j' (both 'ch' in the RTGS).

Consonants

th	as the 't' in 'tea'
ph	as the 'p' in 'put' (never as the 'ph' in phone)
kh	as the 'k' in 'kite'
k	as the 'k' in 'skin'; similar to 'g' in 'good', but unaspirated (no accompanying puff of air) and unvoiced
t	as the 't' in 'forty', unaspirated; similar to 'd' but unvoiced
p	as the 'p' in 'stopper', unvoiced and unaspirated (not like the 'p' in 'put')
ng	as the 'ng' in 'sing'; used as an initial consonant in Thai (practice by saying 'sing' without the 'si')
r	similar to the 'r' in 'run' but flapped (tongue touches palate); in everyday speech often pronounced like 'l'
w	as the 'w' in 'walk'

All the remaining consonants correspond closely to their English counterparts.

Vowels

i	as the 'i' in 'it'
ii	as the 'ee' in 'feet'
ai	as the 'i' in 'pipe'
aa	as the 'a' in 'father'
a	half as long as 'aa'
ae	as the 'a' in 'bat' or 'tab'
e	as the 'e' in 'hen'
eh	as the 'a' in 'hate'
oe	as the 'u' in 'hut' but more closed
u	as the 'u' in 'flute'
uu	as the 'oo' in 'food', longer than u
eu	as the 'eu' in French 'deux', or the 'i' in 'sir'
ao	as the 'ow' in 'now'
aw	as the 'aw' in 'jaw'
o	as the 'o' in 'bone'; with the exception of *ko*, which is pronounced 'kaw'
oh	as the 'o' in 'toe'
eua	diphthong, or combination, of *eu* and *a*
ia	as 'ee-ya', or as the 'ie' in French 'rien'

ua as the 'ou' in 'tour'
uay as the 'ewy' in 'Dewey'
iu as the 'ew' in 'yew'
iaw as the 'io' in 'Rio' or Italian 'mio' or 'dio'

A few extra hints to help you with the alphabetic tangle:

1) Remember that 'ph' is not meant to be pronounced like the 'ph' in phone but like the 'p' in 'pound' (the 'h' is added to distinguish this consonant sound from the Thai 'p' which is closer to the English 'b'). Can be seen written as 'p', 'ph', and even 'bh'.

2) There is no 'v' sound in Thai; Sukhumvit is pronounced Sukhumwit and Viang is really Wiang.

3) 'L' or 'r' at the end of a word is always pronounced like an 'n'; hence, Satul is pronounced Satun, Wihar is really Wihan. The exception to this is when 'er' or 'ur' are used to indicate the sound 'oe', as in 'ampher' *(amphoe)*. In the same way 'or' is sometimes used for the sound 'aw' as in 'Porn' *(phawn)*.

4) 'L' and 'r' are often used interchangeably in speech and this shows up in some transliterations. For example, *naliga* (clock) may appear as 'nariga' and *râat nâa* (a type of noodle dish) might be rendered 'laat naa' or 'lat na'.

5) 'U' is often used to represent the short 'a' sound, as in *tam* or *nam*, which may appear as 'tum' and 'num'.

6) Phonetically all Thai words end in a vowel ('a', 'e', 'i', 'o', 'u'), a semi-vowel ('y', 'w') or one of three stops: 'p', 't' and 'k'. That's it. Words transcribed with 'ch', 'j' or 'd' endings – like Panich, Raj and Had – should be pronounced as if they end in 't', as in Panit, Rat and Hat. Likewise 'g' becomes 'k' (Ralug is actually Raluk) and 'b' becomes 'p' (Thab becomes Thap).

7) Finally, the 'r' in 'sri' is *always* silent, so that word should be pronounced 'sii' (extended 'i' sound, too).

Transliteration

Writing Thai in Roman script is a perennial problem – no truly satisfactory system has yet been devised to assure both consistency and readability. The Thai government uses the Royal Thai General System of transcription for official government documents in English and for most highway signs. However, local variations crop up on hotel signs, city street signs, menus, and so on in such a way that visitors often become confused. Add to this the fact that even the government system has its flaws. For example, 'o' is used for two very different sounds ('o' and the 'aw' in the Language section above), as is 'u' ('u' and 'eu' above). Likewise for 'ch', which is used to represent two different consonant sounds ('ch' and 'j'). The government transcription system also does not distinguish between short and long vowel sounds, which affect the tonal value of every word.

To top it off, many Thai words (especially people and place names) have Sanskrit and Pali spellings, but the actual pronunciation bears little relation to that spelling if Romanised strictly according to the original Sanskrit/Pali. Thus, Nakhon Si Thammarat, if transliterated literally, becomes 'Nagara Sri Dhammaraja'. If you tried to pronounce it using this Pali transcription, very few Thais would be able to understand you.

Generally, names in this book follow the most common practice or, in the case of hotels for example, simply copy their Roman script name, no matter what devious process was used in its transliteration! When this transliteration is especially distant from actual pronunciation, I've included the pronunciation (following the system given in the Language section) in parentheses after the transliteration. Where no Roman model was available, names were transliterated phonetically directly from Thai. Of course, this will only be helpful to readers who bother to acquaint themselves with the language – I'm constantly amazed at how many people manage to stay great lengths of time in Thailand without learning a word of Thai.

Problems often arise when a name is transliterated differently, even at the same place. 'Thawi', for example, can be Tavi, Thawee, Thavi, Tavee or various other versions. With the exception of the International Phonetic Alphabet, there is no 'proper' way to transliterate Thai – only wrong ways. The Thais themselves are incredibly inconsistent in this matter, often using English letters that have no equivalent sound in Thai: Faisal for Phaisan, Bhumiphol for Phumiphon, Vanich for Wanit, Vibhavadi for Wiphawadi. Sometimes they even mix literal Sanskrit transcription with Thai pronunciation, as in King Bhumibol (which is pronounced Phumiphon and if transliterated according to the Sanskrit would be Bhumibala).

Greetings & Civilities

When being polite the speaker ends their sentence with
khráp (for men) or *khâ* (for women). It's the speaker's
gender that is being expressed here; it's also the common
way to answer 'yes' to a question or show agreement.

Greetings./Hello.
　Sawàt-dii (khráp/khâ).　สวัสดี (ครับ/ค่ะ)
How are you?
　Pen yangai?　เป็นอย่างไร?
I'm fine.
　Sabàay dii.　สบายดี
Thank you.
　Khàwp khun.　ขอบคุณ

Small Talk

you	*khun* (peers)	คุณ
	thâan (respectful)	ท่าน
I	*phŏm* (for men)	ผม (ผู้ชาย)
	diichăn (for women)	ดีฉัน (ผู้หญิง)

What is your name?
　Khun chêu arai?　คุณชื่ออะไร?
My name is ...
　Phŏm chêu ... (men)　ผมชื่อ..
　Diichăn chêu ... (women)　ดีฉันชื่อ...
Do you have ...?
　Mii ... măi? / ... mii măi?　มี...ไหม?　(...มีไหม?)
Do you have noodles?
　Mii kŭuayth īaw măi?　มีก๋วยเตยวไหม?
I/you/he/she/it does
　not have
　mâi mii　ไม่มี

No.	*Mâi châi.*	ไม่ใช่
No?	*Măi? / Châi măi?*	ไหม?/ใช่ไหม?
When?	*Mêu-arai?*	เมื่อไหร่?
It doesn't matter.	*Mâi pen rai.*	ไม่เป็นไร
What is this?	*Níi arai?*	นี้อะไร?

What do you call this in Thai?
　Níi phaasăa thai rîak wâa arai?　นี้ภาษาไทยเรียกว่าอะไร?
I understand.
　Khâo jai.　เข้าใจ

Do you understand?	
Khâo jai mãi?	เข้าใจไหม?
I don't understand.	
Mâi khâo jai.	ไม่เข้าใจ
a little	
nít nawy	นิดหน่อย

Some Verbs

go	*pai*	ไป
will go	*jà pai*	จะไป
come	*maa*	มา
will come	*jà maa*	จะมา
(I) like ...	*châwp ...*	ชอบ...

(I) do not like ...	
mâi châwp ...	ไม่ชอบ...
(I) would like (+ verb) ...	
yàak jà ...	อยากจะ...
(I) would not like ...	
mâi yàak jà ...	ไม่อยากจะ...
(I) would like to eat ...	
yàak jà thaan ...	อยากจะทาน...
(I) would like ... (+ noun)	
yàak dâi ...	อยากได้...

Getting Around

I would like a ticket.	
Yàak dâi tũa.	อยากได้ตั๋ว
I would like to go ...	
Yàak jà pai ...	อยากจะไป...
Where is (the) ...?	
... yàu thîi nãi?	...อยู่ที่ไหน?

motorcycle	*rót maw-toe-sai*	รถมอเตอร์ไซ
train	*rót fai*	รถไฟ
bus	*rót meh or rót bát*	รถเมล์/รถบัส
car	*rót yon*	รถยนต์
hotel	*rohng raem*	โรงแรม
station	*sathãanii*	สถานี
post office	*praisanii*	ไปรษณีย์
restaurant	*ráan aahãan*	ร้านอาหาร
hospital	*rohng phayaabaan*	โรงพยาบาล
airport	*sanãam bin*	สนามบิน
market	*talàat*	ตลาด
beach	*hàat*	หาด
food (rice)	*khâo*	ข้าว

Accommodation

bathroom	*hâwng náam*	ห้องน้ำ
toilet	*hâwng sûam*	ห้องส้วม
room	*hâwng*	ห้อง
hot	*ráwn*	ร้อน
cold	*năo*	หนาว
bath/shower	*àap náam*	อาบน้ำ
towel	*phâa chét tua*	ผ้าเช็ดตัว

Shopping

How much is this?
  Níi thâo rai? / Kìi bàat? นี่เท่าไรฝ(กี่บาท)
How much?
  Thâo rai? เท่าไร?
too expensive
  phaeng pai แพงไป
cheap/inexpensive
  thùuk ถูก

Emergencies

(I) need a doctor.
  Tâwng-kaan măw. ต้องการหมอ
Help!
  Chûay dûay! ช่วยด้วย
Call the police!
  Chûay rîak tam-rùat dûay! ช่วยเรียกตำรวจด้วย
Fire!
  Fai mâi! ไฟไหม้
I am lost.
  Chăn lŏng thaang. ฉันหลงทาง

Time

today	*wan níi*	วันนี้
tomorrow	*phrûng níi*	พรุ่งนี้
yesterday	*mêua waan*	เมื่อวาน

Numbers

0	*sŭun*	ศูนย์
1	*nèung*	หนึ่ง
2	*săwng*	สอง
3	*săam*	สาม
4	*sìi*	สี่
5	*hâa*	ห้า

6	*hòk*	หก
7	*jèt*	เจ็ด
8	*pàet*	แปด
9	*kâo*	เก้า
10	*sìp*	สิบ
11	*sìp-èt*	สิบเอ็ด
12	*sìp-sāwng*	สิบสอง
13	*sìp-sāam*	สิบสาม
14	*sìp-sìi*	สิบสี่
20	*yîi-sìp*	ยี่สิบ
21	*yîi-sìp-èt*	ยี่สิบเอ็ด
22	*yîi-sìp-sāwng*	ยี่สิบสอง
23	*yîi-sìp-sāam*	ยี่สิบสาม
30	*sāam-sìp*	สามสิบ
40	*sìi-sìp*	สี่สิบ
50	*hâa-sìp*	ห้าสิบ
100	*nèung ráwy*	ร้อย
200	*sāwng ráwy*	สองร้อย
300	*sāam ráwy*	สามร้อย
1000	*phan*	พัน
10,000	*mèun*	หมื่น
100,000	*sāen*	แสน
1 million	*láan*	ล้าน
1 billion	*phan láan*	พันล้าน

Facts for the Visitor

WHEN TO GO

The best overall months for visiting Bangkok vis-à-vis climate are November and February – during these months it rains least and is not so hot. The most difficult months weatherwise are April – the peak of the hot season – and October, the end of the rainy season. If you're in Bangkok during these months, be prepared to roast in April and do some wading in October.

Peak months for tourism are November, December, February, March and August, with secondary peak months in January and July. Consider travelling during the least crowded months of April, May, June, September and October if avoiding crowds of vacationers is your main objective and you want to take advantage of discounted rooms and other low-season rates.

ORIENTATION

The 560 sq km city is situated approximately 14° north of the equator, a latitude shared by Madras, Manila, Guatemala and Khartoum. Metropolitan Bangkok covers 1569 sq km in the middle of the fertile Chao Phraya River Delta, often called 'the rice bowl of Asia', just a few km inland from the Gulf of Thailand. This area also encompasses Thonburi, the older part of the city (and former capital), which is across the Chao Phraya River to the west.

The east side of the river, Bangkok proper, can be divided into two by the main north-south railway line. The portion between the river and the railway is old Bangkok (often called Ko Ratanakosin) where most of the older temples and the original palace are located, as well as the Chinese and Indian districts. That part of the city east of the railway, which covers more than twice as much area as the old districts, is 'new' Bangkok. This latter part can be divided again into the business/tourist district wedged between Charoen Krung (New) Rd and Rama IV Rd, and the sprawling residential/tourist district stretching along Sukhumvit and New Phetburi Rds.

This leaves the hard-to-classify areas below Sathon Tai Rd (which includes Khlong Toey, Bangkok's main port), and the area above Rama IV Rd between the railway and Withayu (Wireless) Rd (which comprises an infinite variety of businesses, several movie theatres, civil service offices, the shopping area of Siam Square, Chulalongkorn University and the National Stadium). The areas along the east bank of the Chao Phraya River are undergoing a surge of redevelopment and many new buildings, particularly hotels, are going up.

On the opposite (west) side of the Chao Phraya River is Thonburi, which was Thailand's capital for 15 years before Bangkok was founded. Few tourists ever step foot on the Thonburi side except to visit Wat Arun, the Temple of Dawn. Fang Thon (Thon Bank), as it's often called by Thais, seems an age away from the glittering high-rises on the river's east bank, although it is an up-and-coming area for condo development.

Finding Addresses

Any city as large and unplanned as Bangkok can be tough to get around. Street names often seem unpronounceable to begin with, compounded by the inconsistency of Romanised Thai spellings. For example, the street often spelt as Rajdamri is actually pronounced Ratchadamri (with the appropriate tones, of course), or, in abbreviated form, Rat'damri. The 'v' in Sukhumvit should be pronounced like a 'w'. The most popular location for foreign embassies is known both as Wireless Rd and Withayu Rd (*wítháyú* is Thai for 'radio').

Many street addresses show a string of numbers divided by slashes and hyphens, for example, 48/3-5 Soi 1, Sukhumvit Rd. The reason is that undeveloped property in Bangkok was originally bought and sold in lots. The number before the slash refers to the original lot number; the numbers following the slash indicate buildings (or entrances to buildings) constructed within that lot. The pre-slash numbers appear in the order in which they were added to city plans, while the post-slash numbers are arbitrarily assigned by developers. As a result numbers along a given street don't always run consecutively.

A *soi* is a small street or lane that runs off a larger street. In our example, the address referred to as 48/3-5 Soi 1, Sukhumvit Rd will be located off Sukhumvit Rd on Soi 1. Alternative ways of writing the same address include 48/3-5 Sukhumvit Rd Soi 1, or even just 48/3-5 Sukhumvit 1.

MAPS

A map is essential for finding your way around Bangkok. The best one is the *Bangkok Bus Map (Walking Tours)*

RICHARD I'ANSON

Caught in the traffic: bustling Chinatown, east of the Chao Phraya river.

published by Bangkok Guide because it clearly shows all the bus routes. The map costs 35B (some places ask 40B) and although it's regularly updated, some bus routes will inevitably be wrong, so take care. Other companies put out similar maps called *Bangkok Thailand Tour 'n Guide Map* and *Latest Tour's Map to Bangkok & Thailand* that will also do the job. For more detail on bus routes you'll have to get the *Bus Guide*, a small booklet published by Bangkok Guide for 35B. It contains maps and a listing of all the public bus routes in Bangkok as well as a Bangkok railway schedule. To use it properly takes some patience since much of the guide is in Thai and the English is horrendous.

A second map to consider is Nancy Chandler's *Map of Bangkok* which costs 70B. This map has a whole host of information on out-of-the-way places, including lots of stuff on where to buy unusual things around the city. There's a similar companion map to Chiang Mai. The Fine Arts Commission of the Association of Siamese Architects produces a pack of four unusual maps showing temples and important places of cultural interest. The maps are *Bangkok, Grand Palace, Canals of Thonburi* and *Ayuthaya*. The Tourism Authority of Thailand (TAT) issues a *Sightseeing & Shopping Map* of Bangkok that has lively 3-D drawings of popular tourist spots along Ratchadamri, Rama IV, Rama I and Phayathai Rds.

TOURIST OFFICES

TAT is a government-operated tourist information/promotion service, attached to the prime minister's office, with several branch offices within the country and overseas. In 1991 the TAT was granted regulatory powers to monitor tourism-related businesses throughout Thailand, including hotels, tour operators, travel agencies and transport companies, in an effort to upgrade the quality of these services and prosecute unscrupulous operators.

Bangkok

The TAT has a desk in the arrivals area at Bangkok International airport that's open 8 am to midnight. The authority's main office (☎ 226-0060, 226-0072/6, 280-1305, fax 224-6221) is in a large government compound on the corner of Bamrung Meuang and Worachak Rds. English-speaking staff dispense information from a small round building at the centre of the compound. The TAT produces the usual selection of colourful brochures, but they're also one of the best tourist offices in Asia for putting out useful hard facts – on plain but quite invaluable duplicated sheets. This main office is open daily from 8.30 am to 4.30 pm.

Smaller TAT offices with fewer materials can be found at Chatuchak (Weekend) Market (Map 3) and opposite Wat Phra Kaew (Map 5) on Na Phra Lan Rd; these two are open daily from 8.30 am to 7.30 pm.

The TAT also maintains a Tourist Assistance Centre, or TAC (☎ 282-8129, 281-5051) in the same compound for matters relating to theft and other mishaps; it's open from 8 am to midnight. The paramilitary arm of the TAT, the tourist police, can be quite effective in dealing with such matters, particularly 'unethical' business practices – which sometimes turn out to be cultural misunderstandings. Note that if you think you've been overcharged for gems (or any other purchase) there's very little the TAC can do.

Tourist Offices Abroad

Australia
   7th floor, National Australia Bank House, 255 George St, Sydney, NSW, 2000 (☎ (02) 9247-7549, fax 251-2465)
France
   Office National de Tourisme de Thailande, 90 Ave des Champs Elysées, 75008 Paris
   (☎ (01) 4562-8656, fax 4563-7888)

Germany
> Thailandisches Fremdenverkehrbüro, Bethmannstrasse 58, 60311 Frankfurt/Main
> (☎ (069) 295704/804, fax 281468)

Hong Kong
> Rm 401, Fairmont House, 8 Cotton Tree Drive, Central
> (☎ 2868-0732, fax 2868-4585)

Italy
> Via Barberini 50, 00187 Rome
> (☎ (06) 487-3479, fax 487-3500)

Japan
> 2nd floor, South Tower, Yurakucho Denki Bldg, 1-7-1 Yurakucho, Chiyoda-ku, Tokyo 100
> (☎ (03) 3218-0337, fax 3218-0655)
> 5th floor, Hiranomachi Yachiyo Bldg, 1-8-13 Hiranomachi, Chuo-ku, Osaka 541
> (☎ (06) 231-4434, fax 231-4337)

Korea
> Rm No 2003, 20th floor, Coryo Daeyungek Center Bldg 25-5, 1-ka, Chungmu-Ro, Chung-Ku, Seoul 100-706
> (☎ (02) 779-5417, fax 779-5419)

Malaysia
> c/o 206 Jalan Ampang, 504505 Kuala Lumpur
> (☎ 248-0958, fax 241-3002)

Singapore
> c/o 370 Orchard Rd 238870 (☎ 235-7694, fax 733-5653)

Taiwan
> 13th floor, Boss Tower, 109-111 Sung Chiang Rd, Taipei 104
> (☎ (02) 502-1600, fax 502-1603)

UK
> 49 Albemarle St, London W1X 3FE
> (☎ (0171) 499-7679, fax 629-5519)

USA
> 5 World Trade Center, Suite 3443, New York, NY 10048
> (☎ (212) 432-0433, fax 912-0920)
> 3440 Wilshire Blvd, Suite 1100, Los Angeles, CA 90010
> (☎ (213) 382-2353/2355, fax 389-7544)
> 303 East Wacker Drive, Suite 400, Chicago, IL 60601
> (☎ (312) 819-3990, fax 565-0359)

DOCUMENTS

Passports

Entry into Thailand requires a passport valid for at least three months from the time of entry. If you anticipate your passport may expire while you're in Thailand, you should obtain a new one before arrival or enquire from your government whether your embassy in Thailand (if one exists – see the Embassies list further on) can issue a new one after arrival.

Visas

Whichever type of visa you have, be sure to check your passport immediately after stamping. Overworked officials sometimes stamp 15 or 30 days on arrival even when you hold a longer visa; if you point out the error before you've left the immigration area at your port of entry, officials will make the necessary corrections. If you don't notice this until you've left the port of entry, go to Bangkok and plead your case at the central immigration office.

Once a visa is issued, it must be used (ie you must enter Thailand) within 90 days.

Transit & Tourist Visas The Thai government allows 56 different nationalities to enter the country without a visa for 30 days at no charge. Shining exceptions are visitors with New Zealand, Swedish or South Korean passports, who may enter Thailand for up to 90 days without a visa!

Seventy-six other nationalities – those from smaller European countries like Andorra or Liechtenstein or from West Africa, South Asia or Latin America – can obtain 15-day Transit Visas on arrival upon payment of a 300B fee.

A few nationalities – eg Hungarians – must obtain a visa in advance of arrival or they'll be turned back. Check with a Thai embassy or consulate in advance to be sure if you plan to try arriving without a visa.

Without proof of an onward ticket and sufficient funds for one's projected stay any visitor can be denied entry, but in practice your ticket and funds are rarely checked if you're dressed neatly for the immigration check. See Exchange Control in the Money section in this chapter for officially required amounts for each visa type.

Next in length of validity is the Tourist Visa, which is good for 60 days and costs US$15. Three passport photos must accompany all applications.

Non-Immigrant Visas Good for 90 days, these visas must be applied for in your home country, cost US$20 and are not difficult to obtain if you can offer a good reason for your visit. Business, study, retirement and extended family visits are among the purposes considered valid.

Re-Entry & Multiple-Entry Visas If you need to leave and re-enter the kingdom before your visa expires, say for a return trip to Laos, apply at the immigration office on Soi Suan Phlu, Bangkok (Map 8). The cost is 500B;

you'll need to supply one passport photo. There is no limit to the number of Re-Entry Permits you can apply for and use during the validity of your visa.

Thailand does not issue multiple-entry visas. If you want a visa that enables you to leave the country and then return, the best you can do is to obtain a visa permitting two entries; this will cost double the single-entry visa. For example, a two-entry three-month Non-Immigrant Visa will cost US$40 and will allow you six months in the country, as long as you cross a border with immigration facilities by the end of your first three months. The second half of your visa is validated as soon as you re-cross the Thai border, so there is no need to go to a Thai embassy/consulate abroad. All visas acquired in advance of entry are valid for 90 days from the date of issue.

Visa Extensions

Sixty-day Tourist Visas may be extended up to 30 days at the discretion of Thai immigration authorities. The Bangkok office (☎ 287-3101) is on Soi Suan Phlu, Sathon Tai (South) Rd (Map 8), but you can apply at any immigration office in the country – every province that borders a neighbouring country has at least one. The usual fee for the extension of a Tourist Visa (up to one month) is 500B. Bring along one photo and one copy each of the photo and visa pages of your passport. Normally, only one 30-day extension is granted.

The 30-day no-visa stay can be extended for seven to 10 days (depending on the immigration office) for 500B. You can also leave the country and return immediately to obtain another 30-day stay. There is no limit on the number of times you can do this, nor is there a minimum interval you must spend outside the country.

Extension of the 15-day, on-arrival Transit Visa is only allowed if you hold a passport from a country that has no Thai embassy.

If you overstay your visa, the usual penalty is a fine of 100B per day of your overstay, with a 20,000B limit; fines can be paid at the airport or in advance at the Investigation Unit (☎ 287-3129, ext 2204), Immigration Bureau, Room 416, 4th floor, Old Bldg, Soi Suan Phlu, Sathon Tai Rd.

Foreigners with Non-Immigrant Visas who have resided in Thailand continuously for three years – on one-year extensions – may apply for permanent residency at Section 1, Subdivision 1, Immigration Division 1, Room 301, 3rd floor, Immigration Bureau, Soi Suan Phlu, (☎ 287-3117 or 287-3101). Foreigners who receive permanent residence must carry an 'alien identification card' at all times.

Tax Clearance Anyone who receives income while in Thailand must obtain a tax clearance certificate from the Revenue Department before they'll be permitted to leave the country. The Bangkok office (☎ 281-5777, 282-9899) of the Revenue Department is on Chakkapong Rd not far from the Democracy Monument (Map 5).

Old Thai hands note: The tax clearance requirement no longer applies to those who have simply stayed in Thailand beyond a cumulative 90 days within one calendar year – this regulation was abolished in 1991. This makes it much easier for expats or other long-termers who live in Thailand on Non-Immigrant Visas – as long as they don't receive income. Hence, there's no more hustling for tax clearance for every visa trip to Penang or Vientiane.

Photocopies

It's a good idea to keep photocopies of all vital documents – passport data page, credit card numbers, airline tickets, travellers cheque serial numbers and so on – separate from the originals. Replacement will be much easier to arrange if you can provide issuing agencies with copies. You might consider leaving extra copies of these documents with someone at home or in a safe place in Bangkok or other point of entry.

Onward Tickets

Thai immigration does not seem very concerned with whether or not you arrive with proof of onward travel. Legally speaking, all holders of Tourist Visas or the no-visa 30-day stay permit are *supposed* to carry such proof. In all my years of frequent travel in and out of the Kingdom, my onward travel documents haven't once been checked.

Travel Insurance

A travel insurance policy to cover theft, loss and medical problems is strongly recommended. Though Thailand is generally a safe country to travel in, sickness, accidents and theft do happen. There are a wide variety of policies available and your travel agent could give recommendations. Check the small print to see if the policy covers any potentially dangerous sporting activities you may do, such as diving or trekking, and make sure that it adequately covers your valuables. A few credit cards offer limited, sometimes full, travel insurance to the holder.

Driving Licence & Permits

An International Driving Permit is necessary for any visitor who intends to drive a motorised vehicle while in Thailand. These are usually available from motoring organisations such as AAA (US) or BAA (UK) in your home country.

Hostel Card

Hostelling International (formerly known as International Youth Hostel Federation) issues a membership card that will allow you to stay at Thailand's member hostels. Without such a card or a temporary membership you won't be admitted. There is only one hostel in Bangkok, and it's not particularly recommended, so if your visit is limited to Bangkok a card may not be of much use.

Memberships are sold at any member hostel worldwide or from the head office: Hostelling International, 9 Guessens Rd, Welwyn Garden City, Hertfordshire AL8 6QW, UK.

Student Cards

The International Student Identity Card (ISIC), issued by the International Student Travel Confederation (☎ 3393-9303, fax 3393-7377), Box 9048, DK1000, Copenhagen, Denmark, can be used for the rare student discount at some museums in Thailand. It's probably not worth getting just for a visit to Thailand, but if you already have one, or plan to use one elsewhere in Asia, then bring it along. Fake ISICs are available on Khao San Rd in Bangkok, but it's doubtful these will be recognised outside Thailand.

EMBASSIES & CONSULATES

Thai Embassies Abroad

To apply for a visa, contact one of Thailand's diplomatic missions in any of the following countries. In many cases if you apply in person you may receive a Tourist or Non-Immigrant Visa on the day of application; by mail it generally takes anywhere from two to six weeks.

Facts for the Visitor

Australia
111 Empire Circuit, Yarralumla, Canberra, ACT 2600
(☎ (06) 273-1149/2937)
Canada
180 Island Park Drive, Ottawa, Ontario K1Y OA2
(☎ (613) 722-4444)
China
40 Guanghua Lu, Beijing 100600 (☎ (010) 532-1903)
France
8 Rue Greuze, 75116 Paris (☎ 01 47 27 80 79, 01 47 24 32 22)
Germany
Ubierstrasse 65, 53173 Bonn 2 (☎ (0228) 355-065/068)
Hong Kong
8th floor, Fairmont House, 8 Cotton Tree Drive, Central
(☎ 2521-6481/6482)
India
56-N Nyaya Marg, Chanakyapuri, New Delhi, 110021
(☎ (11) 605679, 607289)
Indonesia
Jalan Imam Bonjol 74, Jakarta (☎ (021) 390-4052/4053/4054)
Italy
Via Bertoloni 26B, 00197 Rome (☎ (06) 807-8955)
Japan
3-14-6 Kami-Osaki, Shinagawa-ku, Tokyo 141
(☎ (03) 3441-1386/1387)
Laos
Route Phonkheng, Vientiane Poste 128
(☎ (21) 214582/214583)
Malaysia
206 Jalan Ampang, Kuala Lumpur (☎ (03) 248-8222/350)
Myanmar (Burma)
91 Pyi Rd, Yangon (☎ (01) 282471, 276555)
Nepal
Jyoti Kendra Bldg, Thapathali, Kathmandu
(☎ (01) 213-910/912)
Netherlands
Buitenrustweg 1, 2517 KD The Hague
(☎ (070) 345-2088/9703)
New Zealand
2 Cook St, Karori, Wellington 5 (☎ (04) 476-8618/8619)
Philippines
107B Rada St, Legaspi Village, Makati, Metro Manila
(☎ (02) 810-3833, 815-4219)
Singapore
370 Orchard Rd (☎ 235-4175, 737-2158/3372)
Sweden
5th floor, Sandhamnsgatan 36, Stockholm
(☎ (08) 667-2160/8090)
Switzerland
3rd floor, Eigerstrasse 60, 3007 Bern
(☎ (031) 372-2281/2282)
UK
29-30 Queen's Gate, London SW7 5JB
(☎ (0171) 589-0173/2944)

USA
    1024 Wisconsin Ave NW, Washington, DC 20007
    (☎ (202) 944-3600)
Vietnam
    63-65 Hoang Dieu St, Hanoi (☎ (04) 235-092/094)

Foreign Embassies & Consulates

Bangkok is a good place to collect visas for onward travel. The visa sections of most embassies and consulates are open from around 8.30 to 11.30 am, Monday through Friday only (call first to be sure).

Countries with diplomatic representation in Bangkok include:

Australia
    37 Sathon Tai Rd (☎ 287-2680)
Bangladesh
    727 Soi 55, Sukhumvit Rd (☎ 392-9437)
Brunei
    19 Soi 26, Sukhumvit Rd (☎ 260-5884)
Canada
    Boonmitr Bldg, 138 Silom Rd (☎ 234-1561/1568, 237-4126)
China
    57 Ratchadaphisek Rd (☎ 245-7032/49)
France
    35 Customs House Lane, Charoen Krung Rd
    (☎ 234-0950/0956); consular section (visas): 29 Sathon Tai Rd (☎ 213-2181/2184)
Germany
    9 Sathon Tai Rd (☎ 286-4223/4227, 213-2331/2336)
India (Map 4)
    46 Soi Prasanmit (Soi 23), Sukhumvit Rd(☎ 258-0300/0306)
Indonesia
    600-602 Phetburi Rd (☎ 252-3135/3140)
Ireland
    205 United Flour Mill Bldg, Ratchawong Rd (☎ 223-0876)
Israel
    31 Soi Lang Suan, Ploenchit Rd (☎ 252-3131/3134)
Italy
    399 Nang Linchi Rd (☎ 286-4844/4846, 287-2054)
Japan
    1674 New Phetburi Rd (☎ 252-6151/6159)
Korea (North)
    81 Soi Ari 7, Phahonyothin Rd (☎ 278-5118)
Korea (South)
    23 Thiam-Ruammit Rd, Huay Khwang, Sam Saen Nok
    (☎ 247-7537)
Laos
    193 Sathon Tai Rd (☎ 254-6963, 213-2573)
Malaysia
    35 Sathon Tai Rd (☎ 286-1390/1392)

Myanmar (Burma)
    132 Sathon Neua Rd (☎ 233-2237, 234-4698)
Nepal
    189 Soi Phuengsuk (Soi 71), Sukhumvit Rd (☎ 391-7240)
New Zealand
    93 Withayu Rd (☎ 251-8165)
Pakistan (Map 4)
    31 Soi Nana Neua (Soi 3), Sukhumvit Rd (☎ 253-0288/0289)
Philippines
    760 Sukhumvit Rd (☎ 259-0139)
Singapore
    129 Sathon Tai Rd (☎ 286-2111/1434)
South Africa
    6th floor, Park Place, 231 Sarasin Rd (☎ 253-8473)
Sri Lanka
    48/3 Soi 1, Sukhumvit Rd (☎ 251-2789)
Taiwan
    Far East Trade Office, 10th floor Kian Gwan Bldg, 140 Withayu Rd (☎ 251-9274/9276)
UK
    1031 Ploenchit Rd (☎ 253-0191/0199)
USA
    95 Withayu Rd (☎ 252-5040/5049)
Vietnam
    83/1 Withayu Rd (☎ 251-7201/7203)

CUSTOMS

Like most countries, Thailand prohibits the import of illegal drugs, firearms and ammunition (unless registered in advance with the police department) and pornographic media. A reasonable amount of clothing

JOE CUMMINGS

Gold ornaments are sold at good rates in Bangkok.

for personal use, toiletries and professional instruments are allowed in duty-free, as is one still or one movie/video camera with five rolls of still film or three rolls of movie film or videotape. Up to 200 cigarettes can be brought into the country without paying duty, or for other smoking materials a total of up to 250g. One litre of wine or spirits is allowed in duty-free.

Electronic goods like personal stereos, calculators and computers can be a problem if the customs officials have reason to believe you're bringing them in for resale. As long as you don't carry more than one of each, you should be OK. Occasionally, customs will require you to leave a hefty deposit for big-ticket items (eg a lap-top computer or midi-component stereo) which is refunded when you leave the country with the item in question. If you make the mistake of saying you're just passing through and don't plan to use the item while in Thailand, they may ask you to leave it with Customs until you leave the country.

For information on currency import or export, see Exchange Control in the Money section of this chapter.

Antiques & Art

When leaving Thailand, you must obtain an export licence for any antiques or *objets d'art* you want to take with you. An antique is any 'archaic movable property whether produced by man or by nature, any part of ancient structure, human skeleton or animal carcass, which by its age or characteristic of production or historical evidence is useful in the field of art, history or archaeology'. An objet d'art is a 'thing produced by craftsmanship and appreciated as being valuable in the field of art'. Obviously these are very sweeping definitions, so if in doubt go to the Department of Fine Arts for inspection and licensing.

Export licence applications can be made by submitting two front-view photos of the object(s) (no more than five objects to a photo) and a photocopy of your passport, along with the object(s) in question, to the Bangkok National Museum. You need to allow three to five days for the application and inspection process to be completed.

Thailand has special regulations for taking a Buddha or other deity image (or any part thereof) out of the country. These require not only a licence from the Department of Fine Arts but a permit from the Ministry of Commerce as well. The one exception to this are the small Buddha images *(phrá phim)* that are meant to be worn on a chain around the neck; these may be exported without a licence as long as the reported purpose is religious.

Temporary Vehicle Importation

Passenger vehicles (car, van, truck or motorcycle) can be brought into Thailand for tourist purposes for up to six months. Documents needed are: a valid International Driving Permit; passport; vehicle registration papers (or in the case of a borrowed or hired vehicle, authorisation from the owner); and a cash or bank guarantee equal to the value of the vehicle plus 20%. For entry through Khlong Toey port or Bangkok airport, this means a letter of bank credit; for overland crossings via Malaysia a 'self-guarantee' filled in at the border is sufficient.

MONEY

ATM & Credit/Debit Cards

An alternative to carrying around large amounts of cash or travellers cheques in Bangkok is to open an account at a Thai bank. Most major banks in Thailand now have automatic teller machines (ATMs) in provincial capitals and in many smaller towns as well. Request an ATM card and you'll be able to withdraw cash at machines throughout Thailand, whether those machines belong to your bank or not. For example, ATM cards issued by Thai Farmers Bank or Bangkok Bank can be used at the ATMs of 14 major banks – and there were over 2500 machines nationwide as of 1996. A 10B transaction charge is usually deducted for using an ATM belonging to a bank with whom you don't have an account.

Debit cards (also known as cash cards or cheque cards) issued by a bank in your own country can also be used at several Thai banks to withdraw cash (in Thai baht only) directly from your cheque or savings account back home, thus avoiding all commissions and finance charges. You can use MasterCard debit cards to buy baht at foreign exchange booths or desks at either Bangkok Bank or Siam Commercial Bank. Visa debit cards can buy cash though Thai Farmers Bank exchange services.

These cards can also be used at many Thai ATMs, though a surcharge of around US$1 is usually subtracted from your home account each time you complete a machine transaction. As a general rule, debit cards issued under the MasterCard name work best at Bangkok Bank ATMs, while Visa debit cards work best with Thai Farmers Bank machines. Some travellers now use debit cards in lieu of travellers cheques because they're quicker and more convenient, although it's a good idea to bring along an emergency travellers cheque fund in case you lose your card. One disadvantage of debit card accounts – as opposed to credit card accounts – is that you can't arrange a 'chargeback' for unsatisfactory purchases after the transaction is completed – once the money's drawn from your account it's gone.

Plastic money is becoming increasingly popular in Thailand and many shops, hotels and restaurants now accept credit as well as debit cards. The most commonly accepted cards are Visa and MasterCard, followed by Diner's Club and Japan Card Bureau (JCB). American Express and Carte Blanche are less useful.

Card Problems Occasionally when you try to use a Visa or MasterCard at upcountry hotels or shops, the staff tell you that only Thai Farmers Bank or Siam Commercial Bank cards are accepted. With a little patience, you should be able to make them understand that the Thai Farmers Bank will pay them and that your bank will pay the Thai Farmers Bank – that any Visa or MasterCard issued anywhere in the world is indeed acceptable.

Another problem is illegal surcharges on credit-card purchases. It's against Thai law to pass on to the customer the 3% merchant fee charged by banks, but almost all merchants in Thailand do it anyway. Some even ask 4 or 5%! The only exception seems to be hotels (although even a few hotels will hit you with a credit-card surcharge). If you don't agree to the surcharge they'll simply refuse to accept your card. Begging and pleading or pointing out the law doesn't seem to help.

The best way to get around the illegal surcharge is to politely ask that the credit-card receipt be itemised with cost of product or service and the surcharge listed separately. Then when you pay your bill, photocopy all receipts showing the surcharge and request a 'charge back'. If a hotel or shop refuses to itemise the surcharge, take down the vendor's name and address and report them to the TAT tourist police – they may be able to arrange a refund. Not all banks in all countries will offer such refunds – banks in the UK, for example, refuse to issue such refunds, while banks in the US usually will.

To report a lost or stolen credit/debit card, call the following telephone hotlines in Bangkok:

American Express	☎ 273-0022, 273-0044
Diners Club	☎ 238-3660
MasterCard	☎ 299-1990
Visa	☎ 273-1199, 273-7449

See the Dangers & Annoyances section in this chapter for important warnings on credit-card theft and fraud.

International Transfers

If you have a reliable place to receive mail in Thailand, one of the safest and cheapest ways to get money from overseas is to have an international cashiers cheque (or international money order) sent by courier. It usually takes no more than four days for courier mail to reach Thailand from anywhere in the world.

If you have a bank account in Thailand or your home bank has a branch in Bangkok, you can have money wired direct via a telegraphic transfer. This costs a bit more than having a cheque sent; telegraphic transfers take anywhere from two days to a week to arrive. International banks with branches in Bangkok include Hongkong Bank, Standard Chartered Bank, Sakura Bank, Bank of America, Banque Indosuez, Citibank, Banque Nationale de Paris, Chase Manhattan Bank, Bank of Tokyo, Deutsche Bank, Merrill Lynch International Bank, HongKong & Shanghai Bank, United Malayan Bank and many others.

Western Union (☎ 251-9201) had an office on the 3rd floor of Central Department Store, 1027 Ploenchit Rd, before this building burnt down in late 1995. It should be operating again by the time you read this.

Currency

The basic unit of Thai currency is the baht. There are 100 satang in one baht; coins include 25-satang and 50-satang pieces and baht in 1B, 5B and 10B coins. Older coins exhibit Thai numerals only, while newer coins have Thai and Roman numerals. At the time of writing, 1B coins come in three sizes: only the middle size works in public pay phones! Likewise, 5B coins also come in three sizes; a large one with a Thai numeral only and two smaller coins that have Thai and Roman numerals (one of the smaller 5B coins has nine inset edges along the circumference). The copper-and-silver 10B coin has Thai and Roman-Arabic numerals. Eventually, Thailand will phase out the older coins, but in the meantime, counting out change is confusing.

Twenty-five satang equals one saleng in colloquial Thai, so if you're quoted a price of six saleng in the market, say, for a very small bunch of bananas or a bag of peanuts, this means 1.50B. The term is becoming increasingly rare as inflation makes purchases of less than 1B or 2B almost extinct.

Paper currency comes in denominations of 10B (brown), 20B (green), 50B (blue), 100B (red), 500B (purple) and 1000B (beige). A 10,000B bill is on the way.

The 10B bills are being phased out in favour of the relatively new 10B coin and have become rather uncommon. Fortunately for newcomers to Thailand, numerals are printed in their Western as well as Thai forms. Notes are also scaled according to their value; the larger the denomination, the larger the note. Large denominations – 500B and especially 1000B bills – can be hard to change in small towns, but banks will always change them.

Currency Exchange

Australia	A$1	=	19.84B
Canada	C$1	=	18.62B
France	FF1	=	5.01B
Germany	DM1	=	17.07B
Japan	¥100	=	23.49B
Malaysia	M$1	=	9.99B
New Zealand	NZ$1	=	17.27B
Singapore	S$1	=	17.98B
United Kingdom	UK£1	=	38.72B
United States	US$1	=	25.28B

Changing Money

There is no black-market money exchange for baht, so there's no reason to bring in any Thai currency. Banks or legal moneychangers offer the best exchange rate within the country. The baht is firmly attached to the US dollar and is equally stable.

Exchange rates are listed in the *Bangkok Post* and *The Nation* every day. For buying baht, US dollars are the most readily accepted currency and travellers cheques get better rates than cash. Since banks charge 10B commission and duty for each travellers cheque cashed, you will save if you cash larger cheque denominations (eg a US$50 cheque will only cost 10B while five US$10 cheques will cost 50B). Note that you can't exchange Indonesian rupiah, Nepalese rupees, Cambodian riel, Lao kip, Vietnamese dong or Myanmar kyat into Thai currency at banks, though some Bangkok moneychangers carry these currencies. The latter can in fact be good places to buy these currencies if you're going to any of these countries. Rates are comparable with black-market rates in countries with discrepancies between the 'official' and free-market currency values.

Visa and MasterCard credit-card holders can get cash advances of up to US$500 (in baht only) per day through some branches of the Thai Farmers Bank, Bangkok Bank and Siam Commercial Bank (and also at the night-time exchange windows in well-touristed spots like Banglamphu).

American Express card holders can also get advances, but only in travellers cheques. The Amex agent is SEA Tours (☎ 216-5757), Suite 88-92, Payathai Plaza, 8th floor, 128 Phayathai Rd, Bangkok.

Many Thai banks also have currency exchange offices, which are open from 8.30 am to 8 pm (some even later) every day of the year. You'll find them in several places along Sukhumvit, Nana Neua, Khao San, Patpong, Sur-awong, Ratchadamri, Rama IV, Rama I, Silom and Charoen Krung Rds. If you're after currency for other countries in Asia, try the moneychangers along Charoen Krung Rd near the GPO.

Costs

While food and accommodation outside the capital are usually cheaper, costs in Bangkok are also very reason-able, especially considering the value vis-à-vis other countries in South and South-East Asia.

In Bangkok there's almost no limit to the amount you *could* spend, but if you live frugally, avoid the tourist ghettos and ride the public bus system you can get by on only slightly more than you would spend upcountry. Where you stay in Bangkok is of primary importance, as accommodation is generally a good deal more expensive than in the provinces. Outside Bangkok, budget-squeez-ers should be able to get by on 200B per day – this estimate includes basic guesthouse accommodation, food, nonalcoholic beverages and local transport, but not camera film, souvenirs, tours, long-distance trans-port or vehicle hire. Add another 50 to 75B per day for every large beer (25 to 35B for small bottles) you drink.

However, in Bangkok, the visitor typically spends more than 300B per day just for accommodation – this is generally the minimum for air-con (in a twin room). On the other hand, if you can do without air-con, rooms can be found for as little as 60B per person. It is usually the noise, heat and pollution in Bangkok that drives many budget travellers to seek more comfort than they might need upcountry.

Those seeking international-class accommodation and food will spend at least 1500B a day for a room with all the modern amenities – IDD phone, 24-hour hot water and air-conditioning, carpeting, a fitness centre and all-night room service.

Food is somewhat more expensive in Bangkok than in the provinces. However, in Thonburi (Bangkok's 'left bank'), where I lived for some time, many dishes are often *cheaper* than they are upcountry, due to the avail-ability of fresh ingredients. This is also true for the working-class districts on the Bangkok side, like Khlong Toey or Makkasan. Bangkok is the typical 'primate city' cited by sociologists, meaning that most goods produced by the country as a whole end up in Bangkok. The glaring exception is Western food, which Bangkok has more of than anywhere else in the kingdom, but charges the most for. Eat only Thai and Chinese food if you're trying to spend as little as possible. After all, why go to Thailand to eat steak and potatoes?

Tipping & Bargaining

Good bargaining, which takes practice, is another way to cut costs. Anything bought in a market should be bargained for; prices in department stores and most nontourist shops are fixed. Sometimes accommodation rates can be bargained down. Bargain hard in heavily touristed areas as the one-week, all-air-con type of visitor often pays whatever's asked, creating an artificial price zone between the local and tourist market.

On the other hand, the Thais aren't *always* trying to rip you off, so use some discretion when going for the bone on a price. There's a fine line between bargaining and niggling – getting hot under the collar over 5B makes both seller and buyer lose face. Some more specific suggestions about costs can be found in the Places to Stay and Shopping chapters of this book.

The cost of transport within Bangkok and between it and other cities is very reasonable; again, bargaining

RICHARD NEBESKY

Be prepared to bargain when hiring a tuk-tuk.

(when hiring a vehicle) can save you a lot of baht. See the Getting Around chapter.

Tipping is not normal practice in Thailand, although they're getting used to it in expensive hotels and restaurants. Elsewhere, don't bother. In taxis where you have to bargain the fare, it certainly isn't necessary.

Consumer Taxes

In January 1992 Thailand instituted a 7% value-added tax (VAT) for certain goods and services. Unfortunately no-one seems to know what's subject to VAT and what's not, so the whole situation is rather confusing. It doesn't mean that consumers are to be charged 7% over retail – the tax is supposed to be applied to a retailer's cost for the product. For example, if a merchant's wholesale price is 100B for an item that retails at 200B, the maximum adjusted retail price including VAT should be 207B, not 214B. In practice the tax is supposed to have caused a net decrease in prices for most goods and services since the VAT replaces a graduated business tax that averaged 9%. But this doesn't always stop Thai merchants from trying to add 'VAT' surcharges to their sales. Like the credit-card surcharge, a direct VAT surcharge is illegal and should be reported to the TAT tourist police.

Tourist hotels add a 7% to 11% hotel tax, and sometimes an 8 to 10% service charge as well, to your room bill.

Carrying Money

Give some thought in advance to how you're going to carry your money – whether travellers cheques, cash, credit and debit cards, or a combination of these. Many travellers favour hidden pouches worn beneath clothing. Hip-pocket wallets are easy targets for thieves. Pickpockets work markets and crowded buses throughout the country, so it pays to keep your money concealed. See the Dangers & Annoyances section later in this chapter for more on petty crime.

It's a good idea not to keep all your money in one place; keep an 'emergency' stash well-concealed in a piece of luggage separate from other money. Long-term travellers might even consider renting a safety deposit box at a bank. Keep your onward tickets, a copy of your passport, a list of all credit-card numbers and some money in the box just in case all your belongings are stolen while you're on the road. It's not likely, but it does happen.

Safety Deposit Boxes

Travellers can rent safety deposit boxes at Bangkok's Safety Deposit Centre, 3rd floor, Chan Issara Tower, 942/81 Rama IV Rd (near the Silom Rd intersection) for 150B a month plus 2000B for a refundable key deposit. The centre is open from 10 am to 7 pm on weekdays, and from 10 am to 6 pm Saturday, Sunday and public holidays. A few banks rent safety deposit boxes, but generally you need to open an account with them first.

Exchange Control

Legally, any traveller arriving in Thailand must have at least the following amount of money in cash, travellers cheques, bank draft, or letter of credit, according to visa category: Non-Immigrant Visa, US$500 per person or US$1000 per family; Tourist Visa, US$250 per person or US$500 per family; Transit Visa or no visa, US$125 per person or US$250 per family. This may be checked if you arrive on a one-way ticket or if you look as if you're at 'the end of the road'.

According to 1991 regulations, there are no limits to the amounts of Thai or foreign currency you may bring into the country. Upon leaving Thailand, you're permitted to take no more than 50,000B per person without special authorisation; export of foreign currencies is unrestricted.

It's legal to open a foreign-currency account at any commercial bank in Thailand. As long as the funds originate from abroad, there are no restrictions on their maintenance or withdrawal.

DOING BUSINESS

Thailand's steady economic growth over the past 15 years has attracted much trade and investment, so the Thais – at least Bangkok Thais – are quite used to doing business with foreigners. See Society & Conduct in the previous chapter for a discussion of social taboos and important information on social relationships, status and Thai concepts of saving face.

Government Contacts

For a complete rundown of investment regulations, contact the Office of the Board of Investment (BOI), (☎ (2) 537-8111, fax 537-8177555) Vibhavadi Rangsit Rd, Bangkok, Thailand 10900. Investment law in Thailand is quite complicated, but the government does offer certain tax deferments and other concessions for foreign businesses – depending on the business arena.

The BOI has offices in Australia, the USA, Germany, France and Japan – these can be contacted through the relevant Thai embassy in each of these countries. There are also four regional offices within Thailand for the central, southern, northern and north-eastern regions.

Those interested in import/export possibilities should contact the Thai Chamber of Commerce, 150 Ratchabophit Rd (☎ (2) 255-0086, fax 225-3372) and the Board of Trade of Thailand, (same address, ☎ (02) 221-9350, fax 225-3995).

Other Resources

The daily newspaper *Business Day*, published in Bangkok, focuses on business news, including Thai politics as it relates to trade and investment. Three helpful books are: *Working with Thais*, *Thais Mean Business* and *Starting and Operating a Business in Thailand*, all of which are available at bookstores in Bangkok (see Books further on for bookstore information).

On the Internet, you can find the latest news on investments, trade, labour policy and other topics relevant to the Thai business world by doing a search for Thailand under: www.businessmonitor.co.uk.

Business Services

Most of the major hotels have business centres where fax, telecommunications, translation and secretarial services can be arranged for standard fees. Several private companies around the city also offer such services.

Computer Equipment Rental
The following companies rent a wide variety of computer equipment – usually not the latest hardware, but adequate for most business needs.

Computer System Connection, 212 Intharaphitak Rd
   (☎ 466-2393)
Computerist Company, Tada Bldg, 55 Ratchaprarop Rd
   (☎ 247-1282/1283)
Cybernetics Company, 62/17-8 Thaniya Rd (☎ 235-2916)
Microway Ltd, 727 Sukhumvit Rd (☎ 258-8922)
Quantum Systems, 1400 Rama IV Rd (☎ 249-3996)
Shinawatra Computer Co, 526 Rama V Rd (☎ 241-3161)

Translation Services These companies can provide Thai-English and English-Thai translations, often very quickly.

Interlanguage Translation Center, 554 Ploenchit Rd
      (☎ 252-4307/9177, fax 252-9177)
International Translations Office, 22 Silom Rd
      (☎ 233-7714, fax 235-6619)
Siam Translation Center, 57/4 Withayu (Wireless) Rd
      (☎ 254-5582, 250-1656, fax 254-5582)
World Translation Center, 1107 New Phetburi Rd (☎ 251-7545)

Business Centres These offices provide a mixed bag of services, including secretarial, translation and fax services.

Adisorn Business Center, 23/15 Royal City Avenue, Rama IX
      Rd (☎ 203-0330)
Bangkok Business & Secretarial Office, 5/6 Soi Sala Daeng,
      Silom Rd (☎ 233-4768, 233-3572)
Ecco Services, Insurance Bldg, Surawong Rd
      (☎ 235-4667, fax 237-0887)
Girl Friday Business and Secretarial Services, 107 Silom Soi 9
      (☎ 233-9293, fax 237-6132)
Inter-Asian Enterprises (IAE), 1426 New Phetburi Rd
      (☎ 251-6671, fax 255-3529)

POST & COMMUNICATIONS

Post

Thailand has a very efficient postal service and within the country postage is very cheap. Bangkok's GPO on Charoen Krung (New) Rd (Map 8) is open from 8 am to 8 pm weekdays and from 8 am to 1 pm weekends and holidays.

The vintage 1927 Thai Art Deco building is a treat in itself. During the short-lived Japanese assault on Bangkok in 1941, a bomb came through the roof and landed on the floor of the main hall without exploding. Italian sculptor Corrado Feroci, considered the father of Thai modern art, crafted the garuda sculptures perched atop either side of the building's central tower. The easiest way to get to the GPO is via the Chao Phraya River Express, which stops at Tha Meuang Khae at the river end of Soi Charoen Krung 34, next to Wat Meuang Khae, just south of the GPO. A 24-hour international telecommunications service (including telephone, fax, telex and telegram) is located in a separate building behind and to the right of the main GPO building.

The American Express office (☎ 216-5757), Suite 88-92, Payathai Plaza, 8th floor, 128 Phayathai Rd, will also take mail on behalf of Amex card holders. The hours are from 8.30 am to noon and 1 to 4.30 pm on weekdays, and 8.30 to 11.30 am Saturday. Amex won't accept courier packets that require your signature. The mail window staff have a well-deserved reputation for rudeness – one staff member has been known to shut the window on patrons' fingers!

Poste Restante & Packaging The poste restante counter at the GPO on Charoen Krung Rd is open week-days from 8 am to 8 pm, and on weekends from 8 am to 1 pm. Each letter you collect costs 1B, parcels 2B, and the staff are very efficient. Poste-restante service is very reliable, though during high tourist months you may have to wait in line. As with many Asian countries, confusion with poste restante is most likely to arise over given names and surnames. Ask people who are writing to you to print your surname clearly and to underline it. If you're certain a letter should be waiting for you and it cannot be found, it's always wise to check it hasn't been filed under your given name.

There's also a packaging service at the GPO where parcels can be wrapped for 4 to 10B plus the cost of materials (up to 35B). Or you can simply buy the mate-rials at the counter and do it yourself. The packaging counter is open weekdays from 8 am to 4.30 pm and Saturday from 9 am to noon. When the parcel counter is closed (weekday evenings and Sunday mornings) an informal packing service (using recycled materials) is open behind the service windows at the centre rear of the building.

Branch post offices throughout the city also offer poste restante and parcel services. In Banglamphu, the post office at the east end of Trok Mayom, near Sweety Guest House, is very conveniently located; packaging services are available here as well.

Postal Rates Air-mail letters weighing 10g or less cost 13B to Europe, Australia and New Zealand and 16B to the Americas.

Aerograms cost 10B regardless of destination; post-cards are 9B.

Letters sent by registered mail cost 20B in addition to regular airmail postage. International express mail (EMS) fees vary according to the country of destination. Sample rates for items weighing 100g to 250g are: Japan 250B; Australia, Germany and the UK 215B; and France,

Canada and the USA 235B. Within Thailand, this service costs only 20B (100g to 250g) in addition to regular postage.

Rates for parcels shipped by post vary according to weight (rising in one-kg increments), country of destination and whether they're shipped by surface (takes up to two months) or air (one to two weeks).

You can insure a package's contents for 8.50B for each 1740B of the goods' value.

Courier Services The following companies will pick up mail or parcels anywhere in Bangkok for overnight delivery to other towns in Thailand or to most places in the world within three to four days. DHL has the best reputation for punctuality and efficiency. Be sure to allow plenty of time between your call and the expected pick-up time for traffic jams.

DHL Worldwide
    22nd floor, Grand Amarin Tower, New Phetburi Rd
    (☎ 207-0600)
Federal Express
    8th floor, Green Tower, Rama IV Rd (☎ 367-3222)
TNT Express
    599 Chong Non Sii Rd, Khlong Toey (☎ 249-0242)

Telephone

The telephone system in Thailand, operated by the government-subsidised but privately-owned Telephone Organisation of Thailand (TOT) under the Communications Authority of Thailand (CAT), is quite efficient, and from Bangkok you can usually direct dial most major centres with little difficulty.

International Calls To direct dial an international number (other than those in Malaysia and Laos; see the next heading) from a private phone, simply dial 001 before the number. For operator-assisted international calls, dial 100. A service called Home Direct is available at Bangkok's GPO on Charoen Krung Rd (Map 8), Bangkok International airport, Queen Sirikit National Convention Centre (Map 8), World Trade Center (Map 7), Sogo department store (Map 7) and at the Banglamphu (Map 5) and Hualamphong post offices. Home Direct phones offer easy one-button connection to international operators in 20-odd countries around the world.

You can also direct-dial Home Direct access numbers from any private phone (most hotel phones won't work) in Thailand. For Home Direct, dial 001-999 followed by:

Australia	61-1000
Canada	15-1000
Denmark	45-1000
Germany	49-1000
Hawaii	14414
Hong Kong	852-1086
Indonesia	62-1000
Italy	39-1000
Japan	81-0051
Korea	82-1000
Netherlands	31-1035
New Zealand	64-1066
Norway	47-1000
Philippines	63-1000
Singapore	351-1000
Taiwan	886-1000
UK	44-1066
USA (AT&T)	1111
USA (MCI)	12001
USA (Sprint)	13877

Hotels generally add surcharges (sometimes as much as 30% over and above the TOT rate) for international long-distance calls; it's always cheaper to call abroad from a CAT telephone office. A useful CAT office is the one near the GPO (Map 8). You can also make long-distance calls and faxes at the TOT office on Ploenchit Rd (Map 7) – but this office accepts cash only, no reverse-charge or credit-card calls. Hence the CAT office is generally your best choice.

Once you've found the proper office and window, the procedure for making an international long-distance call (*thorásàp ráwàang pràthêt*) begins with filling out a bilingual form with your name and details pertaining to the call's destination. Except for collect calls, you must estimate in advance the time you'll be on the phone and pay a deposit equal to the time/distance rate. There is always a minimum three-minute charge, refunded if your call doesn't go through.

Usually, only cash or international phone credit cards are acceptable at CAT offices. If the call doesn't go through you must pay a 30B service charge anyway – unless you're calling collect (*kèp plai-thaang*). For collect calls it's the reverse, you must pay the 30B charge only if the call goes through. Depending on where you're calling, reimbursing someone later for a collect call to your home country may be less expensive than paying

CAT/TOT charges – it pays to compare rates. For calls between the USA and Thailand, for example, AT&T collect rates are less than TOT's direct rates.

There are also private long-distance telephone offices but these are usually only for calls within Thailand. Private offices with international service always charge more than the government offices, although private office surcharges are usually lower than hotel rates.

Whichever phone service you use, the least expensive time of day to make calls is from 10 pm to 7 am (66% discount from standard rates), followed by 6 pm to 10 pm (50% discount). You pay full price from 7 am to 6 pm.

Malaysia & Laos CAT does not offer long-distance service to Malaysia or Laos. To call these countries you must go through TOT. For Vientiane, you must dial 101 to reach a TOT operator and arrange an operator-assisted call. Malaysia can be dialled direct by prefixing the Malaysian number (including area code) with the code 09.

Telephone Office Hours Bangkok's CAT international phone office at the Charoen Krung Rd GPO is open 24 hours.

Pay Phones There are two kinds of public pay phones in Thailand: 'red' and 'blue'. The red phones are for local city calls and the blue are for long-distance calls (within Thailand). Local calls from pay phones cost 1B. Although there are three different 1B coins in general circulation, only the middle-sized coin fits the coin slots. Some hotels and guesthouses have private pay phones that cost 5B per call; these take only nine-sided 5B coins.

Card phones are available at most Thai airports as well as major shopping centres and other public areas throughout urban Thailand. Telephone cards come in 25B, 50B, 100B, 200B and 240B denominations, all roughly the same size as a credit card; they can be purchased at any TOT office. In airports you can usually buy them at the airport information counter or at one of the gift shops.

The newest phone booth service in Thailand – found mostly in Bangkok – is called Telepoint (formerly Fonepoint), a system which uses a one-way mobile phone network operated by TOT. Such mobile phones can be used within 100 to 200m of a Telepoint location to communicate with other mobile phones and pagers. For a Telepoint account, the TOT charges a monthly service fee of 350B plus 1B per minute (three-minute minimum) in Bangkok, or normal TOT rates for upcountry and overseas calls, plus registration fees.

Cellular Phones TOT authorises the use of private cell phones using two systems, NMT 470 MHZ and Cellular 900 NMT. The latter system is more common, with at least 10 dealer agencies around the country and more base stations.

It costs 1000B to register a phone and 500B per month for 'number rental'. Rates are 3B per minute within the same area code, 8B per minute to adjacent area codes and 12B per minute to other area codes. Cell phone users must pay for incoming as well as outgoing calls. Keep this in mind whenever you consider calling a number that begins with the code (01) – this means you're calling a cell phone number and will be charged accordingly.

Area Codes The country code for Thailand is 66. Area codes include:

02	Bangkok, Thonburi, Nonthaburi, Pathum Thani, Samut Prakan
032	Phetburi, Cha-am, Prachuap Khiri Khan Pranburi, Ratchaburi
034	Kanchanaburi, Nakhon Pathom, Samut Sakhon, Samut Songkhram
035	Ang Thong, Ayuthaya, Suphanburi
036	Lopburi, Saraburi, Singburi
037	Nakhon Nayok, Prachinburi, Aranya Prathet
038	Chachoengsao, Chonburi, Pattaya, Rayong, Si Racha
039	Chanthaburi, Trat
042	Loei, Chiang Khan, Mukdahan, Nakhon Phanom, Nong Khai, Sakon Nakhon, Udon Thani
043	Kalasin, Khon Kaen, Mahasarakham, Roi Et
044	Buriram, Chaiyaphum, Nakhon Ratchasima (Khorat)
045	Si Saket, Surin, Ubon Ratchathani, Yasothon
053	Chiang Mai, Chiang Rai, Lamphun, Mae Hong Song
054	Lampang, Nan, Phayao, Phrae
055	Kamphaeng Phet, Phitsanulok, Sukhothai, Tak, Mae Sot, Uttaradit
056	Nakhon Sawan, Phetchabun, Phichit, Uthai Thani
073	Narathiwat, Sungai Kolok, Pattani, Yala
074	Hat Yai, Phattalung, Satun, Songkhla
075	Krabi, Nakhon Si Thammarat, Trang
076	Phang-Nga, Phuket
077	Chumphon, Ranong, Surat Thani, Chaiya, Ko Samui

Fax, Telex & Telegraph
GPO telephone offices offer fax, telegraph and telex services in addition to regular phone service. There's no need to bring your own paper as the post offices supply

their own forms. International faxes typically cost a steep 100 to 140B for the first page, 65 to 110B per page for following pages, depending on the size of the paper and destination.

Larger hotels with business centres offer the same telecommunication services, but always at higher rates.

BOOKS

Lonely Planet

Thailand, by the same author as *Bankgok city guide*, has gone through seven editions since its first publication in 1982. At over 800 pages, this book remains the most comprehensive guidebook to Thailand in existence. Lonely Planet also publishes a *Thailand travel atlas*, *Thai phrasebook* and *Thai Hill Tribes phrasebook*.

History & Politics

One of the more readable general histories written in the latter half of the 20th century is David Wyatt's *Thailand: A Short History*.

Concentrating on post-revolutionary Thailand, *The Balancing Act: A History of Modern Thailand*, by Joseph Wright Jr, starts with the 1932 revolution and ends with the February 1991 coup. Wright's semi-academic chronicle concludes that Thai history demonstrates a continuous circulation of elites governed by certain 'natural laws'. Though the book is packed with detail, such deep structure theorising brings to mind the way Anglo scholars until very recently identified all French political trends as 'Bonapartiste'. Wright's most demonstrable thesis is that, despite the 1932 revolution, democracy has never gained a firm foothold in Thai society.

The best source of information on Thailand's political scene during the turbulent 1960s and 1970s is *Political Conflict in Thailand: Reform, Reaction, Revolution* by David Morrell & Chai-anan Samudavanija.

Thailand's role in the international narcotics trade is covered thoroughly in Alfred McCoy's *The Politics of Heroin in Southeast Asia* and Francis Belanger's *Drugs, the US, and Khun Sa*.

Although it's fiction, ex-prime minister Kukrit Pramoj's 1961 *Red Bamboo* vividly portrays and predicts the conflict between the Thai communist movement and the establishment during the 60s and 70s. His book *Si Phaendin: Four Reigns*, the most widely read novel ever published in Thailand, covers the Ayuthaya era. Both novels are available in English language versions.

Axel Aylwen's novel *The Falcon of Siam* and its sequel *The Falcon Takes Wing* are not up to Kukrit's literary standards, but nonetheless capture the feel and historical detail of 17th-century Siam; Aylwen obviously read other foreign authors like Collis, Loubére and Tachard closely.

Although it's tough to find, *The Devil's Discus* by Rayon Kurgan focuses on the circumstances surrounding the mysterious death of Rama VIII. It's banned in Thailand, of course, for its police-blotter-style analysis of a taboo topic.

Abha Bhamorabutr's crudely translated *The History of Bangkok*, available through DK Book House, contains some interesting trivia on early Bangkok.

People, Culture & Society

Culture Shock! Thailand by Robert & Nanthapa Cooper is an interesting outline on getting along with the Thai way of life, with particular emphasis on Bangkok. *Letters from Thailand* by Botan (translated by Susan Fulop Kepner) and Carol Hollinger's *Mai Pen Rai Means Never Mind* can also be recommended for their insights into traditional Thai culture. *Bangkok Post* reporter Denis Segaller's *Thai Ways* and *More Thai Ways* present yet more expat insights into Thai culture.

Ramakian: The Thai Ramayana by Naga Books (anonymous author) is a thorough exposition of the Thai version of Indian poet Valmiki's timeless epic.

For a look at rural life in Thailand, the books of Pira Sudham are unparalleled. Sudham is a Thai author who was born to a poor family in north-east Thailand and has written *Siamese Drama*, *Monsoon Country* and *People of Esarn (Isaan)*. These books are not translations – Sudham writes in English in order to reach a worldwide audience. These fiction titles are fairly easy to find in Bangkok but can be difficult overseas – the publisher is Siam Media International, GPO Box 1534, Bangkok 10501.

Behind the Smile: Voices of Thailand by Sanitsuda Ekachai is a very enlightening collection of interviews with Thai peasants from all over the country. The Siam Society's (on Soi Asoke, Map 4) *Culture & Environment in Thailand* is a collection of scholarly papers delivered at a 1988 symposium that examined the relationship between Thai culture and the natural world. Topics range from the oceanic origins of the Thai race and nature motifs in Thai art to evolving Thai attitudes toward the environment.

Jack Reynolds' 1950s *A Woman of Bangkok* (republished in 1985), a well-written and poignant story of a young Englishman's descent into the world of Thai brothels, remains the best novel yet published with this theme. Expat writer Christopher G Moore covers the Thai underworld in his 1990s novels *A Killing Smile, Spirit House* and *A Bewitching Smile*, but with a rose-tinted view of the go-go bar scene.

Food & Shopping

Amongst the explosion of Thai cookbooks that have appeared in recent years, one of the best remains *Thai Cooking* (formerly *The Original Thai Cookbook*) by Jennifer Brennan. For those without access to a complete range of Thai herbs and spices, *Cooking Thai Food in American Kitchens* by Malulee Pinsuvana makes reasonable substitutions. Though expensive and unwieldy, the huge, coffee-table-style *Thailand the Beautiful Cookbook* by Panurat Poladitmontri contains excellent photography and very authentic recipes.

Shopping in Exotic Thailand Ronald & Caryl Rae Krannich is packed with general shopping tips as well as lists of speciality shops and markets throughout Thailand. Although it's a bit out of date, John Hoskins' *Buyer's Guide to Thai Gems & Jewellery* is a must for anyone contemplating a foray into Thailand's gem market. *Arts and Crafts of Thailand* (1994), written by William Warren, with photographs by Luca Invernizzi Tettoni, is a useful primer for the world of Thai handicrafts, despite a few iconographical errors (eg the Hindu deity Indra is misidentified as Brahma in one photo).

RICHARD I'ANSON

Evening in Bangkok and small-time traders set up food stalls piled high with trays of freshly fried snacks.

ONLINE SERVICES

A number of online service providers offer information on Thailand. World Wide Web sites with data on Thailand in particular are multiplying quickly. A recent search under the key words 'Bangkok and business' turned up 34,000 references! Many of these were commercial sites established by tour operators or hotels; the ratio of commercial to noncommercial sites is liable to increase over time if current Internet trends continue.

Remember that all URL's (universal resource locaters) mentioned below are subject to change without notice; a couple of them even changed addresses while I was compiling this section. You can of course use your own Web browser to conduct searches; Webcrawler (query.webcrawler.com) and Yahoo (www.yahoo.com) are currently among the best.

The TAT has its own Web site at www.tat.or.th; like many Web sites these days, it contains only basic info crowded with lots of ad-style propaganda. Another Web site sourced from Thailand is one carried by Siam Net (www.siam.net). Pages include general information, a list of tour operators in Thailand, a hotel directory and a golf directory. All hotel lists I have come across on the Net have been sorely incomplete, whether oriented toward budget or luxury properties. Hotel info reflecting the experiences of individual Internet members can be accessed through http://ftp.nectec.or.th/soc.culture.thai/SCTinfo/hotels.

Lonely Planet's Web site (www.lonelyplanet.com) contains Thailand updates from travellers, occasional author updates for this book, and other salient info. (For a direct link to Thailand-related material, go to the site www.lonelyplanet.com.au/dest/sea/thai.html.) Indochina.net (www.icn.net/icn/) links to many Thailand-related Web pages. Mahidol University has a very useful site (mahidol.ac.th/Thailand/Thailand-main.html) that's searchable by key word.

Other online addresses with miscellaneous Thailand material include:

www.ait.ac.th/Asia/infoth.html
sunsite.au.ac.th/thailand/thailandhome.html
www.asiatravel.com/thaiinfo.html
bangkoknet.com
www.sino.net/asean/thailand.html
www.forman.com/thainet

The *Bangkok Post* Web site (www.bkk.post.co.th) runs around 60 pages of stories as well as photos, but overall it's not very good. For information on Bangkok, *Bangkok Metro* magazine's site (www.icn.net/METRO.html), shows promise (note this address is case-sensitive), although so far it hasn't impressed. Utopia, a gay/lesbian centre in Bangkok, maintains an informative page (www.utopia-asia.com/thipsthai.htm). With all of these, links to other Thailand sites may prove useful.

Aside from the Web, another Internet resource is the ftp usenet group culture.thai. It's very uneven, as it's basically a chat outlet for anyone who thinks they have something to say about Thailand. Still it's not a bad place to start if you have a burning question that you haven't found an answer to elsewhere.

Online in Thailand

If you're bringing a computer and modem to Thailand with hopes of staying in the info highway's fast lane, keep in mind that online options are still quite limited and that baud rates are very slow – generally 9600 or less (2400 was the overall practical norm as of mid 1996). Higher baud rates are bottlenecked by low bandwidth and can be very unreliable. This will change rapidly with time and as more global providers are allowed into the market. One big bureaucratic impasse stands in the way: the Communication Authority of Thailand (CAT), which is very much opposed to privatisation of the telecom industry. For the moment CAT isn't content with simply collecting normal local and long-distance phone rates, operating instead on the principle that digital telecommunications is a 'premium' service that requires extra charges. All service, so far, is thus surcharged according to baud rate.

CompuServe and IBM Global are the only 'international' providers so far that include Bangkok nodes. AT&T and MCI have promised global services soon, but sooner or later they will have to deal with CAT, which gets a piece of all the action. Rates are very high, but since it's mostly the Thai and expat elite who are plugged in, virtually no one complains loudly about paying the prevailing price.

CompuServe is available at up to 9600 baud (2400 and occasional 7200 in everyday practice) through InfoNet World for a basic $US10 per hour charge (added to one's home account). If a CompuServe/Pacific deal in the works goes through it will probably be Thailand's best bet since it hopes to offer a 28.8M-baud, CIS-direct node in Thailand. IBM Global offers Net access at an advertised 9600B baud, but in reality service is very slow and unreliable for any purposes except email. CompuServe, incidentally, has a very dynamic travel forum with lots of member input on Thailand in its Asia section; the quality of Thailand material found on America Online – so far – suffers by comparison.

The Net is gaining in popularity in Thailand, especially as more and more local Thai-language pages go online and folks get their Net software installed for Thai language. IBM Global operates at 9600, or you can pay a fat CAT-mandated surcharge for 28.8M service. Microsoft Network is similar. Local Internet providers (KSC, NECTEC, LoxInfo) typically charge around 1500 to 2000B per month for 28.8 service with 20 to 40 hours 'free.' Low-grade, text-only services are available for basic charges of as low as 600B a month, plus per-hour charges once your online time is maxed out.

For the moment, all dial-ups go through Bangkok, which means you must add long-distance charges to your online costs if you plug in outside the capital. RJ11 phone jacks are becoming the standard in new hotels, but in older hotels and guesthouses the phones may still be hard-wired. A pocketknife and pair of alligator clips are useful for stripping and attaching wires, or bring along an acoustic coupler. A few guesthouses (eg Joe Guest House in Banglamphu) and bars/cafes (eg the CyberPub at the Dusit Thani Hotel or Haagen Dazs on Ploenchit Rd) in Bangkok are beginning to offer email and Internet log-ons at house terminals. For the visitor who only needs to log on once in a while, these are a less expensive alternative to getting your own account – and it certainly beats lugging around a laptop. The going rate is 3 or 4B per on and off-line minute.

Loxinfo recently began offering NetAccess cards, prepaid telephone card packages with special uses for modem communications. These cards come in denominations of two hours (300B), four hours (500B) and 10 hours (1000B). Purchasers are provided with a sealed envelope containing a user name, password, local phone access number (currently Bangkok, Chiang Mai and Pattaya) and log-on procedures. Follow the latter and you'll be able to navigate the Internet, check email at your online home address, and access any online services you subscribe to, such as CompuServe or America Online. Complete details about the NetAccess card, including a list of authorized agents, can be obtained through Loxinfo's home page at www.loxinfo.co.th.

One electronic bulletin board service (BBS) worth checking out is Sala Thai (modem (02) 679-8380), which has a subscriber base of over 700. Topics are diverse. For a list of over 40 other BBS sites in Bangkok, Pattaya, Chiang Mai and Phuket, see a current issue of *Bangkok*

Metro or contact Piyabute Fuangkhon at the Information Center at modem 734-7301.

NEWSPAPERS & MAGAZINES

Thailand's 1991 constitution guarantees freedom of the press, though the national police department has the power to suspend publishing licences for national security reasons. Editors nevertheless exercise self-censorship in certain realms, particularly in regard to the monarchy. Monarchical issues aside, Thailand is widely considered to have the freest print media in South-East Asia. In a recent survey conducted by the Singapore-based Political and Economic Risk Consultancy, 180 expatriate managers in 10 Asian countries ranked Thailand's English-language press the highest in Asia. Surprisingly, these expats cited the *Bangkok Post* and *The Nation* more frequently as their source of regional and global news than the *Asian Wall Street Journal* or the *Far Eastern Economic Review*.

These two English-language newspapers are published daily, the *Bangkok Post* in the morning and *The Nation* in the afternoon. *The Nation* is almost entirely staffed by Thais and presents, obviously, a Thai perspective, while the *Post*, which was Thailand's first English daily (established in 1946), has a mixed Thai and international staff and presents a more international view. For international news, the *Post* is the better of the two papers and is in fact regarded by many journalists as the best English-language daily in the region. *The Nation*, on the other hand, has better regional coverage – particularly with regard to Myanmar and former Indochina, and is to be commended for taking a harder anti-NPKC stance during the 1991 coup.

A third English-language daily, the less widely available *Thailand Times*, is owned by an investment company with obvious biases regarding growth and development. About the only thing this newspaper has going for it is the page of condensed train and air-con bus timetables which appear near the back of each issue. However, the bus fares were out of date when I last checked them.

The Singapore edition of the *International Herald Tribune* is widely available in Bangkok, Chiang Mai and heavily touristed areas like Pattaya and Phuket.

The most popular Thai-language newspapers are *Thai Rath* and *Daily News*, but they're mostly full of blood-and-guts stories. The best Thai journalism is found in the somewhat less popular *Matichon* and *Siam Rath* dailies. Many Thais read the English-language dailies as they consider them better news sources. The *Bangkok Post* also publishes a Thai-language version of the popular English daily.

Outside Thailand one can subscribe to the *Bangkok Post Weekly*, a recapitulation of all the major *Post* news stories of the week printed on Bible-thin paper and sent by air mail round the world.

English-language magazine publishing continues to grow, although the lifespan of individual titles tends to be short. Though mostly devoted to domestic and regional business, the English-language *Manager* occasionally prints very astute, up-to-date cultural pieces. *Bangkok Metro*, a slick and sophisticated lifestyle magazine introduced in 1995 concerned with art, culture, and music.

Many popular magazines from the UK, USA, Australia and Europe – particularly those concerned with computer technology, autos, fashion, music, and business – are available in bookstores that specialise in English-language publications (see Bookshops in the Shopping chapter).

PAUL BEINSSEN

Billboard for new movie. The majority of films shown in Bangkok are comedies and action blockbusters.

Radio & TV

Thailand has more than 400 radio stations, with 41 FM and 35 AM stations in Bangkok alone. Of these, two have English-language programming. FMX, at 95.5 FM, offers pop music and news on the half hour. Bangkok's national public radio station, Radio Thailand (Sathaanii Withayu Haeng Prathet Thai), also uses 95.5 FM to air government-slanted English-language news broadcasts at 7 am, 12.30 pm, 7 pm and 8 pm. The other English-language alternative is Smooth 105 FM, an easy listening station. If you're in search of classical music, tune in to MCOT FM 95, a Thai-language station that broadcasts 24 hours a day. For the latest in the Thai pop-music scene try 89.5 FM.

Thailand has five TV networks based in Bangkok. Following the 1991 coup, the Thai government authorised an extension of telecast time to 24 hours and networks have been scrambling to fill air-time ever since. As a result, there has been a substantial increase in English-language telecasts – mostly in the morning when Thais aren't used to watching TV.

Channel 5 is a military network (the only one to operate during coups) and broadcasts from 6 am to midnight. Between 6 and 10 am this network presents a mix of ABC, CNN International, and English-subtitled Thai news programs; English-language news is broadcast at noon and 7 pm; and then CNN headlines again at 11.30 pm. Channel 9, the national public television station, broadcasts from 6 am until midnight. An English-language soundtrack is simulcast with Channel 9's evening news program weekdays at 7 pm on radio station 107 FM.

Channel 3 is privately owned; broadcast hours vary, but there's an English-language news simulcast at 7 pm on 105.5 FM. Channel 7 is military-owned, but broadcast time is leased to private companies; it offers an English-language news simulcast on 103.5 FM at 7 pm. Channel 11 is run by the Ministry of Education and features educational programs from 5.30 am to 11 pm, including TV correspondence classes from Ramkhamhaeng and Sukhothai Thammathirat open universities. An English-language news simulcast comes over 88 FM at 8 pm.

Upcountry cities will generally receive only two networks – Channel 9 and a local private network with restricted hours.

Satellite & Cable TV As elsewhere in Asia, satellite and cable-television services are swiftly multiplying in

Thailand, and competition for the largely untapped
market is keen. Of the many regional satellite operations
aimed at Thailand, the most successful so far is Satellite
Television Asian Region (STAR), beamed from Hong
Kong via AsiaSat 1 & 2. STAR offers five free 24-hour
channels, including Music TV Asia (a tie-in with
America's MTV music-video channel), Prime Sports
(international sports coverage), BBC World Service Television (news), and two channels showing movies in
Chinese and English. AsiaSat 1 & 2 also supply Channel
V (a Hong Kong-based music video telecast), Zee TV
(Hindi programming), Deutsche Welle (German gov-
ernment network), Pakistan TV and Myanmar TV.

Thailand has launched its own ThaiCom 1 & 2 as
uplinks for AsiaSat and as carriers for the standard Thai
networks as well as for the International Broadcasting
Corporation (IBC, news and entertainment), Vietnam
Television and Thai Sky. The latter includes five channels offering news and documentaries, Thai music
videos, Thai variety programs, the BBC World Service,
and MTV-Asia.

Turner Broadcasting (CNN International), ESPN,
HBO, and various telecasts from Indonesia, Malaysia,
the Philippines, Brunei and Australia are available in
Thailand via Indonesia's Palapa C1 satellite. Other sat-
ellites tracked by dishes in Thailand include China's
Apstar 1 and soon-to-be-launched Apstar 2.

Tourist-class hotels in Thailand often have one or
more satellite TV channels (plus in-house video), including a STAR 'sampler' channel that switches from one
STAR offering to another.

Video The predominant video format in Thailand is
PAL, a system compatible with that used in most of
Europe (France's SECAM format is a notable exception)
as well as in Australia. This means if you're bringing
videotapes from the USA or Japan, which use the NTSC
format, you'll have to bring your own VCR to play them!
Some video shops (especially those which carry pirated
or unlicensed tapes) sell NTSC as well as PAL and
SECAM tapes. A 'multi-system' VCR has the capacity to
play both NTSC and PAL, but not SECAM.

PHOTOGRAPHY

Print film is fairly inexpensive and widely available
throughout Thailand. Japanese print film costs 65 to 70B
per 36 exposures, US print film 75 to 90B. Fujichrome
Velvia and Provia slide films costs around 160B per roll,

Kodak Ektachrome Elite is 140B and Ektachrome 200 about 200B. Slide film, especially Kodachrome, can be hard to find outside Bangkok, so be sure to stock up before heading upcountry. Film processing is generally quite good in the larger cities in Thailand and also quite inexpensive. Kodachrome must be sent out of the country for processing, so it can take up to two weeks to get it back. Dependable E6 processing is available at several labs in Bangkok.

Pack some silica gel with your camera to prevent mould growing on the inside of your lenses. A polarising filter could be useful to cut down on tropical glare at certain times of the day, particularly around water or highly polished glazed-tile work.

TIME

Time Zone

Thailand's time zone is seven hours ahead of GMT/ UTC. Thus, noon in Bangkok is 10 pm the previous day in Los Angeles, 1 am the same day in New York, 5 am in London, 6 am in Paris, 1 pm in Perth and 3 pm in Sydney.

Thai Calendar

The official year in Thailand is reckoned from 543 BC, the beginning of the Buddhist Era, so that 1997 AD is 2540 BE.

ELECTRICITY

Electric current is 220V, 50 cycles. Electrical wall outlets are usually of the round, two-pole type; some outlets also accept flat, two-bladed terminals, and some will accept either flat or round terminals. Any electrical supply shop will carry adaptors for any international plug shape as well as voltage converters.

LAUNDRY

Virtually every hotel and guesthouse in Thailand offers a laundry service. Rates are generally geared to room rates; the cheaper the accommodation, the cheaper the washing and ironing. Cheapest of all are public laundries where you pay by the kilogram.

Many Thai hotels and guesthouses also have laundry areas where you can wash your own clothes at no charge; sometimes there's even a hanging area for drying. Where a laundry area isn't available, do-it-yourselfers can wash their clothes in the sink and hang them out to dry in their rooms. Laundry detergent is readily available in general stores and supermarkets.

For dry cleaning, take clothes to a dry cleaner. Laundries that advertise dry cleaning often don't really dry clean (they just boil everything!) or do it badly. Luxury hotels usually have dependable dry-cleaning services.

Two reliable dry cleaners in Bangkok are Erawan Dry Cleaners (basement of Landmark Plaza, Sukhumvit Rd) and Spotless Dry Cleaning & Laundry (166 Soi 23 Sukhumvit Rd). Both of these companies dry clean large items like sleeping bags as well as clothes.

WEIGHTS & MEASURES

In Thailand, dimensions and weight are usually expressed using the metric system. The exception is land measure, which is often quoted using the traditional system of *waa*, *ngaan* and *râi*. Old-timers in the provinces will occasionally use the traditional Thai system of weights and measures in speech, as will boat-builders, carpenters and other craftspeople when talking about their work. Here are some conversions to use for such occasions:

1 sq *waa*	=	4 sq metres
1 *ngaan* (100 sq waa)	=	400 sq metres
1 *râi* (4 ngaan)	=	1600 sq metres
1 *bàht*	=	15g
1 *taleung*		
or *tamleung* (4 baht)	=	60g
1 *châng* (20 taleung)	=	1.2 kg
1 *hàap* (50 chang)	=	60 kg
1 *níu*	=	about 2 cm (or one inch)
1 *khêup* (12 niu)	=	25 cm
1 *sàwk* (2 kheup)	=	50 cm
1 *waa* (4 sawk)	=	2m
1 *sén* (20 waa)	=	40m
1 *yôht* (400 sen)	=	16 km

HEALTH

Immunisation

There are no requirements for Thailand in terms of required vaccinations unless you are coming from a yellow-fever infected area, in which case you will require that vaccine. Travellers should ensure their tetanus, diphtheria and polio vaccinations are up to date (boosters are required every 10 years). Travellers should also consider having vaccinations for typhoid and

Hepatitis A, which are food and water-borne diseases. It is important to have a Hepatitis B vaccination if sexual contact is a possibility.

You should also check if vaccinations are required by any countries you are going to after visiting Thailand. A Japanese encephalitis vaccination is a good idea for those who think they may be at moderate or high risk while in Thailand. Your doctor may also recommend booster shots against measles or polio.

Health Precautions

Most visitors to Bangkok don't experience any serious health problems. Care in what you eat and drink is the most important health rule; a stomach upset is the most likely problem, but the majority of these upsets will be relatively minor. Don't become paranoid – after all, trying the local food is part of the experience of travel.

Water The number-one rule to remember is *don't drink tap water*. If you don't know for certain that the water is safe always assume the worst. The reputable brands of bottled water or soft drinks are generally fine, although in some places the use of refilled bottles is not unknown. Drinking tea or coffee should be fine as the water is boiled.

Thai soft drinks are safe to drink, as is the weak Chinese tea served in most restaurants. Ice is produced from purified water under hygienic conditions and is therefore theoretically safe. During transit to the local restaurant, however, conditions are not so hygienic (you may see blocks of ice being dragged along the street). The rule of thumb is that if it's chipped ice, it probably came from an ice block (which may not have been handled well), but if it's ice cubes or 'tubes', it was delivered from the ice factory in sealed plastic and is safe.

Food It is best to buy fruit that you can peel and slice yourself (cheaper, too), but most fare at food stalls is reasonably safe. Salads and fruit should be washed with purified water or peeled where possible. Beware of ice cream which is sold in the street or anywhere, it might have been melted and refrozen. Thoroughly cooked food is safest, but not if it has been left to cool or if it has been reheated. Take great care with shellfish or fish and avoid undercooked meat.

If a place looks clean and well run and the vendor also looks clean and healthy then the food is probably safe. In general, places that are packed with travellers or locals will be fine, empty restaurants are questionable.

Malaria According to the Centre for Disease Control and Thailand's National Malaria Centre, there is no malaria risk in Bangkok. No special precautions, such as malaria preventive tablets, are advisable. There is also no risk in the main tourist areas, eg Chiang Mai, Pattaya and Phuket. Outside these areas the usual preventative measures should be taken: apply a good mosquito repellent to skin and clothes whenever and wherever mosquitos are about; sleep under a mosquito net or in a screened room if possible; where screens or nets aren't available, burn mosquito coils.

Sexually Transmitted Diseases & AIDS In Thailand the most statistically common STD is gonorrhoea, followed by non-specific urethritis (NSU). Treatment of gonorrhoea, NSU and syphilis is by antibiotics. Sores, blisters or rashes around the genitals, discharges or pain when urinating are common symptoms.

Two STDs reported in Thailand for which no cures are available are herpes and the human immuno-deficiency virus (HIV), which is known to lead to acquired immune deficiency syndrome (AIDS), a fatal disease. The incubation period (time before an infection registers in lab tests) can extend to several years.

HIV can also be spread through infected blood transfusions or by dirty needles – vaccinations, acupuncture and tattooing can be as dangerous as intravenous drug use if the equipment is not clean. HIV is a major health problem in Thailand although the overall incidence of infection has slowed tremendously over recent years. Any exposure to blood, blood products or bodily fluids may put the individual at risk. In Thailand, transmission is predominantly through heterosexual sexual activity (40%); the second most common source of HIV infection is intravenous injection by drug addicts who share needles (33%). Apart from abstinence, the most effective preventative is always to practise safe sex using condoms. It is impossible to detect the HIV-positive status of an otherwise healthy-looking person without a blood test.

For the casual male visitor the greatest risk of HIV transmission is via sexual contact with prostitutes or any Thai female whose HIV status is unknown. HIV statistics for Bangkok are relatively low compared to provincial areas; an estimated 75% of HIV infections in Thailand have reportedly occurred in the north. For female visitors the main risk is having sexual contact with any male – Thai or foreigner – known to have had intercourse with Thai prostitutes.

The use of condoms greatly decreases but does not eliminate the risk of STD infection. The Thai phrase for 'condom' is *thŭng anaamai*. Latex condoms are more effective than animal-membrane condoms in preventing disease transmission; to specify latex condoms ask for *thŭng yaang anaamai*. Good quality latex condoms are distributed free by offices of the Ministry of Public Health throughout the country – they come in numbered sizes, like shoes! Condoms can also be purchased at any pharmacy, but those issued by the Ministry of Public Health are considered the most effective; a recent ministry survey found that around 11% of commercial Thai condoms were damaged, mostly due to improper storage.

Diarrhoea Simple things like a change of water, food or climate can all cause a mild bout of diarrhoea, but a few rushed toilet trips with no other symptoms is not indicative of a major problem.

Dehydration is the main danger with any diarrhoea, particularly in children or the elderly, as dehydration can occur quite quickly. Under all circumstances *fluid replacement* (at least equal to the volume being lost) is the most important thing to remember. Weak black tea with a little sugar, soda water, or soft drinks allowed to go flat and diluted 50% with clean water are all good. With severe diarrhoea a rehydrating solution is preferable to replace minerals and salts lost. Commercially available oral rehydration salts (ORS) are very useful; add them to boiled or bottled water. In an emergency you can make up a solution of six teaspoons of sugar and a half teaspoon of salt to a litre of boiled or bottled water. You need to drink at least the same volume of fluid that you are losing in bowel movements and vomiting. Urine is the best guide to the adequacy of replacement – if you have small amounts of concentrated urine, you need to drink more. Keep drinking small amounts often. Stick to a bland diet as you recover.

Lomotil or Imodium can be used to bring relief from the symptoms, although they do not actually cure the problem. Only use these drugs if you do not have access to toilets eg if you *must* travel. For children under 12 years Lomotil and Imodium are not recommended. Do not use these drugs if the person has a high fever or is severely dehydrated.

In certain situations antibiotics may be required: diarrhoea with blood or mucous (dysentery), any fever, watery diarrhoea with fever and lethargy, persistent diarrhoea not improving after 48 hours and severe diarrhoea. In these situations gut-paralysing drugs like Imodium or Lomotil should be avoided.

Heat Exhaustion Dehydration and salt deficiency can cause heat exhaustion. Take time to acclimatise to high temperatures, drink sufficient liquids and do not do anything too physically demanding.

Salt deficiency is characterised by fatigue, lethargy, headaches, giddiness and muscle cramps; salt tablets may help, but adding extra salt to your food is better.

Anhydrotic heat exhaustion, caused by an inability to sweat, is quite rare. It is likely to strike people who have been in a hot climate for some time, rather than newcomers.

Medical Services

Bangkok is Thailand's leading health care centre, with three university research hospitals, 12 public and private hospitals and hundreds of medical clinics. Australian, US and UK embassies usually keep up-to-date lists of doctors who speak English. For doctors who speak other languages, contact the relevant embassy or consulate.

Several store-front clinics in the Ploenchit Rd area specialise in lab tests for sexually transmitted diseases. According to *Bangkok Metro* magazine, Bangkok General Hospital has the most sophisticated HIV blood testing program. Bangkok's better hospitals include:

Bangkok Adventist (Mission) Hospital
  430 Phitsanulok Rd (☎ 281-1422, 282-1100)
Bangkok Christian Hospital
  124 Silom Rd (☎ 233-6981/6989, 235-1000)
Bangkok General Hospital
  Soi 47, New Phetburi Rd (☎ 318-0066)
Bangkok Nursing Home
  9 Convent Rd (☎ 233-2610/2619)
Bumrumgrad Hospital (Map 4)
  33 Soi 3, Sukhumvit Rd (☎ 253-0250)
Chao Phraya Hospital
  113/44 Pinklao Nakhon-Chaisi Rd, Bangkok Noi
  (☎ 434-6900)
Phayathai Hospital
  364/1 Si Ayuthaya Rd (☎ 245-2620)
  or 943 Phahonyothin Rd (☎ 270-0780)
Samitivej Hospital (Map 4)
  133 Soi 49, Sukhumvit Rd (☎ 392-0010/0019)
Samrong General Hospital
  Soi 78, Sukhumvit Rd (☎ 393-2131/2135)
St Louis Hospital
  215 Sathon Tai Rd (☎ 212-0033/0048)

Those interested in Chinese medicine will find plenty of Chinese doctors and herbal dispensaries in Bangkok's

Sampeng district, in the vicinity of Ratchawong, Charoen Krung, Yaowarat and Songwat Rds. The Pow Tai Dispensary at 572-574 Charoen Krung Rd has been preparing traditional Chinese remedies since 1941.

Emergency All the hospitals listed above offer 24-hour service. Bangkok does not have an emergency phone system staffed by English-speaking operators. Between the hours of 8 am and midnight, your best bet for English-speaking assistance is the Tourist Assistance Centre (☎ 281-5051, 282-8129). After midnight you'll have to rely on your own resources or on English-speaking hotel staff.

If you can find a Thai to call on your behalf, here are the city's main emergency numbers:

Police	☎ 191 or 123
Fire	☎ 191 or 199
Ambulance	☎ 252-2171/2175

TOILETS & SHOWERS

In Thailand, as in many other South-East Asian countries, the 'squat toilet' is the norm, except in hotels and guesthouses geared toward tourists and international business travellers. Instead of trying to approximate a chair or stool like a modern sit-down toilet, a traditional Asian toilet sits more or less flush with the surface of the floor, with two footpads on either side of the porcelain abyss. For persons who have never used a squat toilet it takes a bit of getting used to. If you find yourself feeling awkward the first couple of times you use one, you can console yourself with the knowledge that, according to those who study such matters, people who use squat toilets are much less likely to develop haemorrhoids than people who use sit toilets.

Next to the typical squat toilet is a bucket or cement reservoir filled with water. A plastic bowl usually floats on the water's surface or sits nearby. This water supply has a two-fold function; toilet-goers scoop water from the reservoir with the plastic bowl and use it to clean the nether regions while still squatting over the toilet. Since there is usually no mechanical flushing device attached to a squat toilet, a few extra scoops must be poured into the toilet basin to flush waste into the septic system. In larger towns, mechanical flushing systems are becoming increasingly common, even with squat toilets. More rustic toilets in rural areas may simply consist of a few planks over a hole in the ground.

Even in places where sit-down toilets are installed, the plumbing may not be designed to take toilet paper. In such cases the usual washing bucket will be standing nearby or there will be a waste basket where you're supposed to place used toilet paper.

Public toilets are common in cinema houses, department stores, bus and railway stations, larger hotel lobbies and airports. On the road between towns and villages it is perfectly acceptable to go behind a tree or bush or even to use the roadside when nature calls.

Bathing

Some hotels and most guesthouses in the country do not have hot water, though most tourist-oriented places in Bangkok do. Very few boiler-style water heaters are available outside larger international-style hotels; in the smaller places hot water is provided by small, in-line electric heaters.

Many private homes and some of the older guest-houses in Bangkok have washrooms where a large jar or cement trough is filled with water for bathing. A plastic or metal bowl is used to sluice water from the jar or trough over the body. Even in homes where showers are installed, heated water is uncommon. Most Thais bathe at least twice a day.

WOMEN TRAVELLERS

Attitudes Towards Women Chinese trader Ma Huan noted in 1433 that among the Thais 'All affairs are managed by their wives, all trading transactions large or small.' In rural areas females typically inherit land and throughout the country they tend to control family finances. The UNDP Human Development Report for 1995 noted that on the gender-related development index (GDI) Thailand ranked 31st of 130 countries, thus falling into the 'progressive' category. The nation's GDI increase was greater than that of any country in the world over the past 20 years. According to the report, Thailand 'has succeeded in building the basic human capabilities of both women and men, without substantial gender imparity'. Thailand's work force is 44% female, ranking it 27th on a world scale, just ahead of China and the United States.

So much for the good news. The bad news is that while women generally fare well in the labour force and in rural land inheritance, their cultural standing is a bit further from parity. An oft-repeated Thai saying reminds us that men form the front legs of the elephant, women

RICHARD I'ANSON

Cooking and cleaning in a street restaurant. Women
comprise 44% of Thailand's work force.

the hind legs (at least they're pulling equal weight). Thai
Buddhism commonly holds that women must be reborn
as men before they can attain nirvana, though many Thai
dharma teachers point out that this presumption isn't
supported by the *suttas* (discourses of the Buddha) or by
the commentaries. But it is a common belief, supported
by the availability of a fully ordained Buddhist monastic
status for men and a less prestigious eight-precept ordination for women. On a legal level, men enjoy more
privileges. They can divorce their wives for committing
adultery, but not vice versa, for example. Men who take
a foreign spouse continue to have the right to purchase
and own land, while Thai women who marry foreign
men lose this right.

Safety Around 38% of foreign visitors to Thailand are
women, a figure equal to the worldwide average as
measured by the World Tourism Organisation, and on a
par with Singapore and Hong Kong. (For all other Asian
countries the proportion of female visitors runs lower
than 35%.) The ratio of women travellers is growing year
by year; the overall visitor increase between 1993 and
1994, for example, was 2.3% while the number of women
visitors jumped 13.8%.

Women visitors to Bangkok report that it's one of the
safest cities in the world for unaccompanied travel. Thai

males seldom hassle women walking down the street; the groping problems common to India, Malaysia or Indonesia are for the most part nonexistent. Nonetheless, women travellers should refrain from walking alone at night in dimly lit or sparsely populated areas; taking a taxi alone late at night is also not advisable.

GAY & LESBIAN TRAVELLERS

Thai culture is very tolerant of homosexuality, both male and female. The nation has no laws that discriminate against homosexuals and there is a fairly prominent gay/lesbian scene in Bangkok and around the country. Since there's no antigay establishment to move against, there is no 'gay movement' in Thailand as such. Whether speaking of dress or mannerisms, 'butch' women and 'feminine' men are generally accepted without comment.

Public displays of affection – whether heterosexual or homosexual – are frowned upon. As the guide *Thai Scene* (Gay Men's Press, Box 247, London N6 4AT, England) has written, 'For many gay travellers, Thailand is a nirvana with a long-established gay bar scene, which, whilst often very Thai in culture, is particularly welcoming to tourists. There is little, if any, social approbation toward gay people, providing Thai cultural mores are respected. What people do in bed, whether straight or gay, is not expected to be a topic of general conversation nor bragged about.'

Utopia (☎ 259-1619, fax 258-3250), on 116/1 Soi 23, Sukhumvit Rd, is a gay and lesbian multipurpose Bangkok centre consisting of a guesthouse, bar, cafe, gallery and gift shop. It maintains an Internet site called Southeast Asia Gay & Lesbian Resources or 'Utopia Homo Page' (www.utopia-asia.com and email address utopia@ksc9.th).

Gay men may be interested in the services of the Long Yang Club (☎ /fax 679-7727), PO Box 1077, Silom Post Office, Bangkok 10504, a 'multicultural social group for male-oriented men who want to meet outside the gay scene' with branches in London, Amsterdam, Toronto, Canberra, Ottawa and Vancouver.

DISABLED TRAVELLERS

Bangkok presents one large, ongoing obstacle course for the mobility-impaired. With its high curbs, uneven sidewalks and nonstop traffic, movement around the city can be particularly difficult – many streets must be crossed via pedestrian bridges flanked with steep stairways, while buses and boats don't stop long enough for even the mildly handicapped. Rarely are there any ramps or other access points for wheelchairs.

The Hyatt International, Novotel Siam Square, Royal Orchid Sheraton, Holiday Inn Crowne Plaza and Westin Banyan Tree are the only hotels in the city that make consistent design efforts to provide handicapped access to their properties. Because of their high employee-to-guest ratios, home-grown luxury hotel chains such as those managed by Dusit, Amari, and Royal Garden Resorts are usually very good about accommodating the mobility-impaired by providing staff help where architecture fails. For the rest, you're pretty much left to your own resources.

For wheelchair travellers, any trip to Thailand will require a good deal of advance planning; fortunately a growing network of information sources can put you in touch with those who have wheeled through Thailand before. There is no better source of information than someone who's done it.

A reader recently wrote with the following tips:

- The difficulties you mention in your book are all there. However, travel in the streets is still possible, and enjoyable, providing you have a strong, ambulatory companion. Some obstacles may require two carriers; Thais are by nature helpful and could generally be counted on for assistance.
- Don't feel you have to rely on organised tours to see the sights – these often leave in the early morning at times inconvenient to disabled people. It is far more convenient (and often cheaper) to take a taxi or hired car. It's also far more enjoyable as there is no feeling of holding others up.
- Many taxis have an LPG tank in the boot (trunk) which makes it impossible to get a wheelchair in and close it. You might do better to hire a private car and driver (this usually costs no more – and sometimes less – than a taxi).
- A tuk-tuk is far easier to get in and out of and can carry two people and a wheelchair better than a taxi can.
- Be ready to try anything – in spite of my worries, riding an elephant proved quite easy.

Three international organisations which act as clearing houses for information on world travel for the mobility-impaired are: Mobility International USA (☎ (541) 343-1284), PO Box 10767, Eugene, OR 97440, USA; Access Foundation (☎ (516) 887-5798), PO Box 356, Malverne, NY 11565, USA; and Society for the Advancement of Travel for the Handicapped (SATH) (☎ 718 858-5483), 26 Court St, Brooklyn, NY 11242, USA.

Abilities magazine (☎ (416) 766-9188, fax 762-8716), PO Box 527, Station P, Toronto, ON, Canada M5S 2T1, carries a new column called 'Accessible Planet', which offers tips on foreign travel for people with disabilities. One story described how two French wheelchair travellers trekked around northern Thailand. The book *Exotic Destinations for Wheelchair Travelers* by Ed Hansen and Bruce Gordon (Full Data Ltd, San Francisco) contains a useful chapter on seven locations in Thailand. Other books of value include *Holidays and Travel Abroad – A Guide for Disabled People* (RADAR, London) and *Able to Travel* (Rough Guides, London, New York).

Accessible Journeys (☎ (610) 521-0339), 35 West Sellers Ave, Ridley Park, Pennsylvania, USA, specialises in organising group travel for the mobility-impaired. Occasionally the agency offers Thailand trips.

In Thailand you can also contact:

Association of the Physically Handicapped of Thailand
    73/7-8 Soi 8 (Soi Thepprasan), Tivanon Rd, Talaat Kawan,
    Nonthaburi, 11000 (☎ 951-0569, fax 580-1098 ext 7)
Disabled Peoples International – Thailand
    78/2 Tivanon Rd, Pak Kret, Nonthaburi 11120
    (☎ 583-3021, fax 583-6518)
Handicapped International
    87/2 Soi 15 Sukhumvit Rd, Bangkok 10110
Thai Disability Organisations
    David Lambertson, Ambassador (☎/fax 254-2990)

SENIOR TRAVELLERS

Senior discounts aren't generally available in Thailand, but the Thais more than make up for this in the respect they typically show for the elderly. In traditional Thai culture, status comes with age; there isn't as heavy an emphasis on youth as in the Western world. Deference for age manifests itself in the way Thais go out of their way to help older people in and out of taxis or with luggage, and – usually, but not always – in serving them first in shops and post offices.

Nonetheless, some cultural spheres are reserved for youth. Cross-generation entertainment in particular is less common than in Western countries. There is strict stratification among discos and nightclubs, for example, according to age group. One place will cater to teenagers, another to people in their early 20s, one for late 20s and 30s, yet another for those in their 40s and 50s, and once you've reached 60 you're considered too old to go clubbing! Exceptions to this rule include the more traditional entertainment venues, such as rural temple fairs and other wat-centred events, where young and old dance and eat together. For men, massage parlours are another place where old and young clientele mix.

BANGKOK FOR CHILDREN

Like many places in South-East Asia, travelling with children in Thailand can be a lot of fun as long as you come well prepared with the right attitudes, physical requirements and the usual parental patience. Lonely Planet's *Travel with Children* by Maureen Wheeler and others contains useful advice on how to cope with kids on the road and what to bring along to make things go more smoothly, with special attention paid to travel in developing countries.

For the most part, parents needn't worry too much about health concerns, though it pays to lay down a few ground rules – such as regular hand-washing – to head off potential medical problems. All the usual health precautions apply (see Health for details); children should especially be warned not to play with animals as rabies is relatively common in Thailand.

Fun for Kids

Bangkok has plenty of attractions for children. Among the most recommended are the centrally located Dusit Zoo, Queen Saovabha Memorial Institute ('Snake Farm') and Lumphini Park. On the outskirts of Bangkok are Samphran Elephant Ground & Zoo, Siam Water Park and Safari World. All of these are described in detail in the Things to See & Do chapter.

LIBRARIES

Besides offering an abundance of reading material, Bangkok's libraries make a peaceful escape from the heat, noise and traffic.

The National Library (☎ 281-5212) on Samsen Rd (Map 1) is an impressive institution with a huge collection of Thai material dating back several centuries as well as smaller numbers of foreign-language books. Membership is free. The Siam Society, off Sukhumvit Rd (Map 4), and National Museum (Map 2) also have collections of English-language materials on the history, art and culture of Thailand.

Both the American University Alumni (AUA), on Ratchadamri Rd (Map 8), and the British Council (Siam Square; Map 7) have lending libraries; the British Council allows only members (residents over 16 years only) to borrow books, while AUA has a free public lending service. Both libraries cater primarily to Thai members, hence the emphasis tends to be on English-language teaching rather than, say, the latest fiction. Their main strengths are their up-to-date periodicals sections – the British Council's selection is strictly British of course while AUA's is all-American.

Although you won't be permitted to borrow books unless you're a Chula student, the library in Chula-longkorn University (south of Siam Square) is a good place to hang out – it's quiet and has air-con.

In a class all of its own, the Neilson Hays Library (☎ 233-1731), at 193 Surawong Rd (Map 8), next to the British Club, is a historical monument as well as a good, all-purpose lending library. Built in 1921 by Dr Heyward Hays as a memorial to his wife Jennie Neilson Hays, the classic colonial Asian edifice is operated by the 100-year-old Bangkok Library Association and is the oldest English-language library in Thailand. The collection encompasses over 20,000 volumes, including a good selection of children's books and titles on Thailand. The periodical section offers a few Thai magazines, and the library even has jigsaw puzzles that can be borrowed.

Although the building isn't air-conditioned (except for one reading room), the ancient ceiling fans do a good job of keeping the sitting areas cool. The library's Rotunda Gallery hosts monthly art exhibitions and occasional art sales. Yearly membership is 1300B for adults, 800B for children or 1700B per family. Opening hours are Monday to Saturday 9.30 am to 4 pm, Sunday 9.30 am to 12.30 pm. Free parking for members is available at the library's small car park near the corner of Surawong and Naret Rds.

CULTURAL CENTRES

Various Thai and foreign associations organise and support cultural events of a wide-ranging nature. They can be good places to meet Thais with an international outlook as well as expat Bangkok residents. Some of the more active organisations include:

Alliance Française (Map 8)
> French language courses; translation services; monthly bulletin; French films; small library and bookshop; French and Thai cafeteria; music, arts and lecture programs – 29 Sathon Tai Rd (☎ 286-3841)

American University Alumni (AUA, Map 8)
> English and Thai language courses; monthly newsletter; American films; TOEFL testing; Thai cafeteria; library;

music, art and lecture programs – 179 Ratchadamri Rd
(☎ 252-7067/7069)

British Council
English language classes; monthly calendar of events;
British films; music, art and drama programs – 428 Soi 2,
Siam Square, Rama I Rd (☎ 252-6136/6138)

Goethe Institute (Map 8)
18/1 Soi Attakanprasit, between Sathon Tai Rd and Soi
Ngam Duphli (☎ 286-9002)

Thailand Cultural Centre (TCC, Map 11)
Hosts a variety of local and international cultural events,
including musical and theatrical performances, art exhibits, cultural workshops and seminars – Ratchadaphisek
Rd, Huay Khwang (☎ 247-0028)

The TCC also sponsors the Cultural Information Service
Centre, an information clearing house that issues a
bimonthly calendar of notable cultural events throughout the country. Many of the events listed are held in
Bangkok at foreign culture associations, universities, art
galleries, film societies, theatres and music centres. This
is the best single source for cultural happenings in Thailand. The calendar is available at the TCC as well as at
the TAT office on Bamrung Meuang Rd.

DANGERS & ANNOYANCES

Precautions

Although Bangkok is in no way a dangerous city to visit,
it's wise to be a little cautious, particularly if you're
travelling alone. Don't take one of Bangkok's very unof-
ficial taxis (black-and-white licence tags) by yourself –
better a licensed taxi (yellow and black tags), the airport
bus or even public bus. Ensure that your hotel room is
securely locked and bolted at night.

When possible, keep valuables in a hotel safe. Make
sure you obtain an itemised receipt for property left with
hotels or guesthouses – note the exact quantity of travellers cheques and all other valuables. Many travellers
have reported unpleasant experiences with leaving
valuables in guesthouses while travelling upcountry.

Credit Cards

When making credit-card purchases, don't let vendors
take your credit card out of your sight to run it through
the machine. Unscrupulous merchants have been
known to rub off three or four or more receipts with one
credit-card purchase; after the customer leaves the shop,
they use the one legitimate receipt as a model to forge

Scams

Thais are generally so friendly and laid-back that some visitors are lulled into a false sense of security that makes them vulnerable to a variety of scams and con schemes. Scammers tend to haunt first-time tourist spots, such as the Grand Palace area, Wat Pho or Siam Square (especially near Jim Thompson's House).

Most scams begin the same way: a friendly Thai male approaches a lone visitor – usually newly arrived – and strikes up a seemingly innocuous conversation. Sometimes the con man says he's a university student or teacher, at other times he may claim to work for the World Bank or a similarly distinguished organisation (some conners even carry cellular phones). If you're on the way to Wat Pho, for example, he may tell you it's closed for a holiday or repairs. Eventually the conversation works its way around to the subject of the scam – the better con men can actually make it seem like *you* initiated the topic. That's one of the most bewildering aspects of the con – afterwards victims remember that the whole thing seemed like their idea, not the con artist's.

The scam itself almost always involves gems or card playing. With gems, the victims are invited to a gem and jewellery shop – your new-found friend is picking up some merchandise for himself and you're just along for the ride. Somewhere along the way he usually claims to have a connection – often a relative – in your home country (what a coincidence!) with whom he has a regular gem export-import business. One way or another, victims are convinced (usually they convince themselves) that they can turn a profit by arranging a gem purchase and reselling the merchandise at home. After all, the jewellery shop just happens to be offering a generous discount today – it's a government or religious holiday, or perhaps it's the shop's 10th anniversary, or maybe they just take a liking to you!

There are a seemingly infinite number of variations on the gem scam, almost all of which end up with the victim purchasing small, low-quality sapphires and posting them to their home countries. (If they let you walk out with them, you might return for a refund after realising you'd been taken.) Once you return home, of course, the cheap sapphires turn out to be worth much less than what you paid for them (perhaps one-tenth to one-half). A jeweller in Perth, Australia, says he sees about 12 people a week who have been conned in Thailand. The con artist who brings the mark into the

shop gets a commission of 10% to 50% per sale – the shop takes the rest.

Many have invested and lost virtually all their savings; some admit they have been scammed even after reading warnings in this guidebook or posted by the TAT around Bangkok. As one letter-writer concluded his story: 'So now I'm US$500 poorer and in possession of potentially worthless sapphires – a very expensive lesson in human nature.'

Even if you were able to return your purchase to the gem shop in question (I knew one fellow who actually intercepted his parcel at the airport before it left Thailand), chances are slim to none they'd give a full refund.

The Thai police are usually of no help, believing that merchants are entitled to whatever price they can get. The main victimisers are a handful of shops who get protection from certain high-ranking government officials. These officials put pressure on police not to prosecute or to take as little action as possible. Even the TAT tourist police have never been able to prosecute a Thai jeweller, even in cases of blatant, recurring gem fraud. A Thai police commissioner was recently convicted of fraud in an investigation into a jewellery theft by Thais in Saudi Arabia, which resulted in the commissioner's replacing the Saudi gems with fakes!

The card-playing scam starts out much the same – a friendly stranger approaches the lone traveller on the street, strikes up a conversation and then invites you to the house or apartment of his sister (or brother-in-law, etc) for a drink or meal. After a bit of socialising, a friend or relative of the con arrives on the scene; it just so happens a little high-stakes card game is planned for later that day. Like the gem scam, the card-game scam has many variations, but eventually the victim is shown some cheating tactics to use with help from the 'dealer', some practice sessions take place and finally the game gets under way with several high rollers at the table. The mark is allowed to win a few hands first, then somehow loses a few, gets bankrolled by one of the friendly Thais, and then loses the Thai's money. Suddenly your new-found buddies aren't so friendly any more – they want the money you lost. Sometimes the con pretends to be dismayed by it all. Sooner or later you end up cashing in most or all of your travellers cheques.

Other minor scams involve tuk-tuk drivers, hotel employees and bar girls who take new arrivals on city tours; these almost always end in high-pressure sales pushes at silk, jewellery or handicraft shops. In this case

greed isn't the ruling motivation – it's simply a matter of weak sales resistance.

Follow the TAT's number-one suggestion to tourists: disregard all offers of free shopping or sightseeing help from strangers – they invariably take a commission from your purchases. I would add this: beware of deals that seem too good to be true – they're usually neither good nor true. You might also try lying whenever a stranger asks how long you've been in Thailand – if it's only been three days, say three weeks! The con artists rarely prey on anyone except new arrivals.

The TAT now has regulatory powers over shops catering to tourists – you should contact the tourist police if you have any problems with consumer fraud. The tourist police headquarters (☎ 255-2964) is at 29/1 Soi Lang Suan, Ploenchit Rd in Bangkok; you can also contact them through the TAT office on Bamrung Meuang Rd (Map 4). There is also a police unit that deals specifically with gem swindles (☎ 254-1067, 235-4017). Telephone hotline number 1699 connects with the tourist police from any phone in Thailand. ■

your signature on the blanks, then fill in astronomical 'purchases'. Sometimes they wait several weeks – even months – between submitting each charge receipt to the bank, so that you can't remember whether you'd been billed at the same vendor more than once.

Touts

Touting – grabbing newcomers in the street or in railway stations, bus terminals or airports to sell them a service – is a long-time tradition in Asia, and while Thailand doesn't have as many as, say, India, it has its share. In the popular tourist spots it seems like everyone – young boys waving flyers, tuk-tuk drivers, samlor drivers, schoolgirls – is touting something, usually hotels or guesthouses. For the most part they're completely harmless and sometimes they can be very informative. But take anything a tout says with two large grains of salt. Since touts work on commission and get paid just for delivering you to a guesthouse, hotel, or shop, they'll say anything to get you to the door.

Often the best (most honest and reliable) places refuse to pay tout commissions – so the average tout will try to steer you away from such places. Tuk-tuk drivers often offer free or low-cost rides to the place they're touting; if you have another place you're interested in, you might agree to go with a driver only if he or she promises to deliver you to your first choice after you've had a look at the place being touted. If drivers refuse, chances are it's because they know your first choice is a better one. Sometimes they'll take off after delivering you to the wrong place. The only way to avoid this is to refuse rides offered by touts.

This type of commission work isn't limited to low-budget guesthouses. Taxi drivers and even airline employees at Thailand's major airports reap commissions from the big hotels as well. At either end of the budget spectrum, the customer ends up paying the commission indirectly through raised room rates. Bangkok International airport employees are notorious for talking newly arrived tourists into staying at badly located, overpriced hotels. (see the Warning section of the Getting There & Away chapter for more info.)

Drugs

Opium, heroin and marijuana are widely used in Thailand, but it is illegal to buy, sell or possess these drugs in any quantity. (The possession of opium for consumption – but not sale – among hill tribes is legal.) Although in certain areas of the country drugs seem to be used with some impunity, enforcement is arbitrary – the only way not to risk getting caught is to avoid the scene entirely. Every year perhaps dozens of visiting foreigners are arrested for drug use or trafficking and end up doing hard time. A smaller but significant number die of heroin overdoses. Penalties for drug offences are stiff; if you're caught using marijuana, you face a fine and/or up to one year in prison, while for heroin, the penalty for use can be anywhere from six months to 10 years imprisonment.

BUSINESS HOURS

Most government offices are open from 8.30 am to 4.30 pm on weekdays, but closed from noon to 1 pm for lunch. Regular bank hours in Bangkok are now 10 am to 4 pm – a new schedule instituted in 1995 in an effort to relieve traffic congestion. Several banks have special foreign-exchange offices which are open longer hours (generally until 8 pm) and every day of the week. Businesses usually operate between 8.30 am and 5 pm on weekdays and sometimes Saturday morning as well. Larger shops usually open from 10 am to 6.30 or 7 pm, but smaller shops may open earlier and close later.

PUBLIC HOLIDAYS & SPECIAL EVENTS

The number and frequency of festivals and fairs in Thailand is incredible – there always seems to be something going on, especially during the cool season from November to February.

Dates for festivals may vary from year to year, either because of the lunar calendar – which isn't quite in sync with the solar calendar – or because local authorities decide to change festival days. The TAT publishes an up-to-date *Major Events & Festivals* calendar each year.

Major upcoming events not listed below include the *13th Asian Games*, which will be held at the National Stadium in Bangkok in 1998. For information contact a TAT office in Thailand or abroad.

On dates noted as public holidays, all government offices and banks will be closed.

January
> *New Year's Day* – a rather recent public holiday in deference to the Western calendar.

February
> *Magha Puja (Makkha Buchaa)* – held on the full moon of the third lunar month to commemorate the preaching of the Buddha to 1250 enlightened monks who came to hear him 'without prior summons'. A public holiday throughout the country culminating in a candle-lit walk around the main chapel at every wat.

Late February to early March
> *Chinese New Year* – called *trùt jiin* in Thai. Chinese communities all over Thailand celebrate their lunar new year (the date shifts from year to year) with a week of housecleaning, lion dances and fireworks. The most impressive festivities take place in the Chinese-dominated province capital of Nakhon Sawan. In Bangkok activities are centred around the Yaowarat district, the city's Chinatown.

March
> *Bangkok International Jewellery Fair* – held in several large Bangkok hotels, this is Thailand's most important annual gem and jewellery trade show. Runs concurrently with the Department of Export Promotion's *Bangkok Gems & Jewellery Fair*.

April
> *Songkran Festival* – the New Year's celebration of the lunar year in Thailand. Buddha images are 'bathed', monks and elders receive the respect of younger Thais by the sprinkling of water over their hands, and a lot of water is tossed about for fun. Songkran generally gives everyone a chance to release their frustration and literally cool off during the peak of the hot season. Hide out in your room or expect to be soaked; the latter is a lot more fun.

BERNARD NAPTHINE

Dressed up for the Chinese New Year.

Chakri Day – a public holiday commemorating the founder of the Chakri Dynasty, Rama I. Held on 6 April.

May

Visakha Puja (Wisakha Buchaa) – a public holiday that falls on the 15th day of the waxing moon in the 6th lunar month. This is considered the date of the Buddha's birth, enlightenment and *parinibbana*, or passing away. Activities are centred around the wat, with candle-lit processions, much chanting and sermonising, etc.

Coronation Day – public holiday. The King and Queen preside at a ceremony at Wat Phra Kaew in Bangkok, commemorating their 1946 coronation.

Royal Ploughing Ceremony – to kick off the official rice-planting season, the king participates in this ancient Brahman ritual at Sanam Luang (the large field across from Wat Phra Kaew) in Bangkok. Thousands of Thais gather to watch, and traffic in this part of the city reaches a standstill.

July

Asanha Puja – full moon is a must for this public holiday which commemorates the first sermon preached by the Buddha.

Khao Phansaa – a public holiday and the beginning of

Buddhist 'lent', this is the traditional time of year for young men to enter the monkhood for the rainy season and for all monks to station themselves in a single monastery for the three months. It's a good time to observe a Buddhist ordination.

August

Queen's Birthday – a public holiday. Ratchadamnoen Klang Rd and the Grand Palace are festooned with coloured lights.

September

Thailand International Swan-Boat Races – these take place on the Chao Phraya River in Bangkok near the Rama IX Bridge.

October

Chulalongkorn Day – a public holiday in commemoration of King Chulalongkorn (Rama V).

Mid-October to mid-November

Thawt Kathin – a one-month period at the end of the Buddhist 'lent', or *phansaa*, during which new monastic robes and requisites are offered to the Sangha.

November

Loi Krathong – on the proper full-moon night, small lotus-shaped baskets or boats made of banana leaves containing flowers, incense, candles and a coin are floated on Thai rivers, lakes and canals. This is a peculiarly Thai festival that probably originated in Sukhothai and is best celebrated in the country's north.

King's Birthday – this is a public holiday which is celebrated with some fervour in Bangkok. As with the Queen's birthday, it features lots of lights along Ratchadamnoen Klang Rd. Some people erect temporary shrines to the King outside their homes or businesses.

December

Constitution Day – public holiday on 10 December.

WORK

Thailand's steady economic growth has provided a variety of work opportunities for foreigners, although in general it's not as easy to find a job as in more developed countries. The one exception is teaching English. As in the rest of East and South-East Asia, there is a high demand for English speakers to provide instruction to locals. This is not due to a shortage of qualified Thai teachers with a good grasp of English grammar, but rather represents the desire to have native-speaker models in the classroom.

Teaching English

Those with academic credentials such as teaching certificates or degrees in English as a second language get first crack at the better-paying jobs, such as those at universities and international schools. But there are perhaps hundreds of private language teaching establishments that hire non-credentialed teachers by the hour throughout the country. Private tutoring is also a possibility. International oil companies pay the highest salaries for English instructors, but are also quite picky.

If you're interested in looking for teaching work, start with the English-language *Yellow Pages* of the Greater Bangkok Metropolitan Telephone Directory, which contains many upcountry as well as Bangkok listings. Check all the usual headings: Schools, Universities, Language Schools (there's over 75 listings in Bangkok alone) and so on. Organisations such as Teachers of English to Speakers of Other Languages (TESOL, 1600 Cameron St, Suite 300, Alexandria, Virginia 22314 USA) and International Association of Teachers of English as a Foreign Language (IATEFL, 3 Kingsdown Chamber, Kingsdown Park, Whitstable, Kent CT52DJ UK) publish newsletters with lists of jobs in foreign countries, including Thailand.

Other Jobs & Volunteer Positions

Voluntary and paying positions with organisations that provide charitable services in education, development or public health are available for those with the right educational and/or experiential backgrounds.

The UN supports a number of ongoing projects in the country. In Bangkok try contacting the UNDP (☎ 282-9619), UN World Food Program (☎ 280-0427), WHO (☎ 2829700), FAO (☎ 281-7844), UNICEF (☎ 280-5931) or UNESCO (☎ 391-0577).

Foreign musicians can sometimes find work in the city's many hotel clubs and independent live music venues. The only way to find out what's available is to hit the streets at night and ask around. The most comprehensive list of such places is published monthly in the magazine *Bangkok Metro*. The better places – including major hotels – can arrange for the proper work permits and visas since music performance is one of the occupations most tolerated by Thai immigration.

Foreigners have also been able to find temporary work in guesthouses that cater to farangs; these are usually quasi-legal at best.

Getting There & Away

AIR

The expense of getting to Bangkok per air-km varies quite a bit depending on your point of departure. However, you can take heart in the fact that Bangkok is one of the cheapest cities in the world to fly out of, due to the Thai government's loose restrictions on airfares and the close competition between airlines and travel agencies. The result is that with a little shopping around, you can come up with some real bargains. If you can find a cheap one-way ticket to Bangkok, take it, because you are virtually guaranteed to find one of equal or lesser cost for the return trip once you get there.

From most places around the world your best bet will be budget, excursion or promotional fares – when inquiring from airlines ask for the various fares in that order. Each carries its own set of restrictions and it's up to you to decide which set works best in your case. Fares fluctuate, but in general they are cheaper from September to April (northern hemisphere) and from March to November (southern hemisphere).

Fares listed here should serve as a guideline – don't count on them staying this way for long (they may go down!).

Australia

The full economy fare from Australia to Bangkok is around A$4000 from Sydney, Melbourne or Brisbane, A$3330 from Perth. However, tickets discounted either by travel agents or airlines are much cheaper. None of these are advance purchase nowadays, but they tend to sell out early – the airlines only allocate a limited number of these super-cheap seats to each flight. Prices start at about A$550 (one way) and A$700 (return) from Melbourne or Sydney on the cheaper carriers (eg Alitalia), and get more expensive the better the airline's 'reputation'.

From Australia to most Asian destinations, including Bangkok, the airlines have recently introduced new seasons: the peak is December to 15 January, mid-year school holiday periods are 'shoulder' season, and the rest of the year is low season. Fares now also vary depending on how long you want to stay away – a fare valid for 28 days' travel is about A$50 to A$60 cheaper than one valid for 90 days. However, there is some variation in this rule so check with individual airlines for the best deal.

At the time of writing, fares available through agents specialising in discount fares on the better-known airlines (eg Thai, Qantas, British Airways and Royal Brunei) are: A$699 to A$1089 (low season) and A$1079 to A$1305 (high season) from Sydney or Melbourne; A$915 to A$1089 (low) and A$1285 to A$1305 (high) from Brisbane; and A$789 to A$935 (low) and A$1079 to A$1129 (high) from Perth.

The UK & Continental Europe

London 'bucket shops' offer quite a range of cheap tickets to Bangkok: a student fare on Kuwait Airways is UK£215 one way and UK£355 return and on THAI its UK£275 and UK£459. KLM offers a fare for UK£350 one way and UK£580 return.

It's also easy to stop over in Bangkok between London and Australia, with return fares for around UK£689 on THAI to the Australian east coast, or UK£550 on Royal Brunei to Brisbane or Perth, UK£730 on KLM to Sydney. Good travel agencies to try for these sorts of fares are Trailfinders on Kensington High St (☎ (0171) 938-3939) and Earls Court Rd (☎ (0171) 938-3366), or STA Travel (☎ (0171) 937-9962) on Old Brompton Rd and at the universities of London, Kent, Birmingham and Loughborough. Or you can simply check the travel ads in *Time Out*, *Evening Standard* and *TNT*. For discounted flights out of Manchester or Gatwick, check with Airbreak Leisure (☎ (0171) 712-0303) at South Quay Plaza 2, 193 Marsh Wall, London, E14 92H.

One of the cheapest deals going is on TAROM (Romanian Air Transport), which has Brussels-Bangkok-Brussels fares valid for a year. Uzbekistan Airways does a London to Bangkok flight via Tashkent. Other cheapies are Lauda Air from London (via Vienna) and Czech Airlines from Prague (via London, Frankfurt and Zurich).

North America

If you fly from the west coast, you can get some great deals through the many bucket shops (which discount tickets by taking a cut in commissions) and consolidators (agencies that buy airline seats in bulk) operating in Los Angeles and San Francisco. Through agencies such as these a return (round-trip) airfare to Bangkok from any of 10 different west coast cities starts at around US$750.

One of the most reliable discounters is Avia Travel (☎ (800) 950-AVIA toll-free, (415) 668-0964, fax (415) 386-8519) at 5429 Geary Blvd, San Francisco, CA 94121. Avia specialises in custom-designed round-the-world fares, for example San Francisco-London-Delhi-Bangkok-Seoul-San Francisco for US$1486 or San Francisco-Tokyo-Kuala Lumpur-Bangkok-Amsterdam/Rome/Madrid/Athens/Paris (choice of one)-London-SFO for US$1512, as well as 'Circle Pacific' fares such as San Francisco-Hong Kong-Bangkok-Singapore-Jakarta-Denpasar-Los Angeles for US$1230. The agency sets aside a portion of its profits for Volunteers in Asia, a nonprofit organisation that sends grassroots volunteers to work in South-East Asia.

Another agency that works hard to get the cheapest deals is Air Brokers International (☎ (800) 883-3273 toll-free, (415) 397-1383, fax (415) 397-4767) at 323 Geary St, Suite 411, San Francisco, CA 94102. One of their 'Circle Pacific' fares, for example, offers a Los Angeles-Hong Kong-Bangkok-Denpasar-Los Angeles ticket for US$975 plus tax during the low season; you can add Honolulu, Singapore, Jakarta or Yogyakarta to this route for US$50 each stop. San Francisco/Los Angeles-Hong Kong-Bangkok-Delhi-Bombay-Rome/London-San Francisco/Los Angeles costs US$1449, or you could go New York-Los Angeles-Bali-Singapore-Bangkok-Hong Kong-New York for US$1399.

While the airlines themselves can rarely match the prices of the discounters, they are worth checking if only to get benchmark prices to use for comparison. Tickets bought directly from the airlines may also have fewer restrictions and/or less strict cancellation policies than those bought from discounters (though this is not always true).

Cheapest from the west coast are: Thai Airways International (THAI), China Airlines, Korean Airlines and CP Air. Each of these has a budget and/or 'super Apex' fare that costs around US$900 to US$1200 return from Los Angeles, San Francisco or Seattle. THAI is the most overbooked of these airlines from December to March and June to August and hence their flights during these months may entail schedule delays (if you're lucky enough to get a seat at all). Several of these airlines also fly out of New York, Dallas, Chicago and Atlanta – add another US$150 to US$250 to their lowest fares.

TAROM, the Romanian carrier, offers one-way excursion fares from New York to Bangkok for US$500.

Canada

Canadian Pacific flies from Vancouver to Bangkok at fares beginning at around C$850 return for advance purchase excursion fares. Travellers living in eastern Canada will usually find the best deals out of New York or San Francisco, adding fares from Toronto or Montreal (see the USA section above).

Asia

There are regular flights to Bangkok from every major city in Asia and it's not so tricky dealing with inter-Asia flights as most airlines offer about the same fares. Here is a sample of current estimated one-way fares:

Singapore	US$110-195
Hong Kong	US$110-195
Taipei	US$220-373
Calcutta	US$170
Kathmandu	US$210-276
Colombo	US$236
New Delhi	US$236
Manila	US$200-231
Kunming	US$250
Vientiane	US$100
Phnom Penh	US$150

ASEAN promotional fares (return from any city, eg a Bangkok-Manila-Jakarta fare allows you to go between Manila, Jakarta, Bangkok and Manila; or Jakarta, Bangkok, Manila and Jakarta; or Bangkok, Manila, Jakarta and Bangkok):

Route Fare

Route	Fare
Bangkok-Manila-Jakarta	US$545
Bangkok-Singapore-Manila	US$440
Bangkok-Jakarta-Kuala Lumpur	US$410
Bangkok-Manila-Brunei-Jakarta-Singapore-Kuala Lumpur	US$580
Bangkok-Singapore-Jakarta-Yogyakarta-Denpasar	US$580

From Bangkok

Although other Asian centres are now competitive with Bangkok for buying discounted airline tickets, it is still a good place for shopping around. Note, however, that some Bangkok travel agencies have a shocking reputation: taking money and then delaying or not coming through with the tickets, providing tickets with limited validity periods or severe use restrictions are all part of the racket. There are a lot of perfectly honest agents, but beware of the rogues.

Some typical one-way discount fares being quoted from Bangkok include:

Around Asia

Calcutta	3100 to 3500B
Colombo	3100 to 4000B
Delhi	4100B
Hong Kong	3150B
Jakarta	5800B
Kathmandu	3900B
Kuala Lumpur	2750B
Penang	2500 to 3300B
Singapore	1850 to 3000B
Yangon	1900 to 3150B
Tokyo	4800B

Australia & New Zealand

Sydney/Brisbane/Melbourne	10,400B
Darwin/Perth	7400B
Auckland	12,000 to 13,200B

Europe

Athens, Amsterdam, Frankfurt, London, Paris, Rome or Zurich	9200 to 9700 B

USA

San Francisco/Los Angeles	11,200B
via Australia	25,000B
New York	13,200B

Regional Services Thailand's Ministry of Transport allows several air carriers to provide regional air services to Myanmar, Vietnam, Laos and Cambodia. Routes to/from Thailand by foreign carriers include Yunnan Airways and China Southwest flights from Kunming to Bangkok; Silk Air between Singapore and Phuket; Dragon Air between Hong Kong and Phuket; MAS between Ipoh, Malaysia, and Hat Yai; Royal Air Cambodge between Bangkok and Phnom Penh; Lao Aviation between Bangkok and Vientiane; Vietnam Airlines between Bangkok and Ho Chi Minh City; and Air Mandalay between Chiang Mai and Mandalay.

Booking Problems During the past few years the booking of flights in and out of Bangkok during the high season (December to March) has become increasingly difficult. For air travel during these months you should book as far in advance as possible. THAI is finally loosening its stranglehold on air routes in and out of Thailand, so the situation has improved since the late 80s when the national carrier refused to give rival airlines permission to add much-needed service through Bangkok.

Also be sure to reconfirm return or ongoing tickets when you arrive in Thailand. Failure to reconfirm can mean losing your reservation.

Departure Tax Airport departure tax is 250B for international flights departing from Bangkok International, 200B for international departures from Phuket and Chiang Mai, and 30B for domestic flights. Children under two are exempt. Airport authorities say there is no longer a tax exemption for passengers in transit, but some travellers report that this is not always enforced.

Airline Offices

Bangkok is a major centre for international flights throughout Asia, and Bangkok's airport is a busy one. Domestic flights operated by THAI and Bangkok Airways also fan out from Bangkok all over the country. Addresses of airline offices in Bangkok are:

Aeroflot
   7 Silom Rd (☎ 233-6965)
Air France
   Ground floor, Chan Issara Tower, 942/51 Rama IV Rd
   (☎ 234-1330/1339; reservations ☎ 233-9477)
Air India
   16th floor, Amarin Tower, Ploenchit Rd
   (☎ 256-9620; reservations ☎ 256-9614/9618)
Air Lanka
   Chan Issara Tower 942/34-5 Rama IV Rd
   (☎ 236-4981, 235-4982)
Air New Zealand
   1053 Charoen Krung Rd (☎ 233-5900/9, 237-1560/1562)
Alitalia
   8th floor, Boonmitr Bldg, 138 Silom Rd (☎ 233-4000/4004)
All Nippon Airways (ANA)
   2nd floor, CP Tower, 313 Silom Rd (☎ 238-5121)
American Airlines
   518/5 Ploenchit Rd (☎ 254-1270)
Asiana Airlines
   14th floor, BB Bldg, 54 Soi Asoke (☎ 260-7700/7704)
Bangkok Airways
   Queen Sirikit National Convention Centre, New Ratch-adaphisek Rd, Khlong Toey
   (☎ 229-3434/3456, fax 229-3450)
   1111 Ploenchit Rd (☎ 254-2903)

Bangladesh Biman
    Chongkolnee Bldg, 56 Surawong Rd
    (☎ 235-7643/7644, 234-0300/0309)
British Airways
    Chan Issara Tower, Rama IV Rd (☎ 236-0038)
Canadian Airlines International
    Maneeya Bldg, 518/5 Ploenchit Rd
    (☎ 251-4521, 254-8376)
Cathay Pacific Airways
    11th floor, Ploenchit Tower, Ploenchit Rd (☎ 263-0606)
China Airlines
    Peninsula Plaza, Ratchadamri Rd
    (☎ 253-5733; reservations ☎ 253-4242)
China Southern Airlines
    1st floor, Silom Plaza Bldg, Silom Rd (☎ 266-5688)
Delta Air Lines
    7th floor, Patpong Bldg, 1 Surawong Rd
    (☎ 237-6855; reservations ☎ 237-6838)
Druk Air (see Thai Airways International)
EgyptAir
    3rd floor, CP Tower, 313 Silom Rd (☎ 231-0504/0508)
Eva Air
    3656/4-5 2nd floor, Green Tower, Rama IV Rd
    (☎ 367-3388; reservations 240-0890
El Al Israel Airlines
    14th floor, Manorom Bldg, Rama IV Rd
    (☎ 671-6145, 249-8818)
Finnair
    175 Sathorn City Tower, Sathon Rd
    (☎ 679-6671; reservations ☎ 251-5075)
Garuda Indonesia
    27th floor, Lumphini Tower, 1168 Rama IV Rd
    (☎ 285-6470/6473)
Gulf Air
    Maneeya Bldg, 518/2 Ploenchit Rd (☎ 254-7931/7940)
Japan Airlines
    254/1 Ratchadaphisek (☎ 274-1400, 274-1435)
KLM Royal Dutch Airlines
    Maneeya Bldg, 518/5 Ploenchit Rd
    (☎ 254-8834; reservations 254-8325)
Korean Air
    Dusit Thani Hotel (☎ 235-6800)
    Kongboonma Bldg, Silom Rd (☎ 235-9221)
Kuwait Airways
    Bangkok International airport (☎ 523-6993)
Lao Aviation
    Silom Plaza, 491/17 Silom Rd (☎ 236-9821/9823)
Lauda Air
    33/33-4 Wall Street Tower, Surawong Rd (☎ 233-2565)
LOT Polish Airlines
    485/11-12 Silom Rd (☎ 235-2223, 235-7092)
Lufthansa
    Bank of America Bldg, 2/2 Wireless Rd (☎ 255-0385)
    Asoke Bldg, Soi 21, Sukhumvit Rd (☎ 264-2400)

National Airlines
Rama Gardens, Vibhavadi Rangsit Rd (☎ 561-3784)
Malaysian Airlines
98-102 Surawong Rd
(☎ 236-5871; reservations ☎ 236-4705/4709)
20th floor, Ploenchit Tower, Ploenchit Rd (☎ 263-0565)
Myanmar Airways International
Chan Issara Tower, Rama IV Rd (☎ 267-5078)
Northwest Airlines
Peninsula Plaza, 153 Ratchadamri Rd (☎ 254-0789)
Pakistan International Airlines
52 Surawong Rd (☎ 234-2961, 266-4548)
Philippine Airlines
Chongkolnee Bldg, 56 Surawong Rd
(☎ 234-2483, 233-2350/2352)
Qantas
Chan Issara Tower, 942/51 Rama IV Rd
(☎ 267-5188, 236-0307)
Royal Air Cambodge
c/o Malaysian Airlines
Royal Brunei Airlines
2nd floor, Chan Issara Tower, 942/52 Rama IV Rd
(☎ 233-0506, 235-4764)
Royal Jordanian Airlines
Yada Bldg, 56 Silom Rd (☎ 236-0030)
Royal Nepal Airlines
Sivadon Bldg, 1/4 Convent Rd (☎ 233-3921/3924)
Sabena Belgian World Airlines
3rd floor, CP Tower, 313 Silom Rd
(☎ 238-2201, 238-2204/2205)
Saudi Arabian Airlines
Ground floor, CCT Bldg, 109 Surawong Rd
(☎ 236-9400/9403)
Scandinavian Airlines System (SAS)
Soi 25, Sukhumvit Rd (☎ 260-0444)
Silk Air
12th floor, Silom Centre Bldg, Silom Rd
(☎ 236-0303; reservations ☎ 236-0440)
Singapore Airlines
12th floor, Silom Center Bldg, 2 Silom Rd
(☎ 236-0303; reservations ☎ 236-0440)
South African Airways
Maneeya Bldg, 518/5 Ploenchit Rd (☎ 254-8206)
Swissair
1 Silom Rd
(☎ 233-2930/2934; reservations ☎ 233-2935/2938)
TAROM Romanian Air Transport
89/12 Bangkok Bazaar, Ratchadamri Rd (☎ 253-1681)
Thai Airways International (THAI)
89 Vibhavadi Rangsit Rd
(☎ 513-0121; reservations ☎ 233-3810)
485 Silom Rd (☎ 234-3100/3119)
6 Lan Luang Rd (☎ 280-0060, 628-2000)
Asia Hotel, 296 Phayathai Rd (☎ 215-2020/2021)

Grand China Tower, 3rd floor, 215 Yaowarat Rd
(☎ 223-9745/9750)
Bangkok International airport, Don Meuang
(☎ 535-2081/2082, 523 6121)
United Airlines
9th floor, Regent House, 183 Ratchadamri Rd (☎ 253-0558)
Vietnam Airlines (Hang Khong Vietnam)
3rd floor, 572 Ploenchit Rd (☎ 251-4242)

Within Thailand

Bangkok's Don Meuang domestic air terminal is only a few hundred metres south of the international terminals. A free shuttle bus runs between the international and domestic terminals every 15 minutes or so between 6 am and 11.20 pm.

Thai Airways International Most domestic air services in Thailand are operated by Thai Airways International (THAI), which covers 22 airports throughout the kingdom. On certain southern routes, domestic flights through Hat Yai continue on to Malaysia (Penang, Kuala Lumpur), Singapore and Brunei (Bandar Seri Begawan). THAI operates Boeing 737s or Airbus 300s on its main domestic routes.

Note that through fares are generally less than combination fares – Chiang Rai to Bangkok, for example, is cheaper than the addition of Chiang Rai to Chiang Mai and Chiang Mai to Bangkok fares. This does not always apply to international fares, however. It's much cheaper to fly from Bangkok to Penang via Phuket or Hat Yai than direct, for example.

THAI offers special four-coupon passes – sold only outside Thailand for foreign currency – in which you can book any four domestic flights for one fare of US$259 as long as you don't repeat the same leg. Unless you plan carefully, this isn't much of a saving since it's hard to avoid repeating the same leg in and out of Bangkok. For information on the four-coupon deal, known as the 'Discover Thailand fare', enquire at any THAI office outside Thailand.

Bangkok Airways Bangkok Airways, owned by Sahakol Air, flies five main routes: Bangkok-Sukhothai-Chiang Mai; Bangkok-Ko Samui-Phuket; Bangkok -Ranong-Phuket; Bangkok-Hua Hin-Samui; and U Taphao (Pattaya)-Ko Samui. The mainstay of the Bangkok Airways fleet is the Franco-Italian ATR-72.

Bangkok Airways' fares are competitive with THAI's, but the company is small and it remains to be seen whether or not it will survive to become a serious contender.

The airline's head office (☎ 229-3434/3456, fax 229-3450) is at the Queen Sirikit National Convention Centre, New Ratchadaphisek Rd, Khlong Toey, Bangkok 10110. There are also offices in Hua Hin, Pattaya, Phuket and Ko Samui.

Orient Express Air Formerly a carrier in Cambodia known as SK Air, relative newcomer Orient Express Air (OEA) operates charter tour-package flights between Chiang Mai and Phuket, along with 20 scheduled domestic routes linking the North with the South and North-East without Bangkok stopovers. The company uses B727-200s for all flights. OEA (☎ (53) 818092, 201566) has headquarters at Chiang Mai International airport.

LAND

Malaysia

Trains, buses and taxis enter Thailand from Malaysia at the western point of entry, Padang Besar, or either of two eastern crossings at Sungai Kolok and Tak Bai. There is also limited public transport via the much less-frequented Betong, near the centre of the Thai-Malaysian border.

Riding the rails from Singapore to Bangkok via Butterworth, Malaysia, is a great way to travel to Thailand – as long as you don't count on making a smooth change between the Malaysian railway (KTM) and State Railway of Thailand (SRT) trains. The Thai train almost always leaves on time; the Malaysian train rarely arrives on time. Unfortunately, the Thai train leaves Padang Besar even if the Malaysian railway express from Kuala Lumpur (or the 2nd class connection from Butterworth) is late. To be on the safe side, purchase the Malaysian and Thai portions of your ticket with departures on consecutive days and plan a Butterworth/Penang stopover.

Laos

Since April 1993 a land crossing from Champasak Province in Laos to Chong Mek in Thailand's Ubon Ratchathani Province has been open to foreign visitors. To use this crossing you must hold a visa valid for Laos.

The Thai-Lao Friendship Bridge, an Australian-financed span across the Mekong near Nong Khai which

Eastern & Oriental Express

In 1993 the State Railway of Thailand, the Kereta Api Tanah Melayu (Malaysia's state railway) and Singapore's Eastern & Oriental Express Co (E&O) inaugurated the Eastern & Oriental Express between Singapore and Bangkok. Finally, an Orient Express that actually begins and ends in the Orient!

The E&O travels at an average speed of 50 km/h, completing the 1943-km Singapore to Bangkok journey in 41 hours, with a two-hour Butterworth stopover and tour of Georgetown, Penang. As in Europe, this new train offers cruise-ship luxury on rails. Passengers dine, sleep and are entertained in 22 railway carriages imported from New Zealand and refurbished in a 1930s style using lots of brass, teak and old-world tapestry by the same French designer who remodelled the Venice Simplon Orient Express in Europe. Aside from the locomotive(s), sleeping coaches, staff coach and luggage cars, the train has two restaurant cars, a saloon car and a bar car, with a combination bar car/open-air observation deck at the rear. All accommodation is in deluxe private cabins with shower, toilet and individually controlled air-conditioning; passengers are attended by round-the-clock cabin stewards in the true pukkah tradition.

Tariffs begin at (brace yourself) US$1400 per person for the full route in the bunk-style sleeper, US$1950 in a more spacious state room; and half-car Presidential suites are available for a mere US$3620. These fares include four complimentary hotel nights at the Oriental Bangkok and Oriental Singapore (two nights each at either end). Half routes from Bangkok or Singapore to Butterworth or vice versa are available for a bit more than half fare, no hotel included. Honeymoon couples comprise a significant part of the clientele.

The train can be booked in Singapore through Eastern & Oriental Express (☎ (65) 227-2068; (02) 251-4862 in Bangkok; fax (65) 224-9265), at Carlton Bldg No 14-03, 90 Cecil St, Singapore 0106.

Elsewhere, E&O reservations and information can be obtained by calling the numbers below.

Australia	☎ (02) 232 7499
France	☎ (1) 45 62 0069
Germany	☎ (211) 16 21 06/7
New Zealand	☎ (9) 379 3708
Switzerland	☎ (22) 366 42 22
UK	☎ (71) 928 6000
USA	☎ (800) 524-2420

leads to Vientiane in Laos, opened in April 1994. Construction began in early 1996 on a second Mekong bridge to span the river between Thailand's Chiang Khong and Laos' Huay Xai. If all goes as planned, this one should be operational by early 1998 and will link Thailand with China by road via Laos' Bokeo and Luang Nam Thai provinces.

A third span is planned for either Tha Khaek (which is opposite Thailand's Nakhon Phanom) or Savannakhet (opposite Mukdahan).

River It is now legal for non-Thai foreigners to cross the Mekong River by ferry between Laos and Thailand at the following points:, Nakhon Phanom (opposite Tha Khaek), Beung Kan (opposite Paksan), Chiang Khong (opposite Huay Xai), and Mukdahan (opposite Savannakhet).

Myanmar

There is currently no legal land passage between Myanmar and Thailand, but several border crossings between the countries are open to day-trippers or short excursions in the vicinity. These include Mae Sai (opposite Tachilek), Three Pagodas Pass (opposite Payathonzu), and Mae Sot (Myawaddy). As yet, none of these link up with routes to Yangon (Rangoon) or Mandalay or any other cities of size. Nor are you permitted to enter Thailand from Myanmar, at least not yet.

Cambodia

The Cambodian border won't be safe for land crossings until mines and booby traps left over from the conflict between the Khmer Rouge and the Vietnamese are removed or detonated.

China

The governments of Thailand, Laos, China and Myanmar recently agreed to the construction of a four-nation ring road through all four countries. The western half of the loop will proceed from Mae Sai, Thailand, to Jinghong, China, via Myanmar's Tachilek (opposite Mae Sai) and Kengtung (near Dalau on the China-Myanmar border), while the eastern half will extend from Chiang Khong, Thailand, to Jinghong via Huay Xai, Laos (opposite Chiang Khong) and Boten, Laos (on the Yunnanese border south of Jinghong).

Once the roads are built and the visa formalities have been worked out, this loop will provide alternative travel connections between China and South-East Asia, in much the same way as the Karakoram Highway has forged new links between China and South Asia. It's difficult to predict when all the logistical variables will be settled, but progress so far points to a cleared path by the end of the decade.

A third way to reach China's Yunnan Province from Thailand is by boat along the Mekong River. Several surveys of the waterway have been completed and a specially constructed express boat made its inaugural run between Sop Ruak, Chiang Rai Province, and China's Yunnan Province in early 1994. For the moment, permission for such travel is restricted to private tour groups, but it's reasonable to assume that in the future – if demand is high enough – some sort of scheduled public service may become available.

WITHIN THAILAND

Government Bus

Several types of buses ply the roads of Thailand. The cheapest and slowest are the ordinary government-run buses (rót tham daa) that stop in every little town and for every waving hand along the highway. For some destinations – smaller towns – these orange-painted buses are your only choice, but at least they leave frequently. The government also runs faster, more comfortable, but less frequent air-conditioned buses called rót ae or rót pràp aakàat; these are painted with blue markings. If these are available to your destination, they are your very best choice since they don't cost that much more than the ordinary stop-in-every-town buses. The government bus company is called Baw Khaw Saw, an abbreviation of Borisàt Khŏn Sòng (literally, Transportation Company). Every city and town in Thailand linked by bus transportation has a Baw Khaw Saw terminal, even if it's just a patch of dirt by the roadside.

The service on the government air-con buses is usually quite good and includes a beverage service and video. On longer routes (eg Bangkok to Chiang Mai, Bangkok to Nong Khai), the air-con buses even distribute claim checks (receipt dockets) for your baggage. Longer routes may also offer two classes of air-con bus, regular and 1st class; the latter have toilets. 'VIP' buses have fewer seats (30 to 34 instead of 44; some routes have Super VIP buses, with only 24 seats) so that each seat reclines more. Sometimes these are called rót nawn or sleepers. Occasionally you'll get a government air-con bus in which the air-con is broken or the seats are not up to standard, but in general I've found them more reliable than the private tour buses.

Private Bus

Private buses run between major tourist and business destinations: Chiang Mai, Surat, Ko Samui, Phuket, Hat Yai, Pattaya, Hua Hin and a number of others. To Chiang Mai, for example, several companies run daily buses out of Bangkok. These can be booked through most hotels or any travel agency, although it's best to book directly through a bus office to be assured that you get what you pay for.

Fares vary from company to company, but usually not by more than a few baht. However, fare differences between the government and private bus companies can be substantial. Using Surat Thani as an example, state-run buses cost 158B for the ordinary bus or 285B (1st class) for the air-con, while the private companies charge up to 385B. On the other hand, to Chiang Mai the private buses often cost less than the government buses, although those that charge less offer inferior service. Departures for some private companies are more frequent than for the equivalent Baw Khaw Saw route.

The private air-con buses are usually no more comfortable than the government air-con buses and feature similarly narrow seats and a hair-raising ride. The trick the tour companies use to make their buses seem more comfortable is to make you think you're not on a bus by turning up the air-con until your knees knock, handing out pillows and blankets and serving free soft drinks. On overnight journeys the buses usually stop en route and passengers are woken up to get off the bus for a free meal of fried rice or rice soup. A few companies even treat you to a meal before a long overnight trip.

Like their state-run equivalents, the private companies offer VIP (sleeper) buses on long hauls. In general, private bus companies that deal mostly with Thais are good, while tourist-oriented ones are the worst as they know very few customers will be returning.

In recent years the service on many private lines has declined, especially on the Bangkok to Chiang Mai, Bangkok to Ko Samui, Surat to Phuket and Surat to Krabi routes.

Sometimes the cheaper lines – especially those booked on Khao San Rd – switch vehicles at the last moment so that instead of the roomy air-con bus advertised, you're stuck with a cramped van with broken air-con. Another problem with private companies is that they generally spend more time cruising the city for passengers before getting under way, meaning that they rarely leave at the advertised departure time.

Out of Bangkok, the safest, most reliable private bus services are the ones which operate from the three official Baw Khaw Saw terminals rather than from hotels or guesthouses. Picking up passengers from any points except these official terminals is actually illegal, and services promised are often not delivered. Although it can be a hassle getting out to the Baw Khaw Saw terminals, you're generally rewarded with safer, more reliable and punctual service.

Safety & Service Statistically, private buses meet with more accidents than government air-con buses. Turnovers on tight corners and head-on collisions with trucks are probably due to the inexperience of the drivers on a particular route. This in turn is probably a result of the companies opening and folding so frequently and because of the high priority given to making good time.

As private bus fares are typically higher than government bus fares, the private bus companies attract a better heeled clientele among the Thais, as well as among foreign tourists. One result of this is that a private bus loaded with money or the promise of money is a temptation for upcountry bandits. Hence, private buses occasionally get robbed by bands of thieves. These incidents are diminishing, however, due to increased security under provincial administration.

Large-scale robberies never occur on the ordinary government buses, very rarely on the government air-con buses and rarely on the trains. Accidents, however, are not unknown on the government buses either, so the train still comes out as the safest means of transport in Thailand.

Keep an eye on your bags when riding buses – pilfering by stealth is still the most popular form of robbery in Thailand, though again the risks are not that great – just be aware. Most pilfering seems to take place on the private bus runs between Bangkok and Chiang Mai, especially on buses booked on Khao San Rd. Keep zippered bags locked and well secured.

Train

The railway network in Thailand, run by the government through the State Railway of Thailand (SRT), is surprisingly good. After travelling several thousand km by train and bus, I have to say that the train wins hands down as the best form of public transport in the kingdom. The SRT operates passenger trains in three classes – 1st, 2nd and 3rd – but each class varies considerably depending on whether you're on an ordinary, rapid or express train. Third class is often the cheapest way to cover a long distance; by 2nd class it's about the same as a private tour bus but much safer and more comfortable. Trains take a bit longer than chartered buses on the same journey, but are worth the extra travel time, on overnight trips especially.

Rail Routes Four main rail lines cover 4500 km along the northern, southern, north-eastern and eastern routes. There are several side routes, notably between Nakhon Pathom and Nam Tok (stopping in Kanchanaburi) in the western Central region, and between Tung Song and Kantang (stopping in Trang) in the South. The southern line splits at Hat Yai, one route going to Sungai Kolok on the Malaysian east-coast border, via Yala, and the other route going to Padang Besar in the west, also on the Malaysian border.

Bangkok Terminals Most long-distance trains originate from Bangkok's Hualamphong station. Before a railway bridge was constructed across the Chao Phraya River in 1932, all southbound trains left from Thonburi's Bangkok Noi station. Today this station services commuter and short-line trains to Kanchanaburi/Nam Tok, Suphanburi, Ratchaburi and Nakhon Pathom (Ratchaburi and Nakhon Pathom can also be reached by train from Hualamphong). A slow night train to Chumphon and Lang Suan, both in Southern Thailand, leaves nightly from Thonburi (Bangkok Noi) station but it's rarely used by long-distance travellers.

Bookings The disadvantage of travelling by rail, in addition to the time factor mentioned earlier, is that trains can be difficult to book. This is especially true around holiday time, eg the middle of April approaching the Songkhran Festival, since many Thais prefer the train. Trains out of Bangkok should be booked as far in advance as possible – a minimum of a week for popular routes such as the northern line to Chiang Mai and southern line to Hat Yai, especially if you want a sleeper. For the north-eastern and eastern lines a few days will suffice.

Advance bookings may be made one to 90 days before your intended date of departure. If you want to book tickets in advance, go to Hualamphong station, walk through the front of the station house and go straight to the back right-hand corner where a sign says 'Advance Booking' (it's open from 8.30 am to 4 pm on weekdays and 8.30 am to noon on weekends and holidays). The other ticket windows, on the left-hand side of the station, are for same-day purchases, mostly 3rd class.

At the Advance Bookings office, reservations are now computerised – you simply take a queue number, wait until your number appears on one of the electronic marquees, report to the correct desk (one for the southern line, one for the north and north-eastern) and make your ticket arrangements. Only cash baht is acceptable here.

Note that buying a return ticket does not necessarily guarantee you a seat on the way back, it only means you do not have to buy a ticket for the return. If you want a guaranteed seat reservation it's best to make that reservation for the return journey immediately upon arrival at your destination.

Booking trains back to Bangkok is generally not as difficult as booking trains out of Bangkok; however, at some stations this can be quite difficult (eg buying a ticket from Surat Thani to Bangkok).

Tickets between any station in Thailand can be purchased at Hualamphong station (☎ 223-3762, 225-6964, 224-7788, fax 225-6068). You can also make advance bookings at Don Meuang station (across from Bangkok International airport) and at the Advance Booking offices at train stations in the larger cities. Advance reservations can be made by phone from anywhere in Thailand. Train tickets can also be purchased at some travel agencies in Bangkok. It is much simpler to book trains through these agencies than to book them at the station; however, they usually add a surcharge of 50 to 100B to the ticket price.

Charges & Surcharges There is a 50B surcharge for express trains (*rót dùan*) and 30B for rapid trains (*rót raew*). These trains are somewhat faster than the ordinary trains, as they make fewer stops. On the northern line during the day there is a 70B surcharge for 2nd class seats in air-con cars. For the special express trains (*rót dùan phísèt)* that run between Bangkok and Padang Besar or between Bangkok and Chiang Mai there is a 70B surcharge.

The charge for 2nd class sleeping berths is 100B for an upper berth and 150B for a lower berth (or 130B and 200B respectively on a special express). The difference between upper and lower is that there is a window next to the lower berth and a little more headroom. The upper berth is still quite comfortable. For 2nd class sleepers with air-con add 250/320B per upper/lower ticket. No sleepers are available in 3rd class.

All 1st class cabins are air-con. A two bed cabin costs 520B per person; single cabins are no longer available.

Following significant fare hikes in the mid-1980s, train travel is not quite the bargain it once was, especially considering that the charge for 2nd class berths is as high as the cost of cheaper hotel rooms outside Bangkok. You can figure on 500 km costing around 180B in 2nd class (not counting the surcharges for rapid/express services), twice that in 1st class and less than half in 3rd.

Eating Facilities Meal service is available in dining cars and at your seat in 2nd and 1st class cars. Menus change as frequently as the SRT changes catering services. For a while there were two menus, a 'special food' menu with 'special' prices (generally given to tourists) and a cheaper, more extensive menu. Nowadays all the meals seem a bit overpriced (75 to 200B on average) – if you're concerned with saving baht, bring your own.

Train staff sometimes hand out face wipes, then come by later to collect 10B each for them – a racket, since there's no indication to passengers that they're not complimentary. (On government buses they're free, and they're available in the station for 1B.) Drinking water is provided, albeit in plastic bottles; sometimes it's free, sometimes it costs 5 to 10B per bottle.

Several readers have written to complain about being overcharged by meal servers on trains. If you do purchase food on board, be sure to check prices on the menu rather than trusting server quotes. Also check the bill carefully to make sure you haven't been overcharged.

Station Services Accurate, up-to-date information on train travel is available at the Rail Travel Aids counter in Hualamphong station. There you can pick up timetables or ask questions about fares and scheduling – one person behind the counter usually speaks a little English.

All train stations in Thailand have baggage storage services (sometimes called the 'cloak room'). The rates and hours of operation vary from station to station. At Hualamphong station the hours are 4 am to 10.30 pm and left luggage costs 20B per piece per day. Hualamphong station also has a 5B shower service in the rest rooms.

Hualamphong station has a travel agency where other kinds of transport can be booked. It also has a post office that's open from 7.30 am to 5.30 pm on weekdays and 9 am to noon on Saturday and holidays; it's closed on Sunday.

Rail Passes Eurotrain International (St Kongensgade 40h, DK-1264 Copenhagen, Denmark) issues a Thailand Explorer Pass that may save on fares if you plan to ride Thai trains extensively within a relatively short interval. To be eligible for the pass you must hold a valid International Student Identity Card (ISIC) or International Teacher Identity Card (ITIC) or be under 26 years of age; accompanying spouses and children are also eligible. The pass must be purchased outside Thailand and is available from most places that issue Eurail passes and ISICs/ITICs. The cost for seven days of unlimited 2nd-class rail travel is US$33, for 14 days US$40 and for 21 days US$48. This includes all rapid or express surcharges, but does not include sleeping berths or air-con charges, which cost extra according to the standard SRT schedule.

WARNING

The information in this chapter is particularly vulnerable to change: prices for travel are volatile, routes are introduced and cancelled, schedules change, special deals come and go, and rules and visa requirements are amended. Airlines and governments seem to take a perverse pleasure in making price structures and regulations as complicated as possible. You should check directly with the airline or a travel agent to make sure you understand how a fare (and ticket you may buy) works. In addition, the travel industry is highly competitive and there are many lurks and perks.

The upshot of this is that you should get opinions, quotes and advice from as many airlines and travel agents as possible before you part with your hard-earned cash. The details given in this chapter should be regarded as pointers and are not a substitute for your own careful, up-to-date research.

Getting Around

Getting around in Bangkok may be difficult at first for the uninitiated, but once you're familiar with the bus system the whole city is accessible. The main obstacle is traffic, which moves at a snail's pace during the day. This means advance planning is a must when you are attending scheduled events or making appointments.

If you can travel by river or canal from one point to another, it's always the best choice. Bangkok was once called the 'Venice of the East', but much of the original canal system has been filled in for road construction. With 10% of Thailand's population living in the capital, water transportation, with a few exceptions, has been relegated to a secondary role. Larger canals, especially on the Thonburi side, remain important commercial arteries, but many of the smaller canals are hopelessly polluted and would probably have been filled in by now if it weren't for their important drainage function.

THE AIRPORT

During the past decade, the airport facilities at Bangkok International airport have undergone a US$200 million redevelopment, including the construction of an international terminal that is one of the most modern and convenient in Asia. However, the very slow immigration lines in the upstairs arrival hall are still a problem. Despite a long row of impressive-looking immigration counters, there never seem to be enough clerks on duty, even at peak arrival times. Even when the booths are fully staffed, waits of 45 minutes to an hour are not unusual. Baggage claim, however, is usually quick and efficient (of course, they have lots of time to get it right while you're inching along through immigration).

The customs area has a green lane for passengers with nothing to declare – just walk through if you're one of these and hand your customs form to one of the clerks by the exit. Baggage trolleys are free for use inside the terminal.

The Thai government has plans to open another international airport about 20 km east of Bangkok at Nong Ngu Hao. This additional airport is expected to be operational by 2004 and will be named Raja Deva (Racha Thewa).

In the meantime, Terminal 2, a second international terminal adjacent to Terminal 1, has opened to accommodate increasing air traffic. Terminal 2 has few facilities other than currency-exchange booths, a public taxi desk and a few restaurants on the 4th floor.

The old Don Meuang terminal, a few hundred metres south of the new terminals, is now used for domestic flights only. A free shuttle bus runs between the international and domestic terminals every 15 minutes between 6 am and 11.20 pm.

To/From Bangkok International Airport

The main international airport is in Don Meuang district, approximately 25 km north of Bangkok. You have a choice of transport modes from the airport to the city ranging from 3.50 to 300B.

THAI Minibus THAI has a minibus service to major hotels (and minor ones if the driver feels like it) for 100B per person. THAI touts in the arrival hall will try to get you into the 350B limo service first, then the 100B minibus.

To Pattaya THAI operates direct air-con buses to Pattaya from the airport thrice daily at 9 am, 11 am and 7 pm; the fare is 200B one way. Private sedans cost 1500B per trip.

Airport Bus In mid 1996 a new airport express bus service began operating from Bangkok International to three Bangkok districts for 70B per person. Buses run every 15 minutes from 5 am to 11 pm. A map showing the designated stops is available at the airport; each route makes approximately six stops in each direction. A great boon to travellers on a budget, these buses mean you can avoid hassling with taxi drivers to get a reasonable fare as well as forgo the slow pace of the regular bus routes.

Since this service is quite new, the routes, fares and hours could change during the first year or two of operation. So far, few airport arrivals seem to be using the service – one hopes it won't be cancelled as a result.

The airport bus counter is around 200m to the left (with your back to the terminal) of the city taxi counter.

A-1 goes to the Silom Rd business district via Pratunam and Ratchadamri Rd, stopping at big hotels like the Indra, Grand Hyatt Erawan, Regent Bangkok and Dusit Thani.
A-2 goes to Sanam Luang via Phayathai Rd, Lan Luang Rd, Ratchadamnoen Klang Rd and Tanao Rd; this is the one you want if you're going to the Siam Square or Banglamphu areas.
A-3 goes to the Phrakhanong district via Sukhumvit Rd.

Public Bus Cheapest of all are the public buses to Bangkok which stop on the highway in front of the airport. There are two non-air-con bus routes and four air-con routes that visitors find particularly useful for getting into the city. The ordinary buses, however, no longer accept passengers carrying luggage.

Air-con bus No 29 costs 16B and plies one of the most useful, all-purpose routes from the airport into the city as it goes to the Siam Square and Hualamphong areas. After entering the city limits via Phahonyothin Rd (which turns into Phayathai Rd), the bus passes Phetburi Rd (where you'll want to get off to change buses for Banglamphu), then Rama I Rd at the Siam Square/ Mahboonkrong intersection (for buses out to Sukhumvit Rd, or to walk to Soi Kasem San 1 for Muangphol Lodging, Reno Hotel, etc) and finally turns right on Rama IV Rd to go to the Hualamphong district (where the main train terminal is located). You'll want to go the opposite way on Rama IV for the Soi Ngam Duphli lodging area. No 29 runs only from 5.45 am to 8 pm, so if you're arriving on a late-night flight you'll miss it.

Air-con bus No 13 (16B, 5.45 am to 8 pm) also goes to Bangkok from the airport, coming down Phahonyothin Rd (like No 29), turning left at the Victory Monument to Ratchaprarop Rd, then south to Ploenchit Rd, where it goes east to Sukhumvit Rd and all the way to Bang Na. This is definitely the one to catch if you're heading for the Sukhumvit area.

Air-con bus No 4 (16B, 5.45 am to 8 pm) begins with a route parallel to that of the No 29 bus – down Mitthaphap Rd to Ratchaprarop and Ratchadamri Rds (Pratunam district), crossing Phetburi, Rama I, Ploenchit and Rama IV Rds, then down Silom, left on Charoen Krung, and across the river to Thonburi.

No backpacks or large luggage are allowed onto the non-air-con, ordinary buses. Ordinary bus No 59 costs only 3.50B (5B from 11 pm to 5 am) and operates 24 hours – it zigzags through the city to Banglamphu (the Democracy Monument area) from the airport, a trip that can take up to an hour and a half or more in traffic.

Ordinary No 29 bus (3.50B, or 5B, 11 pm to 5 am, 24 hours) plies much the same route as air-con No 29. Green bus No 2 (16B, 5.30 am to 8 pm) has a similar route to the air-con No 4; first it goes through Pratunam, then direct to Ratchadamri Rd, Silom Rd and Charoen Krung Rd.

Unless you're really strapped for baht, it's worth the extra 12.50B for the air-con and almost guaranteed seating, especially in the hot season, since the trip downtown by bus usually takes an hour or more. Even better is the 70B airport bus, described above.

Train You can also get into Bangkok from the airport by ordinary commuter train. Just after leaving the passenger terminal, turn right (north), cross the highway via the pedestrian bridge, turn left and walk about 100m towards Bangkok. Opposite the big Amari Airport Hotel is the small Don Meuang train station from where trains depart regularly to Bangkok. The 3rd-class fare from Don Meuang is only 10B if you buy your ticket on the platform, 20B if purchased on the train. Tickets for rapid or express trains cost 50B.

There are trains every 15 to 30 minutes between 5 am and 8 pm and it takes about 45 minutes to reach Hualamphong, the main station in central Bangkok. In the opposite direction, trains run frequently between 4.20 am and 8 pm. From the Hualamphong train station you can walk to the bus stop almost opposite Wat Traimit (Map 8) for bus No 23 to Banglamphu if that's your destination.

Taxi As reported in previous editions, hassles with airport taxi drivers continue to plague Bangkok International (see Warning in Getting There and Away). The taxis which wait near the arrival area of the airport are supposed to be airport-regulated. Ignore all the touts waiting like sharks near the customs area and buy a taxi ticket from the public taxi booth at the southern end of the arrival hall (to the far left as you leave customs). Fares are set according to city destination – no haggling should be necessary. Most destinations in central Bangkok are 200B (eg Siam Square) or 300B (eg Banglamphu). Taxis using this system are not required to use their meters. Two, three, or even four passengers (if they don't have much luggage) can split the fare.

Sometimes unscrupulous drivers will approach you before you reach the desk and try to sell you a ticket for 350 or 400B – ignore them and head straight for the desk. A few touts from the old taxi mafia that used to prowl the arrival area are still around and may approach you with fares of around 150B. Their taxis have white and black plates and are not licensed to carry passengers, hence you have less legal recourse in the event of an incident than if you take a licensed taxi (yellow and black plates).

The real hassle begins if you decide you'd prefer to take a metered taxi rather than pay the rather high 250B most drivers want. You're *supposed* to be able to take a metered taxi from the airport if you so choose, but the reality from 1994 to 1996 was that once you got in the cab most drivers refused to run the meters – in clear violation of the regulations printed on sheets given to all passengers in advance – and asked for 250B. Drivers complain that it really doesn't pay for them to queue up for passengers at the current metered rates. In mid-1996 the Ministry of Transport authorised drivers of metered taxis from the airport to collect a 100B surcharge over the meter reading. With surcharge included you shouldn't have to pay more than 210 to 240B for most destinations in Bangkok. One hopes the new surcharge – if actually followed – will result in fewer arguments between passenger and driver.

Going to the airport from the city, a metered taxi costs from 115B (eg from Siam Square) to 140B (from Banglamphu or the Silom Rd area). The occasional driver will refuse to use his meter and quote a flat rate of 150 to 200B.

On a metered taxi trip to/from the airport, passengers are responsible for the 10B or 20B (depending on which entrance the driver chooses) expressway toll. If you take a flat-rate taxi, the driver should pay. During heavy traffic you can save money by staying on the surface (non-expressway) streets – which are just as speedy as (if not speedier than) the expressway.

One way to get an unsurcharged metered taxi is to go upstairs to the departure area and get an incoming city taxi, one that has just dropped passengers off. These will usually take you to Bangkok on the meter. The downstairs taxi mafia frowns on this practice, however, and you may be hassled.

Metered taxis flagged down on the highway in front of the airport (turn left from the arrival hall) are even cheaper – 100 to 120B for central Bangkok. When the queue at the public taxi desk is particularly long, it's sometimes faster to go upstairs or walk out to the highway and flag one down.

THAI Limousine THAI offers an airport limousine, which is really just a glorified air-con taxi service, for 400B downtown, 300B to the Northern bus terminal or 500B to the Southern bus terminal.

Helicopter The Shangri-La Hotel (☎ 236-7777) continues its own helicopter service – introduced for the World Bank/IMF meeting in 1991 – from Bangkok airport to the hotel rooftop for 3500B per person, minimum three passengers. The flight takes only 10 minutes but is reserved for Shangri-La guests only. If you can afford the copter flight you can certainly afford this hotel, which has one of Bangkok's best river locations.

Boat The Riverjet (☎ 585-9120) is a fast hydrofoil that operates in conjunction with a bus service from the airport to a pier near the Rama VII Bridge in northern Bangkok for service to the following hotels along the river: Oriental, Shangri-La, Royal Orchid Sheraton and the Marriott Royal Garden Riverside. Tickets are a steep 700B and, although the Riverjet boat/bus service is quicker during peak traffic periods (6.30 to 9.30 am, 3.30 to 8 pm), the rest of the time it's faster to take a taxi. Hours of operation are 7 am to 10 pm.

Airport Facilities

Post & Telephone There is a 24-hour post/telephone office with a Home Direct phone service in the departure hall (3rd floor) of Terminal 1. Another 24-hour post office is located in the departure lounge; a third one in the arrival hall is open on weekdays from 9 am to 5 pm.

Currency Exchange The foreign currency booths (Thai Military Bank, Bangkok Bank, Krung Thai Bank) on the ground floor of the arrival hall and in the departure lounge give a good rate of exchange, so there's no need to wait till you're downtown to change money if you need Thai currency. Each of these banks also operates automatic teller machines in the arrival and departure halls.

Left Luggage & Day Rooms Left-luggage facilities (20B per piece per day, three months maximum) are available in the departure hall (3rd floor). In the transit lounge, clean day rooms with washing and toilet facilities can be rented for 900B for six hours.

Places to Eat On the 4th floor of international Terminal 1 is the *Rajthanee Food Mall*, a small 24-hour cafeteria area where you can choose from Thai, Chinese and European dishes at fairly reasonable prices. Next door is the larger *THAI* restaurant with more expensive fare. On the 2nd level above the arrival area is a *coffee shop* open from 6 am to 11 pm, and there is also a small snack bar in the waiting area of the ground floor. The departure lounge has two snack bars which serve beer and liquor.

On the 4th floor of Terminal 2 is a cluster of new fast-food-style places, including *Swenson's, John Bull Pub, Burger King* and *Pizza Hut*. Opposite these is a posh Chinese restaurant. On the arrival floor of this terminal there's also a *KFC*.

The *Airbridge Café*, a European-style coffee shop on the enclosed bridge between Terminal 1 and the Amari Airport Hotel, provides a quiet alternative to the airport places.

Shopping There are several news stands and souvenir shops in the arrival and departure areas of the airport. Duty-free shopping is available in the departure lounge as well. The books and magazine selection at the airport news stands is patchy; if you have enough time to walk across the enclosed footbridge from Terminal 1 to the Amari Airport Hotel, you'll find a much better bookshop in the hotel's shopping arcade (south of reception).

Near the Airport If you cross the expressway on the pedestrian bridge (just north of the passenger terminal), you'll find yourself in Don Meuang town where there are all sorts of shops, a market, small restaurants, food stalls and even a wat, all within 100m or so of the airport.

The modern and luxurious Amari Airport Hotel (☎ 566-1020/1) has its own air-conditioned, enclosed footbridge from Terminal 1 and 'special mini-stay' daytime room rates (8 am to 6 pm) for stays up to three hours for around 500B for singles/doubles, including tax and service. Longer daytime rates are available on request. The Amari also has a very good bookstore – better than anything in the airport itself – as well as a selection of decent restaurants serving Italian, Japanese and Thai food.

For additional information on overnight accommodation in the Don Meuang area, see the Places to Stay chapter.

Warning

Beware of airport touts – this means anyone trying to steer you away from the city taxi counter or asking where you plan to stay while you're in Bangkok. A legion of touts – some in what appear to be airport or airline uniforms – are always waiting for new arrivals in the arrival area, and will begin their badgering as soon as you clear customs. Posing as helpful tourist information agents, their main objective is to get commissions from overpriced taxi rides or hotel rooms. If you're foolish enough to mention the hotel or guesthouse you plan to stay at, chances are they'll tell you it's full and that you must go to another hotel (which will pay them a commission, though they may deny it). Sometimes they'll show you a nice collection of photos; don't get sucked in as these touted hotels are often substandard and badly located.

The THA hotel reservation desk at the back of the arrival hall also takes a commission on every booking, but at least they have a wide selection of accommodation. There have been reports that the THA desk occasionally claims a hotel is full when it isn't, just to move you into a hotel that pays higher commissions. If you protest, the staff may ask you to speak to the 'reservations desk' on the phone – usually an accomplice who confirms the hotel is full. Dial the hotel yourself if you want to be certain.

Now that the TAT supposedly has regulatory powers, one of its first acts should be to clean the touts out of the airport arrival area, as the present situation gives many visitors a rather negative first impression of Thailand. Then again, some see it as part of the challenge of Asian travel!

BUS

You can save a lot of money in Bangkok by sticking to the public buses, which are 2.50B for any journey under 10 km on the ordinary blue or smaller green buses, 3.50B on the red buses or 6B for the first eight km on the air-con lines. The fare on ordinary buses is 4B for longer trips (eg from Chulalongkorn University to King Mongkut's Institute of Technology in Thonburi on bus No 21) and as high as 16B for air-con buses (eg from Silom Rd to Bangkok airport on air-con bus No 4). The air-con buses are not only cooler, but are usually less crowded (all bets are off during rush hours).

One air-con bus service that's never overcrowded is the red microbus, which stops taking passengers once every seat is filled. They collect a 30B flat fare – you deposit the money in a box at the front of the bus rather than wait for an attendant to collect it. Newspapers (usually Thai papers only, occasionally a *Thailand Times)* are available on the microbus. A couple of useful microbus lines are the No 6, which starts on Si Phraya Rd (near the River City complex) and proceeds to the Mahboonkrong-Siam Square area, then out to Sukhumvit Rd (and vice versa); and the No 1, which runs between the Victory Monument area and Banglamphu district.

Bus Maps

To do any serious bus riding you'll need a Bangkok bus map – the easiest to read is the *Bangkok Bus Map (Walking Tours)* published by Bangkok Guide, or

Thaveepholcharoen's *Bangkok Thailand Tour'n Guide Map*. If you plan to do a lot of bus riding, the Bangkok Bus Map is the more accurate, but Tour'n Guide Map also has a decent map of the whole country on the flip side. The bus numbers are clearly marked in red, with air-con buses in larger type. Don't expect the routes to be 100% correct, a few will have changed since the maps last came out, but they'll get you where you're going most of the time. These maps usually retail for 35 to 40B. A more complete 113-page *Bus Guide* is available in some bookshops and news stands for 35B, but it's not as easy to use as the bus maps.

Bus Safety

Be careful with your belongings while riding Bangkok buses. The place you are most likely to be 'touched' is on the crowded ordinary buses. Razor artists abound, particularly on buses in the Hualamphong train station area. These dexterous thieves specialise in slashing your backpack, shoulder bag or even your trouser pockets with a sharp razor and slipping your valuables out unnoticed. Hold your bag in front of you and carry money in a front shirt pocket, preferably (as the Thais do) maintaining a tactile and visual sensitivity to these areas if the bus is packed shoulder to shoulder. Seasoned travellers don't need this advice, as the same precautions are useful all over the world – the trick is to be relaxed but aware.

CAR & MOTORCYCLE

Cars and motorbikes are easily rented in Bangkok, if you can afford to and if you have nerves of steel. The rental rates start at around 1200B per day for a small car; the rates are much less for a motorcycle, not including insurance. For long-term rentals you can usually arrange a discount of up to 35% off the daily rate. An International Driving Permit and passport are required for all rentals.

For long, cross-country trips, you might consider buying a new or used motorcycle and reselling it when you leave – this can end up being cheaper than renting, especially if you buy a good used bike.

Here are the names and addresses of a few car rental companies:

Avis Rent-a-Car
2/12 Withayu (Wireless) Rd (☎ 255-5300/4, fax 253-3734); branch offices at the Dusit Thani, Grand Hyatt Erawan, Sukhothai and Royal Princess hotels

Central Car Rent
   24 Soi Tonson, Ploenchit Rd (☎ 251-2778)
Grand Car Rent
   233-5 Asoke-Din Daeng Rd (☎ 248-2991)
Hertz
   Bangkok domestic airport (☎ 535-3004)
   1620 New Phetburi Rd (☎ 251-7575)
Highway Car Rent
   1018/5 Rama IV Rd (☎ 266-9393)
Inter Car Rent
   45 Sukhumvit Rd, near Soi 3 (☎ 252-9223)
Krung Thai Car Rent
   233-5 Asoke-Din Daeng Rd (☎ 246-0089, 246-1525/7)
Lumpinee Car Rent
   167/4 Withayu (Wireless) Rd (☎ 255-1966, 255-3482)
Petchburee Car Rent
   23171 New Phetburi Rd (☎ 319-1393)
SMT Rent-a-Car
   931/11 Rama I Rd (☎ 216-8020)
Toyota Metro Rent-A-Car
   7th floor, Koolhiran Bldg, 1/1 Vibhavadi Rangsit Rd,
   Chatuchak (☎ 216-2181)
Toyota Rental & Leasing
   Vibultnani Bldg, 3199 Rama IV Rd (☎ 637-5050))
Sathorn Car Rent
   6/8-9 Sathon Neua Rd (☎ 633-8888)
Thongchai Car Rent
   58/117 Si Nakharin Rd (☎ 322-3313)

There are more car rental agencies along Withayu and
New Phetburi Rds. Some also rent motorcycles, but
you're better off renting or leasing a bike at a place that
specialises in motorcycles, such as:

Big Bike Rentals
   Soi 55, Sukhumvit Rd (☎ 391-5670), hires 250 to 750cc
   bikes
Chusak Yont Shop
   1400 New Phetburi Rd (☎ 251-9225)
Visit Laochaiwat
   1 Soi Prommit, Suthisan Rd (☎ 278-1348)

TAXI

Metered taxis were finally introduced in Bangkok in
1993, and now they outnumber the old no-meter taxis.
The ones with meters have signs on top reading 'Taxi
Meter', the others 'Taxi Thai' or just 'Taxi'. Fares for
metered taxis are always lower than for non-metered,
the only problem being that they can be a little harder to
flag down during peak hours. Demand often outstrips
supply from 8 to 9 am and 6 to 7 pm, and also late at

Bangkok Traffic

At times, Bangkok's traffic seems quite hopeless. An estimated three million vehicles (a figure rising by 1000 per day) crawl through the streets at an average of 13 km/h during commuter hours, and nearly half the municipal traffic police are undergoing treatment for respiratory ailments! It's estimated that the typical Bangkok motorist spends a cumulative 44 days per year in traffic; petrol stations in the capital sell the Comfort 100, a portable potty that allows motorists to relieve themselves in their own vehicles during traffic jams. Cellular phones, TVs and food warmers are other commonplace auto accessories among wealthier drivers.

The main culprit, in addition to the influx of motor vehicles, is the lack of road surface, which only represents 8.5% of Bangkok's mass; to reach international standards the road surface needs to be increased to at least 20%. Privately owned automobiles aren't the gridlock's mainstay; only 25% of the city's population use personal cars. Motorcycles, buses, trucks and taxis make up the bulk of Bangkok traffic. In 1996 the government established an excise tax on products and services that harm the environment, beginning with two-stroke motorcycles, a major polluter. Buses are in dire need of attention, as they make up less than 1% of the vehicles on city roads but account for as much as half the air pollutants.

Several mass transit systems (which are either in the planning or very early construction phases) promise much-needed 'decongestion'. The one most likely to be completed first is the Bangkok Metropolitan Authority's (BMA) light rail system, about two-thirds of which will be elevated (Khlong Toey to Lat Phrao via Ratchadaphisek Rd) and a third underground (Hualamphong to Khlong Toey). This project has undergone so many reroutings (initially the north-south leg was to run parallel to Ratchaprarop, Ratchadamri and Sathon Tai Rds) that it's difficult to say whether it will ever actually get off the ground. The BMA also plans to add several more elevated expressways; sceptics say building more roads will simply encourage Bangkokians to buy more cars.

The much ballyhooed Skytrain network, a more extensive elevated rail project proposed in 1986, went from contractor to contractor until construction finally began in 1994. The US$1.3 billion project will initially consist of two lines, the Phrakhanong-Bang Seu (23 km) and Sathon-Lat Phrao (11 km) routes, plus two more lines in each direction to follow later. If all goes as planned, this one should be operating by 1999. A second project, the US$3.2 billion Hopewell Bangkok Elevated Road and Train System (BERTS), is supposed to provide 60 km of light rail and

48 km of expressways; the project is designed so that the railways will be stacked on top of the expressways, both of which are in turn stacked atop existing roadways. Five thousand piles for BERTS have already been driven throughout Bangkok, but this plan, too, has fallen victim to interdepartmental squabbles and problems with the Hong Kong contractor. BERTS may be taken over by the Metropolitan Rapid Transit Authority (MRTA).

Finally, there's the MRTA's own US$3.2 billion underground rail, to consist of one 42-km north-east to south-west main line, with a separate loop around central Bangkok. This one hasn't begun construction yet, though a 2003 completion date has been projected. There has also been serious talk of a monorail loop around outer Bangkok, with a feeder line for the Skytrain.

The problem with every one of these projects is the lack of coherent coordination. With separate contracts and separate supervision, it's doubtful any can remain on schedule. The main villains in all this appear to be BMA principals, who want inflexible control over every project brought to the table even where there are clear conflicts of interest. In 1993 the BMA shot down a reasonable proposal put before the Interior Ministry to split the 560 sq km city into separate townships for ease of traffic administration.

The investments involved in these rail and road projects are enormous, but as current traffic congestion costs the nation over 14 billion baht per year in fuel, the potential savings far exceed the outlay. Bangkok lost to Singapore in a recent bid to be named the site of the new Asia-Pacific Economic Cooperation (APEC) secretariat largely because of the city's appalling traffic congestion.

One cheaper alternative which the government is seriously considering is a toll zone or other area traffic control zone within the central business district. City planners from the Massachusetts Institute of Technology, hired as consultants by BMA, concur that this would be the best approach for quick and lasting traffic congestion relief. This sort of plan has worked very well in nearby Singapore but it remains to be seen whether such a system would work in Bangkok, where even enforcement of traffic lights, parking and one-way streets is shaky.

While you're stuck in a Bangkok traffic jam you can take comfort in knowing that average rush-hour traffic flows are worse in Hong Kong (12.2 km/h), Taipei (11.5 km/h), Bombay (10.4 km/h) and Manila (7.2 km/h). Dirty air? Bangkok didn't even make UNEP/WHO's list of Asia's five worst cities for air pollution – honours went to Delhi, Xian, Beijing, Calcutta and Shenyang. Ambient noise ratios are equal to those measured in Seoul, Chongqing and Saigon. ∎

night when the bars are closing (1 to 2 am). Because metered-taxi drivers use rented vehicles and must return them at the end of their shifts, they sometimes won't take longer fares as quitting time nears.

Metered taxis charge 35B at flag fall for the first two km, then 2B for each half-km increment thereafter when the cab travels at six km/h or more; at speeds under five km/h, a surcharge of 1B per minute kicks in. Freeway tolls – 10 to 20B depending where you start – must be paid by the passenger. Since the introduction of metered cabs (called *tháeksii miitôe* in Thai), the average fare has dropped considerably. An airport trip from Siam Square, for example, previously cost 150 to 250B (depending on your negotiation skills) in a non-metered cab; the typical meter fare for the same trip is now around 115 to 120B. A jaunt to Silom Rd from the same area that previously cost 50 or 60B is now in the neighbourhood of 40B.

A 24-hour 'phone-a-cab' service (☎ 319-9911) is available for an extra 20B over the regular metered fare. This is only really necessary if you're in an area where there aren't a lot of cabs; residents who live down long sois are the main clientele. Previously such residents had to catch a motorcycle taxi or 'baht bus' to the *pàak soi* ('soi mouth', where a soi meets a larger street).

For certain routes it can be very difficult to find a taxi driver who's willing to use the meter. One such instance is going from the Southern bus terminal across the river to Bangkok proper – most drivers will ask for a flat 300B but settle for 200B. In the reverse direction you can usually get them to use the meter. Another route is from Bangkok International airport into town; in this case drivers want a flat 200 or 250B, even if you hired them through the airport taxi desk. Of course in either case it's illegal, but it can be very difficult to persuade them to take you otherwise.

For those times when you're forced to use a non-metered cab, you'll have to negotiate the fare. It's no use telling non-metered cab drivers what a comparable metered trip would cost – they know you wouldn't be wasting your time with them if a metered cab were available. Fares to most places within central Bangkok are 60 to 80B – you should add 10B or so if you're using it during rush hour or after midnight. For airport trips the non-meter guys still want 150 to 200B. Perhaps in the future there won't be any non-metered cabs left on the street – but until that time you'll probably be forced to use them occasionally.

You can hire a taxi all day for 1000 to 1500B depending on how much driving is involved. A better option – in terms of the quality of both car and driver – would be to hire through J&J Car Rent (☎ 531-2262), an agency that specialises in car/driver combos at competitive rates.

A useful *Taxi Guide* brochure distributed by TAT lists Thai and English addresses of hotels, guesthouses, embassies, airlines, shopping centres, temples and various tourist attractions. The guide can be of considerable help in facilitating communication between non-English-speaking drivers and non-Thai-speaking passengers.

TUK-TUK

In heavy traffic, tuk-tuks are usually faster than taxis since they're able to weave in and out between cars and trucks. This is the main advantage to taking a tuk-tuk for short hops. On the down side, tuk-tuks do not have air-conditioning, so you have to breathe all that lead-soaked air (at its thickest in the middle of Bangkok's wide avenues), and they're also more dangerous since they easily flip when braking on a fast curve. The typical tuk-tuk fare offers no savings over a metered cab – around 40B for a short hop (eg Siam Square to Soi 2 Sukhumvit).

Tuk-tuk drivers tend to speak less English than taxi drivers, so many new arrivals have a hard time commu-

---

Tuk-Tuk Wars

In 18th-century Bangkok, residents got around on foot, by canal, or in human-drawn rickshaws called *rót chék* or 'Chinese vehicles' by the Thais. During the early 20th century the rickshaw gave way to the three-wheeled pedicab or samlor, which were then fitted with inexpensive Japanese two-stroke engines after WWII to become the onomatopoeic *tu'k tu'k*.

These three-wheeled taxis sound like power saws gone berserk and commonly leave trails of blue smoke whenever they rev up. Objecting Bangkokians have been trying for years to enact a ban on tuk-tuks. Several years ago the city supposedly forbade the further production of any new three-wheel taxis, but every time I go to Bangkok I see hordes of brand new ones. It's a bit of a moral dilemma actually, since the tuk-tuk drivers are usually poor north-easterners who can't afford to rent the quieter, less polluting Japanese auto-taxis. You can buy one for around US$1200 from Tuk-Tuk Industry Thailand (☎ (02) 437-6983), 463-465 Prachathipok Rd, Bangkok. ■

nicating their destinations. Although some travellers have complained about tuk-tuk drivers deliberately taking them to the wrong destination (to collect commissions from certain restaurants or silk shops), other folks never seem to have a problem with tuk-tuks, and swear by them. Beware tuk-tuk drivers who offer to take you on a sightseeing or factory tour for 10B or 20B – it's a touting scheme designed to pressure you into purchasing overpriced goods.

MOTORCYCLE TAXI

As passengers become more desperate to beat rush-hour gridlocks, motorcycle taxis have moved from the sois to the main avenues. Fares for a motorcycle taxi are about the same as tuk-tuks except during heavy traffic, when they may cost a bit more.

Riding on the back of a speeding motorcycle taxi is even more of a kamikaze experience than riding in a tuk-tuk. Keep your legs tucked in – drivers are used to carrying passengers with shorter legs than those of the average farang and they pass perilously close to other vehicles while weaving in and out of traffic.

WALKING

At first glance Bangkok doesn't seem like a great town for walking – its main avenues are so choked with traffic that the noise and thick air tend to drive one indoors. Quiet spots where walks are rewarding – Lumphini Park, for example, or neighbourhoods off the main streets – do exist. And certain places are much more conveniently seen on foot, particularly the older sections of town along the Chao Phraya River where the roads are so narrow and twisting that bus lines don't operate there.

BOAT

Although many of Bangkok's canals (*khlongs*) have been paved over, there is still plenty of transport along and across the Chao Phraya River and up adjoining canals. River transport is one of the nicest ways to get around Bangkok as well as often being much faster than road-based alternatives. For a start you get a quite different view of the city; secondly, it's much less of a hassle than tangling with the polluted, noisy, traffic-crowded streets. (Just try getting from Banglamphu to the GPO as fast by road.)

Over the past few years the Bangkok Metropolitan Authority (BMA) has revived four lengthy and useful canal routes: Khlong Saen Saep (Banglamphu to Bang Kapi), Khlong Phrakhanong (Sukhumvit to Sinakarin campus), Khlong Bang Luang/Khlong Lat Phrao (New Phetburi Rd to Phahonyothin Bridge) and Khlong Phasi Charoen in Thonburi (Kaset Bang Khae port to Rama I Bridge). The canal boats can be crowded but they are generally much faster than either an auto taxi or bus.

Chao Phraya River Express

The first step in using river transport is to know your boats. The main ones, the rapid Chao Phraya Express boats *(reua dùan)*, are a sort of river bus service. They cost 5 to 10B (depending on the distance) and follow a regular route; a trip from Banglamphu to the GPO, for example, costs 6B. They may not stop at each pier if there are no people waiting, or no-one wants to get off. You buy your tickets on the boat. Chao Phraya Express boats are big, long boats with numbers on their roofs; the last boat from either end of the route departs at 6 pm.

This company has a new competitor called Laemthong Express which for the most part serves outlying areas to the north and south of central Bangkok. It stops at some of the same piers but not necessarily at all of them. It also runs less frequently than Chao Phraya River Express. The latter usually feature white bodies with red stripes, while Laemthong boats have blue or red bodies. If you're heading for one of the Chao Phraya Express piers listed in this book (Map 9), be sure not to get on the wrong boat.

BERNARD NAPTHINE

A ferry plies the Chao Phraya River.

Cross-River Ferry

From the main Chao Phraya stops and also from almost every other jetty, there are slower cross-river ferries *(reua khâam fâak)* which simply shuttle back and forth across the river. Standard fares are 1B and you usually pay at the entrance to the jetty. Be careful, there will probably be a pay window at the jetty and also a straight-through aisle for people taking other boats.

Long-Tail Taxi

Finally there are the long-tail boats *(reua haang yao)* which operate a share-taxi system off the main river and up the smaller khlongs. Fares usually start from 5B – you've really got to know where you're going on these. There are also river charter taxis where you take the whole boat – you'll find them at certain jetties (primarily Tha Chang, Tha Si Phraya), and you can charter them for trips around the river-canal system for a standard 300B per hour.

One of the most useful canal services runs along Khlong Saen Saep. It provides a quicker alternative to road transport between the river and eastern Bangkok (ie outer Sukhumvit and Bang Kapi). The boat to the Ramkhamhaeng University area from Banglamphu, for example, costs 10B and takes only 40 minutes. A bus would take at least an hour under normal traffic conditions. The main detraction of this route is the seriously polluted canal – passengers typically hold newspapers over their clothes and faces to prevent being splashed by the stinking black water. It's not the best choice of transport if you're dressed for a formal occasion.

A handy little run along this route is by long-tail boat (5B) from the Siam Square area (from Tha Ratchathewi – see Map 7 – by the bridge near the Asia Hotel) to the Banglamphu pier near Wat Saket and the Democracy Monument. At its western end this route intersects a north-south boat route along Khlong Banglamphu and Khlong Phadung Krung Kasem. You can catch a boat east from the Khlong Banglamphu pier near the corner of Phra Sumen and Samsen Rds (north side of the canal) all the way to Hualamphong station in 15 minutes for 5B.

Things to See & Do

Bangkok caters to diverse interests: there are temples, museums and other historic sites for those interested in traditional Thai culture; an endless variety of good restaurants, clubs, international cultural and social events; movies in several languages and modern art galleries for those seeking contemporary Krung Thep. As the dean of expat authors in Thailand, William Warren, has said, 'The gift Bangkok offers me is the assurance I will never be bored'.

HIGHLIGHTS

If your visit to Bangkok is short, you won't begin to be able to see all the city has to offer. For visits of four or five days, must-dos include Wat Phra Kaew and the Grand Palace along with nearby Wat Pho, the National Museum, either the Lak Meuang or Erawan shrines, Jim Thompson's House, either Vimanmek Teak Mansion or Wang Suan Phakkard, and a river or canal trip.

For a three-day stopover, leave out the National Museum and the shrines. If you have longer – say a week or more – add the Weekend Market, a Thai boxing match and a *khŏn* performance at the Chalermkrung Royal Theatre. Looking for another temple or two? Wat Traimit's Golden Buddha never fails to impress; Wat Arun also makes a pleasant cross-river excursion.

Evenings can be devoted to sampling Bangkok's incredible Thai restaurants – try at least one riverside place to soak up the languid ambience of old Bangkok. You should also seek out at least one Thai musical performance, whether traditional (at a dinner theatre) or modern (at one of the city's many nightclubs).

MUSEUMS & GALLERIES

National Museum (Maps 2 & 5)

On Na Phra That Rd, on the west side of Sanam Luang, the National Museum is the largest museum in South-East Asia and an excellent place to learn something about Thai art before heading upcountry. All periods and styles are represented from Dvaravati to Ratanakosin, and English-language literature is available. Room 23 contains a well-maintained collection of traditional

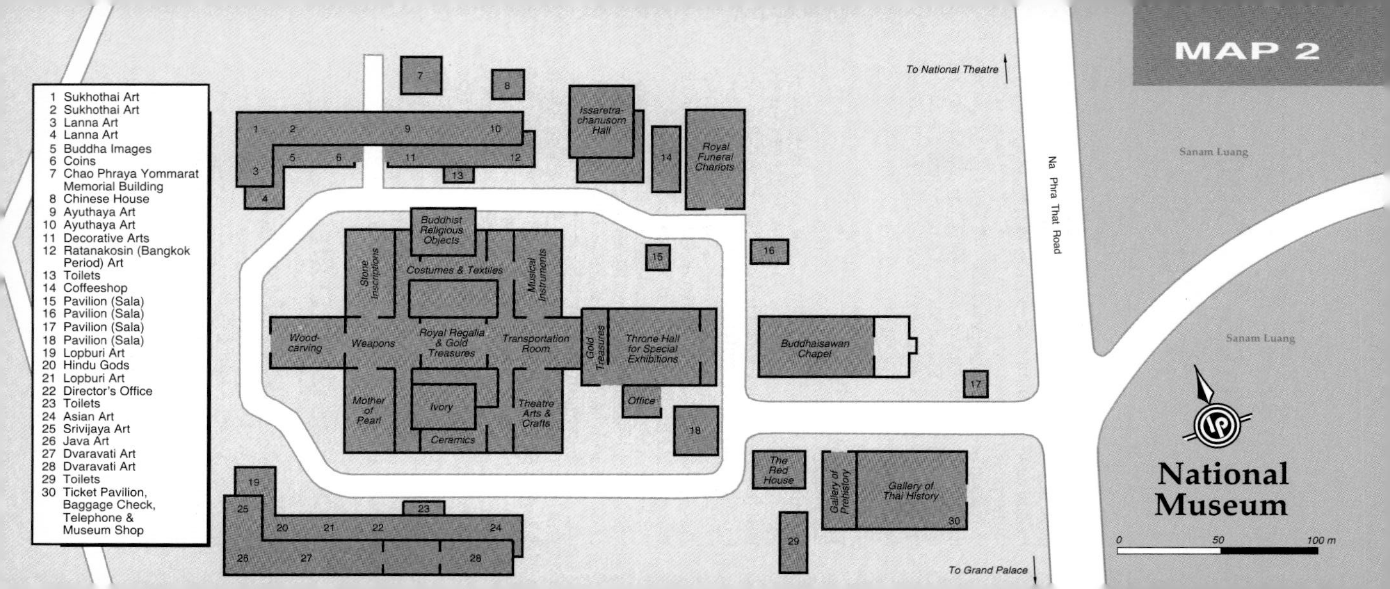

MAP 2

Na Phra That Road

To National Theatre

Sanam Luang

Sanam Luang

National Museum

0   50   100 m

To Grand Palace

1 Sukhothai Art
2 Sukhothai Art
3 Lanna Art
4 Lanna Art
5 Buddha Images
6 Coins
7 Chao Phraya Yommarat
  Memorial Building
8 Chinese House
9 Ayuthaya Art
10 Ayuthaya Art
11 Decorative Arts
12 Rattanakosin (Bangkok
   Period) Art
13 Toilets
14 Coffeeshop
15 Pavilion (Sala)
16 Pavilion (Sala)
17 Pavilion (Sala)
18 Pavilion (Sala)
19 Lopburi Art
20 Hindu Gods
21 Director's Office
22 Toilets
23 Toilets
24 Asian Art
25 Srivijaya Art
26 Java Art
27 Dvaravati Art
28 Dvaravati Art
29 Toilets
30 Ticket Pavilion,
   Baggage Check,
   Telephone &
   Museum Shop

Isaratra-
chanusom
Hall

Royal
Funeral
Chariots

Buddhaisawan Chapel

Gallery of
Thai History

Gallery
of
Prehistory

The
Red
House

Stone Inscriptions

Buddhist
Religious
Objects

Costumes & Textiles

Musical Instruments

Gold Treasures

Throne Hall
for Special
Exhibitions

Office

Weapons

Wood-
carving

Mother
of
Pearl

Royal Regalia
& Gold
Treasures

Ivory

Ceramics

Transportation
Room

Theatre
Arts &
Crafts

musical instruments from Thailand, Laos, Cambodia and Indonesia. Other permanent exhibits include ceramics, clothing and textiles, woodcarving, royal regalia, Chinese art and weaponry.

The museum buildings themselves were built in 1782 as the palace of Rama I's viceroy, Prince Wang Na. Rama V (Chulalongkorn) turned it into a museum in 1884.

In addition to the exhibition halls, the museum grounds contain the restored **Buddhaisawan (Phutthaisawan) Chapel**. Inside the chapel (built in 1795) are some well-preserved original murals and one of the country's most revered Buddha images, Phra Phut Sihing. Legend says the image came from Ceylon, but art historians attribute its provenance to 13th century Sukhothai.

Free English-language tours of the museum are given by National Museum volunteers on Wednesday (Buddhism) and Thursday (Thai art, religion and culture), starting from the ticket pavilion at 9.30 am. These guided tours are excellent and many people have written to recommend them. The tours are also conducted in German (Thursday), French (Wednesday) and Japanese (Wednesday). For more information on the tours, contact the volunteers (☎ 215-8173). The museum is open from 9 am to 4 pm Wednesday to Sunday; admission is 20B.

Jim Thompson's House (Map 7)

Though it may sound corny when described, this is a great spot to see authentic Thai residential architecture and South-East Asian art. At the end of an undistinguished soi next to Khlong Saen Saep, the premises once belonged to American silk entrepreneur Jim Thompson, who deserves most of the credit for the current worldwide popularity of Thai silk.

Born in Delaware in 1906, Thompson was a New York architect who briefly served in the Office of Strategic Services (the forerunner of the CIA) in Thailand during WWII. After the war, Thompson found New York too tame and moved to Bangkok. Thai silk caught his connoisseur's eye; he sent samples to fashion houses in Milan, London and Paris, gradually building a steady worldwide clientele for a craft that had been in danger of dying out. A tireless promoter of traditional Thai arts and culture, Thompson collected parts of various derelict Thai homes from central Thailand and reassembled them in the current location in 1959. For the most part put together in typical Thai style, one striking departure from tradition was the way each wall was installed with its exterior side facing the house's interior, thus exposing the wall's bracing system.

While out for an afternoon walk in the Cameron Highlands of west Malaysia in 1967, Thompson disappeared under mysterious circumstances; he has never been heard from since. That same year his sister was murdered in the USA, fuelling various conspiracy theories about the disappearance. Was it a man-eating tiger? Communist spies? Business rivals? The most recent theory – for which there is apparently some hard evidence – has it that the silk magnate was accidentally run over by a Malaysian truck driver who hid his remains.

William Warren's *The Legendary American – The Remarkable Career & Strange Disappearance of Jim Thompson* (Houghton Mifflin, 1970), is an excellent book on Thompson's life, his house and his intriguing disappearance. In Thailand, it has been republished for Asian distribution as *Jim Thompson: The Legendary American of Thailand* (Jim Thompson Thai Silk Co, Bangkok).

On display in the main house is his small but splendid Asian art collection as well as his personal belongings. The Jim Thompson Foundation has a table at the front where you can buy prints of old Siam maps and Siamese horoscopes in postcard and poster form.

The house, on Soi Kasem San 2, Rama I Rd, is open Monday to Saturday, 9 am to 5 pm. Admission is 100B (proceeds go to Bangkok's School for the Blind) but you may wander around the grounds for free. Students under 25 years get in for 40B. The rather sleazy khlong at the end of the soi is one of Bangkok's most lively. Beware of well-dressed touts in the soi who will tell you Thompson's house is closed – it's just a ruse to take you on a buying spree.

Wang Suan Phakkard (Phakkat) (Map 7)

The Lettuce Farm Palace, once the residence of Nakhon Sawan's Princess Chumbot, is a collection of five traditional wooden Thai houses containing art, antique and furnishing displays. The landscaped grounds are a peaceful oasis complete with ducks and swans and a semi-enclosed garden reminiscent of Japanese landscaping.

The diminutive **Lacquer Pavilion**, at the back of the complex, dates from the Ayuthaya period (the building originally sat in a monastery compound on the Chao Phraya River, just south of Ayuthaya) and features gold-leaf *jataka* as well as scenes from daily Ayuthaya life. Larger residential structures at the front of the complex contain displays of Khmer Hindu and Buddhist art, Ban Chiang ceramics and a nice collection of historic Buddhas, including a beautiful late U Thong-style image. In the noise and confusion of Bangkok, the gardens offer a tranquil retreat.

The grounds are open daily except Sunday from 9 am to 4 pm and admission is 150B (students 30B). It's on Si Ayuthaya Rd, between Phayathai and Ratchaprarop Rds; air-con bus No 3 passes right in front.

Vimanmek Teak Mansion (Phra Thii Nang Wimanmek) (Map 1)

Originally constructed on the island of Ko Si Chang in 1868 and moved to the present site in 1910, this beautiful L-shaped, three storey mansion contains 81 rooms, halls and anterooms and is said to be the world's largest golden teak building. Teak was once one of Thailand's greatest natural resources (it has since all but disappeared) and its durability makes it an especially good wood for building houses. A special oil in teak makes it resistant to heavy rain and hot sun and also repels insects. A solid piece of teak can easily last 1000 years.

Vimanmek was the first permanent building on the Dusit Palace grounds. It served as King Rama V's residence in the early 1900s, was closed in 1935 and reopened in 1982 for the Ratanakosin bicentennial. Inside the mansion are various personal effects of the king, and a treasure trove of early Ratanakosin art objects and antiques.

English-language tours leave every half hour beginning at 9.45 am, with the last one at 3.15 pm. The tour covers around 30 rooms and lasts an hour. Smaller adjacent buildings display historic photography documenting the Chakri dynasty. Traditional Thai classical and folk dances are performed in the late morning and early afternoon in a pavilion off the canal side of the mansion.

Vimanmek is open from 9.30 am to 4 pm daily; admission is 50B for adults, 20B for children. It's free if you've already been to the Grand Palace/Wat Phra Kaew and kept the entry ticket for Vimanmek/Abhisek. As this is royal property, visitors wearing shorts or sleeveless shirts will be refused entry.

Abhisek Dusit Throne Hall (Phra Thii Nang Aphisek Dusit)
This is a smaller wood, brick and stucco structure completed in 1904 for Rama V. Typical of the finer architecture of this era, the Victorian-influenced gingerbread and Moorish porticoes blend to create a striking and distinctly Thai exterior. The hall houses an

Rama V Cult
Since 1991 a new spirit cult has swept the Thai public,
involving the veneration of the spirit of King Rama V
(1868-1910, also known as King Chulalongkorn or, to
the Thais, as Chunla Jawm Klao). The cult is particularly
strong in Bangkok and other large urban centres, since
its members tend to be middle-class and nouveau riche
Thais with careers in commerce and the professions.

In Bangkok the most visible devotional activities are
focused on a bronze statue of Rama V standing in Royal
Plaza – opposite the south-east corner of the Viman-
mek/Abihisek throne hall compound from whence the
venerated king once ruled the kingdom as absolute
monarch. Although originally intended as mere historical commemoration, the statue has quite literally
become a religious shrine, where every Tuesday
evening thousands of Bangkokians come to offer
candles, flowers (predominantly pink roses), incense
and bottles of whisky to the newly ordained demigod.
Worship of the statue begins around 9 pm and continues till early in the morning.

All over Thailand Rama V portraits are selling briskly.
Some devotees place the portraits at home altars, while
others wear tiny, coloured porcelain likenesses of the king
on gold chains around their necks in place of the usual
Buddhist amulet. In some social circles Rama V amulets
are now more common than any other phra phim.

No single event occurred to ignite the Rama V movement but rather its growth can be traced to a series of
events beginning with the 1991 military coup – which
caused the intelligentsia to once again lose faith in the
constitutional monarchy – on top of the 1990-92 economic recession. Along with worsening traffic and a host
of other problems, these events brought about an unfo-
cussed, general mistrust of modern politics, technology
and affluence among many Thais, who began looking
for a new spiritual outlet with some historical relevancy.
They seized on Rama V, a king who – without the help
of a parliament or the military – brought Thai nationalism
to the fore while fending off European colonialism. He is
also considered a champion of the common person for
his abolition of slavery and corvée (the requirement that
every citizen be available for state labour when called).

Ironically few Rama V cultists realise that the much-
revered Rama V conceded substantial Thai territory to
French Indo-China and British Malaya during his reign
– for a total loss of land greater than any Thai king had
allowed since before the Sukhothai era. Rama V also
deserves more of the blame for 'westernisation' than

any other single monarch. He was the first king to travel to Europe, which he did in 1897 and again in 1907. After seeing Europeans eating with forks, knives and spoons, he discouraged the Thai tradition of taking food with the hands; he also introduced chairs to the kingdom (before his reign, Thais sat on the floor or on floor cushions). Following one European visit he asked his number-one concubine to grow her hair long after the European fashion; by custom Thai women had kept their hair cropped short since the Ayuthaya period. ■

excellent display of regional handiwork crafted by members of the Promotion of Supplementary Occupations & Related Techniques (SUPPORT) foundation, an organisation sponsored by the queen. Among the exhibits are *mát-mìi* cotton and silk, *málaeng tháp* collages (made from metallic, multi-coloured beetle wings), damascene ware, nielloware and *yaan lipao* basketry.

Abhisek is open 10 am to 4 pm daily and admission is 50B (or free with a Wat Phra Kaew/Grand Palace/Vimanmek ticket). There is souvenir shop here. As at Wat Phra Kaew and Vimanmek, visitors must be properly dressed – no sleeveless shirts or shorts.

JOE CUMMINGS

Vimanmek teak mansion, former residence of King Rama V.

Vimanmek and Abhisek lie toward the north end of the Dusit Palace grounds, off U-Thong Nai Rd (between Si Ayuthaya and Ratwithi Rds), across from the west side of the Dusit Zoo. Air-con bus No 3 (Si Ayuthaya Rd), air-con bus No 10 (Ratwithi Rd) or red microbus No 4 (Ratwithi Rd) will drop you nearby.

Siam Society & Ban Kamthieng (Map 4)

At 131 Soi Asoke, Sukhumvit Rd, the Siam Society is the publisher of the renowned *Journal of the Siam Society* and its members are valiant preservers of traditional Thai culture. The society headquarters are a good place to visit for those with a serious interest in Thailand – a reference library is open to visitors and Siam Society monographs are for sale. Almost anything you'd want to know about Thailand (outside the political sphere, since the society is sponsored by the royal family) can be researched here. An ethnological museum of sorts, exhibiting Thai folk art is located on the Siam Society grounds in the northern-Thai style Kamthieng House. Ban Kamthieng is open Tuesday to Saturday from 9 am to noon and 1 to 5 pm. Admission is 25B. For information call ☎ 258-3491.

The Siam Society and Ban Kamthieng are within walking distance from the intersection of Sukhumvit Rd and Soi Asoke.

Other Museums

The **Museum of the Dept of Forensic Medicine**, on the ground floor of the Forensic Medicine Bldg, Siriraj Hospital (Map 5) in Thonburi (Phrannok Rd, near Bangkok Noi train station), is the most famous of ten medical museums on the hospital premises. Among the grisly displays are the preserved bodies of famous Thai murderers. It's open weekdays from 9 am to 4 pm; admission is free.

The **Hall of Railway Heritage**, just north of Chatuchak Park, displays steam locomotives, model trains and other artefacts related to Thai railroad history. It's open on Sunday only from 5 am to noon; admission is free. Call the Thai Railfan Club (☎ 243-2037) for further information.

The **Bangkok Doll Factory & Museum** (☎ 245-3008) at 85 Soi Ratchataphan, (Soi Mo Leng), off Ratchaprarop Rd in the Pratunam district, houses a colourful selection of traditional Thai dolls, both new and antique. Dolls are also available for purchase. It's open from Monday to Saturday, 8 am to 5 pm; admission is free.

Military aircraft aficionados shouldn't miss the **Royal Thai Air Force Museum**, on Phahonyothin Rd near Wing 6 of the Don Meuang domestic airport terminal. Among the world-class collection of historic aircraft is the only existing Japanese Tachikawa trainer, along with a Spitfire and several Nieuports and Breguets. The museum is open from 8.30 am to 4.30 pm on weekdays and on the first weekend of each month; admission is free.

Bangkok also has a **Museum of Science** and a **Planetarium**, both on Sukhumvit Rd between sois 40 and 42.

Art Galleries

Opposite the National Theatre, on Chao Fa Rd, the **National Gallery** (☎ 281-2224) displays traditional and contemporary art. Most of the art here is by artists who receive government support; the general consensus is that it's not Thailand's best, but the gallery is worth a visit for die-hard art fans or if you're in the vicinity. The gallery is closed on Monday and Tuesday, and open from 9 am to 4 pm on other days. Admission is 10B.

At the forefront of the new Buddhist art movement is the **Visual Dhamma Art Gallery** (☎ 258-5879) at 44/28 Soi Asoke (Soi 21, Sukhumvit Rd). Works by some of Thailand's most prominent muralists are sometimes displayed here, along with the occasional foreign exhibition. The gallery is open on weekdays from 1 to 6 pm, Saturday from 10 am to 5 pm, or at other times by appointment. Although the address is Soi Asoke, the gallery is actually off Asoke – coming from Sukhumvit Rd, take the second right into a small lane opposite Singha Bier Haus.

Silpakorn University (near Wat Phra Kaew; Map 5) is Bangkok's fine arts university and has a gallery of student works. The **Thailand Cultural Centre** (Map 11) on Ratchadaphisek Rd (in the Huay Khwang district, between Soi Tiam Ruammit and Din Daeng Rd) has a small gallery with rotating contemporary art exhibits, as does the **River City shopping complex** (Map 8) next to the Royal Orchid Sheraton on the river. Bangkok's foreign cultural centres hold regular exhibits of foreign and local artists – check the monthly bulletins issued by American University Alumni (AUA), Alliance Française, the British Council and the Goethe Institute. For addresses, see Cultural Centres in the Facts for the Visitor chapter.

Several of Bangkok's luxury hotels display top-quality contemporary art in their lobbies and other public areas. The **Grand Hyatt Erawan** (on the corner of Ratchadamri and Ploenchit Rds, Map 7) and the **Landmark Hotel** (Sukhumvit Rd, Map 7) have the best collections of contemporary art in the country. The Erawan alone has over 1900 works exhibited on a rotating basis.

The **Neilson Hays Library** at 195 Surawong Rd (see Map 8) occasionally hosts small exhibits in its Rotunda Gallery.

Gallery Pubs

Bangkok's latest trend in public art is the 'gallery pub', an effort to place art in a social context rather than in sterile galleries and museums.

Why Art? Pub & Gallery, behind Cool Tango in the Royal City Avenue complex (Soi Sunwichai, Rama IX Rd) has a pub on the first two floors with copies of Michaelangelo and Botticelli murals done by Silpakorn University art students, and an art display space on the 3rd floor. **Seri Art Gallery**, at the Premier entertainment complex, is similar in concept. The place that actually initiated this trend, **Ruang Pung Art Community**, opposite section 13 in Chatuchak Market (Map 3), has been in business for around 12 years. It's open weekends from 11 am to 6 pm and features rotating exhibits. Also at Chatuchak Market is the very active **Sunday Gallery** (Sunday Plaza), which, contrary to its name, is open Monday, Wednesday and Friday from 10 am to 5 pm, Saturday and Sunday from 7 am to 7 pm.

Utopia Gallery, a gallery-pub-social centre opposite Tia Maria Restaurant at 116/1 Soi 23, Sukhumvit Rd, specialises in gay and lesbian art and is open daily noon to 10 pm.

TEMPLES & SHRINES

Wat Phra Kaew & Grand Palace (Map 5)

Also called the Temple of the Emerald Buddha (official name: Wat Phra Si Ratana Satsadaram), Wat Phra Kaew adjoins the Grand Palace on common ground, which was consecrated in 1782, the first year of Bangkok rule. The 945,000-sq-metre compound encompasses over 100 buildings that represent 200 years of royal history and architectural experimentation. Most of the architecture can be classified as Bangkok or Ratanakosin style.

Extremely colourful, the wat combines gleaming, gilded chedis (stupas), polished orange and green roof tiles, mosaic-encrusted pillars and rich marble pediments. Extensive murals depicting scenes from the Ramakian

GLENN BEANLAND

The Chakri Palace, residence of Rama V.

RICHARD NEBESKY

Temple guardian, Wat Phra Kaew.

The Emerald Buddha

The so-called Emerald Buddha or Phra Kaew, 60 to 75 cm high (depending on how it is measured), is made of either a type of jasper or of nephrite (a type of jade), depending on who you believe. A definite aura of mystery surrounds the image, enhanced by the fact that it cannot be examined closely – it sits in a glass case, on a pedestal high above the heads of worshippers – and photography within the bòt is forbidden. Its mystery further adds to the occult significance of the image, which is considered the 'talisman' of the Thai kingdom, the legitimator of Thai sovereignty.

No-one knows for certain where the image originated or who sculpted it, but it first appeared on record in 15th-century Chiang Rai. Legend says it was sculpted in India and brought to Siam by way of Ceylon, but stylistically it seems to belong to the Chiang Saen or Lanna (Lan Na Thai) period (13th to 14th century). Sometime in the 15th century, the image is said to have been covered with plaster and gold leaf and placed in Chiang Rai's Wat Phra Kaew (literally, 'temple of the jewel holy image'). While being transported elsewhere after a storm had damaged the chedi in which it had been kept, the image supposedly lost its plaster covering in a fall. It next appeared in Lampang where it enjoyed a 32-year stay (again at a Wat Phra Kaew) until it was brought to Wat Chedi Luang in Chiang Mai.

Laotian invaders took the image from Chiang Mai in the mid-16th century and brought it to Luang Prabang in Laos. Later it was moved to Wiang Chan (Vientiane). When Thailand's King Taksin waged war against Laos 200 years later, the image was taken back to the then Thai capital of Thonburi by General Chakri, who later succeeded Taksin as Rama I, the founder of the Chakri Dynasty. Rama I had the Emerald Buddha moved to the new Thai capital in Bangkok and had two royal robes made for it, one to be worn in the hot season and one for the rainy season. Rama III added another to the wardrobe – to be worn in the cool season. The three robes are still solemnly changed at the beginning of each season by the king himself. ∎

(the Thai version of the Indian epic Ramayana) line the inside walls of the compound. Painted during Rama I's reign (1782-1809), the murals have undergone several restorations, including a major one finished in time for the 1982 Bangkok/Chakri Dynasty bicentennial. Divided into 178 sections, the murals illustrate the epic in its entirety, beginning at the north gate and moving clockwise around the compound.

Except for an anteroom here and there, the **Grand Palace** (Phra Borom Maharatchawong) is today used by the king only for certain ceremonial occasions such as Coronation Day and is closed to the public. (The king's current residence is Chitlada Palace in the north of the city.) The exteriors of the four buildings are worth a swift perusal, however, for their royal bombast.

Borobiman Hall (east end), a French-inspired structure that served as a residence for King Rama VI, is occasionally used to house visiting foreign dignitaries. In April 1981 General San Chitpatima used it as headquarters for an attempted coup. **Amarindra Hall** to the west, was originally a hall of justice, but is used today for coronation ceremonies.

The largest of the palace buildings is the triple-winged **Chakri Mahaprasat,** literally Great Holy Hall of Chakri, but usually translated as Grand Palace Hall. Built in 1882 by British architects using Thai labour, the exterior shows a peculiar blend of Italian renaissance and traditional Thai architecture. This style is often referred to as *faràng sài chá-daa*, or European wearing a Thai classical dancer's headdress, because each wing is topped by a *mondòp*, a layered and heavily ornamented spire representing a Thai adaptation of the Hindu *mandapa*, or shrine.

The tallest of the mondops, in the centre, contains the ashes of each Chakri king who has passed away; the flanking mondops enshrine the ashes of Chakri princes who never inherited the throne. Thai kings traditionally housed their huge harems in the Mahaprasat's inner palace area, which was guarded by combat-trained female sentries.

Last from east to west is the Ratanakosin-style **Dusit Hall,** which initially served as a venue for royal audiences and later as a royal funerary hall.

Admission to the Wat Phra Kaew/Grand Palace compound is 125B, and hours are 8.30 to 11.30 am and 1 to 3.30 pm. The admission fee includes entry to the Royal Thai Decorations & Coins Pavilion (on the same grounds) and to both Vimanmek Teak Mansion and Abhisek Dusit Throne Hall (see earlier in this chapter for details).

Wats are a sacred place to Thai Buddhists – particularly this one because of its monarchical associations – so visitors should dress and behave decently. If you wear shorts or a sleeveless shirt you may be refused admission; sarongs and baggy pants are sometimes available on loan at the entry area. For walking in the courtyard areas you must wear shoes with closed heels and toes – thongs aren't permitted. As in any temple compound,

RICHARD NEBESKY

GLENN BEANLAND

Ramakian murals at Wat Phra Kaew.

RICHARD NEBESKY

JOE CUMMINGS

Details of murals, Wat Phra Kaew.

shoes should be removed before entering the main chapel *(bòt)* or sanctuaries *(wihāan)* of Wat Phra Kaew.

The cheapest way of reaching Wat Phra Kaew and the Grand Palace is by air-con bus No 8 or 12. By the Chao Phraya River Express, disembark at Tha Chang (Map 9).

Wat Pho (Wat Phra Chetuphon) (Map 5)

A long list of superlatives for this one: the oldest and largest wat in Bangkok, it features the largest reclining Buddha and the largest collection of Buddha images in Thailand and was the earliest centre for public education. As a temple site Wat Pho dates back to the 16th century, but its current history really begins in 1781 with the renovation of the original monastery.

Narrow Chetuphon Rd divides the grounds in two, with each section surrounded by huge whitewashed walls. The most interesting part is the northern compound, which includes a very large bòt enclosed by a gallery of Buddha images and four wihāans, four large chedis commemorating the first three Chakri kings (Rama III has two chedis), 91 smaller chedis, an old Tripitaka (Buddhist scriptures) library, a sermon hall, the large wihāan, which houses the reclining Buddha, and a school building for classes in Abhidhamma (Buddhist philosophy), plus several less important structures. The temple is currently undergoing a 53-million-baht renovation.

Wat Pho is the national headquarters for the teaching and preservation of traditional Thai medicine, including Thai massage. A massage school convenes in the afternoons at the eastern end of the compound; a massage costs 180B per hour, 100B for a half hour. You can also study massage in seven to 10-day courses.

The tremendous reclining Buddha, 46m long and 15m high, illustrates the passing of the Buddha into *parinibbana* (post-death nirvana). The figure is modelled out of plaster around a brick core and finished in gold leaf. Mother-of-pearl inlay ornaments the eyes and feet of the colossal image, the feet displaying 108 different auspicious *laksanas*, or characteristics of a Buddha. The images on display in the four wihāans surrounding the main bòt in the eastern part of the compound are interesting. Particularly beautiful are the Phra Jinnarat and Phra Jinachi Buddhas, in the west and south chapels, both from Sukhothai.

The galleries extending between the four chapels feature no less than 394 gilded Buddha images. King Rama I's remains are interred in the base of the presiding Buddha image in the bòt.

The temple rubbings for sale at Wat Pho and else-where in Thailand come from 152 Ramakian reliefs, carved in marble and obtained from the ruins of Ayu-thaya, sculpted in the base of the large bòt. The rubbings are no longer taken directly from the panels but are rubbed from cement casts of the panels made years ago.

You may hire English, French, German or Japanese-speaking guides for 150B for one visitor, 200B for two, 300B for three. Also on the premises are a few astrologers and palm-readers.

The temple is open daily from 8 am to 5 pm; admission is 10B. The ticket booth is closed from noon to 1 pm. Air-con bus No 6, 8 and 12 stop near Wat Pho. The nearest Chao Phraya Express pier is Tha Tien (Map 9).

Wat Mahathat (Map 5)

Founded in the 1700s, Wat Mahathat is a national centre for the Mahanikai monastic sect and houses one of Bangkok's two Buddhist universities, Mahathat Raja-vidyalaya. On weekends, a large produce market is held on the grounds. Opposite the main entrance on the other side of Maharat Rd is a large religious market selling amulets, or magic charms (phrá phim).

The temple is open to visitors from 9 am to 5 pm every day and on wan phrá – Buddhist holy days (the full and new moons every fortnight). Also in the temple grounds is a daily open-air market that features traditional Thai herbal medicine.

The monastery's International Buddhist Meditation Centre offers meditation instruction in English on the second Saturday of every month from 2 to 6 pm in the Dhamma Vicaya Hall. Those interested in more inten-sive instruction should contact the monks in Section 5 of the temple compound.

Wat Mahathat is right across the street from Wat Phra Kaew, on the west side of Sanam Luang. Air-con bus No 8 and 12 both pass by it, and the nearest Chao Phraya Express pier is Tha Maharat (Map 9).

Wat Traimit (Map 8)

The attraction at the Temple of the Golden Buddha is, of course, the impressive three-metre tall, 5½ tonne solid-gold Buddha image, which gleams like no other gold artefact I've ever seen.

Sculpted in the graceful Sukhothai style, the image was 'rediscovered' some 40 years ago beneath a stucco or plaster exterior when it fell from a crane while being moved to a new building within the temple compound.

RICHARD I'ANSON

Buddha at Wat Pho.

It has been theorised that the covering was added to protect it from 'marauding hordes', either during the late Sukhothai period or later in Ayuthaya when the city was under siege by the Burmese. The temple itself is said to date from the early 13th century.

The golden image can be seen every day from 9 am to 5 pm, and admission is 10B. Nowadays lots of camera-toting tour groups haunt the place (there's even a moneychanger on the premises), so it pays to arrive in the early morning if you want a more traditional feel. Wat Traimat is near the intersection of Yaowarat and Charoen Krung Rds, near Hualamphong station.

Wat Arun (Map 5)

The Temple of Dawn is named after the Indian god of dawn, Aruna. It appears in all the tourist brochures and is located on the Thonburi side of the Chao Phraya River. The present wat is built on the site of 17th century Wat Jang, which was the palace and royal temple of King Taksin when Thonburi was the Thai capital; hence, it was the last home of the Emerald Buddha before Rama I brought it across the river to Bangkok.

The 82m-high *prang* (Khmer-style tower) was constructed during the first half of the 19th century by Rama II and Rama III. The unique design elongates the typical

RICHARD I'ANSON

Wat Arun from across the busy waterways
of the Chao Phraya River.

PAUL WENTFORD

Novice monks climbing Wat Arun.

Khmer prang into a distinctly Thai shape. Its brick core has a plaster covering embedded with a mosaic of broken, multi-hued Chinese porcelain. (The use of broken porcelain for temple ornamentation was common in the early Ratanakosin period when Chinese ships calling at Bangkok used tonnes of old porcelain as ballast.) Steep stairs reach a lookout point about halfway up the prang from where there are fine views of Thonburi and the river. During certain festivals, hundreds of lights illuminate the outline of the prang at night.

Also worth a look is the interior of the bòt (ordination chapel). The main Buddha image is said to have been designed by Rama II himself and the murals date to the reign of Rama V. Particularly impressive is one that depicts Prince Siddhartha encountering examples of birth, old age, sickness and death outside his palace walls. According to Buddhist legend it was the experience of seeing these phenomena for the first time that led Siddhartha to abandon the worldly life. The ashes of King Rama II are interred in the base of the bòt's presiding Buddha image.

The temple looks more impressive from the river than up close, though the peaceful wat grounds make a nice retreat from the hustle and bustle of Bangkok. Between the prang and the ferry pier is a huge sacred banyan tree.

Wat Arun is open daily from 8.30 am to 5.30 pm; admission is 10B. To reach Wat Arun from the Bangkok side, catch a cross-river ferry from Tha Tien at Thai Wang Rd (Map 9). Crossings are frequent and cost only 1B.

Wat Benchamabophit (Map 1)

This wat of white Carrara marble (hence its tourist name, Marble Temple) was built at the turn of the century under Chulalongkorn (Rama V). The large bòt is a prime example of modern Thai architecture. The courtyard behind the bòt exhibits 53 Buddha images (33 originals and 20 copies), representing famous images and styles from all over Thailand and other Buddhist countries – an education in itself if you're interested in Buddhist iconography.

Wat Ben is at the corner of Si Ayuthaya and Rama V Rds, diagonally opposite the south-west corner of Chitlada Palace; it's open daily and admission is 10B. Air-con bus No 2 and ordinary bus No 72 stop nearby.

Wat Saket (Map 5)

Saket is an undistinguished temple except for the Golden Mount (Phu Khao Thong) on the west side of the grounds, which provides a good view of Bangkok's rooftops. The artificial hill was created when a large chedi under construction by Rama III collapsed because the soft soil beneath would not support it. The resulting mud-and-brick hill was left to sprout weeds until Rama IV built a small chedi on its crest.

Frank Vincent, a well-travelled American writer of the New England school, describes his 1871 ascent in *Land of the White Elephant*:

From the summit . . . may be obtained a fine view of the city of Bangkok and its surroundings; though this is hardly a correct statement, for you see very few of the dwelling-houses of the city; here and there a wat, the river with its shipping, the palace of the King, and a waving sea of cocoa-nut and betel-nut palms, is about all that distinctly appears. The general appearance of Bangkok is that of a large, primitive village, situated in and mostly concealed by a virgin forest of almost impenetrable density.

Rama V later added to the structure and housed a Buddha relic from India (given to him by the British government) in the chedi. The concrete walls were added during WWII to prevent the hill from eroding. Every November a large festival held on the grounds of Wat Saket includes a candle-lit procession up the Golden Mount.

Admission to Wat Saket is free except for the final approach to the Golden Mount summit, which costs 5B. Wat Saket is within walking distance of the Democracy Monument; air-con bus No 11 and 12 pass nearby.

Wat Rajanadda (Ratchanatda) (Map 5)

Across Mahachai Rd from Wat Saket and behind the old Chalerm Thai movie theatre, this temple dates from the mid 19th century. Built under Rama III, it is an unusual specimen, possibly influenced by Burmese models.

The wat has a well-known market selling Buddhist amulets or magic charms in all sizes, shapes and styles. The amulets not only feature images of the Buddha, but famous Thai monks and Indian deities. Full Buddha images are also for sale. In Thai, Buddhas or *phrá phim* are never 'bought' or 'sold', they are 'rented'. The images are purported to protect the wearer from physical harm, though some act as 'love charms'. Amulets that are considered to be particularly powerful tend to cost thousands of baht and are worn by soldiers, taxi drivers and other Thai believers working in high-risk professions. Wat Rajanadda is an expensive place to purchase a charm, but a good place to look.

Wat Bovornives (Bowonniwet) (Map 5)

Wat Bowon, on Phra Sumen Rd, is the national head-quarters for the Thammayut monastic sect, the minority sect in Mahanikai Buddhism. King Mongkut, founder of the Thammayuts, began a royal tradition by residing here as a monk – in fact he was the abbot of Wat Bowon for several years. King Bhumibol and Crown Prince Vajiralongkorn, as well as several other males in the royal family, have temporarily ordained as monks here. The temple was founded in 1826, when it was known as Wat Mai.

Bangkok's second Buddhist university, Mahamakut University, is housed at Wat Bowon. Across the street from the main entrance to the wat are an English-language Buddhist bookshop and a Thai herbal clinic.

Because of its royal status, visitors should be particularly careful to dress properly for admittance to this wat – no shorts or sleeveless shirts.

Lak Meuang (City Pillar) (Map 5)

The City Pillar is across the street from the eastern wall of Wat Phra Kaew, at the southern end of Sanam Luang. This shrine encloses a wooden pillar erected by Rama I in 1782 to represent the founding of the new Bangkok capital. Later, during the reign of Rama V, five other idols were added to the shrine. The spirit of the pillar is considered to be the city's guardian deity and it receives the daily supplications of countless Thai worshippers, some of whom commission classical Thai dancers to perform *lákhon chaa-trii* at the shrine. Some of the offerings include severed pigs' heads with sticks of incense sprouting from their foreheads.

Maha Uma Devi Temple (Map 8)

This small Hindu temple sits alongside busy Silom Rd (near the Pan Rd intersection) in Bangrak, a district with a high concentration of Indian residents. The principal temple structure, built in the 1860s by Tamil immigrants, features a six-metre facade of intertwined, full-colour Hindu deities, topped by a gold-plated copper dome.

The temple's main shrine contains three principal deities: Jao Mae Maha Umathewi (Uma Devi, also known as Shakti, Shiva's consort) at the centre; her son Phra Khanthakuman (Khanthakumara or Subramaniam) on the right; and her elephant-headed son Phra Phikhkane-sawora (Ganesha) on the left. Along the left interior wall sit rows of Shivas, Vishnus and other Hindu deities, as well

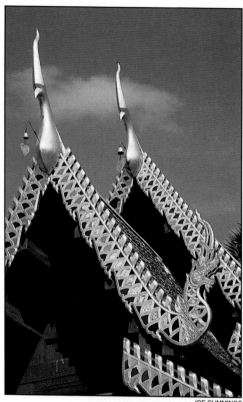

JOE CUMMINGS

These hook-like gable fixtures' spiritual function is to
protect the temple interior from any unsavoury
spirits that may fall out of the sky.

as a few Buddhas, so that just about any non-Muslim
Asian can worship here – Thai and Chinese devotees
come to pray along with Indians. Bright yellow mari-
gold garlands are sold at the entrance for this purpose.

An interesting ritual takes place in the temple at noon
on most days, when a priest brings out a tray carrying
an oil lamp, coloured powders and holy water. He sprin-
kles the water on the hands of worshippers who in turn
pass their hands through the lamp flame for purification;

then they dip their fingers in the coloured powder and daub prayer marks on their foreheads. On Friday at around 11.30 am, *prasada* (blessed vegetarian food) is offered to devotees.

Thais call this temple Wat Khaek – *khàek* is a Thai colloquial expression for persons of Indian descent. The literal translation is guest, an obvious euphemism for a group of people you don't particularly want as permanent residents; hence most Indians living permanently in Thailand don't appreciate the term.

Wat Thammamongkhon

East of Bangkok on Sukhumvit Soi 101, this 95m-high *chedi* came about as the result of a monk's vision. While meditating in 1991, Phra Viriyang Sirintharo saw a giant jade boulder; at around the same time a 32-tonne block of solid jade was discovered in a Canadian riverbed. Viriyang raised funds to purchase the block (US$560,000) and commissioned a 14-tonne Buddha sculpture (executed by Carrara sculptors) to be placed in a pavilion at Thammamongkhon; an image of this magnitude deserved a massive chedi. The chedi, which contains a hair of the Buddha presented to Thailand by Bangladesh's Sangharaja (head of a Theravada monastic order), features a lift so you can ride to the top. The chedi's grand opening ceremony was held in 1993.

A leftover 10-tonne chunk of jade is to be carved into a figure of Kuan Yin (the Chinese Buddhist goddess of compassion). Smaller leftovers – a total of nearly eight tonnes – will be made into amulets and sold to worshippers for US$20 each, raising money to pay for 5000 daycare centres throughout Thailand.

Other Temples & Shrines

Marked by its modern-style 32m-high standing Buddha, **Wat Intharawihan** (Map 1) borders Wisut Kasat Rd, at the northern edge of Banglamphu. Check out the hollowed-out air-con stupa with a lifelike image of Luang Phaw Toh, a famous monk associated with Wat In. Entry is by donation.

At **Sao Ching-Cha**, the Giant Swing, a spectacular Brahman festival in honour of the Hindu god Shiva used to take place each year until it was stopped during the reign of Rama VII. Participants would swing in ever-heightening arcs in an effort to reach a bag of gold suspended from a 15m bamboo pole – many died trying. The Giant Swing is a block south of the Democracy Monument.

Nearby **Wat Suthat** (Map 5), begun by Rama I and completed by Ramas II and III, boasts a *wihāan* with gilded bronze Buddha images (including Phra Si Sakayamuni, one of the largest surviving Sukhothai bronzes) and colourful Jataka murals. Wat Suthat holds a special place in the Thai national religion because of its association with Brahman priests who perform important annual ceremonies, such as the Royal Ploughing Ceremony in May. These priests perform rites at two Hindu shrines near the wat – the Thewa Sathaan (Deva Sthan) across the street to the north-west and the smaller Saan Jao Phitsanu to the east. The former contains images of Shiva and Ganesh while the latter is dedicated to Vishnu. The wat holds the rank of Rachavoramahavihan, the highest royal temple grade; the ashes of King Rama VIII (Ananda Mahidol, the current king's older brother) are contained in the base of the main Buddha image in Suthat's wihāan.

Wat Chong Nonsii, off Ratchadaphisek Rd in the south-west of the city, contains notable Jataka murals painted between 1657 and 1707. It is the only surviving unrenovated Ayuthaya-era temple in which both the murals and architecture are of the same period. As a single, 'pure' architectural and painting unit, it's considered quite important for the study of late Ayuthaya art; the painting style is similar to that found in the Phetburi monasteries of Wat Yai Wannaram and Wat Ko Kaew Sutharam.

There are also numerous temples on the Thonburi side of the river which are less visited. These include **Wat Kalayanimit** (Map 5) with its towering Buddha statue and, outside, the biggest bronze bell in Thailand; **Wat Pho Bang-O** (Map 9) with its carved gables and Rama III-era murals; **Wat Chaloem Phrakiat** (Map 9), a temple with tiled gables; and **Wat Thawng Nophakhun** (Map 1) with its Chinese-influenced *uposatha* (bòt). Get the Fine Arts Commission *Canals of Thonburi* map for more information on these wats. **Wat Yannawa** (Map 9), on the Bangkok bank of the river near Tha Sathon, was built during Rama II's reign (1824-51) and features a building built to resemble a Chinese junk.

Just off Chakraphet Rd near Pahurat Market is a **Sikh Temple** (Sri Gurusingh Sabha) (Map 5) where visitors are welcome to walk around. Basically it's a large hall – somewhat reminiscent of a mosque interior – devoted to the worship of the Guru Granth Sahib, a 16th-century Sikh holy book which is considered the last of the religion's ten great gurus or teachers. Prasada (blessed food offerings) is distributed among devotees every morning around 9 am.

At the corner of Ratchaprarop and Ploenchit Rds, next to the Grand Hyatt Erawan Hotel, is a large shrine called Saan Phra Phrom, also known as the **Erawan Shrine** (Map 7). It was originally built to ward off bad luck during the construction of the first Erawan Hotel (torn down to make way for the Grand Hyatt Erawan some years ago). The four-faced deity at the centre of the shrine is Brahma (Phra Phrom), the Hindu god of creation. Apparently, the developers of the original Erawan – named for Brahma's three-headed elephant mount – first erected a typical Thai spirit house but decided to replace it with the more impressive Brahma shrine after several serious mishaps delayed the hotel construction. Worshippers who have a wish granted may return to the shrine to commission the musicians and dancers always on hand for an impromptu performance.

Since the success of the Erawan Shrine, several other flashy Brahma shrines have been erected next to large hotels and office buildings around the city. Next to the **World Trade Center** on Ploenchit Rd is a large shrine containing a standing Brahma, a rather unusual posture for Thai Brahmas.

Another hotel shrine worth seeing is the *lingam* (phallus) shrine behind the Hilton International (Map 7) in tiny Nai Loet Park off Withayu Rd. Clusters of carved stone and wooden lingam surround a spirit house and shrine built by millionaire businessman Nai Loet to honour **Jao Mae Thapthim**, a female deity thought to reside in the old banyan tree on the site. Someone who made an offering had a baby shortly thereafter, and the shrine has received a steady stream of worshippers – mostly young women seeking fertility – ever since. Nai Loet Park is fenced off in such a way that you must now wind through the Hilton complex to visit the shrine. Or come via the Khlong Saen Saep canal taxi; ask to get off at Saphaan Withayu (Radio Bridge) – look for the TV 3 building on the north side of the canal.

CHURCHES

Several Catholic churches were founded in Bangkok in the 17th to 19th century. Ones worth seeing include the **Holy Rosary Church** (known in Thai as Wat Kalawan, from the Portuguese 'Calvario') in Talaat Noi near the River City shopping complex (Map 8). Built in 1787 by the Portuguese, the Holy Rosary was rebuilt by Vietnamese and Cambodian Catholics around the turn of the century – hence the French inscriptions beneath the stations of the cross. The church has a splendid set of Romanesque stained-glass windows, gilded ceilings and a very old statue of Christ that is carried through the streets during Easter celebrations. The alley leading to the church is lined with old Bangkok shophouse architecture.

The **Church of the Immaculate Conception**, near Krungthon Bridge (north of Phra Pinklao Bridge), was also founded by the Portuguese and later taken over by Cambodians fleeing civil war. The present building is an 1837 reconstruction on the church's 1674 site. One of the original church buildings survives and is now used as a museum housing holy relics. Another Portuguese-built church is the 1913-vintage **Santa Cruz** (Map 5) on the Thonburi side near Memorial Bridge (Saphaan Phut). The architecture shows Chinese influence, hence the Thai name Wat Kuti Jiin, meaning Chinese monastic residence.

Christ Church, at 11 Convent Rd next to the Bangkok Nursing Home in the Silom Rd area, was established as an 'English Chapel' in 1864. The current gothic-style structure, opened in 1904, features thick walls and a tiled roof braced with teak beams; the carved teak ceiling fans date to 1919.

OLD CITY SIGHTS

Royal Barges (Maps 1, 5 & 9)

The Royal Barges are fantastically ornamented boats used in ceremonial processions on the river. The largest is 50m long and requires a rowing crew of 50, plus seven umbrella bearers, two helmsmen, two navigators, a flagman, a rhythm-keeper and a chanter. The barges are kept in sheds on the Thonburi side of the river. They're on Khlong Bangkok Noi, near the Phra Pinklao Bridge. *Suphannahong*, the king's personal barge, is the most important of the boats. One of the best times to see the fleet in action on the river is during the royal *kathin* ceremony at the end of *phansaa* (the Buddhist Rains Retreat, ending with an October or November new moon), when new robes are offered to the monastic contingent.

The barge shed is open daily from 8.30 am to 4.30 pm and admission is 10B. To get there, take a ferry to Tha Rot Fai, then walk down the street parallel to the railway tracks until you come to a bridge over the khlong. Follow the bridge to a wooden walkway that leads to the barge sheds. You can also get there by taking a khlong taxi (5B) up the canal and getting off near the bridge.

Chinatown/Sampeng (Maps 5 & 7)

Bangkok's Chinatown, off Yaowarat and Ratchawong Rds, comprises a confusing and crowded array of jewellery, hardware, wholesale food, automotive and fabric shops, as well as dozens of other small businesses. It's a good place to shop since goods are cheaper than almost anywhere else in Bangkok and the Chinese proprietors like to bargain, especially along Soi Wanit 1 (also known as Sampeng Lane). Chinese and Thai antiques of varying age and authenticity are sold at the so-called Thieves' Market (Nakhon Kasem), but it's better for browsing than buying these days.

During the annual Vegetarian Festival, celebrated fervently by Thai Chinese for the first nine days of the ninth lunar month (September-October), Chinatown becomes a virtual orgy of vegetarian Thai and Chinese food. The festivities are centred around **Wat Mangkon Kamalawat (Neng Noi Yee)**, one of Chinatown's largest temples, on Charoen Krung Rd. All along Charoen Krung Rd in this vicinity, as well as on Yaowarat Rd to the south, restaurants and noodle shops offer hundreds of vegetarian dishes.

Chinese have been living in this area ever since 1782, when they were moved from Bang Kok (today's Ko Ratanakosin) by the royal government to make room for the new capital. A census of the area taken exactly 100 years later found 245 opium dens, 154 pawnshops, 69 gambling establishments and 26 brothels. Pawnshops, along with a myriad of gold shops, remain popular Chinatown businesses, while the three other vices have gone underground. Brothels continue under the guise of 'tea halls' *(róhng chaa)*, back-street heroin dealers have replaced the opium dens and illicit card games convene in the private upstairs rooms of certain restaurants. The four Chinese newspapers printed and distributed in the district have a total circulation of over 160,000.

At the south-eastern edge of Chinatown stands **Hualamphong train station**, built by Dutch architects and engineers just before WWI. One of the city's earliest and most outstanding examples of Thai Art Deco, the station's vaulted iron roof and neoclassical portico demonstrate engineering that was state-of-the-art in its time, while the patterned, two-toned skylights exemplify pure de Stijl-style Dutch modernism.

Fully realised examples of Thai Deco from the 20s and 30s can be found along Chinatown's main streets, particularly Yaowarat Rd. Towers over main doorways are often surmounted with whimsical Deco-style sculptures – the Eiffel Tower, a lion, an elephant, a Moorish dome.

Atop one commercial building on Songwat Rd near Tha Ratchawong is a rusting model of a WWII-vintage Japanese Zero warplane, undoubtedly placed there by the Japanese during their brief 1941 occupation of Bangkok; in style and proportion it fits the surrounding Thai Deco elements.

Pahurat (Map 5)

At the edge of Chinatown, around the intersection of Pahurat (Phahurat) and Chakraphet (Chakkaphet) Rds, is a small but thriving Indian district, generally called Pahurat. Here dozens of Indian-owned shops sell all kinds of fabric and clothes, and this is the best place in the city to bargain for such items, especially silk. The selection is unbelievable, and Thai shoulder bags (*yaams*) sold here are the cheapest in Bangkok, perhaps in Thailand.

Behind the more obvious store fronts along these streets, in the 'bowels' of the blocks, is a seemingly endless Indian bazaar selling not only fabric, but household items, food and other necessities. There are some good, reasonably priced Indian restaurants in this area, too, and a Sikh temple off Chakraphet Rd.

PARKS

Lumphini Park (Map 8)

Named after the Buddha's birthplace in Nepal, this is Bangkok's largest and most popular park. The park is bordered by Rama IV Rd to the south, Sarasin Rd to the north, Withayu Rd to the east and Ratchadamri Rd to the west, with entrance gates on all sides. A large artificial lake in the centre is surrounded by broad, well-tended lawns, wooded areas and walking paths – in other words, it's the best outdoor escape from Bangkok without leaving town.

One of the best times to visit the park is in the early morning before 7 am when the air is fresh (well, relatively so for Bangkok) and legions of Chinese are practising t'ai chi. Also in the morning, vendors set up tables to dispense fresh snake blood and bile, considered health tonics by many Thais and Chinese. Rowing boats and paddle boats can be rented at the lake. A weightlifting area in one section becomes a miniature 'muscle beach' on weekends. Other facilities include a snack bar, several areas with tables and benches for picnics and a couple of tables where ladies serve Chinese tea. Rest rooms are placed at intervals throughout the park.

During kite-flying season, mid-February to April, Lumphini becomes a favoured flight zone; kites (wâo) can be purchased in the park in these months.

Rama IX Royal Park (Map 11)

Opened in 1987 to commemorate King Bhumibol's 60th birthday, Bangkok's newest green area covers 80 hectares and includes a water park and botanical gardens. Since its opening, the latter has developed into a significant horticultural research centre. A museum with an exhibition on the life of the king sits at the centre of the park. Take bus No 2 or No 23 to Soi Udomsuk (Soi 103), off Sukhumvit Rd in Phrakhanong district, then a green minibus to the park. The park is open from 6 am to 6 pm daily; admission is 10B.

Sanam Luang (Map 5)

Sanam Luang (Royal Field), just north of Wat Phra Kaew, is the traditional site for royal cremations, and for the annual Ploughing Ceremony, in which the king officially initiates the rice-growing season. The most recent ceremonial cremation took place in March 1996, when the king presided over funeral rites for his mother (HRH Princess Mother). Before that, the previous Sanam Luang cremations were held in 1976 for Thai students killed in the demonstrations of that year. A statue of Mae Thorani, the Earth Goddess (borrowed from Hindu mythology's Dharani), stands in a white pavilion at the north end of the field. Erected in the late 19th century by King Chulalongkorn, the statue was originally attached to a well that provided drinking water to the public.

Before 1982, Bangkok's famous Weekend Market was held at Sanam Luang (it is now held at Chatuchak Park – see the Shopping chapter for details). Nowadays the large field is most popularly used as a picnic and recreational area and a large kite competition is held during the kite-flying season, February to April.

WALKING TOURS (Map 5)

Temples & River Walking Tour

This walk covers **Ko Ratanakosin** (Ratanakosin Island), which rests in a bend of the river in the middle of Bangkok and contains some of the city's most historic architecture – Wat Phra Kaew, the Grand Palace, Wat Pho, Wat Mahathat and Wat Suthat (each described in detail earlier) – and prestigious universities. The river bank in this area is busy with piers and markets, worthwhile attractions in themselves. Despite its name, Ko Ratanakosin is not an island at all, though in the days when Bangkok was known as the 'Venice of the East', Khlong Banglamphu and Khlong Ong Ang – two lengthy adjoining canals to the east that run parallel to the river – were probably large enough that the area seemed like an island.

This circular walk (one to three hours depending on your pace) begins at **Lak Meuang** (City Pillar), a shrine to Bangkok's city spirit. At the intersection of Ratchadamnoen Nai and Lak Meuang Rds (opposite the southern end of Sanam Luang (Royal Field), the shrine can be reached by taxi, by air-con bus No 3, 6, 7 or 39, by ordinary bus No 39, 44 or 47, or on foot if you're already in the Royal Hotel area. (If the Chao Phraya River Express is more convenient, you can start this walk from Tha Tien – see Map 9). Traditionally, every city in

RICHARD NEBESKY

Ornately decorated door, Wat Phra Kaew.

Thailand must have a foundation stone that embodies the city spirit *(phǐi meuang)* and from which intercity distances are measured. This is Bangkok's most important site of animistic worship; believers throng the area day and night, bringing offerings of flowers, incense, whisky, fruit and even cooked food.

From the City Pillar, walk south across Lak Meuang Rd and along Sanamchai Rd with the Grand Palace/Wat Phra Kaew walls to your right until you come to Chetuphon Rd on the right (the second street after the palace walls end, approximately 500m from the pillar). Turn right onto Chetuphon Rd and enter **Wat Pho** through the second portico. Officially named Wat Phra Chetuphon, this is Bangkok's oldest temple and is famous for its huge reclining Buddha (see the earlier Wat Pho section for more details) and for its massage school. The massage school is the oldest in Thailand and is part of a traditional medical college that archives the country's principal texts on Thai medicine. After you've done the rounds of the various sanctuaries within the monastery grounds, exit through the same door and turn right onto Chetuphon Rd, heading towards the river.

Chetuphon Rd ends at Maharat Rd after a hundred metres or so; turn right at Maharat and stroll north, passing the **market** area to your left. At the end of this block, Maharat Rd crosses Thai Wang Rd. On the southwestern corner is an older branch of the Bangkok Bank, turn left on Thai Wang to glimpse a row of rare early Ratanakosin-era **shophouses.** If you continue along Thai Wang Rd to the river you'll arrive at Tha Tien, one of the pier stops for the Chao Phraya River Express. From an adjacent pier you can catch one of the regular ferries (1B) across the Chao Phraya to **Wat Arun,** which features one of Bangkok's most striking prang, a tall Hindu/Khmer-style pagoda (Wat Arun is described in more detail earlier in this chapter).

Stroll back along Thai Wang Rd to Maharat Rd and turn left to continue the walking tour. On the left along Maharat are two government buildings serving as headquarters for the departments of Internal Trade and Public Welfare. On the right are the whitewashed west walls of the Grand Palace. Two air-con city buses, Nos 8 and 12, stop along this stretch of Maharat – something to keep in mind when you've had enough walking. About 500m from the Thai Wang Rd intersection, Maharat Rd crosses Na Phra Lan Rd; turn left to reach Tha Chang, another express boat stop; or right to reach the entrance to the Grand Palace and Wat Phra Kaew grounds.

The entrance to the **Grand Palace & Wat Phra Kaew** is on the right (south) side of Na Phra Lan Rd less than a hundred metres from Maharat Rd. All visitors to the palace and temple grounds must be suitably attired, ie no shorts, tank tops or other dress considered unacceptable for temple visits. Temple staff can provide wraparound sarongs for bare legs. Shops opposite the main entrance to the complex sell film, cold drinks, curries and noodles; there is also a small post office. The Grand Palace has been supplanted by Chitlada Palace as the primary residence of the royal family, but it is still used for ceremonial occasions. Wat Phra Kaew is a gleaming example of Bangkok temple architecture at its most baroque – see earlier in this chapter for details.

After you've had enough of wandering around the palace and temple grounds, exit via the same doorway and turn left toward the river again. On the right you'll pass the entrance to **Silpakorn University**, Thailand's premier university for fine arts studies. Originally founded as the School of Fine Arts by Italian artist Corrado Feroci, the university campus includes part of an old Rama I palace. A small bookshop inside the gate to the left offers a number of English-language books on Thai art.

At Maharat Rd, turn right (past the Siam City Bank on the corner) and almost immediately you'll see vendor tables along the street. On the tables are cheap amulets representing various Hindu and Buddhist deities. Better quality religious amulets (*phrá phim* or *phrá khrêuang*) are found a bit farther north along Maharat Rd in the large **amulet market** between the road and the river. Walk back into the market area to appreciate how extensive the amulet trade is. Opposite the amulet market on Maharat Rd is **Wat Mahathat**, another of Bangkok's older temples and the headquarters for the country's largest monastic sect.

If you're hungry by now, this is a good place on the circuit to take time out for a snack or meal. Head back along Maharat from the amulet market just a few metres and turn right at Trok Thawiphon (the sign reads 'Thawephon'). This alley leads to Tha Maharat, yet another express boat stop; on either side of the pier is a riverside restaurant – Maharat to the left and Lan Theh to the right. Although the food at both of these restaurants is quite adequate, most local residents head past the Lan Theh (no English sign) along the river and into a warren of smaller restaurants and food vendors along the river. The food here is very good and very inexpensive – to order, all you'll need is a pointing index finger. Rumour has it that these vendor stalls may soon be forced to leave to accommodate plans for a Ko Ratanakosin restoration project.

JOE CUMMINGS

Upper terrace, golden chedi and other
buildings, Wat Phra Kaew.

Renewed and refuelled, start walking north again
along Maharat past the amulet market and Wat Mahathat
to Phra Chan Rd, around 80m from Trok Thawiphon.
Turn left to reach Tha Phra Chan if you want to catch an
express boat north or south along the river, or turn right
to reach Sanam Luang, the end of the tour. If you take the
latter route, you'll pass **Thammasat University** on the left.
Thammasat is known for its law and political science
faculties; it was also the site of the bloody demonstrations
of October 1976, in which hundreds of Thai students
were killed or wounded by military troops. Opposite the
university entrance are several very good noodle shops.

Chinatown-Pahurat Walking Tour (Map 5)

This route meanders through Bangkok's busy Chinese
and Indian market districts – best explored on foot since
vehicular traffic in the area is in almost constant gridlock. Depending on your pace and shopping intentions,
this lengthy route could take from 1½ to three hours. You
can also do this tour in reverse, beginning from the
Pahurat fabric market.

Be warned that the journey should only be under-taken by those who can withstand extended crowd contact as well as the sometimes unpleasant sights and smells of a traditional fresh market. The rewards for tolerating this attack on the senses are numerous glimpses into the 'real' day-to-day Bangkok, away from the glittering facade of department stores and office buildings along Bangkok's main avenues – not to mention the opportunity for fabulous bargains. If you plan to buy anything, you'd better bring along either a phrasebook or an interpreter – very little English is spoken in these areas.

Start at **Wat Mangkon Kamalawat (Neng Noi Yee)**, one of Chinatown's largest and liveliest temples (the name means Dragon Lotus Temple), on Charoen Krung Rd between Mangkon Rd and Soi 21. A taxi direct to the temple is recommended over taking a bus, simply because the district is so congested and street names don't always appear in Roman script. If you're deter-mined to go by bus, No 1, 4, 7, 25, 35, 40, 53 and 73 pass the temple going east (the temple entrance will be on the left), or you could take air-con buses No 1, 7 or 8 and get off near the Mangkon Rd intersection on Yaowarat Rd, a block south of Charoen Krung. Another option is to arrive by Chao Phraya River Express at Tha Ratchawong, then walk four blocks north-east along Ratchawong Rd to Charoen Krung Rd, make a right and walk 11\2 blocks to the temple.

To help pinpoint the right area on Charoen Krung Rd look for neighbouring shops selling fruit, cakes, incense and ritual burning paper for offering at the temple. Inscriptions at the entrance to Wat Mangkon Kamalawat are in Chinese and Tibetan, while the labyrinthine inte-rior features a succession of Buddhist, Taoist and Confucianist altars. Virtually at any time of day or night this temple is packed with worshippers lighting incense, filling the ever-burning altar lamps with oil and praying to their ancestors.

Leaving the temple, walk left along Charoen Krung Rd about 20m to the nearest crossing, then turn right and head down the alley on the other side. You're now heading south-west on **Trok Itsaranuphap**, one of Chinatown's main market lanes. This section is lined with vendors purveying ready-to-eat or preserved food-stuffs, including cleaned chickens, duck and fish. Though not for the squeamish, it's one of the cleanest-looking fresh markets in Bangkok.

About a hundred metres down Trok Itsaranuphap you'll cross **Yaowarat Rd**, a main Chinatown thorough-fare. This section of Yaowarat is lined with large and small gold shops; for price and selection this is probably the best place in Thailand to purchase a gold chain (they are sold by the *bàht*, a unit of weight equal to 15g). From the trok entrance, turn right onto Yaowarat Rd, walk 50m to the crossing and, using a couple of savvy-looking Chinese crones as screens, navigate your way across the street.

Trok Itsaranuphap continues southward on the other side. Down the lane almost immediately on your left is the Chinese-ornamented entrance to **Talaat Kao (Old Market)**. This market section off Trok Itsaranuphap has been operating for over 200 years. All manner and size of freshwater and saltwater fin and shellfish are displayed here, alive and filleted – or sometimes half alive and half filleted.

About a hundred metres farther down Itsaranuphap, past rows of vendors selling mostly dried fish, you'll come to a major Chinatown market crossroads. Running perpendicular to Itsaranuphap in either direction is famous **Sampeng Lane (Soi Wanit 1)**. Turn right onto Sampeng. This is usually the most crowded of Chinatown's market sois, a traffic jam of pedestrians, pushcarts and the occasional annoying motorbike twisting through the crowds. Shops along this section of Sampeng sell dry goods, especially shoes, clothing, fabric, toys and kitchenware.

About 25m along, Sampeng Lane crosses Mangkon Rd. On either side of the intersection are two of Bangkok's oldest commercial buildings, a Bangkok Bank and the venerable **Tang To Kang** gold shop, both over 100 years old. The exteriors of the buildings are classic early Bangkok, showing lots of European influence; the interiors are heavy with hardwood panelling. Continue walking another 60m or so to the Ratchawong Rd crossing (a traffic cop is usually stationed here to part the vehicular Red Sea for pedestrians), cross and re-enter Sampeng Lane on the other side.

At this point, there are lots of fabric shops – many of them operated by Indian (mostly Sikh) merchants – as the edge of Chinatown approaches the Indian district of Pahurat. If you're looking for good deals on Thai textiles you're in the right place. But hold off buying until you've had a chance to look through at least a dozen or more shops – they get better the farther you go. After about 65m is the small Mahachak Rd crossing and then after another 50m or so is the larger Chakrawat (Chakkawat) Rd crossing, where yet another traffic cop assists. Along Chakrawat Rd in this vicinity, as well as farther ahead along Sampeng Lane on the other side of Chakrawat, there are many gem and jewellery shops.

If you were to turn right and follow Chakrawat Rd
north from Soi Wanit, you could have a look around the
Chinese-Thai antique stores of **Nakhon Kasem,** between
Yaowarat and Charoen Krung Rds. Nakhon Kasem is
also known as the Thieves' Market, a name based on its
past reputation for being a market where stolen goods
were commonly sold. After you re-enter Soi Wanit on the
other side of Chakrawat Rd the jewellery shops are
mixed with an eclectic array of houseware and clothing
shops until you arrive, after another 50m, at the **Saphaan
Han** market area, named after a short bridge *(saphāan)*
over Khlong Ong Ang. Clustered along the khlong on
either side of the bridge is a bevy of vendors selling
noodles and snacks. On the other side of the bridge,
Sampeng Lane ends at Chakraphet Rd, the eastern edge
of the Pahurat district.

Chakraphet Rd is well known for its Indian restaurants and shops selling Indian sweets. One of the best
eateries in the area is the Royal India Restaurant, which
serves north Indian cuisine. This restaurant is justly
famous for its tasty selection of Indian breads. To get
there, turn left onto Chakraphet Rd and walk about 70m
along the east (left) side of the road; look for the Royal
India sign pointing down an alley on the left.

On the opposite side of Chakraphet Rd from the Royal
India is another Chinese temple. North of this temple, in
a back alley on the west side of the road, is a large **Sikh
temple** – turn left before the ATM department store to
find the entrance. Visitors to the temple – reportedly the
second-largest Sikh temple outside India – are welcome,
but you must remove your shoes. If you happen to arrive
on a Sikh festival day you can partake of the *langar*, or
traditional communal Sikh meal, which is served in the
temple.

Several inexpensive Indian food stalls are found in an
alley alongside the department store. Behind the store,
stretching westward from Chakraphet Rd to Triphet Rd,
is the **Pahurat Market**, devoted almost exclusively to
textiles and clothing. Pahurat Rd itself runs parallel to
and just north of the market.

If you're ready to escape the market hustle and bustle,
you can catch city buses on Chakraphet Rd (heading
north and then east to the Siam Square and Pratunam
areas) or along Pahurat Rd (heading west and then north
along Tri Thong Rd to the Banglamphu district). Or walk
to the river and catch a Chao Phraya Express boat from
Tha Saphaan Phut, which is just to the north-west of
Memorial Bridge (Saphaan Phut). If you're doing this
route in reverse, you can arrive by Chao Phraya River
Express at Tha Saphaan Phut.

OTHER ATTRACTIONS

Dusit Zoo (Khao Din Wana) (Map 1)

The collection of animals at Bangkok's 19-hectare zoo comprises over 300 mammals, 200 reptiles and 800 birds, including relatively rare indigenous species such as banteng, gaur, serow, and rhinoceros. Originally a private botanical garden for King Rama V (Chulalong-korn), the grounds were converted into a zoo in 1938. The shady terrain features trees labelled in English, Thai, and Latin – as well as a lake in the centre where paddle boats can be rented. There's also a small children's play-ground.

If nothing else, the zoo is a nice place to get away from the noise of the city and observe how the Thais amuse themselves – mainly by eating. A couple of lake-side restaurants serve good, inexpensive Thai food. Entry to the zoo is 20B for adults, 5B for children, 10B for those over 60; it's open 9 am to 6 pm daily. A small circus performs on weekends and holidays between 11 am and 2 pm. Sunday can be a bit crowded – if you want the zoo mostly to yourself, go on a weekday.

The zoo is in the Dusit district between Chitlada Palace and the National Assembly Hall; the main entrance is off Ratwithi Rd. Buses that pass the entrance include the ordinary No 18 and 28 and the air-con No 10.

Queen Saovabha Memorial Institute (Snake Farm) (Map 8)

At this research institute (☎ 252-0161) on Rama IV Rd (near Henri Dunant Rd), venomous snakes are milked daily to make snake-bite antidotes, which are distributed throughout the country. The milking sessions – at 10.30 am and 2 pm weekdays, 10.30 am only on week-ends and holidays – have become a major Bangkok tourist attraction. Unlike other 'snake farms' in Bang-kok, this is a serious herpetological research facility; a very informative half-hour slide show on snakes is presented before the milking sessions. This will be boring to some, fascinating to others. Feeding time is 3 pm. Admission is 70B.

A booklet entitled *Guide to Healthy Living in Thailand*, published jointly by the Thai Red Cross and US Embassy, is available here for 100B. You can also get common vaccinations against diseases such as cholera, typhoid, hepatitis A and smallpox.

Monk's Bowl Village (Map 5)

This is the sole survivor of three such villages established in Bangkok by King Rama I for the handcrafting
of monk's bowls *(bàat)*. The black bowls, used by Thai
monks to receive alms-food from faithful Buddhists
every morning, are still made in this village in the traditional manner. Due to the expense of purchasing a
handmade bowl, the 'village' has been reduced to a
single alley in a district known as Ban Baht *(bâan bàat,*
Monk's Bowl Village). About half a dozen families
hammer the bowls together from eight separate pieces
of steel, representing the eight spokes of the wheel of
dharma (which in turn symbolise Buddhism's Eightfold
Path). The joints are fused in a wood fire with bits of
copper, the bowl is polished and coated with several
layers of black lacquer. A typical bowl-smith makes one
bowl per day.

To find it, walk south on Boriphat Rd south of Bamrung Meuang Rd, then left into Soi Baan Baht. The
artisans who fashion the bowls are not always at work,
so it's largely a matter of luck whether you'll see them
in action. At any of the houses which make them, you can
purchase a fine-quality alms bowl for around 400 to 500B.
To see monks' robes and bowls for sale, wander down
Bamrung Meuang Rd in the vicinity of the Giant Swing.

RIVER & CANAL TRIPS

In 1855 British envoy Sir John Bowring wrote, 'The
highways of Bangkok are not streets or roads but the
river and the canals. Boats are the universal means of
conveyance and communication'. The wheeled motor
vehicle has long since become Bangkok's conveyance of
choice, but fortunately it hasn't yet become universal. A
vast network of canals and river tributaries surrounding
Bangkok still carries a motley fleet of watercraft, from
paddled canoes to rice barges. In these areas, many
homes, trading houses and temples remain oriented
toward water life and provide a fascinating glimpse into
the past, when Thais still considered themselves *jâo
nâam,* or water lords. While the Thonburi side canals are
wonderful for sightseeing, the Bangkok-side routes are
good for getting around the city quickly.

Chao Phraya River Express

You can observe urban river life from the water for 1½
hours for only 7B by climbing aboard a Chao Phraya
River Express boat at Tha Ratchasingkhon, just north of

The Original Siamese Twins

While walking along Bangkok's Chao Phraya River one afternoon in 1824, English trader Robert Hunter spotted what he thought was a creature with eight limbs and two heads swimming in the river. When the oddity lifted itself onto a canoe, Hunter was surprised to see it was in fact two 13-year-old boys who were fused together at the chest. The Briton was so intrigued that he sponsored a medical examination for the boys (which showed they couldn't be surgically separated) and later introduced them to Bangkok's Western social circuits.

The boys, named Chang and Eng, left Siam five years later to tour Europe and the USA as physiological celebrities. They eventually settled in North Carolina, where they married two sisters and sired 22 children. In 1874 Chang passed away in his sleep; Eng followed him two hours later.

Thais have no known genetic disposition toward joined births (Chang and Eng were actually of Chinese descent), but ever since Hunter's 'discovery', the non-medical world has used the term 'Siamese twins' to describe the phenomena. ∎

Krungthep Bridge (Map 9). If you want to ride the entire length of the express route north all the way to Nonthaburi, this is where you must begin. Ordinary bus Nos 1, 17, and 75 and air-con bus No 4 pass Tha Ratchasingkhon. Or you can board at any other express boat pier in Bangkok for a shorter ride to Nonthaburi; for example, 20 minutes from Tha Phayap (the first stop north of Krungthon Bridge), or 30 minutes from Tha Phra Athit (near the Phra Pinklao Bridge). Express boats run about every 15 minutes from 6 am to 6 pm daily. See the Getting Around chapter for more information on the Chao Phraya River Express service.

Khlong Bangkok Noi Taxi

Another good boat trip is the Bangkok Noi canal taxi route, which leaves from Tha Maharat (Map 9) next to Silpakorn University. The fare is only a few baht and the further up Khlong Bangkok Noi you go, the better the scenery becomes, with teak houses on stilts, old wats and plenty of greenery.

Stop off at Wat Suwannaram to view 19th century Jataka murals painted by two of early Bangkok's foremost religious muralists. Art historians consider these the best surviving temple paintings in Bangkok. A one-way fare anywhere is 10B.

Other Canal Taxis

From Tha Tien near Wat Pho (Map 9), get a canal taxi along **Khlong Mon** (leaving every half hour from 6.30 am to 6 pm, 5B) for more typical canal scenery, including orchid farms. A longer excursion could be made by making a loop along khlongs Bangkok Noi, Chak Phra and Mon, an all-day trip. An outfit called Chao Phraya Charters (☎ 433-5453) runs a tour boat to Khlong Mon from Tha Tien each afternoon from 3 to 5 pm for 300B per person, including refreshments.

Boats from Tha Chang to **Khlong Bang Yai** (10B) leave every half hour from 6.15 am to 10 pm – this is the same trip that passes the Bang Khu Wiang Floating Market (see Floating Markets later in this chapter). Though the market itself is over by 7 am, this trip is worthwhile later in the day as it passes a number of interesting wats, traditional wooden homes and the Royal Barges.

From the Tha Phibun Songkram in Nonthaburi you can board a boat taxi up picturesque **Khlong Om** and see durian plantations. Boats leave every 15 minutes.

Boats to **Khlong Bangkok Yai**, available from either Tha Tien or Tha Ratchini, pass Wat Intharam, where a chedi contains the ashes of Thonburi's Kin Taksin Maharaj. Taksin was assassinated by his own ministers in 1782 after they decided he'd gone mad. The fine gold-and-black lacquer work adorning the main bòt doors depicts the mythical *naariiphŏn* tree, which bears beautiful girls as fruit.

It is possible to go as far as Suphanburi and Ratch-aburi (Ratburi) by boat from Bangkok, though this typically involves many boat connections.

For details on boat transport on the Bangkok side of the river, where four lengthy canal routes have been revived, see the Getting Around chapter. Although they provide quick transport, none of the four right-bank canal routes can be recommended for sightseeing.

Boat Charters

If you want to see the Thonburi canals at your own pace, the best thing to do is charter a long-tail boat – it needn't be expensive if you get a small group together to share the costs. The usual price is 300B per hour and you can choose from eight canals in Thonburi alone. Beware of 'agents' who will try to put you on the boat and rake off an extra commission. Before travelling by boat, establish the price – you can't bargain when you're in the middle of the river!

The best piers for hiring a boat are **Tha Chang, Tha Saphaan Phut** and **Tha Si Phaya**. Close to the latter, at the rear of the River City complex, the **Boat Tour Centre** charges the same basic hourly price (300B) and there are no hassles with touts. Of these four piers, Tha Chang usually has the largest selection of boats.

Those interested in seeing Bangkok's deep-water port can hire long-tail boats to Khlong Toey or as far downriver as Pak Nam, which means river mouth. It's about two hours each way by boat, or a bit quicker if you take a bus or taxi one way.

Dinner Cruises

A dozen or more companies in Bangkok run regular cruises along the Chao Phraya for rates ranging from 40 to 750B per person, depending on how far they go and whether dinner is included. Most require advance phone reservations.

The less expensive, more casual boats allow you to order as little or as much as you want from moderately priced menus; a modest charge of 40 to 70B per person is added to the bill for the cruise. It's a fine way to dine outdoors when the weather is hot, away from city traffic and cooled by river breezes. Several of the dinner boats cruise under the illuminated Rama IX Bridge, the longest single-span cable-suspension bridge in the world. This engineering marvel supports the elevated expressway joining Bangkok's Thanon Tok district with Thonburi's Ratburana district. Those dinner cruises offering the à la carte menu plus surcharge include:

Ban Khun Luang Restaurant
    Ban Khun Luang Restaurant to Tha Oriental, Thursday, Friday, Saturday (☎ 243-3235)
Khanap Nam Restaurant
    Krungthon Bridge to Sathon Bridge, twice daily
    (☎ 433-6611)
Riverside Company
    Krungthon Bridge to Rama IX Bridge, daily (☎ 434-0090)
River Sight-Seeing Ltd
    Tha Si Phraya to Wat Arun or Rama IX Bridge (depending on current), daily (☎ 437-4047)
Yok-Yor Restaurant
    Yok-Yor Restaurant (Tha Wisut Kasat) to Rama IX Bridge, daily (☎ 281-1829, 282-7385)

Swankier dinner cruises charge a set price of 300 to 750B per person for the cruise and dinner; beer and liquor cost extra.

Wanfah Cruise
    River City to Krungthon Bridge, twice daily
    (☎ 433-5453, 424-6218)
Loy Nava Co
    Tha Si Phraya to Tha Wasukri, twice daily
    (☎ 437-4932/7329)
Oriental Hotel
    Tha Oriental to Nonthaburi, Wednesday only
    (☎ 236-0400/9)
Loy Nava Co
    Tha Si Phraya to Tha Wasukri, twice daily
    (☎ 437-4932/7329)
Manohra Cruises
    Marriott Royal Garden Riverside Hotel to Krung Thep
    Bridge, nightly (☎ 476-0021)

Sunset Cruise Before its regular 2½ hour dinner cruise begins at 7.30 pm, the *Manohra* sails from the Marriott Royal Garden Riverside Hotel for an hour-long sunset cocktail cruise. Boarding is free; passengers are only charged for drinks purchased from the well-stocked bar on board. A free river taxi operates between the River City Pier and the Royal Garden Pier at 5 pm, just in time for the 5.30 pm cruise departure. Call ☎ 476-0021 for more info.

Longer Cruises All-day and overnight cruises on the river are also available. The Chao Phraya River Express Boat Co (☎ 222-5330, 225-3002/3) does a reasonably priced tour on Sunday only, starting from Tha Maharat at 8 am and returning at 5.30 pm, that includes visits to the Thai Folk Arts & Handicrafts Centre in Bang Sai, Bang Pa-In Palace in Ayuthaya, and the bird sanctuary at Wat Phailom. The price is 180B per person lower deck, 250B upper deck, not including lunch, which you arrange on your own in Bang Pa-In.

Mit Chao Phraya Express Boat Co (☎ 225-6179) operates another moderately priced program through several Thonburi canals, with stops at Wat Arun, the Royal Barges, an orchid farm and the Snakes & Crocodiles Farm. The tour departs from Tha Maharat at 8.30 am and returns at 6 pm. The cost is 150B, not including admission fees to the aforementioned attractions.

The Oriental Hotel's luxurious all air-con *Oriental Queen* (☎ 236-0400/9) also does a cruise to Bang Pa-In that leaves at 8 am from Tha Oriental and returns by air-con bus at 5 pm. The *Oriental Queen* cruise costs 1300B including lunch and guided tour. Note that neither of the above cruises really allows enough time to see Ayuthaya properly, so if that's your primary intention, go on your own. On the other hand I've had letters from history-weary readers who thought 15 to 30 minutes was plenty of time to see the ruins! Two other companies running similar Bang Pa-In/Ayuthaya tours for 1000 to 1200B per person are Horizon Cruise (☎ 538-3491) and River Sun Cruise (☎ 237-7608).

Royal Garden Resorts and Siam Exclusive Tours maintain three restored half century-old teak rice barges that have been transformed into four and 10-cabin cruisers. Decorated with antiques and Persian carpets, these craft represent the ultimate in Chao Phraya River luxury, the nautical equivalent of the Eastern & Oriental Express train. These barges – two named *Mekhala*, one called *Manohra Song* – usually leave Bangkok in the afternoon and head upriver towards Ayuthaya (or downriver towards Bangkok). In the evening they anchor at Wat Praket, where a candle-lit dinner is served. The next morning passengers offer food to the monks from the wat, and then the barge moves on to Bang Pa-In. After a tour of the Summer Palace, a long-tail boat takes passengers on a tour of the ruins of Ayuthaya.

At present, four Ayuthaya cruises per week are scheduled. The cost for the two-day cruise is variable depending on which barge is used, starting at around 3000B per person for the *Mekhala* and from 7000B per person for the super-deluxe, four-cabin *Manohra Song*, depending on the time of year. Prices include all meals and nonalcoholic beverages, accommodation, guide services, admission fees in Ayuthaya and hotel transfers. Shorter cruises are available by charter. Call the Marriott Royal Garden (☎ 476-0021) for details.

Floating Markets

Among the most heavily published photo images from Thailand are those that depict wooden canoes laden with multi-coloured fruits and vegetables, paddled by Thai women wearing indigo-hued clothes and wide-brimmed straw hats. Such floating markets (*talàat náam*) exist in various locations throughout Bangkok's huge canal system – but if you don't know where to go you may end up at a very inauthentic tourist show.

Bang Khu Wiang Floating Market

At Khlong Bang Khu Wiang in Thonburi a small floating market operates between 4 and 7 am. Boats to the Khu Wiang

Market (Talaat Naam Khuu Wiang) leave from the Tha Chang near Wat Phra Kaew every morning between 6.15 and 8 am; take the earliest one to catch the market before it's over, or charter a long-tail boat at an earlier hour.

Damnoen Saduak Floating Market There is a larger if somewhat more commercial floating market on Khlong Damnoen Saduak in Ratchaburi Province, 104 km south-west of Bangkok, between Nakhon Pathom and Samut Songkhram. You can get buses from the Southern bus terminal on Charan Sanitwong Rd in Thonburi to Damnoen Saduak starting at 5 am. Get there as early as possible to escape the hordes. For more information, see Floating Markets in the Excursions chapter.

Wat Sai Floating Market In recent years, visitors to the floating market near Wat Sai on Khlong Sanam Chai (off Khlong Dao Khanong) have outnumbered vendors to the point that opinions are now virtually unanimous – don't waste your time at this so-called market. Go to Bang Khu Wiang or Damnoen Saduak instead – or find your own.

If you're set on doing the Wat Sai trip, take one of the floating market tours that leave from Tha Oriental (Soi Oriental) or Tha Maharat near Silpakorn University – your only alternative is to charter a whole boat (at Tha Oriental) and that can be quite expensive. Floating market tours cost from 50B, which only gives you 20 minutes or so at the market (which is probably more than enough for this non-event). Most tours charge 300 to 400B for an hour and a half. Be prepared for a very touristy experience.

ACTIVITIES

Athletic Facilities

The first and grandest of the city's sports facilities gyms, see sports clubsis the **Royal Bangkok Sports Club** (RBSC) (Map 7) between Henri Dunant and Ratchadamri Rds (the green oval marked 'Turf' on the Bangkok bus maps). Facilities include a horse track, polo grounds (located elsewhere off Withayu Rd), swimming pool, sauna, squash and tennis courts (both hard and grass) and 18-hole golf course. There's a waiting list for membership so the only way you're likely to frolic at this prestigious club is to be invited by a RBSC member.

Membership at the **British Club** (☎ 234-0247) is open to citizens of Australia, Canada, New Zealand and the

TAT

RICHARD I'ANSON

Bangkok's bustling floating markets.

UK or to others by invitation. Among the sports facilities are a pool and squash and tennis courts.

The least expensive swimming facility in Bangkok is operated by the **Dept of Physical Education** (☎ 215-1535) at the National Stadium on Rama I Rd, next to Mahboonkrong Centre (Map 7); memberships cost just 200B per year plus 20B per hour.

Hollywood Gym (☎ 208-9298), 420 Hollywood Street Center, Phetburi Rd (opposite the Asia Hotel), offers a fully-equipped gym, sauna and lounge. This is where many of Thailand's champion weightlifters work out. It's open daily from 10 am to midnight, and English, French, Spanish and Italian are spoken. Drop-in fees are 150B per session or you can pay heavily discounted fees in one-week, one-month, three-month, six-month and year-long increments. The top-class **Clark Hatch Physical Fitness Centres**, with weight machines, pool, sauna and massage, can be found at the Hilton International, Amari Watergate and DeVille Palace hotels; non-hotel guests are welcome.

Other sports clubs open to the public include:

Amorn & Sons – 8 Soi Amorn 3, Soi 39, Sukhumvit Rd (☎ 392-8442); tennis, squash, badminton

Asoke Sports Club – 302/81- 81 Asoke-Din Daeng Rd (☎ 246-2260); tennis, swimming

Bangkhen Tennis Court – 47/2 Vibhavadi Rangsit Hwy (☎ 579-7629); tennis

The Bangkok Gym – 9th fl, Delta Grand Pacific Hotel, 259 Sukhumvit Rd, Soi 19 (☎ 255-2440); weights, sauna, swimming, aerobics

Central Tennis Court – 13/1 Soi Atakanprasit, Sathon Tai Rd (☎ 213-1909); tennis

Gold Health & Fitness Club – 40th fl, 408 Phahonyothin Place (☎ 619-0460); weights, sauna, swimming, aerobics

Kanpaibun Tennis Court – 10 Soi 40, Sukhumvit Rd (☎ 391-8784, 392-1832); tennis

NTT Sports Club – 612/32 Soi Laoladda, Arun Amarin Rd, Thonburi (☎ 433-4623); swimming, weights, aerobics

Saithip Swimming Pool – 140 Soi 56, Sukhumvit Rd (☎ 331-2037); tennis, badminton, swimming

Santhikham Court – 217 Soi 109, Sukhumvit Rd (☎ 393-8480); tennis

Sivalai Club Tennis Court & Swimming Pool – 168 Soi Anantaphum, Itsaraphap Rd, Thonburi (☎ 411-2649); tennis, swimming

Soi Klang Racquet Club – 8 Soi 49, Sukhumvit Rd (☎ 391-0963, 382-8442); squash, tennis, racquetball, swimming, aerobics

Sukhavadee Swimming Pool – 107/399 Gp 6, Soi 91 Lat Phrao Rd (☎ 538-6879); swimming

Swim & Slim Family Club – 918 Soi 101/1, Sukhumvit Rd
(☎ 393-0889); badminton, swimming, weights

Golf

Golfing in Thailand? It's not my sport, but golf addicts
can get a fix at any of nearly 50 courses in Thailand.
Green fees range from 500 to 1500B, depending on the
day of the week and quality of the course. Caddy fees
are 50 to 150B (caddies are often women) and clubs can
be rented for 150 to 300B. Here are a few courses in
Bangkok that accept non-members:

Krungthep Kretha Golf Course – Si Nakharin Rd (☎ 374-6063);
closest course to central Bangkok aside from the Royal
Dusit; more than 900 caddies work here
Navatanee Golf Course, 5679m, par 72 – 22 Mu 1, Sukhaphiban 2 Rd, Bangkapi, Bangkok (☎ 374-7077); top-rated
course designed by Robert Trent Jones; also has gymna-
sium and swimming pool
Railway Training Centre Golf Course, 6052m, par 72 – Vibhavadi Rangsit Rd, Bangkhen, Bangkok (☎ 271-0130);
Thailand's first 36-hole course, fairly flat, near the airport;
also has swimming pool and tennis courts
Rose Garden Golf Course, 5856m, par 72 – Rose Garden
Resort, Highway 4 (☎ 253-0295); one of Thailand's most
beautiful courses, tight fairways, and usually empty
during the week
Royal Dusit Golf Course, 4476m, par 66 – Phitsanulok Rd; in
the Royal Turf Club in central Bangkok (☎ 281-4320);
closed on race days

COURSES

Cooking

More and more travellers are coming to Thailand just to
learn how to cook. In Bangkok I often meet foreign chefs
seeking out recipe inspirations for the 'east-west' sort of
cuisine that seems to be taking the world by storm. You
too can amaze your friends back home after attending a
course in Thai cuisine at one of the following places:

Modern Housewife Centre – 45/6-7 Sethsiri Rd (☎ 279-2834)
Oriental Hotel Cooking School – Soi Oriental, Charoen Krung
Rd (☎ 236-0400/0439); a five day course under the direction of well-known chef Chali (Charlie) Amatyakul
UFM Food Centre – 593/29-39 Soi 33/1, Sukhumvit Rd
(☎ 259-0620/0633); most classes offered in Thai; need at
least four people to offer an English-language class
Bussaracum Restaurant – 35 Soi Phiphat 2, Convent Rd
(☎ 235-8915)

Martial Arts Training

Many Westerners have had martial arts training in Thailand (especially since the release of Jean-Claude Van Damme's flick, *The Kickboxer*, which was filmed on location in Thailand), but few last more than a week or two in a Thai camp – and fewer still have gone on to compete on Thailand's pro circuit.

Thai Boxing (Muay Thai) An Australian, Patrick Cusick, occasionally directs muay thai seminars for farangs in Thailand. Contact him at Thai Championship Boxing (☎ 234-5360, fax 237-6303), Box 1996, Bangkok. The Pramote Gym (☎ 215-8848) at 210-212 Phetburi Rd, Ratthewi, offers training in Thai boxing as well as other martial arts (judo, karate, tae kwon do, krabi-krabong) to foreigners as well as locals. Those interested in training at a traditional muay thai camp might try the Fairtex Boxing Camp outside Bangkok, c/o Bunjong Busarakamwongs, Fairtex Garments Factory, 734-742 Trok Kai, Anuwong Rd, Bangkok. Be forewarned though – muay thai training is gruelling and features full-contact sparring, unlike tae kwon do, kenpo, kung fu and other East Asian martial arts.

For more information about Thai boxing, see the Spectator Sports section of the Entertainment chapter.

Krabi-Krabong Krabi-krabong (a traditional Thai martial art; see Spectator Sports further on) is taught at several Thai colleges and universities, but the country's best training venue is the Buddhai Sawan Fencing School of Thailand, 5/1 Phetkasem Rd, Thonburi, where Ajaan Samai Mesamarna carries on traditions passed down from Wat Phutthaisawan. Several farangs have trained here, including one American who became the first foreigner to attain *ajaan* (master) status. Pramote Gym (see Thai Boxing earlier) also provides krabi-krabong training.

Meditation Study

Although at times Bangkok may seem like the most un-Buddhist city on earth, there are several places where interested foreigners can learn about Theravada Buddhist meditation. (See the Religion section in the Facts about Bangkok chapter for background information on Buddhism in Thailand.)

Wat Mahathat (Map 5) This 18th-century wat opposite Sanam Luang provides meditation instruction

Muay Thai (Thai Boxing)

Almost anything goes in this martial sport, both in the ring and in the stands. If you don't mind the violence (in the ring), a Thai boxing match is worth attending for the pure spectacle – the wild musical accompaniment, the ceremonial beginning of each match and the frenzied betting around the stadium.

Thai boxing is also telecast on Channel 7 every Sunday afternoon; if you're wondering where everyone is, they're probably inside watching the national sport.

History Most of what is known about the early history of Thai boxing comes from Burmese accounts of warfare between Myanmar (Burma) and Thailand during the 15th and 16th centuries. The earliest reference (1411 AD) mentions a ferocious style of unarmed combat that decided the fate of Thai kings. A later description tells how Nai Khanom Tom, Thailand's first famous boxer and a prisoner of war in Myanmar, gained his freedom by roundly defeating a dozen Burmese warriors before the Burmese court. To this day, many martial art aficionados consider the Thai style the ultimate in hand-to-hand fighting. Hong Kong, China, Singapore, Taiwan, Korea, Japan, the USA, Netherlands, Germany and France have all sent their best challengers, but none have been able to defeat top-ranked Thai boxers. On one famous occasion, Hong Kong's top five Kung Fu masters were all dispatched in less than 6½ minutes, all knock-outs.

King Naresuan the Great (1555-1605) was supposed to have been a top-notch boxer, and he made muay thai a requisite of Thai military training. Later, Phra Chao Seua (the Tiger King), further promoted Thai boxing as a national sport by encouraging prize fights and the development of training camps in the early 18th century. There are accounts of massive wagers and bouts to the death during this time. Phra Chao Seua himself is said to have been an incognito participant in many of the matches during the early part of his reign. Combatants' fists were wrapped in thick horsehide for maximum impact with minimum knuckle damage. They also used cotton soaked in glue and ground glass and later hemp. Tree bark and sea shells were used to protect the groin from lethal kicks.

Modern Thai Boxing The high incidence of death and physical injury led the Thai government to institute a ban on muay thai in the 1920s, but in the 1930s the sport was revived under modern regulations based on the international Queensberry rules. Bouts were limited to five three-minute rounds separated by two-minute breaks. Contestants had to wear international-style gloves and trunks (always either red or blue) and their feet were taped – to this day no shoes are worn.

There are 16 weight divisions in Thai boxing, ranging from mini-flyweight to heavyweight, with the best fighters said to be in the welterweight division (67-kg maximum). As in international-style boxing, matches take place on a 7.3-sq-metre canvas-covered floor with rope retainers supported by four padded posts, rather than the traditional dirt circle.

In spite of these concessions to safety, today all surfaces of the body are still considered fair targets and any part of the body except the head may be used to strike an opponent. Common blows include high kicks to the neck, elbow thrusts to the face and head, knee hooks to the ribs and low crescent kicks to the calf. A contestant may even grasp an opponent's head between his hands and pull it down to meet an upward knee thrust. Punching is considered the weakest of all blows and kicking merely a way to 'soften up' one's opponent; knee and elbow strikes are decisive in most matches.

The training of a Thai boxer, and particularly the relationship between boxer and trainer, is highly ritualised. When a boxer is considered ready for the ring, he is given a new name by his trainer, usually with the name of the training camp as his surname. For the public, the relationship is perhaps best expressed in the

TAT

ram muay (boxing dance) that takes place before every match. The ram muay ceremony usually lasts about five minutes and expresses obeisance to the fighter's guru *(khruu)*, as well as to the guardian spirit of Thai boxing. This is done through a series of gestures and body movements performed in rhythm to the ringside musical accompaniment of Thai oboe (pii) and percussion. Each boxer works out his own dance, in conjunction with his trainer and in accordance with the style of his particular camp.

The woven headbands and armbands worn by fighters in the ring are sacred ornaments, which bestow blessings and divine protection; the headband is removed after the ram muay ceremony, but the armband, which actually contains a small Buddha image, is worn throughout the match. After the bout begins, the fighters continue to bob and weave in rhythm until the action begins to heat up. The musicians play throughout the match and the volume and tempo of the music rise and fall along with the events in the ring.

As Thai boxing has become more popular among Westerners (as both spectators and participants) there are increasing numbers of bouts staged for tourists in places like Pattaya, Phuket and Ko Samui. In these, the action may be genuine but the judging below par. Nonetheless, dozens of authentic matches are held daily at the major Bangkok stadiums and in the provinces (there are about 60,000 full-time boxers in Thailand), and these are easily sought out.

Several Thai *nák muay* have also won world championships in international-style boxing. Khaosai Galaxy, the greatest Asian boxer of all time, chalked up 19 WBA bantamweight championships in a row before retiring undefeated in December 1991. As of 1995 Thailand had five concurrent international boxing champions – all in the flyweight and bantamweight categories.

Meanwhile, in some areas of the country a pre-1920s version of muay thai still exists. In north-eastern Thailand *muay boraan* is a very ritualised form that resembles tai qi chuan or classical dance in its adherence to set moves and routines. In pockets of southern Thailand, fighters practicing *muay katchii* still bind their hands in hemp. And each year around the lunar new year (Songkhran) in April, near the town of Mae Sot on the Thai-Burmese border, a top Thai fighter challenges a Burmese fighter of similar class from the other side of the Moei River to a no-holds barred, hemp-fisted battle that ends only after one of the opponents wipes blood from his body.

International Muay Thai In Thailand, the English-language periodical called *Muay Thai World* appears annually in Bangkok, Chiang Mai and Phuket bookshops that sell English-language material. The annual includes features on muay thai events abroad as well as in Thailand, and contains current rankings for Bangkok's Lumphini and Ratchadamnoen stadiums. The World Muay Thai Council (WMTC), a newly recognised organisation sanctioned by Thailand's Sports Authority with headquarters at the Thai Army Officers Club in Bangkok, has begun organising international muay thai bouts in Bangkok stadiums and elsewhere. So far the largest number of WMTC-affiliated muay thai training facilities is found in the USA, followed by Australia, the Netherlands, Canada, Japan and France. Dutch fighter Ivan Hippolyte took the middleweight WMTC championship in November 1995 at Lumphini Stadium, reportedly the first foreigner ever to win a Lumphini fight.

Krabi-Krabong

Another traditional Thai martial art still practised in Thailand is *kràbìi-kràbong* (literally, 'sword-staff'). As the name implies, this sport focuses on hand-held weapons techniques, specifically the *kràbìi* (sword), *plông* (quarterstaff), *ngao* (halberd), *dàap sǎwng meu* (a pair of swords held in each hand) and *mái sun-sàwk* (a pair of clubs). Although for most Thais krabi-krabong is a ritual artefact to be displayed at festivals or tourist venues, the art is still solemnly taught according to a 400-year-old tradition handed down from Ayuthaya's Wat Phutthaisawan. The King of Thailand's elite bodyguards are trained in krabi-krabong; many Thai cultural observers perceive it as a 'purer' tradition than muay thai.

Like the muay thai of 70 years ago, modern krabi-krabong matches are held within a marked circle, beginning with a *wâi khruu* ceremony and accompanied throughout by a musical ensemble. Thai boxing techniques and judo-like throws are used along with weapons techniques. Although sharpened weapons are used, the contestants refrain from striking their opponents – the winner is decided on the basis of stamina and technical skill displayed. Although an injured fighter may surrender, injuries do not automatically stop a match.

For information on muay thai and krabi-krabong training courses in Thailand, see Martial Arts Training in the Courses section earlier in this chapter. ■

several times daily at Section 5, a building near the monks' residences. Some of the Thai monks here speak English and there are often Western monks or long-term residents available to translate. There is also a special Saturday session for foreigners at the Dhamma Vicaya Hall. Instruction is based on the Mahasi Sayadaw system of *satipatthana*, or mindfulness. Air-con bus No 8 and 12 both pass near the wat; the nearest Chao Phraya River Express pier is Tha Maharat.

Wat Pak Nam (Map 9) This very large wat, where hundreds of monks and nuns reside during the Buddhist Rains Retreat, has hosted many foreigners (especially Japanese) over the years. The meditation teacher, Phra Khru Phawana, speaks some English and there are usually people around who can translate. The emphasis is on developing concentration through *nimittas* (acquired mental images), in order to attain trance-absorption states. There is also a small English library. Pak Nam is on Thoet Thai Rd, Phasi Charoen, Thonburi. Take bus No 4, 9 or 103; the wat can also be reached by chartered long-tail boat from Tha Chang or Tha Saphaan Phut along the river and Thonburi canals.

Wat Rakhang Khositaram (Map 5) Only a few foreigners have studied at this temple, but the meditation teacher, Ajaan Mahathawon, from Ubon Province in the north-east, has quite a good reputation. The teaching tradition at Wat Rakhang is strongly Abhidhamma-based, with much emphasis given to Buddhist psychology. Vipassana is considered attainable without strong concentration by means of a dialectic process similar to Krishnamurti's 'choiceless awareness'. To study here, one ought to be able to speak Thai fairly well; otherwise, an interpreter will have to be arranged. Wat Rakhang is on Arun Amarin Rd, Thonburi. Cross-river ferries leave frequently from Tha Chang on the opposite bank of the Chao Phraya River.

Wat Cholaprathan Rangsarit The teachers here, Ajaan Pañña (the abbot) and Ajaan Khao, employ a modified version of the Mahasi Sayadaw system of satipatthana practice. Occasionally there's someone around who can translate; otherwise it will be necessary to arrange in advance for translation. This wat also serves as the Bangkok headquarters for monks from Wat Suanmok in Chaiya, Southern Thailand. Wat Chola-prathan is in Pak Kret, Nonthaburi Province; although not actually part of Bangkok, Nonthaburi is so connected to Bangkok's urban sprawl that you can hardly tell the difference.

World Fellowship of Buddhists The WFB, at 33 Sukhumvit Rd (Map 4), is a clearing house for information on Theravada Buddhism as well as dialogue between various schools of Buddhism. The centre hosts meditation classes from 2 to 5.30 pm on the first Sunday of every month.

Thai Language Study

Several language schools in Bangkok offer courses for foreigners in Thai language. Tuition fees average around 250B per hour. Some places will let you trade English lessons for Thai lessons, or, if not, you can usually teach English on the side to offset tuition costs. If you have an opportunity to 'shop around' it's best to enrol in programs that offer plenty of opportunity for linguistic interaction rather than rote learning or the passé 'natural method', which has been almost universally discredited for the over-attention given to teacher input.

Schools in Bangkok with the best reputations include:

Union Language School – CCT Bldg, 109 Surawong Rd (☎ 233-4482). Generally recognised as the best and most rigorous course (many missionaries study here). Employs a balance of structure and communication-oriented methodologies in 80-hour, four-week modules. Private tuition is also available.

AUA Language Center (Map 8) – 179 Ratchadamri Rd (☎ 252-8170). American University Alumni (AUA) runs one of the largest English-language teaching institutes in the world so this is a good place to meet Thai students. On the other hand, farangs who study Thai here complain that there's not enough interaction in class because of an emphasis on the 'natural approach'; others find the approach useful.

Nisa Thai Language School – YMCA Collins House, 27 Sathon Tai Rd (☎ 286-9323). This school has a fairly good reputation, though teachers may be less qualified than at Union or AUA language schools. In addition to all the usual levels, Nisa offers a course in preparing for the Baw Hok or Grade 6 examination, a must for anyone wishing to work in the public school system.

Bangkok's Chulalongkorn University (Map 7), the most prestigious university in Thailand, offers an intensive Thai studies course called 'Perspectives on Thailand'. The eight-week program includes classes in Thai language, culture, history, politics and economics, plus a

10-day upcountry field trip. Classes run six hours a day, six days a week (Saturday is usually a field trip) and are offered once a year from the first Monday in July to the last Friday in August. Students who have taken the course say they have found the quality of instruction excellent. Tuition costs around US$2400, including meals, transport and accommodation on the 10-day field trip. Room and board on campus are available, though it's much less expensive to live off campus. For further information write to Perspectives on Thailand, Continuing Education Center (☎ 218-3393, fax 214-4515) 5th Floor, Vidhyabhathan Bldg, Soi Chulalongkorn 12 (2), Chulalongkorn University, Bangkok 10330.

The YWCA's Siri Pattana Thai Language School (☎ 286-1936), 13 Sathon Tai Rd, gives Thai language lessons as well as preparation for the Baw Hok exam. Siri Pattana has a second branch at 806 Soi 38, Sukhumvit Rd.

Places to Stay

Bangkok has perhaps the best variety and quality of places to stay of any Asian capital – which is one of the reasons why it's such a popular destination for roving world travellers. Because of the wide distribution of places, your choice actually depends on what part of the city you want to be in – the tourist ghettos of Sukhumvit Rd and Silom-Surawong Rds, the backpackers' ghetto of Banglamphu (north of Ratchadamnoen Klang Rd), the central Siam Square area, Chinatown, the elegant hotels along the river or the old travellers' centre around Soi Ngam Duphli, off Rama IV Rd.

Chinatown, Hualamphong station and Banglamphu are the best all-round areas for seeing the real Bangkok, and are the cheapest districts for eating and sleeping. The Siam Square area is well located, in that it's more or less in the centre of Bangkok – this, coupled with the good selection of city buses that pass through the Rama I and Phayathai Rd intersection, makes even more of the city accessible. Siam Square also has good bookshops, several banks, excellent middle-range restaurants, travel agencies and eight movie theatres within 10 to 15 minutes walk.

In this chapter, bottom-end accommodation has been taken to mean places costing 60 to 500B per night; mid-range is roughly 500 to 1500B per night, and top end from 2000B up.

PLACES TO STAY – BOTTOM END

Banglamphu (Map 5)

If you're really on a tight budget, head for the Khao San Rd area, near the Democracy Monument, parallel to Ratchadamnoen Klang Rd. Ordinary bus No 2, 15, 17, 44, 56 or 59 will get you there, also air-con bus No 11 and 12. This is the main travellers' centre these days and new guesthouses are continually springing up.

Rates in Banglamphu are generally the lowest in Bangkok and although some of the places are barely adequate (bedbugs are sometimes a problem), a few are excellent value if you can pay just a bit more. At the bottom end, rooms are quite small and the walls dividing them are thin – in fact most are indistinguishable from one another. Some have small attached cafes with limited menus. Bathrooms are usually down the hall or out the back somewhere; mattresses may be on the floor.

The least expensive rooms are 80/120B (60/100B with haggling in the low season) for singles/doubles, though these are hard to come by due to the hordes of people seeking them out. More common are the 100/140B rooms. Occasionally, triple rooms are available for as low as 160B and dorm beds for 50B. During most of the year, it pays to visit several guesthouses before making a decision, but in the high season (December to February), you'd better take the first vacant bed you come across. The best time of day to find a vacancy is from 9 to 10 am. At night during the peak months (December to March), Khao San Rd is bursting with life.

A decade or so ago there were only two Chinese-Thai hotels on Khao San Rd, the Nith Jaroen Suk (now called New Nith Jaroen Hotel) and the Sri Phranakhon (now the Khao San Palace Hotel). Now there are close to 100 guesthouses in the immediate vicinity, too many to list exhaustively here. If you haven't already arrived with a recommendation in hand, you might best use the Banglamphu and Khao San Rd area maps and simply pick one at random for your first night. If you're not satisfied you can stow your gear and explore the area till something better turns up. A tip: the guesthouse rooms along Khao San Rd tend to be cubicles in modern shophouses, while those in Banglamphu's quieter lanes and alleys are often in old homes, some with a lot of character.

At the cheaper places it's not worth calling ahead as the staff usually won't hold a room for you unless you pay in advance. For places that *may* take phone reservations I've included phone numbers.

Central Banglamphu (Map 6) Simple, adequate places with rooms for 60 to 100B single, 80 to 120B double on or just off Khao San Rd – the hub of Bangkok's swirling backpacker universe – include:

Chada Guest House (with air-con, 250B), *CH Guest House* (dorm available for 40B), *Classic Place* (with air-con 380/480B), *Siri Guest House, Marco Polo Guest House* (also called *160 Guest House*), *Good Luck Guest House, VIP Guest House* (all rooms 80B), *Tong Guest House, Nat Guest House, Bonny Guest House* (dorm beds for 60B), *Top Guest House, Dior Guest House, Grand Guest House, PB Guest House* (dorm beds for 40B, snooker hall & gym), *Khao San Guest House, Buddy Guest House, Lek Guest House, Mam's Guest House, Hello Guest House* (with downstairs restaurant – has a word-of-mouth reputation for rudeness), *Prakorp's House & Restaurant* (highly recommended), *Chart Guest House* (with air-con 450B), *NS Guest House, Thai Guest House, Sitdhi Guest House* and, right on the corner of Khao San and Chakraphong Rds, *Ploy Guest House*.

The *Khaosan Palace Hotel* (☎ 282-0578), down an alley at 139 Khao San Rd, has seen a facelift; rooms cost 250/350B single/double with ceiling fan and private bath, 450/500B with air-con and hot water. Down a parallel alley, the *New Nith Jaroen Hotel* (☎ 281-9872) has similar rates and rooms to the Khaosan Palace, but slightly better service. The new *Nana Plaza Inn* (☎ 281-6402), near the Siri Guest House towards Khao San's east end, is a large, hotel-like enterprise built around a restaurant; air-con/hot water rooms go for 400/500B a single/double.

Two narrow alleys between Khao San and Rambutri Rds feature a string of cramped places that nonetheless manage to fill up. The alley furthest west off Khao San sports *Doll, Suneeporn, Leed, Jim's, AT* and *Green House* (☎ 281-0323). Except for Green House, all feature small, luggage-crammed lobbies with staircases leading to rooms layered on several floors and which cost around 60 to 100B. Green House is a bit more expansive, with a pleasant restaurant downstairs and rooms with fan and private bath for 150 to 200B. East down Khao San Rd is a wider alley that's a bit more open, with the small, Indian-run *Best Aladdin Guest House & Restaurant* (90/160B) and the hotel-like *Marco Polo Hostel* (120 to 250B, most rooms with private bath). Further south-east another alley has only one guesthouse, *New Royal* with nothing-special rooms from 100/150B with shared bath, 200 to 250B with attached bath. A final, very narrow alley just before you come to Tanao Rd has three standard-issue places, the *Harn, Nisa* and *VS*.

Parallel to Khao San Rd, but much quieter, is Trok Mayom, an alley reserved mostly for pedestrian traffic. *J & Joe* (☎ 281-2949, fax 281-1198) is an old teak home with pleasant rooms for 90 to 160B; not surprisingly, it's almost consistently full. There's also a *New Joe* (☎ 281-2948) on Trok Mayom, a rather modern-looking place set off the alley a bit with an outdoor cafe downstairs. Rooms cost 170/250B single/double with private bath, 350B with air-con; email and fax services are available. Farther east, towards Tanao Rd, *Ranee Guest House* charges 90/160B for single/double rooms with shared bath.

Orchid House (☎ 280-2691), a spiffy guesthouse near the Viengtai Hotel on Rambutri Rd (north of Khao San Rd), offers clean apartment-style rooms for 300B single with fan and bath, 350/400B single/double with air-con, or 450B for larger air-con rooms.

West Banglamphu (Map 5) Several long-running guesthouses are on sois between Chakraphong Rd and the Chao Phraya River, putting them within walking distance of the Phra Athit pier where you can catch express boats down or up the river. This area is also close to the Thonburi (Bangkok Noi) train station across the river, the National Museum and the National Theatre.

West of Chakraphong on Soi Rambutri, *Sawasdee House* (☎ 281-8138) follows the trend towards hotel-style accommodation in the Khao San Rd area, with a large restaurant downstairs and small to medium-sized rooms on several floors upstairs, all with private bath in the 120 to 300B range. Next along Soi Rambutri are the *Chusri* and *Terrace* guesthouses, all of which have adequate rooms for 50 to 60B per person but are nothing special. Right where Soi Rambutri makes a sharp turn to the south-west, the *Super Siam* catches the overflow from more preferred houses in the area.

Right around the bend along Soi Rambutri is the popular *Merry V Guest House* (☎ 282-9267) with rooms from 100 to 160B; the cosy, similarly priced *Green* is next door. At *My House*, on the same soi, the Thai-style downstairs sitting area looks nice, but the rooms upstairs are bare cubicles with open transoms – at 150B not much of a bargain. *Mango*, in a tin-roofed wooden house set back from Soi Rambutri, is the cheapest in the area at 60/120B.

Also in this vicinity, off the southern end of Soi Rambutri near Chao Fa Rd, the family-run *Chai's House* offers clean rooms for 100/200/300B single/double/triple, or 300B single/double with air-con, all with shared bath. It's a quiet, security-conscious place with a sitting area out front. The food must be cheap and good, as it's a favourite gathering spot for Thai college students on weekends.

Backtracking along Soi Rambutri and turning left into Soi Chana Songkhram, you'll find the *New Siam Guest House*, where quiet rooms cost 250B with shared bath, 350B with private bath, 450B with air-con.

Continue on towards the river and you'll reach Phra Athit Rd. On the eastern side of the road the *Peachy Guest House* (☎ 281-6471) and *New Merry V* are more like small hotels than family-type guesthouses. Peachy has a pleasant garden restaurant and singles/doubles cost 85/130B, 250/320B with air-con. The New Merry V, a bit north of Peachy, has comfortable rooms with private hot water showers for 260B, or with shared bath for 140B. Both are quite popular.

Parallel to Soi Chana on Trok Rong Mai, off Phra Athit Rd, are a few old-timers, most with only two-bed rooms. The *Apple Guest House*, at 10/1 Trok Rong Mai, may not look like much, but it's popular at 70/100B, plus dorm beds for 50B. There's also an *Apple Guest House II*, out on

Trok Kai Chae (off Phra Sumen Rd), for 100/120B, which one traveller recommended as being better.

East Banglamphu (Maps 5 & 6) There are several guesthouses clustered in the alleys east of Tanao Rd. In general, rooms are bigger and quieter here than at places on or just off Khao San Rd. *Central Guest House* (☎ 282-0667) is just off Tanao Rd on Trok Bowonrangsi (Map 6) – look for the rather inconspicuous signs. This is a very pleasant guesthouse, with clean, quiet rooms for 60B per person. There are some more spacious doubles for 120B.

Farther south, off Trok Bowonrangsi, the *Srinthip* (Map 6) has dorm beds at 50B, and singles/doubles from 70/100B. Around the corner on a small road parallel to Ratchadamnoen Klang Rd is *Sweety Guest House* (Map 5) with decent rooms for 70/80B single, 100/150B double. Sweety has a roof terrace for lounging and for hanging clothes. Opposite Sweety and next to the post office are the *Nat II* (Map 5) and *CH II*, both more like Khao San Rd standard issue, for 80/120B.

If you follow Trok Mayom east, away from Tanao Rd, you'll reach Din So Rd. Cross Din So, walk away from the roundabout and you'll see a sign for *Prasuri Guest House* (☎ 280-1428), down Soi Phra Suri on the right (Map 5); clean singles/doubles/triples cost 190/220/300B with fan, 330/360/390B with air-con – all rooms come with private bath.

South Banglamphu (Map 5) On the other side of Ratchadamnoen Klang Rd, south of the Khao San Rd area, are a couple of independent hotels and at least one guesthouse worth investigating. If you walk south along Tanao Rd from Ratchadamnoen Klang Rd, then left at the first soi, you'll come to *Hotel 90* (☎ 224-1012). It's mostly a short-time place but large, clean rooms with fan and private bath are 200/250B, 400B with air-con and TV.

Return to Tanao Rd, turn left and then take the right at Trok Sa-Ke towards the upper mid-range Royal Hotel, and after 50m or so you'll come to the *Palace Hotel* (☎ 224-1876) – an all air-con version of Hotel 90 with singles/doubles at 330/400B – and the friendly *P Guest House* nearby at 80/120B.

North Banglamphu (Map 5) Up on Phra Sumen Rd, opposite the north entrances to Wat Bowon, is the *Canalside Guest House* which, as its name suggests, overlooks a khlong. Basic rooms are 100B single/double – nothing to get excited about – but at least it's away from the Khao San ghetto.

At 11/1 Soi Surao, off Chakraphong Rd towards the Banglamphu department store and market, the friendly *BK Guest House* (☎ 281-3048) offers clean rooms with shared bath for 120/150B with fan, 300/350B with air-con. *PS Guest House* (☎ 282-3932), a Peace Corps favourite, is all the way at the end of Phra Sumen Rd towards the river, off the south side of Khlong Banglam-phu; its well-kept rooms go for 110 to 160B. Next door is the similar *Gipsy Guest House*, and further south-east the more modern-looking *Banglamphu Square Guest House*, which has a coffee shop downstairs. Across Phra Sumen Rd in this area is an alley with a couple of cheapies, friendly *KC* and cold *Sak*; although the latter is signed, they never seem interested in renting rooms!

Facing the north side of Khlong Banglamphu off Samsen Rd (the northern extension of Chakraphong Rd), the *New World House Apartment & Guest House* (☎ 281-5596) does both short and long-term room rentals starting at 400B per night. Rooms come with private hot water shower, air-con and a small balcony.

Also off Samsen Rd, farther north off Khlong Banglam-phu, is a small cluster of guesthouses in convenient proximity to the Tha Samphraya river express landing. On Soi 1 Samsen, just off Samsen Rd, the Khao San Rd-style *Truly Yours* (☎ 282-0371) offers 100/160B rooms over a large downstairs restaurant. A bit farther along Soi 1, *Villa Guest House* offers a quiet, leafy, private home with 10 rooms from 200 to 450B; it's often full. Up on Soi 3 Samsen (also known as Soi Wat Samphraya), are the *River House* (☎ 280-0876), *Home & Garden* (☎ 280-1475) and *Clean & Calm*, each with small but clean rooms with shared bath for 60 to 120B. Note that Soi 3 zigs left, then zags right before reaching these three guesthouses – a good 10 minute walk from Samsen Rd. River House is the best of the three; I've received complaints of an attempted sexual assault on a guest at the Clean & Calm. *Vimol Guest House* on Soi 4 (east of Samsen Rd) rounds out the Samsen Rd offerings, with rooms in a wooden house for 60 to 80B single, 100 to 120B double, 150 to 200B triple.

Out on noisy Samsen Rd itself, the grungy *Sukwawasdi (Suksawat) Hotel* offers air-con rooms for 350 to 450B with private bath – plus hot and cold running hookers. Farther north along Samsen, turn east on Soi 6 Samsen, and find *Nakhon Pink Hotel*, *Mitr Paisarn Hotel* and *Vorapong Guest House*, all places with overpriced rooms and a penchant for short-time trade. Continue along the zigzag soi almost all the way to the end and you'll come to the *AP*, a 70/140B guesthouse near Wat Mai Ama-ratarot.

The next river express stop north – and the last in the Banglamphu district – is next to Wisut Kasat Rd, where there are a couple of decent choices. The *MD Guest House* (☎ 280-3069), near Wat Intharawihan at 12 Wisut Kasat Rd (actually on a trok off Wisut Kasat), has very comfortable rooms with fan for 150B; the staff are very lax. The comfortable, mid-range *Trang Hotel* (☎ 282-2141), at 99/8 Wisut Kasat Rd, has air-con rooms from 1150B single/double, 1350B triple. Each of these is located east of Samsen Rd, so they're a good walk from the river.

Tha Thewet & National Library Area (Map 1)

The next district north of Banglamphu, near the National Library and the Chao Phraya Express stop of Tha Thewet, is another little travellers' enclave. Heading north up Samsen Rd from Wisut Kasat Rd, you'll come to *TV Guest House* (☎ 282-7451) at 7 Soi Phra Sawat, just off Samsen Rd to the east. It's clean, modern and good value at 40B for a dorm bed, 80B a double.

Continue for another half a km or so and cross the canal to the place where Phitsanulok, Samsen and Si Ayuthaya Rd intersect. Just beyond this junction is the National Library. On two parallel sois off Si Ayuthaya Rd towards the river (west from Samsen) are five guesthouses run by various members of the same extended family: *Tavee Guest House* (☎ 282-5983), *Sawatdee Guest House* (☎ 282-5349), *Backpacker's Lodge* (☎ 282-3231), *Shanti Lodge* (Map 1) (☎ 281-2497) and *Original Paradise Guest House* (☎ 282-8673). All are clean, well kept, fairly quiet and cost 50B for a dorm bed and from 100/150B for singles/doubles.

A sixth, independently run place on the same soi as Paradise is *Little Home Guest House* (☎ 282-1574), which is similar to the others in this area except that it has a busy travel agency in front. There's a good market across the road from both sois, and a few small noodle and rice shops along Krung Kasem Rd, the next parallel street south of Si Ayuthaya (and west of Samsen Rd), which leads to Tha Thewet.

Another way to get to and from the National Library area is by taking advantage of Tha Thewet, a Chao Phraya River Express pier. From the pier you walk east along Krung Kasem Rd to Samsen Rd, turn left, cross the canal and then take another left into Si Ayuthaya Rd. Ordinary bus No 16, 30 and 53, and air-con bus No 56 and 6 pass Si Ayuthaya Rd while going up and down Samsen Rd; ordinary bus No 72 terminates on the corner

of Phitsanulok and Samsen Rds, a short walk from Si
Ayuthaya. Air-con bus No 10 from the airport also
passes close to the area along Ratwithi Rd to the north,
before crossing Krungthon Bridge.

East of Samsen Rd, the *Bangkok International Youth
Hostel* (☎ 282-0950, 281-0361) is in the same neighbourhood at 25/2 Phitsanulok Rd. A bed in the fan dorm cost
70B a night, while in the air-con dorm it's 80B. Rooms with
fan and bath are 200B, while air-con singles/doubles
with hot water are 250/300B. The rooms with fan are
larger than the air-con rooms, and there's a cafeteria
downstairs. In 1992 the hostel stopped accepting non-
members as guests. Hostelling International (formerly
IYHF) annual membership costs 300B, or you can purchase a temporary membership for 50B. The Bangkok
hostel gets mixed reports – the rooms seem nice enough
but the staff can be quite rude.

If you want to be close to Ratchadamnoen Boxing
Stadium, or simply away from the river guesthouse
scene, have a look at *Venice House* (☎ 281-8262) at 548-
546/1 Krung Kasem Rd. This friendly, well-maintained
guesthouse is next to Wat Somanat, just around the
corner from Ratchadamnoen Nok Rd (walk north on
Ratchadamnoen Nok from the stadium, turn right on
Krung Kasem and walk about 80m till you see a sign for
Venice House). Rooms are air-con and cost 300/350B. It's
about a 15 minute walk from the Tha Thewet landing.

Chinatown & Hualamphong Station

This area is central and colourful although rather noisy.
There are numerous cheap hotels, but it's not a
travellers' centre like Soi Ngam Duphli or Banglamphu.
Watch your pockets and bag around the Hualamphong
area, both on the street and on the bus. The cream of the
razor artists operate here as the train passengers make
good pickings.

The *New Empire Hotel* (☎ 234-6990/6) is at 572
Yaowarat Rd (Map 8), near the Charoen Krung Rd intersection, a short walk from Wat Traimit. Air-con singles/
doubles with hot water are 450B, with a few more expensive rooms for up to 800B – a bit noisy but a great location
if you like Chinatown. The New Empire is a favourite
among Chinese Thais from the south.

Other Chinatown hotels of this calibre, most without
English signs out the front, can be found along Yaowarat,
Chakraphet and Ratchawong Rds (Map 5). The *Burapha
Hotel* (☎ 221-3545/9), situated at the intersection of
Mahachai and Charoen Krung Rds, on the edge of
Chinatown, is a notch better than the Empire and costs

500B single/double, and up to 1000B for a deluxe room. Likewise for the *Somboon Hotel* (☎ 221-2327), at 415 Yaowarat Rd.

Straddling the bottom and mid-range is the *River View Guest House* (☎ 234-5429, 235-8501) (Map 8) at 768 Soi Phanurangsi, Songwat Rd in the Talaat Noi area – wedged between Bangrak (Silom) and Chinatown. The building is behind the Jao Seu Kong Chinese Shrine, about 400m from the Royal Orchid Sheraton, in a neighbourhood filled with small machine shops. To get there, turn right from the corner of Si Phraya Rd (facing the River City shopping complex), take the fourth left, then the first right. Large rooms are 450B with fan and private bath, 700 to 800B with air-con and hot water. As the name suggests, many rooms have a Chao Phraya River view; the view from the 8th floor restaurant is superb, though you might have to wake up the staff to get a meal. If you call from the River City complex, someone from the guesthouse will pick you up.

Not far from the River View Guest House on Songwat Rd, the *Chao Phraya Riverside Guest House* has decent rooms for 250/300B single/double.

Along the eastern side of Hualamphong station is Rong Meuang Rd which has several dicey Chinese hotels. The *Sri Hualamphong Hotel*, at No 445, is one of the better ones – all rooms are 120B with fan. The *Sahakit (Shakij) Hotel* is a few doors down from the Sri Hualamphong towards Rama IV Rd and is quite OK too. Rooms are 100B up; if you stay here, try to get a room on the 4th floor which has a terrace with a view and the occasional breeze.

The market area behind the Station Hotel is full of cheap food stalls, and on a small soi parallel to Rong Meuang Rd is the *Hoke Aan Hotel*, yet another 100/120B Chinese hole-in-the-wall (but at least it's away from Rong Meuang traffic). Also off Rong Meuang Rd next to the Chinese market is the noisy but adequate *Nam Ia Hotel* for only 100B.

At least four other cheap Chinese hotels can be found west of the station along Maitrichit Rd, all in the 70 to 100B range.

Also convenient to the Hualamphong station – and more suitable for stays of more than a night or two – are the TT guesthouses. The somewhat easier to find *TT 2 Guest House* (☎ 236-2946) is at 516-518 Soi Sawang, Si Phraya Rd near the Mahanakhon Rd intersection. Rooms here are 180B. To find the TT 2 from the train station, turn left onto Rama IV Rd, right on Mahanakhon Rd, left on Soi Kaew Fa and then right on Soi Sawang. Or from Si Phraya Rd (take microbus No 6) turn directly onto Soi Sawang. To find the more hidden *TT 1 Guest House* (☎ 236-3053), at 138 Soi Wat Mahaphuttharam, off Mahanakhon Rd from the station, cross Rama IV Rd, walk left down Rama IV, then right onto Mahanakhon Rd, and follow the signs for TT 1. It's only about a 10 minute walk from the station. Dorm beds are just 40B; singles/doubles go for 150B. Baggage storage and laundry service are available; both TTs enforce a strict midnight curfew.

FF Guest House has a similar setup for 120B single, 150B double. From Hualamphong station, walk 200m east on Rama IV Rd and look for a small sign pointing down an alley to the guesthouse.

Siam Square (Map 7)

Several good places can be found in this centrally located area, which has the additional advantage of being located on the Khlong Saen Saep canal taxi route.

There are several lower mid-range places on or near Soi Kasem San 1, off Rama I Rd near the Jim Thompson House and National Stadium. The eight storey *Muangphol (Muangphon) Mansion* (☎ 215-0033), on the corner of Soi Kasem San 1 and Rama I Rd (931/8 Rama I Rd), has singles/doubles for 450/550B. It's good value – with aircon, hot water, a 24-hour restaurant and good service. Behind the Muangphol, off this soi, is the apartment-style *Pranee Building* (☎ 216-3181), which has one entrance next to the Muangphol and another on Rama I Rd. Fan-cooled rooms with private bath are 300 to 350B; air-con rooms with hot water start at 400B. There are no lifts. The Pranee also does long-term rentals at a 10% discount.

White Lodge (☎ 216-8867, 216-8228), at 36/8 Soi Kasem San 1, past the more expensive Reno Hotel on the left, offers clean if somewhat small rooms for 400B for singles/doubles. There's a pleasant terrace cafe out front. The next one down on Soi Kasem San 1 is the three storey *Wendy House* (☎ 216-2436), where small but clean rooms with air-con, hot shower and TV go for 400/450B. If you're carrying unusually heavy bags, note there's no lift. A small restaurant is on the ground floor.

Next up the soi is the ancient *Star Hotel* (☎ 215-3381) at 36/1 Soi Kasem San 1, a classic mid-60s Thai no-tell motel, with fairly clean, comfortable, air-con rooms with bath and TV for 550 to 650B a double, depending on the room – a bit steep for this area. Perhaps the higher rate is due to the curtained parking slots next to ground floor rooms, which hide cars belonging to guests from casual passers-by.

Opposite the Star is *A-One Inn* (☎ 215-3029, fax 216-4771) at No 25/12-15 Soi Kasem San 1, a friendly and pleasant place that gets a lot of return business. Fair-sized air-con doubles with bath and hot water are 400B; spacious triples are 500B (rates may drop 100B in low season). The similar *Bed & Breakfast Inn* diagonally opposite the A-One has room rates that fluctuate from 350 to 500B depending on demand; air-con rooms are substantially smaller than the A-One's but rates include continental breakfast.

Over on Soi Kasem San 2 – same soi as Jim Thompson's House – the efficient, 54-room *MP Villa* (☎ 214-4495) offers good 500B single/double rooms with air-con, phone, TV and fridge, plus a downstairs restaurant.

Silom & Surawong Rds Area (Map 8)

Several guesthouses and hotels can be found in the Silom and Surawong Rds area. The Indian-owned *Madras Lodge* (☎ 235-6761), on Vaithi Lane off Silom Rd, not far from the Uma Devi temple, has rooms with fan starting at 220B. The proprietor is a friendly Indian man from Madras (a retired gem dealer) and his kitchen serves delicious south Indian food.

Opposite the GPO, on Charoen Krung Rd, are a couple of guesthouses catering mostly to middle-class north Indians, Pakistanis and Bangladeshis – *Naaz* and *Kabana Inn* – each charging a reasonable 400 to 500B for air-con rooms.

Soi Ngam Duphli (Map 8)

This area off Rama IV Rd is where most budget travellers used to come on their first trip to Bangkok. With a couple of notable exceptions, most of the places to stay here are not especially cheap or even good value any more, and the area has taken on a rather seedy atmosphere. Overall, the Banglamphu area has better-value accommodation, although some travellers till prefer less crowded Soi Ngam Duphli. Several countries (Canada, Australia, Germany, Singapore, CIS, Korea, Laos, Myanmar) maintain embassies on nearby Sathon Tai Rd, so it's a convenient location for those with visa/passport business.

The entrance to the soi is on Rama IV Rd, near the Sathon Tai Rd intersection, and within walking distance of verdant Lumphini Park and the Silom Rd business district. Ordinary bus No 4, 13, 14, 22, 45, 47, 74, 109 and 115, and air-con bus No 7 all pass by the entrance to Soi Ngam Duphli along Rama IV Rd.

At the northern end of Soi Ngam Duphli near Rama IV Rd is *ETC Guest House* (☎ 286-9424, 287-1478), an efficiently run, multistorey place with a travel agency downstairs. Rooms are small and uninspiring but clean; rates are 120B with shared bath, 160/200B for singles/doubles with private bath. All room rates include a breakfast of cereal, fruit, toast and coffee or tea.

The cheerless *Tokyo Guest House* is farther south down Ngam Duphli; rooms are 100/140B for singles/doubles with shared bath.

Next south on the left is the *Anna Guest House* above the Anna Travel Agency. The odd place on the block, it reeks of cloying incense and has dilapidated rooms with shared bath for 100 to 180B; not recommended unless all else is full.

Further down Soi Ngam Duphli, the *Malaysia Hotel* (☎ 286-3582/7263), at 54 Soi Ngam Duphli, was once Bangkok's most famous travellers' hotel. Its 120 air-con, hot water rooms cost from 498B for a standard single or double, 586B with a TV and small fridge, and 700B with a TV, larger fridge and carpet. The Malaysia has a swimming pool which may be used by visitors for 50B per day (it's free for guests of course).

Since the 1970s, the Malaysia has made a conscious effort to distance itself from the backpackers' market; for a while it seemed to be catering directly to the lonely male hired-sex market. The big sign out front advertising 'Day-Off International Club – Paradise for Everyone' has dropped the final phrase 'You'll Never Be Alone Again' and there seem to be fewer hookers around the lobby than in the old days – at least before midnight. After the Patpong bars close, bar girls who didn't pick up an outside customer earlier in the evening tend to congregate in the hotel coffee shop.

The *Tungmahamek Privacy Hotel* (☎ 286-2339/8811), across the road to the south of the Malaysia, is also fully air-con and costs 300 to 400B for a double. Many 'short-time' residents here give the place a sleazy feel, though it's less of a 'scene' than the Malaysia. South of the Privacy on Soi Ngam Duphli is *Honey*, an apartment building on the left with tiny, cheap rooms which mostly cater to prostitutes, procurers and their clients for 100 to 400B per night.

In the other direction from the Malaysia is the *LA Hotel* (the English sign just says 'Hotel'), which generally refuses Western guests unless brought there by a prostitute.

Turn from Ngam Duphli into Soi Si Bamphen and before you reach the Boston Inn there is an alley to the right. Near the end of the alley, *TTO Guest House* (☎ 286-6783, fax 287-1571) offers clean air-con rooms with private bath for 350 to 400B, plus a few fan rooms for 250B. Though it isn't cheap, it's a well-managed place with spacious rooms and reasonably friendly staff.

Across Soi Si Bamphen in another alley is the *Home Sweet Home Guest House*. It's a friendly place with rooms at 120/150B for singles/doubles. Rooms facing Si Bamphen are newer, nicer and noisier; rooms on the alley are quieter. Farther down Si Bamphen is another alley on the right with guesthouses on both corners that change their names on average every other year; at the moment they're called *Kenny* and *Turkh*. Both have dingy rooms upstairs that go for 150 to 250B; don't be fooled by the OK-looking restaurants downstairs – the rooms are quite shabby. Down this same alley on the right is the even more miserable-looking *Freddy 3 Guest House* with basic accommodation for 80 to 100B. Let's not mince words; this alley has a reputation for harbouring junkies.

The notorious *Boston Inn* is still a blight on Soi Si Bamphen. Decaying rooms have slid to 60/120B for singles/doubles, but neither the fan nor the water in the attached bath have been functioning for the last couple of years. A suspicious number of drug overdoses in Boston Inn rooms have been reported to the police; among travellers the hotel has a reputation as a Hell's Fawlty Towers. Rumour has it the owner was planning to renovate (at one time the Boston was one of the better places in the Soi Ngam Duphli area), but for now this one's definitely at the very bottom of the list.

If you turn left at the next soi down Si Bamphen, then take the first right, you'll end up in a cul-de-sac with four guesthouses of varying quality. First up on the right as you enter the soi is the clean, secure and well-managed *Lee 4 Guest House*, with rooms for 120B with shared bath, or 150/180B with private bath. Around the corner, *Madam Guest House* gets mixed reports for its 100 to 120B rooms and nightly drinking parties. Next door, the *Lee 3 Guest House*, the best of the three Lee guesthouses, is also quite pleasant and has large rooms from 100B. The *Sala Thai Daily Mansion* (☎ 287-1436) is at the end of the alley and has large, very clean rooms for 150 to 200B. A sitting area with TV on the 3rd floor makes for a pleasant gathering place, and there is a breezy rooftop terrace. The owner speaks English and her design background is evident in the tasteful furnishings. Many repeat or long-term guests fill the rooms here.

If you go north along the soi off Si Bamphen that passes the previously mentioned guesthouses you'll come to a left turn which dead-ends at Soi Saphan Khu (parallel to Soi Ngam Duphli). Turn right and you'll come to two guesthouses on your left, *Charlie House* and

Four Brothers Best House. Well-run Charlie House (☎ 679-8330, fax 679-7308) aims for a slightly more upscale market with carpeted rooms with air-con, phone and TV starting at 450B. Smoking is prohibited; a sign reads 'Decently dressed ladies, gentlemen and their children are welcome'. Four Brothers (☎ 678-8822) costs 400B per day for air-con rooms; the game arcade downstairs can be a bit noisy.

Back out on Soi Si Bamphen heading south-east are two more guesthouses. First on the left is the original *Lee 1 Guest House*, with decaying rooms from 80B, followed by the better *Freddy 2*, a clean, well-run place with 80/150B and a contingent of resident Thai bar girls.

Sukhumvit Rd (Map 4)

Staying in this area puts you in the newest part of Bangkok and the furthest from old Bangkok near the river. Except to the lower-numbered sois, taxis take longer to get here because of the one-way street system. The majority of the hotels in this area are in the middle price range.

The oldest hostelry in the Sukhumvit area is the historic *Atlanta Hotel* (Map 4) (☎ 252-1650, 252-6069), at 78 Soi 2 (Soi Phasak), Sukhumvit Rd (Map 7). Owned since its 1950s construction by Dr Max Henn, a former secretary to the maharaja of Bikaner and owner of Bangkok's first international pharmacy, the Atlanta is a simple but reliable stand-by with clean, comfortable rooms in several price categories. Rooms with private shower, fan, balcony and one large double bed cost 300/400B single/double, while similar rooms with twin beds (no balcony) go for 300/400/500B single/double/triple. Air-con rooms with hot showers and built-in safe boxes go for 450/550/605B single/double/triple on the 3rd floor, 50B extra for lower floors. Monthly stays paid in advance warrant a 10% discount; children under 12 can stay with parents for 50B over the single or double-room rate.

The Atlanta's 1954-vintage swimming pool was the first hotel pool in Thailand; the original 50s-era hotel lobby is occasionally used as a backdrop for fashion shoots. The subdued, simply decorated coffee shop – formerly part of the Continental, a restaurant that once served royalty and foreign diplomats – features a heavily annotated menu (itself a crash course in Thai cuisine), a selection of British, German and French newspapers, a sound system playing Thai, classical and jazz (including an hour of King Bhumibol compositions beginning at noon) and evening video selections which include film classics with Thailand themes (eg *Chang, Bridge on the River Kwai*). A map room and letter-writing lounge round out the offerings at this Bangkok institution.

The *Golden Palace Hotel* (Map 4), at 15 Soi 1, Sukhumvit Rd, has a swimming pool, is well situated and costs 400 to 500B for a double with air-con and bath. The clientele here are mostly middle-class tourists 'on a budget', but the Golden Palace has seen better days. On the next soi east, the quiet *Best Inn* (☎ 253-0573) at 75/5-6 Soi 3, Sukhumvit Rd, provides smallish rooms with fan for 350B and air-con rooms for 450B. Another entry in the inner Sukhumvit area is *Thai House Inn* (☎ 255-4698, fax 253-1780), between sois 5 and 7. Rooms with air-con and hot water are 500B a single or double; facilities include a safety-deposit service and a coffee shop. Back on the other side of Sukhumvit Rd, *Uncle Rey* (☎ 252-5565) at 7/10 Soi 4, offers simple air-con lodging for 400B.

Moving farther out on Sukhumvit Rd, the *Miami Hotel* (Map 4, ☎ 252-5140/4759/5036), at Soi 13, Sukhumvit Rd, dates back to the 60s and 70s R&R days. The room and service quality seems to seesaw every three years or so, but recent reports reckon it's decent value at 500/550B single/double for air-con rooms and a swimming pool. The *Crown Hotel* (Map 4) (☎ 258-0318), at Soi 29, Sukhumvit Rd, is in decline and mostly gets short-time traffic these days.

Disra House (☎ 258-5102), on the access street to Villa Theatre between sois 33 and 33/1, has similar rooms for 80 to 120B.

Thonburi (Map 1)

The Artists Place (☎ 852-0056, fax 862-0074), at 63 Soi Thiam Bunyang off Soi Krung Thonburi 1 (near Wong Wian Yai) was recently opened by Thai artist Charlee Sodprasert as a place for visiting artists to congregate and work. Singles and doubles cost 80 to 120B, while more expensive rooms go for 350B. Studio space is available. It's a bit difficult to find, so call for directions first. Very few farangs or other tourists stay on the Thonburi side of the river, so this is a good choice for people who want to be in the Bangkok milieu while getting away from the tourist scene.

Airport

The well-run *We-Train Guest House* (☎ 566-1774, 566-2288, fax 566-3481) at 501/1 Mu 3, Dechatung Rd, Sikan, Don Meuang, has rooms from as low as 150B (dorm

rooms) to 770B air-con rooms. For more details see
Airport, Middle range.

PLACES TO STAY – MIDDLE

Bangkok is saturated with small and medium-sized
hotels in this category. The clientele at hotels in this range
are a very mixed bunch of Asian business travellers,
Western journalists on slim expense accounts, economy-
class tour groups, along with a smattering of independent
tourists who seem to have chosen their hotels at random.
Not quite 'international class', these places often offer
guests a better sense of being in Thailand than the luxury
hotels.

During the late 1980s, when there was a shortage of
tourist accommodation, many mid-range hotels
doubled their rates in a grab for short-term profit over
long-term goodwill. In the off-season (March to November) you may be able to get a low-occupancy discount
off the rates listed below.

Banglamphu (Maps 5 & 6)

Before Khao San Rd was 'discovered', the most popular
Banglamphu hotel was the *Viengtai Hotel* (☎ 280-5434,
fax 281-8153) at 42 Rambutri Rd (Map 6). Over the past
decade or so the Viengtai has continually raised its prices
(not always concomitant with an upgrading of facilities)
until it now sits solidly in the middle price range of
Bangkok hotels; singles/doubles are 1400B.

On Phra Athit Rd, close to the Tha Phra Athit river-
boat stop, the apartment-style *Phra Athit Mansion* offers
rooms with air-con, TV, hot water showers and fridge for
650B single/double and 850B triple.

Besides the Oriental and the Atlanta, the oldest continually operating hotel in the city is the *Royal Hotel*
(☎ 222-9111/20), still going strong on the corner of
Ratchadamnoen Klang and Atsadang Rds near the
Democracy Monument. The Royal's 24-hour coffee shop
is a favourite local rendezvous; this is one of the few
upper mid-range places where there are as many Asian
as non-Asian guests. Singles/doubles start at 960B;
during low season this can sometimes be negotiated
down to around 700B. Incidentally, most of the taxi
drivers know this hotel as the 'Ratanakosin' (as the Thai
sign on top of the building reads), not as the Royal.
During the bloody May 1992 protests against General
Suchinda's appointment as prime minister, the Royal
served as a makeshift hospital for injured demonstra-
tors. A place of similar vintage and atmosphere, the

Majestic Hotel (☎ 281-5000, fax 280-0965), can be found right around the corner at 97 Ratchadamnoen Klang Rd near the Democracy Monument. Here rooms start at 1200B.

Another mid-range place in this area is the *Thai Hotel* (☎ 282-2833), at 78 Prachatipatai Rd, which has singles/doubles at 1100/1250B.

Chinatown (Map 5)

Mid-range hotels in the Chinatown area of Bangkok are tough to find. Best bets are the 80-room *Chinatown* (☎ 226-1267), at 526 Yaowarat Rd, which has rooms for 700 to 1200B, and the *Miramar Hotel* (☎ 222-4191), 777 Mahachai Rd, where standard singles/doubles cost 780 to 1800B.

Siam Square & Pratunam (Map 7)

This area tends to offer either upper-end budget or top-end luxury hotels, with little in the middle. *Krit Thai Mansion* (☎ 215-3042), out on busy Rama I Rd opposite the National Stadium, costs 700 to 800B for rooms with air-con, hot water, private bath, telephone, colour TV/video, fridge and security parking. The coffee shop downstairs is open 24 hours. Reports are mixed on this one – some like it, others don't. An old Siam Square stand-by, the *Reno Hotel* (☎ 215-0026) on Soi Kasem San 1 is a veteran from the Vietnam War days when a spate of hotels opened in Bangkok with names of US cities. Singles/doubles/triples with air-con and hot water cost 550 to 990B; there's a pool on the premises.

The *Siam Orchid Inn* (☎ 255-2119, fax 255-3144), off Soi Gaysorn close to Le Meridien President Hotel, offers well-appointed rooms with all the amenities for around 1500B.

The multistorey *Tong Poon Hotel* (☎ 216-0020, fax 215-0450), at 130 Soi 8 Rama VI Rd (formerly called Soi 4 Rong Meuang) is a mid-price place favoured for low-budget conventions and Asian tour groups. Although rack rates for large rooms with air-con, colour TV and phones are 1800/2000B single/double, discounts to around 1000 to 1500B are sometimes available. The Tong Poon has a coffee shop and pool, and it's a short tuk-tuk ride from Hualamphong station.

Very near the heart of Pratunam, the *Opera Hotel* (☎ 252-4031, fax 253-5360), at 16 Soi Somprasong 1, Phetburi Rd, features air-con doubles with hot water from 550 to 800B. The Opera also has a swimming pool and coffee shop.

Bangkok Noorie (☎ 252-3340) at 178/7 Soi Wuttiphan, Ratchaprarop Rd near the Indra Hotel, charges 650 to 850B for reasonable air-con rooms. Nearby *Classic Inn* (☎ 208-0496) off Ratchaprarop Rd costs around 400B for decent air-con rooms. A long walk east along the soi almost opposite the Indra (off Ratchaprarop Rd) leads eventually to *Borarn House* (☎ 246-4525, fax 253-3639), a Thai-style apartment building at 487/48 Soi Wattanasin, with singles/doubles for 850/950B with air-con and TV. The OK *Siam Hotel* (☎ 252-5081), at 1777 Phetburi Rd, has 120 rooms; singles/doubles cost 880/1060B.

Just north of Siam Square, in the Victory Monument area, are several hotels, including the decent *Century Hotel* (☎ 246-7800) at 9 Ratchaprarop Rd. This hotel has 96 rooms at 972B for singles or doubles. At the more upmarket *Continental Hotel* (☎ 278-1596/8), 971/16 Phahonyothin Rd, singles cost from 1200 to 2400B. The Indochina War-era *Florida Hotel* (Map 7) (☎ 247-0990), at 43 Phayathai Square, Phayathai Rd, has singles/doubles at 700/800B.

Silom & Surawong Rds Area (Map 8)

This area is packed with upper mid-range places; discounts are often given from April to October. Bangkok has a YMCA and YWCA, both in the Silom and Surawong Rds area. The *YMCA Collins International House* (☎ 287-1900/2727, fax 287-1996), at 27 Sathon Tai Rd, has air-con rooms with TV, telephone and private bath from 1377B. Guests may use the Y's massage room, gym, track and swimming pool. The *YWCA* (☎ 286-1936) is at 13 Sathon Tai Rd and has cheaper air-con rooms starting at 567B.

Off the south side of Silom Rd *Niagara Hotel* (☎ 233-5783/4) at 26 Soi Seuksa Withaya, offers clean air-con rooms with hot water and telephone for 550 to 600B.

A decent upper middle-range choice is the *Newrotel* (☎ 237-1094, fax 237-1102) at 1216/1 Charoen Krung Rd, which is near the GPO and the river. Air-con singles/doubles cost 1200B.

Also off Silom Rd is *Bangkok Christian Guest House* (☎ 253-3353) at 123 Sala Daeng Soi 2, Convent Rd. It has very nice air-con rooms from 650B including breakfast. Offering good service is the *Woodlands Inn*, on the soi that runs along the northern side of the GPO. Clean, air-con rooms with hot water, TV and fridge are 600B for singles/doubles. Downstairs is an air-con Indian restaurant, the Cholas. The two hotels nearest Patpong Rd – the *Suriwong* and the *Rose* – are in the 700 to 800B range. They can't really be recommended for light sleepers as

they suffer from heavy people-traffic from Patpong bars.
The Rose has a primarily gay clientele.

Classic mid-range hotels along Surawong Rd include
the *New Fuji* (☎ 234-5364) at No 299-310 with rooms from
1124 to 1338B and the *New Trocadero Hotel* (☎ 234-
8920/8929) at No 34, where singles or doubles are 770 to
1400B. Because they both offer good service and amenities for under 1500B, these two have been favourites
among journalists. A fair number of package tours stop
here as well. A newer entry at No 173/8-9, *La Residence*
(☎ 235-4795, fax 233-3301), is an intimate 23 room place
with rates of 750 to 1550B.

For anyone who wants to be near the Royal Orchid
Sheraton, River City complex and river (Tha Si Phraya
landing), the *Orchid Inn* (☎ 234-8934, fax 234-4159) at
719/1 Si Phraya Rd provides decent mid-range value at
750/900B (discounts of 100 to 150B often available) for
tidy air-con rooms with TV and mini-fridge. Along with
its proximity to the river, another advantage here is that
the ordinary No 36 bus and microbus No 6 each terminate almost directly opposite the hotel. The downside is
the high number of touts and big-spending tourists in
the neighbourhood.

Sukhumvit Rd (Map 4)

This area is choked with hotels costing 800 to 1500B.
Stick to the lower numbered sois to save crosstown
travel time.

The *Federal Hotel* (Map 4, ☎ 253-0175), at 27 Soi 11,
Sukhumvit Rd, is a favourite among Vietnam War and
Peace Corps vets but I've found the accommodation
overpriced at 700 to 1050B, especially for the added-on
rooms at ground level; these occasionally flood in the
rainy season, when they're available for 550B. The
modest pool and coffee shop are the main attractions.
The well-run *Parkway Inn*, on Sukhumvit Rd at Soi 4,
next to the Landmark Hotel (Map 4) is better value at 800
to 1000B a night; amenities include a rooftop pool.

Moving farther east along Sukhumvit Rd, the well-
run *Carlton Inn* (☎ 258-0471, fax 258-3717) at 22/2-4 Soi
21, Sukhumvit Rd, has decent rooms from 750B. A bit
nicer are the two *City Lodges* on sois 9 (☎ 253-7680) and
19 (☎ 254-4783). Rooms at either location are 1016B for a
single or double, and include air-con, telephone, TV/
video and mini-bar. Other mid-range hotels in the
Sukhumvit Rd area include:

Asoke Place, 4/49 Soi 21, Sukhumvit Rd (☎ 258-3742); 20
rooms, singles/doubles 650 to 850B

Business Inn, 155/4-5 Soi 11, Sukhumvit Rd (☎ 254-7981); 70 rooms, singles/doubles 500 to 700B

China Inn, 19/27-28 Soi 19, Sukhumvit Rd (☎ 255-7571); 27 rooms, singles/doubles 650 to 750B

Comfort Inn, 153/11 Soi 11, Sukhumvit Rd; 60 rooms, singles/doubles 810 to 1300B

Dynasty Inn, 5/4-5 Soi 4, Sukhumvit Rd (☎ 250-1397); 55 rooms, singles/doubles 850 to 950B

Euro Inn, 249 Soi 31, Sukhumvit Rd (☎ 259-9480); 82 rooms, singles/doubles 1100 to 1570B

Fortuna Hotel (Map 4), 19 Sukhumvit Rd (☎ 251-5121); 110 rooms, singles/doubles 900/1100B

Grace Hotel (Map 4), 12 Nana Neua (Soi 3), Sukhumvit Rd (☎ 253-0651); 542 rooms, 760 to 1507B

Grand Inn, 2/7-8 Soi 3, Sukhumvit Rd (☎ 254-9021); 24 rooms, 800 to 1200B

Manhattan (Map 4), Soi 15, Sukhumvit Rd (☎ 252-7141/9); 206 rooms, 1400B up

Nana Hotel (Map 4), 4 Nana Tai, Sukhumvit Rd (☎ 255-0122); 224 rooms, 960 to 1500B

Rajah Hotel (Map 4), 18 Soi 4, Sukhumvit Rd (☎ 255-0040); 450 rooms, singles/doubles from 1287B

Rex Hotel, 762/1 Soi 32; Sukhumvit Rd (☎ 259-0106); 131 rooms, singles/doubles 1100 to 1310B

White Inn, 41 Soi 4, Sukhumvit Rd (☎ 251-1662); 11 rooms, singles/doubles 750B

Airport

Finding decent, moderately priced accommodation near the airport is difficult. Most of the hotels in this area charge nearly twice as much as comparable hotels in the city. Typical among these price-gougers is *Don Meuang Mansion* (☎ 566-3095) at 118/7 Soranakom Rd, Don Meuang, which looks classy on the outside but asks 1000 to 1200B for a small, stuffy room that would cost at the most 500 to 750B in Bangkok. It's possible to negotiate a lower rate of 800B.

Alternatively, you could stay at the well-run *We-Train Guest House* (☎ 566-1774, 566-2288, fax 566-3481), at 501/1 Mu 3, Dechatung Rd, Sikan, Don Meuang. Simple but very clean fan rooms with two beds and private bath cost 450B single/double or 770B with air-con (extra beds cost 150B). You can also get a bed in a fan-cooled dorm for 150B, air-con 200B. To these rates add the usual 10% service charge, but no tax since it's operated by a non-profit women's organisation (male guests are welcome). Facilities include a pool, Thai massage, laundry service, coffee shop and beauty salon. One major drawback is We-Train's distance from the airport – you must get a taxi to cross the highway and railway, then go about three km west along Dechatung Rd to the Thung Sikan school (rohng rian thûng sĭi-kan). If you don't have much luggage, walk across the airport pedestrian bridge to reach Don Meuang, then get a taxi – it's much cheaper that way because you avoid the high taxi-desk fees. From the guesthouse there are usually no taxis in the area when you're ready to return to the airport or continue on to Bangkok, but We-Train can organise transport to and from the airport for a steep 200B one way.

Other Areas

North of central Bangkok in Nonthaburi – about 40 minutes away by Chao Phraya express boat – *Thai House*, (☎ 280-0740, fax 280-0741) at 3677/4 Muu 8 Tambon Bang Meuang, Amphoe Bang Yai, is popular with repeat visitors for its traditional Thai decor and for the cooking courses taught on the premises. Rates run 900B for a single, 1200B for a double. Thai House maintains a reservation office in Banglamphu at 22 Phra Athit Rd.

Aquarius Guest House (☎ /fax 286-217), at 243 Soi Hutayan, Soi Suan Phlu, off Sathon Tai Rd, is a quiet Thai-style place that courts a gay male clientele. It has satellite TV and a shady courtyard. Rooms cost 750B per night.

Other medium-priced hotels include:

Baron Hotel, 544 Soi Huay Khwang, Ratchadaphisek Rd, Huay Khwang (☎ 246-4525); 155 rooms, singles/doubles 600/ 650B

Golden Dragon, 20/21 Ngam Wongwan Rd (10 km from the airport) (☎ 588-4414/4415); 114 rooms, 770 to 1320B

Golden Horse Hotel, 5/1 Damrongrak Rd (☎ 281-6909); 130 rooms, 600 to 1800B

Liberty Hotel, 215 Pratipat Rd, Saphan Khwai (☎ 271-0880); 209 rooms, singles/doubles 475B to 871B

Royal Lake View, 649/1-76 Asoke-Din Daeng Rd; 176 rooms, 1200B

PLACES TO STAY – TOP END

Bangkok has all sorts of international standard tourist hotels, from the straightforward package places to some of Asia's classic hotels. Three of Bangkok's luxury hotels consistently make Condé Nast *Traveler's* annual world-wide top 25 list: the Oriental, the Regent and the Shangri-La. Although there's no single area for top-end hotels, you'll find quite a few of them around the Siam Square area, along the parallel Surawong and Silom Rds, and along the river, while many of the slightly less expensive 'international standard' places are scattered along Sukhumvit Rd.

Due to an overall room glut, at all but the top-rated places such as the Oriental, Regent Bangkok or Grand Hyatt Erawan, recent rates quoted are often lower than those from 1994. With lower occupancy rates, you should still be able to negotiate discounts of up to 40% on the rates listed. Booking through a travel agency almost always means lower rates – also try asking for a hotel's 'corporate' discount. Several luxury hotels have even lowered their rack rates since last edition.

A welcome trend in Bangkok hotels in the past few years has been the appearance of several European-style 'boutique' hotels – small, business-oriented places of around 100 rooms or fewer with rates in the 2000 to 3000B range – like the *Mansion Kempinski* (Map 4, Soi 11 Sukhumvit Rd), *Princess* (269 Lan Luang Rd), *Somerset* (Soi 15 Sukhumvit Rd) and *Swiss Lodge* (Convent Rd). Many experienced Bangkok business travellers prefer this type of hotel because they get personal service for about 1000B less than the bigger hotels; also these smaller hotels don't accept tour groups, so regular guests don't have to wade through crowds in the lobby.

Newer hotel standouts include the *Chateau de Bangkok* (☎ 290-0125, fax 290-0167) at 25 Soi Ruam Rudi, Ploenchit Rd, behind the US embassy. Owned by the French hotel group Accor, it offers 139 service studios – one and two-bedroom apartments, each with walk-in closet, IDD phone and fax – for 2500B a night.

The less expensive, tastefully decorated *Hotel Rembrandt* (Map 4) (☎ 261-7100, fax 261-7107) at Soi 18, Sukhumvit Rd, has 406 large rooms that were going for 2700B in 1996 though rack rates were listed at 3000B and over. Facilities include a swimming pool and the best Mexican restaurant in Bangkok, Señor Pico's of Los Angeles. Another advantage is the Rembrandt's proximity to Queen Sirikit National Convention Centre, off Soi 16.

All of the hotels in this category will add a 10% service charge plus 7% tax to hotel bills on departure.

On the River

The 120-year-old *Oriental Hotel* (☎ 236-0400/39), on the Chao Phraya River (Map 8), is one of the most famous hotels in Asia, right up there with the Raffles in Singapore or the Peninsula in Hong Kong. What's more, it's also rated as one of the very best hotels in the world, as well as being just about the most expensive in Bangkok. The hotel prides itself on providing highly personalised service with a staff of 1200 (for 398 rooms) – once you've stayed here they'll remember your name, what you like to eat for breakfast, even what type of flowers you prefer in your room.

Nowadays the Oriental is looking more modern and less classic – the original Author's Wing is dwarfed by the Tower (built in 1958) and River (1976) wings. Authors who have stayed at the Oriental and had suites named after them include Joseph Conrad, Somerset Maugham, Noel Coward, Graham Greene, John le Carré, James Michener, Gore Vidal and Barbara Cartland. The hotel sits at 48 Oriental Ave; room rates start at 6500B, suites as much as 10 times that. It's worth wandering in if only to see the lobby (no shorts, sleeveless shirts or thongs allowed – dress politely or you'll be refused entry).

On the Thonburi bank of the Chao Phraya River, a bit south of central Bangkok, the tastefully appointed, 420-room *Marriott Royal Garden Riverside Hotel*, at 257/1-3 Charoen Nakhon Rd, near Krungthep Bridge (☎ 476-0021, fax 460-1805), is highly valued for its serene atmosphere and expansive, airy public areas. The grounds encompass a large swimming pool, lush gardens, two lighted tennis courts and a world-class health club. Trader Vic's and Benihana are among the hotel's six restaurants; the *Manohra*, a luxury rice-barge dinner cruiser, is also moored here. A free water-taxi service shuttles guests back and forth to the Oriental and River City piers every hour from 7 am to 11 pm. Rack rates for very spacious rooms are 4200B, or 4800B with a river view.

Two other luxury gems along the river are the *Shangri-La* (☎ 236-7777, fax 236-8570) at 89 Soi Wat Suan Phlu, Charoen Krung Rd (Map 8); and the *Royal Orchid Sheraton* (☎ 266-0123, fax 236-8320), 2 Captain Bush Lane, Si Phraya Rd (Map 8). The Shangri-La has 694 rooms starting from 5265B, and its own helicopter transport from the airport, while the Sheraton (776 rooms, from 5649B) is known for crisp, efficient service (the business centre is open 24 hours).

The *Menam* (☎ 289-1148/9, fax 291-9400), towering over the river at 2074 Charoen Krung Rd, Yannawa, has 718 rooms from 4237B up. The *Royal River* (☎ 433-0300, fax 433-5880), at 670/805 Charan Sanitwong Rd, Thonburi, has 458 rooms from 2300B; the latter receives lots of tour groups.

Siam Square & Pratunam (Map 7)

People accustomed to heady hotels claim the plush *Regent Bangkok* (☎ 251-6127, fax 253-9195), at 155 Ratchadamri

Rd, tops the Oriental in overall quality for the money. Local calls are free at the Regent – probably the only luxury hotel in the city to offer this courtesy; it's also one of the city's top choices for visiting business travellers because of its efficient business centre and central location. The hotel also offers (for 1650B an hour) an 'office on wheels', a high-tech, multi-passenger van equipped with computers, cell phones, fax machines, TVs/VCRs and swivelling leather seats so that small business conferences can be held while crossing town in Bangkok's turgid traffic. The Regent's 415 rooms start at 5885B.

Another top executive choice is the *Hilton International Bangkok* (☎ 253-0123, fax 253-6509) on Withayu Rd, where you won't find tour groups milling around in the lobby; its 343 rooms start at 4400B. The expansive grounds are a major plus; only Bangkok's older hotel properties are so fortunate.

Another of this generation, the 400-room *Siam Intercontinental* (☎ 253-0355, fax 253-0355), ensconced on spacious grounds at 967 Rama I Rd (near Siam Square), takes in a mix of well-heeled pleasure and business travellers. Standard rooms start at 5179B.

The *Grand Hyatt Erawan* (☎ 254-1234, fax 253-5856), at the intersection of Ratchadamri and Ploenchit Rds, was built on the site of the original Erawan Hotel five years ago (which went up at the same time as the Royal but was torn down some years ago) and has obvious ambitions to become the city's number-one hotel. The neo-Thai architecture has been well executed; inside is the largest collection of contemporary Thai art in the world. Adding to the elite atmosphere, rooms at the rear of the hotel overlook the Bangkok Royal Sports Club racetrack. For most visitors – whether for business or leisure – it vies with the Novotel Bangkok on Siam Square for having the best location of all the city's luxury hotels vis-à-vis transport and proximity to shopping. Huge rooms start at 5000B.

Thailand's own Amari Hotels & Resorts opened the 34 storey *Amari Watergate* (☎ 267-653-9000, fax 653-9045) at the end of 1994, right in the centre of Bangkok's busiest district, Pratunam. The neo-classic interior design blends Thai and European motifs, guest rooms are large and facilities include a 900-sq-metre Clark Hatch fitness centre, free-form pool, two squash courts, Thai massage, a 24 hour business centre, an American-style pub and very highly rated Cantonese and Italian restaurants. The hotel stands on Phetburi Rd near the Ratchaprarop Rd intersection. Tour groups check in via a separate floor and lobby while individually booked guests use the main lobby, a boon to business travellers. Huge rooms cost 4200/4600B single/double; the three top floors contain more luxuriously appointed executive rooms at 5200/5800B.

Other brand new Amari hotels in downtown Bangkok include the *Amari Atrium* (☎ 318-5295, fax 319-0789) on Phetburi Tat Mai Rd east of Soi Asoke (3000/3200B single/double) and the *Amari Boulevard* (Map 4, ☎ 255-2930, fax 255-2950) at Soi 5, Sukhumvit Rd (3000 to 4200B). Amari also has an airport hotel – see the Airport section below.

Another extremely well-located hotel for business or leisure is the 429-room *Novotel Bangkok* (☎ 366-8666, fax 366-8699) in Siam Square. Just steps away from one of Bangkok's most vibrant shopping and entertainment districts, the Novotel boasts a full business centre, bakery, pool and various restaurants. Huge rooms list for 4100/4500B.

Other top-notch hotels in the Siam Square & Pratunam area include:

Asia Hotel, 296 Phayathai Rd (☎ 215-0808, fax 215-4360); 640 rooms, 2600B up; it's in a good location, but often full of tour groups and conventioneers

Felix Arnoma Swissotel, 99 Ratchadamri Rd (☎ 255-3410, fax 255-3456); 400 rooms, 2400B up

Mercure Hotel Bangkok, 1091/336 New Phetburi Rd (☎ 253-0500, fax 253-0556); 678 rooms, 2825B; contains several lounges, coffee shops, and massage parlours

Imperial Hotel, Withayu (Wireless) Rd (☎ 254-0023, fax 253-3190); 370 rooms, 2719B up

Indra Regent, Ratchaprarop Rd (☎ 208-0033, fax 208-0388); 500 rooms, 3400B up

Le Meridien President, 135/26 Gaysorn Rd (☎ 253-0444, fax 253-7565); 387 rooms, 3531B up

Siam City Hotel, 477 Si Ayuthaya Rd (☎ 247-0130, fax 247-0178); 535 rooms, 4300B up

Sol Twin Towers Hotel, 88 Soi Rong Muang, New Rama VI Rd (near Hualamphong train station) (☎ 216-9555, fax 216-9544); 660 rooms, 3178B up

Silom & Surawong Rds Area (Map 8)

There are many hotels which have similar amenities to the Regent, Hilton and Sheraton, but which are a step down in price because of their location or smaller staff-to-guest ratios. In the Silom and Surawong Rd areas these include the *Montien* (☎ 234-8060, fax 234-8060) at 54 Surawong Rd (500 rooms, 4680B up), a very Thai hotel; the *Dusit Thani* (☎ 233-1130, fax 2366400) at Rama IV Rd (520 rooms, from 6120B), a great hotel in a busy location; the *Narai* (☎ 237-0100, fax 236-7161) at 222

Silom Rd (520 rooms, 3200B up); and the *Holiday Inn Crowne Plaza* (☎ 238-4300/34, fax 238-5289) at 981 Silom Rd (662 rooms, 3200B up).

Another entry in the luxury/executive market is the 190-room *Beaufort Sukhothai* (☎ 287-0222, fax 287-4980) at 13/3 Sathon Tai Rd. The Sukhothai features Asian minimalist decor, including an inner courtyard with lily ponds; the same architect and interior designer created Phuket's landmark Amanpuri. Standard rooms start at 5297B.

The recently refurbished, Thai-style *Manohra Hotel* (☎ 234-5070) at No 412 offers singles/doubles starting at 2600B. New to the scene is the ultramodern *Westin Banyan Tree* (☎ 679-1200, fax 679-1199), which towers over Sathon Tai Rd with 216 business suites. The hotel is ensconced on the lower two and top 28 floors of the 60 storey Thai Wah Tower II, the tallest building in Thailand. The Banyan Tree's huge rooms feature separate work and sleep areas, two-line speaker phones and data ports and two TV sets, along with all the other amenities expected of lodgings that cost over 6000B a night. The spa-fitness centre spans four floors.

Other top-end hotels in this area include:

Clarion Trinity, 150 Soi 5, Silom Rd (☎ 231-5333, fax 231-5417); 109 rooms, 2400 to 3100B

Mandarin Hotel, 662 Rama IV Rd (☎ 233-4980/4989, fax 237-1620); 343 rooms, 3178 to 8828B

New Peninsula, 295/3 Surawong Rd (☎ 234-3910, fax 236-5526); 102 rooms, 2225 to 3895B

Silom Plaza, 320 Silom Rd (☎ 236-8441/8484, fax 236-7566); 209 rooms, 2589B up

Swiss Lodge, 3 Convent Rd (☎ 233-5345, fax 236-9425); 57 rooms, 2419B up

Sukhumvit Rd (Map 4)

Top-end hotels in this area include:

Ambassador Hotel (Map 4), Soi 11, Sukhumvit Rd (☎ 254-0444, fax 253-4123); 1050 rooms, 2119B up; an amazing conglomeration of restaurants, food centres, night clubs and cocktail lounges

Bel-Aire Princess (Map 4), 16 Soi 5, Sukhumvit Rd (☎ 253-4300, fax 255-8850); 160 rooms, 2800B up

Delta Grand Pacific Hotel Soi 17-19, Sukhumvit Rd (☎ 233-2922/2927, fax 237-5740); easy access to Queen Sirikit National Convention Centre; 400 rooms, 4914B up

Impala Hotel, Soi 24, Sukhumvit Rd (☎ 258-8612/8616, fax 259-2896); 200 rooms, 2314 to 2708B up

Landmark (Map 4), 138 Sukhumvit Rd (☎ 254-0404, fax 255-8419); 415 rooms, 4826 to 9416B; has a Videotex in every room, very good business centre

Mansion Kempinski (Map 4), 75/23 Soi 11, Sukhumvit Rd (☎ 255-7200, fax 253-2329); 127 rooms, 2750B up

Novotel Lotus Bangkok (Map 4), 1 Soi Daeng Udom, Soi 33 Sukhumvit Rd (☎ 261-0111, fax 262-1700); 219 rooms, 4826B

Park Hotel, 6 Soi 7, Sukhumvit Rd (☎ 255-4300, fax 255-4309); 128 rooms, 2000B to 6000B

Windsor Hotel (Map 4), 3 Soi 20, Sukhumvit Rd (☎ 258-0160, fax 258-1491); 235 rooms, 2589 to 9416B

Airport

The 434-room *Amari Airport Hotel* (☎ 566-1020, fax 566-1941), directly opposite the airport, has undergone recent renovations and is quite well appointed. The executive floor features huge suites and 24 hour butler service. Rates start at 4200B for a standard double.

Another luxury-class hotel towards the airport is the *Central Plaza Bangkok* (☎ 541-1234, fax 541-1087) at 1695 Phahonyothin Rd, overlooking the Railway Golf Course and Chatuchak Park. There are 600 rooms, starting at 3955B for a standard room. The 150-room *Comfort Inn Airport* (☎ 552-8929, fax 552-8920), about five minutes south of the airport by car at 88/117 Vibhavadi (Vipavadee) Rangsit Rd. Large rooms with all the amenities (satellite TV, air-con, hot water bath/shower) cost 1500 to 1800B if you book through a Bangkok travel agent, 2500 to 2800B for walk-ins. Best of all, the hotel provides a free shuttle to and from the airport every hour. Other facilities include a coffee shop, pool, sauna and health club; about the only drawback is that you can hear planes landing and taking off until around midnight.

A new top-end project, the *Asia Airport Hotel*, is due to open nearby in late 1997.

Other Areas

Top-end hotels in other areas include:

The Emerald, 99/1 Ratchadaphisek Rd, Huay Khwang (☎ 276-4567, fax 276-4555); 640 rooms, 2600B up

Quality Hotel Lumphini, 17 Soi Ngam Duphli, Rama IV Rd (☎ 287-3411, fax 287-3420); 170 rooms, 2590/2825B

Rama Gardens, 9/9 Vibhavadi Rangsit Rd (☎ 561-0022, fax 561-1025); 380 rooms, 3800B up

Royal Princess Hotel, 269 Lan Luang Rd (☎ 281-3088, fax 280-1314); 170 rooms, 3300B up

Places to Eat

FOOD

Some people take to the food in Thailand immediately while others don't; Thai dishes can be pungent and spicy – a lot of garlic and chillies are used, especially *phrík khîi nũu* (literally, 'mouse-shit peppers') – these are the small torpedo-shaped devils which can be pushed aside if you are timid about red-hot curries. Almost all Thai food is cooked with fresh ingredients, including vegetables, poultry, pork and some beef. Plenty of lime juice, lemon grass and fresh coriander leaf are added to give the food its characteristic tang, and fish sauce *(náam plaa,* generally made from anchovies) or shrimp paste *(kà-pì)* to make it salty. Rice is eaten with most meals.

Other common seasonings include 'laos' or galanga root *(khàa),* black pepper, three kinds of basil, ground peanuts (more often a condiment), tamarind juice *(náam makhãam),* ginger *(khĩng)* and coconut milk *(kà-tí).* The Thais eat a lot of what could be called Chinese food, which is generally, but not always, less spicy. In the north and north-east 'sticky', or glutinous rice *(khâo nĩaw),* is common and is traditionally eaten with the hands.

Where to Eat

Most restaurants in Bangkok's tourist districts have bilingual or English menus; for those places outside the usual tourist venues, it's worthwhile memorising a small standard 'repertoire' of dishes. Many restaurants have their own local specialities in addition to the standards and you might try asking for 'whatever is good', allowing the proprietors to choose for you. Of course, you might get stuck with a large bill this way, but with a little practice in Thai social relations you may get some very pleasant results.

The most economical places to eat – and the most dependable – are noodle shops *(ráan kũaytĩaw),* curry-rice shops *(ráan khâo kaeng)* and night markets *(ta-làat tôh rûng).*

What to Eat

Thai food is served with a variety of condiments and sauces, including ground red pepper *(phrík bon),* ground peanuts *(thùa),* vinegar with sliced chillies *(náam sôm phrík),* fish sauce with chillies *(náam plaa phrík),* a spicy red sauce called *náam phrík sīi raachaa* (from Si Racha, of course) and any number of other dipping sauces *(náam jîm)* for particular dishes. Soy sauce *(náam sīi-yú)* can be requested, though this is normally used as a condiment for Chinese food only.

Except for the 'rice plates' and noodle dishes, Thai meals are usually ordered family-style, which is to say that two or more people order together, sharing different dishes. Traditionally, the party orders one of each kind of dish, eg one chicken, one fish, one soup, etc. One dish is generally large enough for two people. One or two extras may be ordered for a large party. If you come to eat at a Thai restaurant alone and order one of these 'entrees', you had better be hungry or know enough Thai to order a small portion. This latter alternative is not really too acceptable socially: Thais generally consider eating alone in a restaurant unusual – but then as a farang you're an exception anyway.

A cheaper alternative is to order dishes 'over rice' or *râat khâo*. Curry *(kaeng)* over rice is called *khâo kaeng*; in a standard curry shop khao kaeng is only 10 to 15B a plate. Another category of Thai food is called *kàp klâem* – dishes meant to be eaten while drinking alcoholic beverages. On some menus these are translated as 'snacks' or 'appetisers'. Typical kap klaem include *thùa thâwt* (fried peanuts), *kài sāam yàang* (literally 'three kinds of chicken', a plate of chopped ginger, peanuts, mouse-shit peppers and bits of lime – to be mixed and eaten by hand) and various kinds of *yam*, Thai-style salads made with lots of chillies and lime juice.

Vegetarian Those visitors who wish to avoid eating all animal food while in Thailand can be accommodated with some effort. Vegetarian restaurants are increasing in number throughout the country, thanks largely to Bangkok's ex-governor Chamlong Srimuang, who's strict vegetarianism has inspired a nonprofit chain of vegetarian restaurants (Thai: *ráan aahāan mangsàwírát)* in Bangkok and several provincial capitals. Look for the green sign out front with one or two large Thai numerals – each restaurant is numbered according to the order in which it was established. The food at these restaurants is usually served buffet style and is very inexpensive – 5 to 8B per dish. Many modern Thai restaurants in the city (eg the S&P Bakery chain) now have vegetarian sections on their menus.

Another easy though less widespread venue for vegetarian meals include Indian restaurants, which usually feature a vegetarian section on the menu. Chinese restaurants are also a good bet since many Chinese

Buddhists eat vegetarian food during Buddhist festivals, especially in southern Thailand.

Table Etiquette

Using the correct utensils and eating gestures will garner much respect from the Thais, who are of the general opinion that Western table manners are rather coarse.

Thais eat most dishes with a fork *(sáwm)* and tablespoon *(cháwn)*, except for noodles, which are eaten with chopsticks *(tà-kìap)*; noodle soups are eaten with a spoon and chopsticks. Another exception to the fork-and-spoon routine is sticky rice (common in the north and north-east), which is rolled into balls and eaten with the right hand, along with the food accompanying it.

The fork is held in the left hand and used as a probe to push food onto the spoon, which you eat from. To the Thais, pushing a fork into one's mouth is as uncouth as putting a knife in the mouth in Western countries.

When serving yourself from a common platter, put no more than one or two spoonfuls onto your plate at a time. It's customary at the start of a shared meal to eat a spoonful of plain rice first – a gesture that recognises rice as the most important part of the meal. If you're being hosted by Thais, they'll undoubtedly encourage you to eat less rice and more curries, seafood, etc as a gesture of

TAT

Tasty Thai tidbits.

their generosity (since rice costs comparatively little). The humble guest, however, takes rice with every spoonful.

Always leave some food on the serving platters as well as on your plate. To clean your plate and leave nothing on the serving platters would be a grave insult to your hosts. This is why Thais tend to over-order at social occasions – the more food is left on the table, the more generous the host appears.

The following list gives standard dishes in Thai script with a transliterated pronunciation guide, using the system outlined in the Language section, and an English translation and description.

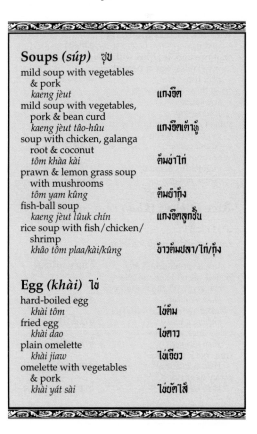

Soups (súp) ซุป

mild soup with vegetables
& pork
  kaeng jèut แกงจืด

mild soup with vegetables,
pork & bean curd
  kaeng jèut tâo-hûu แกงจืดเต้าหู้

soup with chicken, galanga
root & coconut
  tôm khàa kài ต้มข่าไก่

prawn & lemon grass soup
with mushrooms
  tôm yam kûng ต้มยำกุ้ง

fish-ball soup
  kaeng jèut lûuk chín แกงจืดลูกชิ้น

rice soup with fish/chicken/
shrimp
  khâo tôm plaa/kài/kûng ข้าวต้มปลา/ไก่/กุ้ง

Egg (khài) ไข่

hard-boiled egg
  khài tôm ไข่ต้ม

fried egg
  khài dao ไข่ดาว

plain omelette
  khài jiaw ไข่เจียว

omelette with vegetables
& pork
  khài yát sài ไข่ยัดไส้

scrambled egg
khài kuan   ไข่กวน

Noodles (*kũaytĩaw/bà-mii*)
ก๋วยเตี๋ยว/บะหมี่

wide rice noodle soup with
  vegetables & meat
  kũaytĩaw náam   ก๋วยเตี๋ยวน้ำ
wide rice noodles with
  vegetables & meat
  kũaytĩaw hâeng   ก๋วยเตี๋ยวแห้ง
wide rice noodles with gravy
  râat nâa   ราดหน้า
thin rice noodles fried with tofu,
  vegetables, egg & peanuts
  phàt thai   ผัดไทย
fried thin noodles with
  soy sauce
  phàt sii-yíw   ผัดซีอิ๊ว
wheat noodles in broth with
  vegetables & meat
  bà-mii náam   บะหมี่น้ำ
wheat noodles with
  vegetables & meat
  bà-mii hâeng   บะหมี่แห้ง

Rice Dishes (*khâo râat nâa*)
ข้าวราดหน้า

fried rice with pork/chicken/
  shrimp
  khâo phàt mǔu/kài/kûng   ข้าวผัดหมู/ไก่/กุ้ง
boned, sliced Hainan-style
  chicken with marinated rice
  khâo man kài   ข้าวมันไก่
chicken with sauce over rice
  khâo nâa kài   ข้าวหน้าไก่
roast duck over rice
  khâo nâa pèt   ข้าวหน้าเป็ด
'red' pork with rice
  khâo mǔu daeng   ข้าวหมูแดง
curry over rice
  khâo kaeng   ข้าวแกง

Curries (*kaeng*) แกง

hot Thai curry with chicken/
  beef/ pork
   kaeng phèt kài/néua/mǔu   แกงเผ็ดไก่/เนื้อ/หมู
rich & spicy, Muslim-style curry
  with chicken/beef & potatoes
   kaeng mátsàman kài/néua   แกงมัสมั่นไก่/เนื้อ
mild, Indian-style curry with
  chicken
   kaeng kari kài   แกงกะหรี่ไก่
hot & sour, fish & vegetable
  ragout
   kaeng sôm   แกงส้ม
'green' curry with fish/
  chicken/beef
   kaeng khǐaw-wǎan plaa/   แกงเขียวหวานปลา
    kài/néua   /ไก่/เนื้อ
savoury curry with
  chicken/beef
   kaeng phánaeng kài/néua   แกงพะแนงไก่/เนื้อ
chicken curry with bamboo
  shoots
   kaeng kài nàw mái   แกงไก่หน่อไม้
catfish curry
   kaeng plaa dùk   แกงปลาดุก

Seafood (*aahǎan tháleh*) อาหารทะเล

steamed crab
  puu nêung   ปูนึ่ง
steamed crab claws
  kâam puu nêung   ก้ามปูนึ่ง
shark-fin soup
  hǔu chalǎam   หูฉลาม
crisp-fried fish
  plaa thâwt   ปลาทอด
fried prawns
  kûng thâwt   กุ้งทอด
batter-fried prawns
  kûng chúp   กุ้งชุบแป้งทอด
   pâeng thâwt
grilled prawns
  kûng phǎo   กุ้งเผา

JOE CUMMINGS

Unlike Indian curries, which are usually cooked for hours, Thai curries have relatively short cooking times; the preparation of the actual ingredients is often the more time-consuming task.

BERNARD NAPTHINE

Crispy fried fish prepared in the traditional way with a chilli and shallot garnish on a bed of banana leaves.

steamed fish
   plaa nêung   ปลานึ่ง
grilled fish
   plaa phão   ปลาเผา
whole fish cooked in ginger,
   onions & soy sauce
   plaa jĭan   ปลาเจี๋ยน

RICHARD I'ANSON

Drying fish.

sweet & sour fish
  plaa prîaw wãan ปลาเปรี้ยวหวาน
cellophane noodles baked
  with crab
  wûn-sên òp puu วุ้นเส้นอบปู
spicy fried squid
  plaa mèuk phàt phèt ปลาหมึกผัดเผ็ด
roast squid
  plaa mèuk yâang ปลาหมึกย่าง
oysters fried in egg batter
  hãwy thâwt หอยทอด
squid
  plaa mèuk ปลาหมึก
shrimp
  kûng กุ้ง
fish
  plaa ปลา
catfish
  plaa dùk ปลาดุก
freshwater eel
  plaa lãi ปลาไหล
saltwater eel
  plaa lòt ปลาหลด
tilapia
  plaa nin ปลานิล
spiny lobster
  kûng mangkon กุ้งมังกร
green mussel
  hãwy malaeng phùu หอยแมลงภู่

scallop
  hǎwy phát   หอยพัด
oyster
  hǎwy naang rom   หอยนางรม

Miscellaneous

stir-fried mixed vegetables
  phàt phàk lǎi yàang   ผัดผักหลายอย่าง
spring rolls
  pàw-pía   เปาะปี๊ย
beef in oyster sauce
  néua phàt náam-man hǎwy   เนื้อผัดน้ำมันหอย
duck soup
  pèt tǔn   เป็ดตุ๋น
roast duck
  pèt yâang   เป็ดย่าง
fried chicken
  kài thâwt   ไก่ทอด
chicken fried in basil
  kài phàt bai kà-phrao   ไก่ผัดใบกะเพรา
grilled chicken
  kài yâang   ไก่ย่าง
chicken fried with chillies
  kài phàt phrík   ไก่ผัดพริก
chicken fried with cashews
  *kài phàt mét
  má-mûang*   ไก่ผัดเม็ดมะม่วง
morning-glory vine fried in
  garlic, chilli & bean sauce
  phàk bûng fai daeng   ผักบุ้งไฟแดง
'satay' or skewers of
  barbecued meat
  sà-té   สะเต๊ะ
spicy green papaya salad
  (North-Eastern speciality)
  sôm-tam   ส้มตำ
noodles with fish curry
  khǎnom jiin náam yaa   ขนมจีนน้ำยา
prawns fried with chillies
  kûng phàt phrík phǎo   กุ้งผัดพริกเผา
chicken fried with ginger
  kài phàt khǐng   ไก่ผัดขิง
fried wonton
  kíaw kràwp   เกี๊ยวกรอบ

cellophane noodle salad
　yam wún sên — ยำวุ้นเส้น

spicy chicken or beef salad
　lâap kài/néua — ลาบไก่/เนื้อ

hot & sour, grilled beef salad
　yam néua — ยำเนื้อ

chicken with bean sprouts
　kài sàp thùa ngâwk — ไก่สับถั่วงอก

fried fish cakes with
　cucumber sauce
　thâwt man plaa — ทอดมันปลา

Vegetables *(phàk)* ผัก

angle bean
　thùa phuu — ถั่วภู

bitter melon
　márá-jiin — มะระขึ้น

brinjal (round eggplant)
　mákhěua pràw — มะเขือเปราะ

cabbage
　phàk kà-làm — ผะกกะทา ล่ำ
　　(or *kà-làm plii*) — กะทา ล่ซ่ลี

cauliflower
　dàwk kà-làm — ตอกกะทล่ำ

Chinese radish
　phàk kàat hǔa — ผักกาดหัว

corn
　khâo phôht — ข้าวโพต

cucumber
　taeng kwaa — แตงกวา

eggplant
　mákhěua mûang — มะเขือม่วง

garlic
　kràtiam — กระเทียม

lettuce
　phàk kàat — ผักกาด

long bean
　thùa fàk yao — ถั่วฝักยาว

okra ('ladyfingers')
　krà-jíap — กระเจียบ

onion (bulb)
　hǔa hǎwm — หัวหอม

onion (green, 'scallions')
　tôn hǎwm — ต้นหอม

BERNARD NAPTHINE

Try fruits you've never seen before.

peanuts (ground nuts)
tùa lísõng ถั่วลิสง
potato
man faràng มันฝรั่ง
pumpkin
fák thawng ฟักทอง
taro
pheùak เผือก
tomato
mákhẽua thêt มะเขือเทศ

Fruit *(phõn-lá-mái)* ผลไม้

banana – over 20 varieties
(year-round)
klûay กล้วย
coconut (year-round)
máphráo มะพร้าว
custard-apple
náwy naa น้อยหน่า
durian
thúrian ทุเรียน
guava (year-round)
fa-ràng ฝรั่ง
jackfruit
kha-nūn ขนุน

lime (year-round)
  má-nao   มะนาว
longan – 'dragon's eyes';
  similar to rambutan
  (July to October)
  lam yài   ลำใย
mandarin orange
  (year-round)
  sôm   ส้ม
mango – several varieties
  & seasons
  má-mûang   มะม่วง
mangosteen
  mang-khút   มังคุด
papaya (year-round)
  málákaw   มะละกอ
pineapple (year-round)
  sàp-pàrót   สับปะรด
pomelo
  sôm oh   ส้มโอ
rambeh – small, reddish-
  brown and apricot-like
  (April to May)
  máfai   มะไฟ
rambutan
  ngáw   เงาะ
rose-apple – apple-like texture;
  very fragrant (April to July)
  chom-phûu   ชมพู่
tamarind – sweet and tart   มะขาม
  varieties
  mákhãam
sapodilla – small and oval;
  sweet but pungent
  (July to September)
  lámút   ละมุด
watermelon (year-round)
  taeng moh   แตงโม

Sweets (*khãwng wãan*) ของ หวาน

Thai custard
  sãngkha-yaa   สังขยา
coconut custard
  sãngkha-yaa ma-phráo   สังขยามะพร้าว

sweet shredded egg yolk
  fõy thawng　　　　　ฝอยทอง
egg custard
  mâw kaeng　　　　　หม้อแกง
banana in coconut milk
  klûay bùat chii　　　กล้วยบวชชี
fried, Indian-style banana
  klûay khàek　　　　กล้วยแขก
sweet palm kernels
  lûuk taan chêuam　　ลูกตาลเชื่อม
Thai jelly with coconut cream
  ta-kôh　　　　　　ตะโก้
sticky rice with coconut cream
  khâo nĩaw daeng　　ข้าวเหนียวแดง
sticky rice in coconut cream
  with ripe mango
  khâo nĩaw má-mûang　ข้าวเหนียวมะม่วง

Useful Food Words

(For 'I' men use *phõm*; women use *dii-chãn*)

I eat only vegetarian food.
  Phõm/dii-chãn kin jeh.　ผม/ดีฉัน กินเจ

I can't eat pork.
  Phõm/dii-chãn kin .　　ผม/ดีฉัน
  Mũu mâi dâi.　　　　กินหมูไม่ได้

I can't eat beef.
  Phõm/dii-chãn .　　　ผม/ดีฉัน
  kin néua mâi dâi.　　กินเนื้อไม่ได้

(I) don't like it hot & spicy.
  Mâi châwp phèt.　　ไม่ชอบเผ็ด
(I) like it hot & spicy.
  Châwp phèt.　　　　ชอบเผ็ด
(I) can eat Thai food.
  Kin aahãan thai pen.　กินอาหารไทยเป็น

What do you have that's
  special?
  Mii a-rai phí-sèt?　　มีอะไรพิเศษๆ

I didn't order this.
  Níi phõm/dii-chãn mâi　นี้ ผม/ดีฉัน ไม่ได้สั่ง
  dâi sàng.

Do you have ...?
  Mii ... mãi?　　　　มี...ไหมๆ

DRINKS

Nonalcoholic Drinks

Fruit Juices & Shakes The incredible variety of fruits in Thailand means there's an abundance of nutritious juices and shakes.

Thais prefer to drink most fruit juices with a little salt mixed in. Unless a vendor is used to serving farangs, your fruit juice or shake will come slightly salted. If you prefer unsalted fruit juices, specify *mâi sài kleua* (without salt).

Sugar cane juice *(náam âwy)* is a Thai favourite and a very refreshing accompaniment to curry and rice plates. Many small restaurants or food stalls that don't offer any other juices will have a supply of freshly squeezed náam âwy on hand.

Water Purified water is simply called *náam dèum* (drinking water), whether boiled or filtered. *All* water offered to customers in restaurants or to guests in an office or home will be purified, so don't fret about taking a sip (for more information on water safety, see Health in the Facts for the Visitor chapter).

Alcoholic Drinks

Drinking in Thailand can be rather expensive in relation to the cost of other consumer activities. The Thai government has placed increasingly heavy taxes on liquor and beer, so that now about 30B out of the 50 to 70B you pay for a large beer is tax. Whether this is an effort to raise more tax revenue (the result has been a sharp decrease in the consumption of alcohol for perhaps a net decrease in revenue) or to discourage consumption, drinking can wreak havoc with your budget. One large bottle (630 ml) of Singha beer costs more than half the minimum daily wage of a Bangkok worker.

According the Food and Agriculture Organisation (FAO), Thailand ranks fifth worldwide in alcohol consumption, behind South Korea, the Bahamas, Taiwan and Bermuda, and well ahead of Portugal, Ireland and France.

Beer Three brands of beer are brewed in Thailand by Thai-owned breweries: Singha, Amarit and Kloster. Singha (pronounced *Sĭng*) is by far the most common in Thailand, with some 66% of the market. The original recipe was formulated in 1934 by nobleman Phya Bhirom Bhakdi and his son Prachuap, who was the first Thai to earn a brew-master's diploma from Munich's

Beverages (khreûang dèum)
เครื่องดื่ม

plain water	
náam plào	น้ำเปล่า
hot water	
náam ráwn	น้ำร้อน
boiled water	
náam tôm	น้ำต้ม
cold water	
náam yen	น้ำเย็น
ice	
náam khǎeng	น้ำแข็ง
Chinese tea	
chaa jiin	ชาจีน
weak Chinese tea	
náam chaa	น้ำชา
iced Thai tea with milk & sugar	
chaa yen	ชาเย็น
iced Thai tea with sugar only	
chaa dam yen	ชาดำเย็น
no sugar (command)	
mâi sài náam-taan	ไม่ใส่น้ำตาล
hot Thai tea with sugar	
chaa dam ráwn	ชาดำร้อน
hot Thai tea with milk & sugar	
chaa ráwn	ชาร้อน
hot coffee with milk & sugar	
kafae ráwn	กาแฟร้อน
traditional filtered coffee with milk & sugar	
kafae thǔng	กาแฟถุง/โกปี๊
(ko-píi in the South)	
iced coffee with sugar, no milk	
oh-liang	โอเลี้ยง
Ovaltine	
oh-wantin	โอวันติน
orange soda	
náam sôm	น้ำส้ม
plain milk	
nom jèut	นมจืด

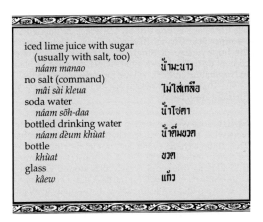

iced lime juice with sugar
(usually with salt, too)
  náam manao   น้ำมะนาว

no salt (command)
  mâi sài kleua   ไม่ใส่เกลือ

soda water
  náam sõh-daa   น้ำโซ่ดา

bottled drinking water
  náam dèum khùat   น้ำดื่มขวด

bottle
  khùat   ขวด

glass
  kâew   แก้ว

Doemens Institute. Singha is a strong, hoppy-tasting
brew thought by many to be the best beer produced in
Asia. The barley for Singha is grown in Thailand, the
hops are imported from Germany and the rated alcohol
content is 6%. Singha is sometimes available on tap in
pubs and restaurants. Kloster is quite a bit smoother and
lighter than Singha and generally costs about 5B more
per bottle, but it is a good-tasting brew often favoured
by Western visitors, expats and upwardly mobile Thais
who view it as a status symbol. Amarit NB (the initials
stand for 'naturally brewed', though who knows whether
it is or not) is similar in taste to Singha but a bit smoother,
and is brewed by Thai Amarit, the same company that
produces Kloster. Like Kloster it costs a few baht more
than the national brew. Together Amarit and Kloster
claim only 7% of Thailand's beer consumption. Alcoholic content for each is 4.7%. Boon Rawd Breweries,
makers of Singha, also produce a lighter beer called
Singha Gold which only comes in small bottles; most
people seem to prefer either Kloster or regular Singha to
Singha Gold, which is a little on the bland side. Better is
Singha's new canned draft beer – if you like cans. Carlsberg, jointly owned by Danish and Thai interests, is a
strong newcomer to Thailand. As elsewhere in South-
East Asia, Carlsberg has used an aggressive promotion
campaign (backed by the makers of Mekong whisky) to
grab around 25% of the Thai market in only two years.
The company adjusted its recipe to come closer to
Singha's 6% alcohol content, which may be one reason
why they've surpassed Kloster and Amarit so quickly.

Singha has retaliated with ads suggesting that drinking Carlsberg is unpatriotic. Carlsberg responded by creating 'Beer Chang' (Elephant Beer), which matches the hoppy taste of Singha but ratchets the alcohol content up to 7%. Dutch giant Heineken opened a plant in Nonthaburi in 1995, so look for more sparks to fly.

The Thai word for beer is *bia*. Draught beer is *bia sòt* (literally, fresh beer).

Spirits Rice whisky is a big favourite in Thailand and somewhat more affordable than beer for the average Thai. It has a sharp, sweet taste not unlike rum, with an alcoholic content of 35%. By far the most popular brand is Maekhong (Mekong), which costs around 120B for a large bottle *(klom)* or 60B for the flask-sized bottle *(baen)*. An even smaller bottle, the *kòk*, is occasionally available for 30 to 35B.

More expensive Thai whiskies appealing to the pre-Johnnie Walker set include Singharaj blended whisky (240B a bottle) and VO Royal Thai whisky (260B), each with 40% alcohol.

One company in Thailand produces a true rum (that is, a distilled liquor made from sugar cane) called Sang Thip (formerly Sang Som). Alcohol content is 40% and the stock is supposedly aged. Sang Thip costs several baht more than the rice whiskies, but for those who find Mekong and the like unpalatable, it is an alternative worth trying.

Herbal Liquor Currently, herbal liquors are fashionable throughout the country and can be found at roadside vendors, small pubs and in a few guesthouses. These liquors are made by soaking various herbs, roots, seeds, fruit and bark in lâo khâo (a clear, colourless, distilled rice liquor) to produce a range of concoctions called *yàa dong*. Many of the yaa dong preparations are purported to have specific health-enhancing qualities. Some of them taste fabulous while others are rank.

Wine Thais are increasingly interested in wine, but still manage only a minuscule one glass per capita average consumption per year. Various enterprises have attempted to produce wine in Thailand, most often with disastrous results. The latest is a winery called Chateau de Loei, near Phu Reua in Loei Province. Dr Chaiyut, the owner, spent a lot of money and time studying Western wine-making methods; his first vintage, a Chenin Blanc, is quite a drinkable wine. It's available at many of the finer restaurants in Bangkok.

Imported wines from France, Australia and the US are also widely available in European restaurants and supermarkets.

PLACES TO EAT

No matter where you go in Bangkok you're almost never more than 50m from a restaurant or sidewalk food vendor. The variety of places to eat is simply astounding and defeats all but the most tireless food samplers in the quest to say they've tried everything. As with seeking a place to stay, you can find somewhere to eat in every price range in most districts – with a few obvious exceptions. Chinatown is naturally a good area for Chinese food, while Bangrak and Pahurat (both districts with high concentrations of Indian residents) are good for Indian and Muslim cuisine. Some parts of the city tend to have higher priced restaurants than others (eg Siam Square, Silom and Surawong Rds and Sukhumvit Rd) while other areas are full of cheap eats (eg Banglamphu and Ko Ratanakosin around Tha Maharat).

Because transport can be such a hassle in Bangkok, most visitors choose the most convenient place to eat rather than seeking out a specific restaurant; this section has therefore been organised by area, rather than cuisine.

Banglamphu (Maps 5 & 6)

This area near the river and old part of the city is one of the best for cheap eating. Many of the guesthouses on Khao San Rd have open-air cafes, which are packed with travellers from November to March and July to August. The typical cafe menu here has Thai and Chinese standards plus a variety of traveller favourites like fruit salads, muesli and yoghurt. None of them are particular standouts, though the side-by-side *Orm* and *Wally House* produce fair Thai, Western and vegetarian meals, while *Prakorp's House* makes good coffee. *Arawy Det* (Map 6), an old Hokkien-style noodle shop on the corner of Khao San and Tanao Rds, has somehow managed to stay authentic amidst the cosmic swirl.

Gaylord Indian Restaurant, hidden away in the rear upstairs of a building on Chakraphong Rd opposite the west entrance to Khao San Rd (Map 6), has decent Indian food. *Royal India* on the south side of Khao San Rd (Map 6) used to be good but has slid downhill since it moved across the street (the original Royal India in Pahurat district is still worth trying). *Chabad House*, a Jewish place of worship on Rambutri Rd (Map 6), serves Israeli-style kosher food downstairs.

SARA-JANE CLELAND

Eat-in or take-away, street-market style.

For more authentic (and cheaper) Thai food, check out the next street north of Khao San, Rambutri Rd. At the western end of the street are several open-air restaurants serving excellent Thai food at low prices. A good spot for southern Thai food is a no-name food shop at 8-10 Chakraphong, south of Khao San Rd and two doors south of the Padung Cheep Mask shop. In the mornings this one serves khâo mòk kài (Thai chicken biryani) as well as khâo yam, a kind of rice salad which is a traditional breakfast in southern Thailand. Nearby at No 22 is a cheap and efficient Chinese noodle (bàmìi) and wonton (kíaw) shop; No 28 offers tasty Thai curries.

A small shop called *Roti-Mataba* (no English sign) on the corner of Phra Athit and Phra Sumen Rds near the river has a bilingual menu offering delicious kaeng matsaman (Thai Muslim curry), chicken kurma, chicken or vegetable mátàbà (a sort of stuffed crepe); look for a white sign with red letters. There are several unassuming Chinese dim sum and noodle places along Phra Athit Rd north of the New Merry V Guest Houses, plus a couple of Thai curry shops. The *Raan Kin Deum* (no English sign), a few doors down from New Merry V, is a nice two-storey cafe with wooden tables and chairs, traditional Thai food and live folk music nightly; the laid-back atmosphere reaches its peak in the evenings when Thais and farangs crowd the place.

Farther north of Khao San Rd, in the heart of Banglamphu's market, are two shopping complexes with food centres, fast-food vendors and supermarkets. At the high-rise *New World shopping centre* (Map 5), the ground floor features doughnut shops and meatball vendors, the 5th floor has a supermarket, and on the 8th is a brilliant food centre with city and river views. Vendors here offer seafood, vegetarian, coffee, noodles, curries and more. The 6th floor of *Banglamphu Department Store* between Krai Si and Rambutri Rds, also has a supermarket and small food centre. The department store has been condemned by the BMA for noncompliance with building codes, so who knows how long it will be before it either closes or collapses.

Good curry and rice is available for around 15B at the outdoor dining hall at *Thammasat University* (Map 5) near the river; it's open for lunch only. Opposite the southern entrance of the university there are several good noodle and rice shops. For north-eastern Thai food, try the restaurants next door to the boxing stadium on Ratchadamnoen Nok Rd, near the TAT office.

At Tha Wisut Kasat, in north-western Banglamphu, there's a very good floating seafood restaurant called *Yok Yor*. Especially good is the hàw mòk (fish curry). Yok Yor also offers inexpensive evening dining cruises – you order from the regular menu and pay a nominal 50B charge for the boat service. Nearby is the similar *Chawn Ngoen*; it has no English sign, but there is an English menu. *Wang Ngar*, in west Banglamphu next to the Phra Pinklao Bridge (Map 5), is another decent waterfront place.

At the Democracy Monument circle, Ratchadamnoen Klang Rd, there are a few air-con Thai restaurants, including the *Vijit* (Map 5) and the *Sorn Daeng*, which have reasonable prices considering the food and facilities. At lunchtime on weekdays they're crowded with local government office workers. Both stay open until 11 pm or so.

For authentic, sit-down Thai cuisine, try the long-running *Yod Kum* (Yawt Kham) opposite Wat Bowon on Phra Sumen Rd. Specialities include phàt phèt plaa dùk (catfish stir-fried in basil and curry paste), kaeng khĩaw-wǎan (green curry) and seafood.

For those in the mood for continental food, *Kanit's*, at 68 Tee Thong Rd, is just south of the Sao Ching-Cha (Giant Swing) and is another worthwhile semi-splurge. The lasagne and pizza are probably the best you can find in this part of Bangkok.

Vegetarian Many of the Khao San Rd guesthouse cafes offer vegetarian dishes. For an all-veggie menu at low prices, seek out the *Vegetarian Restaurant* at 117/1 Soi Wat Bowon, near Srinthip Guest House. To find this out-of-the-way spot, turn left on Tanao Rd at the eastern end of Khao San Rd, then cross the street and turn right down the first narrow alley, then left at Soi Wat Bowon – an English sign reads 'Vegetarian'. The fare is basically Western veggie, with wholemeal breads, salads and sandwiches; it's open from 8 am until around 10 pm. A very good Thai vegetarian place is *Arawy* (Map 5, no English sign), which is south of Khao San Rd, across Ratchadamnoen Klang at 152 Din So Rd (opposite the City Hall) near a 7-Eleven. This was one of Bangkok's first Thai vegetarian restaurants, inspired by ex-Bangkok Governor Chamlong Srimuang. It's open daily from 7 am to 7 pm.

Chinatown & Pahurat (Map 5)

Some of Bangkok's best Chinese and Indian food is found in these adjacent districts, but because few tourists stay in this part of town (for good reason – it's simply too congested), they rarely make any eating forays into the area.

A few old Chinese restaurants have moved from Chinatown to locations with less traffic, the most famous being Hoi Tien Lao, now called *Hoi Tien Lao Rim Nam*. It's now next to the River House Condominium on the Thonburi bank of the Chao Phraya River, more or less opposite the Portuguese embassy and River City complex. (The food and decor at Hoi Tien Lao, though far removed from Chinatown, are nonetheless excellent.) But many places are still hanging on to their venerable Chinatown addresses – where the atmosphere is still part of the eating experience.

Most of the city's Chinatown restaurants specialise in southern Chinese cuisine, particularly that of coastal Guangdong and Fujian provinces. This means seafood, rice noodles and dumplings are often the best choices. The large, banquet-style Chinese places are mostly found along Yaowarat and Charoen Krung Rds, and include *Lie Kee* (on the corner of Charoen Krung Rd and Soi Bamrungrat, a block west of Ratchawong Rd), *Laem Thong* (on Soi Bamrungrat just off Charoen Krung Rd) and *Yau Wah Yuen* (near the Yaowarat and Ratchawong Rds intersection). Each of these has an extensive menu, including dim sum before lunchtime.

The best noodle and dumpling shops are hidden away on smaller sois and alleys. At No 54 on Soi Bamrungrat is the funky *Chiang Kii*, where the 100B khâ tôm plaa (rice soup with fish) belies the casual surroundings – no place does it better. *Kong Lee*, at 137/141 Ratchawong Rd, has a very loyal clientele for its dry-fried wheat noodles (bàmii hâeng) – again it's reportedly the best in Bangkok. Another great noodle place, *Pet Tun*

Jao Thaa, is on the south-eastern edge of Chinatown in the direction of the GPO, at 945 Soi Wanit 2 opposite the Harbour Department building. The restaurant's name means 'Harbour Department Stewed Duck' – the speciality is rice noodles (kūaytīaw) served with duck or goose, either roasted or stewed.

All-night food hawkers set up along Yaowarat Rd at the Ratchawong Rd intersection, opposite Yaowarat Market near the Cathay Department Store. This is the least expensive place to dine out in Chinatown. The city reportedly plans to relocate all the vendors from this area to a new 'Chinatown Night Plaza' around the corner on Ratchawong Rd in order to reduce traffic on Yaowarat Rd.

Over in Pahurat, the Indian fabric district, most places serve north Indian cuisine, heavily influenced by Moghul or Persian flavours and spices. For many people, the best north Indian restaurant in town is the *Royal India* at 392/1 Chakraphet Rd. It can be very crowded at lunchtime – almost exclusively with Indian residents – so it might be better to go there after the standard lunch hour or at night. The place has very good curries (both vegetarian and non-vegetarian), dal, breads (including six kinds of paratha), raita, lassi, etc – all at quite reasonable prices. Royal India also has a branch on Khao San Rd in Banglamphu, but it's not as good.

The *ATM Department Store* on Chakraphet Rd near the pedestrian bridge has a food centre on the top floor with several Indian vendors – the food is cheap and tasty and there's quite a good selection. Running alongside the ATM building on Soi ATM are several small teahouses with very inexpensive Indian and Nepali food, including lots of fresh chapatis and strong milk tea. For a good choice of inexpensive vegetarian food, you could try the Sikh-operated *Indrathep* on Soi ATM. In the afternoons, a Sikh man sets up a pushcart on the corner of Soi ATM and Chakraphet Rd and sells vegetarian samousas often cited as the best in Bangkok.

Wedged between the western edge of Chinatown and the northern edge of Pahurat, the three-storey *Old Siam Plaza* shopping centre houses a number of Thai, Chinese and Japanese restaurants. The most economical places are on the 3rd floor, where food centre restaurants serve inexpensive Thai and Chinese meals from 10 am to 5 pm. The 3rd floor also has several reasonably priced, Thai-style coffee shops. Attached to the adjacent Chalermkrung Royal Theatre is a branch of the highly efficient, moderately priced *S&P Restaurant & Bakery*, where the extensive menu encompasses everything from authentic Thai to well-prepared Japanese, European and vegetarian dishes, along with a selection of pastries and desserts.

Vegetarian *Suki Jeh Yuu Seu* (the English sign reads 'Health Food'), a Chinese vegetarian restaurant just 70m down Rama IV Rd from Hualamphong station, serves excellent, moderately priced vegetarian food in a clean, air-con atmosphere. The fruit shakes are particularly well made; this is a great place to fortify oneself with food and drink while waiting for a train.

During the annual Vegetarian Festival (centred around Wat Mangkon Kamalawat on Charoen Krung Rd from September to October), Bangkok's Chinatown becomes a virtual orgy of vegetarian Thai and Chinese food. Restaurants and noodle shops in the area offer hundreds of dishes. One of the best spreads is at *Hua Seng Restaurant*, a few doors west of Wat Mangkon on Charoen Krung Rd.

Siam Square & Pratunam (Map 7)

This shopping area has several low and medium-priced restaurants as well as American fast-food franchises. Chinese food predominates, probably because it's the well-off Chinese Thais that most frequent Siam Square. Soi 1 has three shark-fin places: *Scala*, *Penang* and *Bangkok*. At the other end of Siam Square, on Henri Dunant Rd, the big noodle restaurant called *Coca Garden* (open from 10.30 am to 10.30 pm) is good for Chinese-style sukiyaki.

BERNARD NAPTHINE

Taking a break from the frantic world of retail.

Can't decide what kind of food you're in the mood for? Then head for *S&P Restaurant & Bakery* on Soi 12. The extensive menu features Thai, Chinese, Japanese, European and vegetarian specialities, plus a bakery with pies, cakes and pastries – all high-quality fare at low to moderate prices.

On Soi 11, the Bangkok branch of the *Hard Rock Cafe* serves good American and Thai food; prices are about the same as at other Hard Rocks around the world. Look for the tuk-tuk captioned 'God is my co-pilot' coming out of the building's facade. The Hard Rock stays open till 2 am, a bit later than many Siam Square eateries.

Just to the right of Siam Square's Scala cinema, plunge into the alley that curves behind the Phayathai Rd shops to find a row of cheap, good food stalls. A shorter alley with food stalls also leads off the north end of Siam Square's Soi 2.

On both sides of Rama I in Siam Square and Siam Center you'll find a battery of American fast-food franchises, including *Mister Donut, Dunkin Donuts, Burger King, Pizza Hut, Swensen's Ice Cream, McDonald's, Shakey's Pizza, A&W Root Beer* and *KFC*. Prices are close to what you would pay in the USA. Siam Center once contained a bevy of good Thai coffee shops on its upper floors, but the whole complex saw McDonald's and Pizza Hut on the ground floor closed following the Center's disastrous 1995 fire; at the time of writing they still hadn't re-opened.

If you're staying on or nearby Soi Kasem San 1, you don't have to suck motorcycle fumes crossing Rama I and Phayathai Rds to Siam Square, Siam Center or Mahboonkrong Shopping Centre to find something to eat. Besides the typical hotel and inn coffee shops found on the soi, there are also two very good, inexpensive curry and rice vendors with tables along the east side of the soi. No need to be fluent in Thai, they're used to the 'point and serve' system. Two outdoor cafes on either side of the White Lodge serve more expensive Thai and European food, burgers, pastries, coffees and breakfast.

Right around the corner on Rama I Rd, next to the liquor dealer with the vintage British and US motorcycles out the front, is *Thai Sa Nguan* (no English sign), a fairly clean shop with curry and rice (khâo kaeng) for 12B (two toppings 17B), fried duck with noodles (kūaytĭaw pèt yâang) and Hainanese-style chicken and rice (khâo man kài).

Mahboonkrong Shopping Centre Another building studded with restaurants, MBK is directly across from Siam Square at the intersection of Phayathai

and Rama I Rds. A section on the ground floor called
Major Plaza contains two cinemas and a good food
centre. An older food centre is on the 7th floor; both
places have vendors serving tasty dishes from all over
Thailand, including vegetarian, at prices averaging 20 to
25B per plate. Hours are 10 am to 10 pm, but for the best
selection remember the more popular vendors run out
of food as early as 8.30 or 9 pm. A beer garden on the
terrace surrounding two sides of the 7th-floor food
centre – with good views of the Bangkok nightscape – is
open in the evening.

Scattered around other floors, especially the 3rd and
4th, are a number of popular medium-priced places,
including *Little Home Bakery* (an American-style pancake
house with a few Filipino dishes), *13 Coins* (steak, pizza
and pasta), *Kobune Japanese Restaurant, Chester's Grilled
Chicken, Pizza Hut* and many others.

World Trade Center This relatively new office and
shopping complex on the corner of Ploenchit and
Ratchadamri Rds contains a few up-market restaurants
and the city's trendiest food centre. Located on the
ground floor of this huge glossy building are *Kroissant
House* (coffees, pastries and gelato) and *La Fontana*
(bistro-style Italian). The 6th floor of the centre features
Lai-Lai and *Chao Sua*, two sumptuous Chinese banquet-
style places, plus the elegant traditional Thai *Thanying*
and the more casual *Narai Pizzeria*. There are also two
food centres on the 7th floor with standard Thai and
Chinese dishes, which are only a little more expensive
than at the usual Bangkok food centre.

The basement of *Zen Department Store* contains a
Thai deli with many curries, a good Japanese sushi and
noodle bar (a sizeable plate of sushi costs 60 to 120B), a
bakery, sandwich/coffee bar and Western deli. The basement food centre has very few seats, encouraging
takeaways.

Soi Lang Suan Farther east from Siam Square and the
World Trade Center, off Ploenchit Rd, Soi Lang Suan
offers a number of medium-priced eateries. Despite its
Western name, *Sarah Jane* (☎ 252-6572), on an alley off
the west side of Soi Lang Suan about a block and a half
south of Ploenchit, serves very good isãan food in a
modest air-con dining room. It's open 11 am to 10 pm.

Thang Long (☎ 251-3504), 82/5 Soi Lang Suan, is
favoured by Thais as well as expats for its reasonable
prices and Thai-Vietnamese menu; it's open daily for
lunch and dinner.

The Italian-owned *Pan Pan* (☎ 252-7501) at 45 Soi Lang Suan is very popular with Western residents for wood-fired pizza (takeaway orders accepted), pastas, salads, gelato (the best in Thailand) and pastries. A low-calorie vegetarian menu is available on request. A second Pan Pan (☎ 258-5071) is located on Soi 33.

The *Whole Earth Restaurant* (☎ 252-5574), at 93/3 Soi Lang Suan, is a good Thai and Indian restaurant that's mostly vegetarian, with good service to match, but it's a bit pricey if you're on a tight budget. The upstairs room features low tables with floor cushions. A second branch has opened at 71 Soi 26, Sukhumvit Rd (☎ 258-4900).

Nguan Lee Lang Suan, on the corner of Soi Lang Suan and Sarasin Rd, is a semi-outdoor place specialising in Chinese-style seafood and kài lâo daeng (chicken steamed in Chinese herbs).

Silom & Surawong Rds Area (Map 8)

This area represents the heart of the financial district so it features a lot of pricey restaurants, along with cheaper ones that attract office workers. Many restaurants are found along the main avenues but there's an even greater number tucked away in sois and alleys. The river end of Silom and Surawong Rds towards Charoen Krung Rd (the Bangrak district) is a good hunting ground for Indian food.

Thai & Other Asian The *Soi Pracheun (Soi 20) Night Market*, which assembles each evening off Silom Rd in front of the municipal market pavilion, is good for cheap eats. During the day there are also a few food vendors in this soi. At lunchtime and early evening a batch of food vendors – everything from noodles to raw oysters – set up on Soi 5 next to Bangkok Bank's main branch.

The area to the east of Silom Rd off Convent and Sala Daeng Rds is a Thai gourmets' enclave. Most of the restaurants tucked away here are very good, but a meal for two will cost 600 to 800B. One such up-market spot is *Bussaracum* (☎ 235-8915), pronounced 'boot-sa-ra-kam', at 35 Soi Phipat off Convent Rd. Bussaracum specialises in 'royal Thai' cuisine, that is, recipes that were created for the royal court in days past; these recipes were kept secret until late this century. Every dish is supposedly prepared only when ordered, from fresh ingredients and freshly ground spices. Live classical Thai music, played at a subdued volume, is also provided. This is a fancy place, recommended for a splurge. Two can eat for around 650 to 850B; call ahead to be sure of a table.

BERNARD NAPTHINE

Bite-sized savoury appetisers, marinated and lightly grilled, neatly laid out for hungry passers-by.

Another great place for traditional Thai – at moderate prices – is *Ban Chiang* (☎ 236-7045), a restored wooden house in a verdant setting at 14 Soi Si Wiang, Pramuan Rd (off Silom Rd west of Uma Devi Temple). Owned by a Thai movie star, *Thanying* (☎ 236-4361) at 10 Pramuan Rd off Silom Rd has elegant decor and very good, moderately expensive royal Thai cuisine. It's open daily from 11 am to 10.30 pm; there's another branch at the World Trade Centre on Ploenchit Rd.

Mango Tree (☎ 236-2820) at 37 Soi Anuman Ratchathon, opposite the Tawana Ramada Hotel between Silom and Surawong Rds, offers classic Thai cuisine and live traditional Thai music amidst a decor of historical photos and antiques. Recommended dishes include plaa sāmlii dàet diaw (half-dried, half-fried cottonfish with spicy mango salad) and kài bai toei (chicken baked in pandanus leaves). Prices are moderate and it's open daily for lunch and dinner.

Moving towards the river, just west of Soi 9 at No 160 Silom Rd, you'll find the open-air *Isn't Classic* (the Thai name is 'Isāan Classic', after the Isāan or north-eastern Thai style), a popular restaurant specialising in north-eastern Thai food. Prices are very reasonable for good-quality sticky rice, kài yâang (spicy grilled chicken), lâap (meat salad), sôm-tam (spicy green papaya salad) and other Isāan delights. Over on Surawong Rd at No 173/8-9, *All Gaengs* is a medium-priced modern, air-con place specialising in Thai curries and spicy Thai-style salads (yam).

A good one-stop eating place with a lot of variety is the Silom Village Trade Centre, an outdoor shopping complex off Silom Rd, at Soi 24. Though it's basically a tourist spot with higher than average prices, the restaurants are of high quality and plenty of Thais dine here as well. The centrepiece is *Silom Village*, a place with shaded outdoor tables where the emphasis is on fresh seafood – sold by weight. The menu also has extensive Chinese and Japanese sections. Prices are moderate to high by Thai standards. For the quick and casual, *Silom Coffee Bar* makes a good choice. At night, *Ruen Thep* offers one of the city's better Thai classical dance-and-dinner venues. During the daytime, vendors dressed in traditional Thai clothing sell a variety of traditional snacks like khanŏm khrók (steamed coconut pastries) and mîang kham (savoury titbits wrapped in wild tea leaves) – more than a little corny, but again the food quality is high.

Chaai Karr (☎ 233-2549), on Silom Rd across from the Holiday Inn and a few shops east of Central Department Store, is a simply decorated with Thai antiques. The medium-priced menu is mostly Thai, with a few Western dishes, plus 19 varieties of brewed coffee; the Thai mango salad and spicy seafood soup are very good. Thai folk music plays in the background. Chaai Karr is open daily from 10.30 am to 9.30 pm.

Towards the eastern end of Surawong Rd, about a 10 minute walk west of Montien Hotel, is the famous *Somboon Seafood* (open from 4 pm to midnight), a good, reasonably priced seafood restaurant known for having the best crab curry in town. Soy-steamed seabass (plaa kràphong nêung sii-yíu) is also a speciality. Somboon has a second branch called *Somboon Chinese* farther north, across Rama IV Rd near Chulalongkorn University at Soi Chulalongkorn 8 (711-717 Chula Soi 8, Ban That Thong Rd).

Towards the other end of Surawong Rd at No 311/2-4 (on the corner of Soi Pramot), the economical *Maria Bakery & Restaurant* is well known for its fresh Vietnamese and Thai food as well as French pastries, pizza and vegetarian food. A newer Maria branch can be found at 909-911 Silom Rd opposite Central Department Store. Both are clean and air-con, with reasonable prices.

Mizu's Kitchen on Patpong Rd 1 has a loyal Japanese and Thai following for its inexpensive but good Japanese food, including Japanese steak. Another very good Japanese place – especially for sushi and sashimi – is *Goro* at 399/1 Soi Siri Chulasewok off Silom; prices are reasonable.

Indian & Muslim Farther towards the western end of Silom and Surawong Rds – an area known as Bangrak – Indian eateries begin to appear. Unlike Indian restaurants elsewhere in Bangkok, the menus in Bangrak don't necessarily exhibit the usual, boring predilection toward north Indian Moghul-style cuisine. For authentic south Indian food (dosa, idli, vada, etc), try the *Madras Cafe* (☎ 235-6761) in the Madras Lodge at 31/10-11 Vaithi Lane (Trok 13), off Silom Rd near the Narai Hotel (open daily from 9 am to 10 pm). Another place serving south Indian (in addition to north Indian) food is the very basic *Simla Cafe* at 382 Soi Tat Mai (opposite Borneo & Co) off Silom Rd, in an alley behind the Victory Hotel. Across from the Narai Hotel, near the Maha Uma Devi temple, street vendors sometimes sell various Indian snacks.

India Hut (☎ 237-8812), a new place on Surawong Rd opposite the Manohra Hotel, specialises in Nawabi (Lucknow) cuisine; it's quite good, friendly and medium to high in menu prices (45 to 100B per dish). The vegetarian samousas and fresh prawns cooked with ginger are particularly good. It's three flights of steps off the street, with modern Indian decor.

Himali Cha-Cha (☎ 235-1569), at 1229/11 Charoen Krung Rd, features good north-Indian cuisine at slightly higher prices. Founder Cha-Cha reportedly worked as a chef for India's last viceroy; his son has taken over the kitchen here. It's open daily for lunch and dinner.

The *Cholas*, a small air-con place downstairs in the Woodlands Inn on Soi Charoen Krung 32 just north of the GPO, serves decent, no-fuss north Indian food at 50 to 80B a dish. The open-air *Sallim Restaurant* next door to the Woodlands is a cheaper, more working-class place with north Indian, Malay and Thai-Muslim dishes – it's usually packed.

Around the corner on Soi Phuttha Osot is the very popular but basic-looking *Naaz* (Naat in Thai), often cited as having the richest khâo mòk kài (chicken biryani) in the city. The milk tea is also very good here, and daily specials include chicken masala and mutton kurma. For dessert, the house speciality is firni, a Middle Eastern pudding spiced with coconut, almonds, cardamom and saffron. Naaz is open from 7.30 am to 10.30 pm daily. There are several other Arab/Indian restaurants in this area.

At 1356 Charoen Krung Rd, near the intersection of Charoen Krung and Silom Rds, is the *Muslim Restaurant*, one of the oldest in the area. The faded yellow walls and chrome chairs aren't very exciting, but you can stuff yourself on curries and roti for 40B or less.

On Soi Pracheun (Soi 20) off Silom Rd there's a mosque – Masjid Mirasuddeen – so Muslim food vendors are common.

Vegetarian *Rabianthong Restaurant*, in the Narai Hotel on Silom Rd, offers a very good vegetarian section in its luncheon buffet – but only on *wan phrá* (full moon days) – for 260B per person.

The *Hare Krishna Centre* at 139 Soi Phuttha Osot, off Charoen Krung Rd opposite the GPO (near the above-mentioned Naaz), offers free Indian vegetarian meals on Sunday only at around 7.45 pm (following chanting and a reading of the Bhagavad Gita).

Other Cuisines If you crave Western food, this cuisine is plentiful on and around Patpong Rd. *Bobby's Arms*, an Aussie Brit pub on Patpong 2 (through a garage), has good fish & chips. The *Brown Derby*, on Patpong 1, is good for American-style deli sandwiches. Authentically decorated *Delaney's Irish Pub* (☎ 266-7160) at 1-4 Sivadon Bldg, Convent Rd in the Silom Rd district serves a set lunch menu for 130 to 160B Monday to Friday, plus other pub grub daily. Irish bands play nightly.

Wedged between the go-go bars on Patpong 2 are several fast-food chicken joints, including *KFC*, *Chicken Divine* and *Magic Grill*. Probably the best Patpong find of all is the *Café de Paris* (☎ 237-2776) on Patpong 2, an air-con spot popular with French expats for its decent approximations of Parisian-style bistro fare; it's open daily from 11 am to 1 am. Yet another branch of the *Little Home Bakery & Restaurant* does a booming business serving farang and Filipino food on Soi Thaniya (one soi east of Patpong 2).

Opposite the Silom entrance to Patpong, in the CP Tower building, are a cluster of air-con American and Japanese-style fast-food places: *McDonald's*, *Pizza Hut*, *Chester's Grilled Chicken*, *Suzuki Coffee House* and *Toplight Coffee House*. Several are open late to catch the night-time Patpong traffic.

The tiny *Harmonique* (☎ 237-8175) on Soi Charoen Krung 34, around the corner from the GPO, is a refreshing oasis in this extremely busy, smog-filled section of Charoen Krung. European-managed, the little shop serves a variety of teas, fruit shakes and coffee on Hokkien-style marble-topped tables – a pleasant spot to read poste-restante mail while quenching a thirst. Well-prepared if pricey (60 to 150B per dish) Thai food is also available. The shop discreetly offers silk, silverwork and antiques for sale. It's open daily 10 am to 10 pm.

Soi Ngam Duphli (Map 8)

Hua Hin Restaurant, on Soi Atakanprasit (off Soi Ngam Duphli south-west of the Malaysia Hotel), serves decent Western breakfasts, including fresh brewed coffee, for 35 to 50B; it's open daily from 7.30 am. On the 11th floor of *Lumphini Tower* on busy Rama IV Rd is a cafeteria-style food centre open from 7 am to 2 pm. Opposite Lumphini Tower on the same road is a warren of food vendors with cheap Thai eats.

Air-con *Mai Mawn* (look for a green sign with Thai script and a small English sign reading 'Restaurant – Thai, Chinese, Seafood') on Soi Ngam Duphli itself serves good Thai noodle dishes at lunch for around 25B, excellent Thai and Chinese food at dinner starting at 40B. Another restaurant in the Soi Ngam Duphli area worth mentioning is *Ratsstube* (☎ 287-2822) in the Thai-German Cultural Centre (Goethe Institute), also on Soi Atakanprasit. Home-made sausages and set meals from 120B attract a large and steady clientele; it's open daily 10 am to 10 pm.

Sukhumvit Rd (Map 4)

This avenue, stretching east all the way to the city limits, has hundreds of Thai, Chinese and Western restaurants to choose from.

Thai & Other Asian The ground floor of the Ambassador Hotel between sois 11 and 13 has a good food centre. It offers several varieties of Thai, Chinese, Vietnamese, Japanese, Muslim and vegetarian food at 20 to 40B per dish – you must buy coupons first and exchange them for dishes you order.

Cabbages & Condoms (Map 4) at No 10, Soi 12, is run by the Population & Community Development Association (PDA), the brainchild of Mechai Viravaidya who popularised condoms in Thailand – first for birth control and now for STD prevention. The restaurant offers not only a great selection of condoms, but fine Thai food at very reasonable prices as well. The tôm khàa kài (chicken-coconut soup) is particularly tasty here; the restaurant is open from 11 am to 10 pm. The *Mandalay* (☎ 255-2893), at 23/7 Soi Ruam Rudi (along with a second branch on Surawong Rd), is supposedly the only Burmese restaurant in town; it's good but not cheap.

The *Yong Lee Restaurant* at Soi 15, near Asia Books, has excellent Thai and Chinese food at reasonable prices and is a long-time favourite among Thai and farang residents alike. There is a second Yong Lee between sois 35 and 37.

The famous *Djit Pochana* (☎ 258-1578) has a branch on Soi 20 (see Map 4) and is one of the best-value restaurants in town for traditional Thai dishes. The all-you-can-eat lunch buffet is 90B. This central section of Sukhumvit Rd is loaded with medium-priced restaurants, which feature modern decor but real Thai food. *Baan Kanitha* (☎ 258-4181), 36/1 Soi 23, Sukhumvit Rd, offers traditional decor and authentic Thai food; the seabass in lime sauce (plaa kràphong nêung mánao) and chicken in coconut-galangal broth (tôm hhàa kài) are tops.

For nouvelle cuisine, try the *Lemongrass* (☎ 258-8637) at 5/21 Soi 24, which is atmospherically set in an old Thai house decorated with antiques. The food is exceptional; try the yam pèt (Thai-style duck salad). It is open from 11 am to 2 pm and 6 to 11 pm.

Another restaurant with an inventive kitchen is *L'Orangery*, at 48/11 Soi Ruam Rudi (close to where Ploenchit Rd becomes Sukhumvit Rd). Billed as Pacific Rim cuisine, the food shows the dual influences of Californian and Asian cooking; sometimes it works, sometimes it doesn't.

Yet another hidden gem down Sukhumvit Rd is *Laicram* (Laikhram) at Soi 33 (☎ 238-2337) and at Soi 49/4 (☎ 392-5864). The food is authentic gourmet Thai, but not outrageously priced. One of the house specialities is hàw mòk hãwy, an exquisite thick fish curry steamed with mussels inside the shell. Sôm-tam (spicy green papaya salad) is also excellent here, usually served with khâo man, rice cooked with coconut milk and bai toei (pandanus leaf). Opening hours are from 10 am to 9 pm Monday to Saturday and 10 am to 3 pm Sunday.

There are many restaurants around the major hotels on Sukhumvit Rd with mixed Thai, Chinese, European and American menus – most of average quality and slightly above-average prices.

The upscale *Le Dalat* (☎ 258-0290) at 47/1 Soi 23, Sukhumvit Rd (Map 4), has the most celebrated Vietnamese cuisine in the city. A house speciality is nãem meuang, grilled meatballs which you place on steamed rice-flour wrappers, then add chunks of garlic, chilli, ginger, starfruit and mango along with a tamarind sauce, and finally wrap the whole thing into a lettuce bundle before popping it in your mouth. There are two other branches at Patpong Business Centre, 2nd floor, Surawong Rd (☎ 234-0290) and Premier Shopping Village, Chaeng Wattana Rd (☎ 573-7017). Also good for a stylish Vietnamese meal is *Pho* (☎ 252-5601) on the 3rd floor of Sukhumvit Plaza (Map 4), Soi 12, Sukhumvit Rd. A second branch can be found in the Alma Link Bldg, 25 Soi Chitlom, Ploenchit Rd; both branches are open daily for lunch and dinner.

Indian & Muslim *Mrs Balbir's* (☎ 253-2281) at 155/18 Soi 11 (behind the Siam Commercial Bank) has a good variety of moderately priced vegetarian and non-vegetarian Indian food (mostly north Indian). Mrs Balbir has been teaching Indian cooking for many years and has her own Indian grocery store as well.

The splurge-worthy *Rang Mahal* (☎ 261-7100), a rooftop restaurant in the Rembrandt Hotel on Soi 18, offers very good north and south Indian 'royal cuisine' with cityscape views. On Sunday the restaurant puts on a sumptuous Indian buffet from 11.30 am to 3 pm. Another decent Indian place is *Bangkok Brindawan* (☎ 258-8793) at 15 Soi 35 near the Fuji supermarket. This one specialises in south Indian food; an all-you-can-eat 120B lunch buffet is offered on weekdays from 11 am to 3 pm.

A few medium to expensive restaurants serving Pakistani and Middle Eastern food can be found in the 'Little Arabia' area of Soi 3 (Soi Nana Neua). The best value in the whole area is *Al Hossain*, a roofed outdoor cafe on the corner of a lane (Soi 3/5) off the east side of Soi Nana Neua. A steam table holds a range of vegetarian, chicken, mutton and fish curries, along with dal (curried lentils), aloo gobi (spicy potatoes and cauliflower), nan and rice. Dishes cost 20 to 40B each. *Shiraz* on the same soi is a slightly pricier indoor place that provides hookahs for Middle Eastern gentlemen who while away the afternoon smoking out front. Similar places in the vicinity include *Mehmaan, Akbar's* (Map 4), *Al Hamra* and *Shaharazad*.

Vegetarian *Vegetarian House International* (☎ 254-7357), in an alley off the west side of Soi Nana Neua, serves Indian, Thai and Italian dishes in a 3rd floor walkup; it's open noon to 11 pm.

Western Homesick Brits need look no farther than *Jool's Bar & Restaurant* at Soi 4 (Soi Nana Tai), past Nana Plaza on the left walking from Sukhumvit Rd. The bar downstairs is a favourite expat hang-out while the dining room upstairs serves decent English food.

Several rather expensive West European restaurants (Swiss, French, German, etc) are also found on touristy Sukhumvit Rd. *Bei Otto*, between sois 12 and 14, is one of the most popular German restaurants in town and has a comfortable bar. *Haus München* (☎ 252-57776), 4 Soi 15, Sukhumvit Rd, serves large portions of good German and Austrian food; prices are reasonable and there are recent German-language newspapers on hand. It's open daily for breakfast, lunch and dinner.

Nostalgic visitors from the USA, especially those from southern USA, will appreciate the well-run *Bourbon St Bar & Restaurant* on Soi 22 (behind the Washington Theatre). The menu emphasises Cajun and Creole cooking; some nights there is also free live music.

One of the top French restaurants in the city – and probably the best not associated with a luxury hotel – is *Le Banyan* (☎ 253-5556) at 59 Soi 8 (Map 4) in a charming early Bangkok-style house. The kitchen is French-managed and the menu covers the territory from ragout d'escargot to canard maigret with foie gras. It also has a superb wine list. This is definitely a splurge experience – although the prices are moderate when compared with other elegant French restaurants in the city.

Giverny (☎ 391-1126), 342 Soi 63, Sukhumvit Rd, is also considered one of the better French restaurants in the city. The menu includes all the French standards, and the well-selected wine list is ample. Figure on spending 400 to 500B per person for three courses.

Pomodoro (☎ 252-9090), a place with floor-to-ceiling windows on the ground floor of the Nai Lert Building on Sukhumvit Rd between sois 3 and 5, specialises in Sardinian cuisine. The menu includes over 25 pasta dishes, and special set lunch menus are available for 180 to 240B. The wine list includes vintages from nine regions in Italy, along with others from France, Australia and the USA. Pomodoro is open daily from 10 am to 11 pm.

If you want Mexican, the city's best is at *Señor Pico's of Los Ángeles* (☎ 261-7100), on the 2nd floor of the Rembrandt Hotel, Soi 18 Sukhumvit Rd. Brightly decorated, it offers reasonably authentic Tex-Mex cuisine, including fajitas, carnitas, nachos and combination platters. Expect to spend 200 to 300B for two.

For American-style pizza, there's a *Pizza Mall* on the corner of Soi 33 and Sukhumvit Rd (the *Uncle Ray's Ice Cream* next door has the best ice cream in Bangkok) and a *Pizza Hut* at Soi 39.

The *Little Home Bakery & Restaurant* (☎ 390-0760), at 413/10-12 Soi 55, has an extensive Western menu along with a few Filipino items – this place has a very loyal Thai following.

Other Areas

Mega-Restaurants   *Tum-Nak-Thai (Tamnak Thai)* (☎ 276-7810), 131 Ratchadaphisek Rd, is one of several large outdoor restaurants built over boggy areas of Bangkok's Din Daeng district, north of Phetburi Rd. Built on four hectares of land and water, it can serve up to 3000 diners at once. The menu exceeds 250 items and includes Thai, Chinese, Japanese and European food. One section has Thai classical dance performances. Two can eat here for under 400B including beer.

Tum-Nak-Thai was billed as the largest outdoor restaurant in the world – as verified by the *Guinness Book of Records* – until *Mang Gorn Luang (Royal Dragon) Seafood Restaurant)* (☎ 398-0037) opened recently at Km 1 on the Bang Na-Trat expressway. Around 1200 roller-skating servers in traditional Thai costumes, along with waitresses paddling along artificial canals in 'happy boats', serve up to 10,000 diners per day. Other loony touches include soundproof karaoke pavilions and a dining area housed in a seven-storey pagoda. House specialities on the 440-item menu (not including drinks or desserts) include hàw mòk (thick seafood curry steamed in banana leaves) and yam yong (sweet and salty banana shoot salad). Figure 300 to 500B for two.

Dinner Cruises There are a number of companies that run these. Prices range from 40 to 750B per person depending on how far they go and whether dinner is included in the fare. See the River & Canal Trips section in the Things to See & Do chapter for more information.

Vegetarian One of the oldest Thai vegetarian restaurants, operated by the Buddhist ascetic *Asoke Foundation*, is at Chatuchak Market off Kamphaeng Phet Rd (near the main local bus stop, a pedestrian bridge and a Chinese shrine – look for a sign reading 'Vegetarian' in green letters). It's open only on weekends from 8 am to noon. Prices are very low – around 7 to 12B per dish.

Bangkok Adventist Hospital cafeteria (430 Phitsanulok Rd) serves cheap veggie fare. All the Indian restaurants in town also have vegetarian dishes on their menus.

Hotel Restaurants

For splurge-level food, many of Bangkok's grand luxury hotels provide memorable – if expensive – eating experiences. With Western cuisine particularly, the quality usually far exceeds anything found in Bangkok's independent restaurants. Some of the city's best Chinese restaurants are also located in hotels. If you're on a budget, check to see if a lunchtime buffet is available on weekdays; usually these are the best deals, ranging from 150 to 300B per person (up to 490B at the Oriental). Also check the *Bangkok Post* and the *Nation* for weekly specials by visiting chefs from far-flung corners of the globe – Morocco, Mexico City, Montreal, no matter how obscure, they've probably done the Bangkok hotel circuit.

The Oriental Hotel (Map 8) has six restaurants, all of them managed by world-class chefs – buffet lunches are offered at several. The hotel's *China House* (☎ 236-0400, ext 3378), set in a charming wooden house opposite the hotel's main wing, has one of the best Chinese kitchens in Bangkok, with an emphasis on Cantonese cooking. The lunchtime dim sum is superb and is a bargain by luxury hotel standards at 50B or less per plate or all-you-can-eat for 250B. *Lord Jim's*, with a view of the river, is designed to imitate the interior of a 19th century Asian steamer; the menu focuses on seafood (lunch buffet available).

The new *Bai Yun* (☎ 679-1200), on the 50th floor of the Westin Banyan Tree, specialises in nouvelle Cantonese – an east-west fusion – and is so far the highest restaurant in Thailand.

Dusit Thani's *Chinatown* (Map 8) (☎ 236-0450) was probably the inspiration for the Oriental's China House, though here the menu focuses on Chiu Chau (Chao Zhou) cuisine as well as Cantonese. Dim sum lunch is available, but it's a bit more expensive than the Oriental's. As at the Oriental, service is impeccable. Dusit also has the highly reputed *Mayflower*, with pricey Cantonese cuisine, and the Vietnamese *Thien Duong*.

For hotel dim sum almost as good as that at the Dusit or Oriental – but at less than a third the price – try the *Jade Garden* (☎ 233-7060) at the Montien Hotel (Map 8). Though not quite as fancy in presentation, the food is nonetheless impressive.

For French food, the leading hotel contenders are *Ma Maison* (☎ 253-0123) at the Hilton International (Map 7), *Normandie* (☎ 236-0400, ext 3380) at the Oriental (Map 8), and *Regent Grill* (☎ 251-6127) at the Regent Bangkok (Map 7). All are expensive but the meals and service are virtually guaranteed to be of top quality. The Regent Bangkok also offers the slightly less formal *La Brasserie*, specialising in Parisian cuisine.

Among the best Italian dining experiences in Bangkok is the very posh *Grappino Italian Restaurant* (☎ 653-9000) in the Amari Watergate Hotel, on Phetburi Rd (Map 7), Pratunam. All pasta and breads are prepared fresh daily on the premises, and the small but high-tech wine cellar is one of Bangkok's best. Of course the grappa selection is unmatched. Grappino is open daily for lunch and dinner; reservations suggested.

The minimalist *Colonnade Restaurant* (☎ 287-0222), at the Beaufort Sukhothai Hotel (Map 8), lays out a huge 500B brunch, including made-to-order lobster bisque, from 11 am to 3 pm on Sunday. A jazz trio plays background music. Reservations are suggested.

Caviar Corner, in The Promenade, a small but posh shopping mall on Withayu Rd, offers a variety of Persian caviars. Platters start at 275B for two kinds of caviar, salmon, toast and mascarpone; larger amounts of caviar start at 750B. Vodka, wine and champagne are also sold.

Finally, if eating at one of the above would mean spending your life savings, try this pauper's version. Go to the end of the soi in front of the Shangri-La Hotel (Map 8) and take a ferry (1B) across the river to the wooden pier immediately opposite. Next to this pier is the riverside *Prom*, where you can enjoy an inexpensive Thai seafood meal outdoors with impressive night-time views of the Shangri-La and Oriental hotels opposite. The ferry runs till the Prom closes, around 2 am.

High Tea

Although Thailand was never a colony, influences from nearby Kuala Lumpur and Singapore have made afternoon tea (or high tea) a custom at the more ritzy hotels. One of the best spreads is afternoon tea in the *Regent Bangkok* lobby (Map 7) from 2 to 5.30 pm on weekdays. The cost is 190B for a selection of herbal, fruit, Japanese, Chinese and Indian teas plus a variety of hot scones, Devonshire cream, jam, cakes, cookies and sandwiches. A live string quartet provides musical atmosphere.

At the *Authors Lounge* of the Oriental Hotel, high tea costs 275B (plus tax and service) for a range of sweet and savoury delights and one of the best tea assortments in Bangkok, all taken in the quasi-colonial atmosphere enjoyed by Maugham, Coward and Greene. Tea is served daily from 2 to 6 pm.

Amidst the Asian minimalism of the *Beaufort Sukhothai Hotel*'s lobby salon (Map 8), the usual sandwiches, pastries and tea selections go for just 180B. Add champagne to the afternoon's nosh for 420B. Served daily 2.30 to 6 pm.

Afternoon tea in the lobby-lounge of the *Shangri-La Hotel* (Map 8) costs 220B on weekdays from 2 to 6 pm, for a variety of teas, sandwiches and cakes; on weekends the Shangri-La does a more lavish 40-item 'high tea buffet' for 250B.

Entertainment

In their round-the-clock search for *khwaam sanùk* (fun), Bangkokians have made their metropolis one that never sleeps. To get an idea of what's available, check the daily entertainment listings in the *Bangkok Post* and the *Nation*, the free tourist-oriented weeklies *This Week* and *Angel City* or the relatively new monthly *Bangkok Metro*. Possibilities include classical music performances, rock concerts, videotheque dancing, touring Asian music/theatre ensembles, cinema, art shows, visiting chefs – virtually every type of event known in both the East and West.

NIGHTLIFE

Bangkok's over-publicised, naughty nightlife image is linked to the bars, coffee houses, nightclubs and massage parlours left over from the days when the City of Angels was an R&R stop for GIs serving in Vietnam. By and large these throwbacks are seedy, expensive and cater to men only. Then there is the new breed of S&S (sex & sin) bar, some merely refurbished R&R digs, that are more modest, classy and welcome females and couples. Not everybody's cup of tea, but they do a good business. Contrary to the media image, there are as many places suitable for either gender as there are male-oriented 'girlie bars'.

All the major hotels have upscale nightclubs as well. Many feature live music – rock, country & western, Thai pop music and jazz. Hotels catering to tourists and business-people often contain up-to-date discos. You'll find the latest recorded music in the smaller neighbourhood bars as well as the mega-discos.

All bars and clubs are supposed to close at 1 or 2 am (the latter closing time is for places with dance floors and/or live music) but in reality only a few obey the law.

Live Music

Bangkok's live music scene has expanded rapidly over the past decade or so, with a multiplicity of new, extremely competent bands and new clubs. The three-storey *Saxophone Pub Restaurant* (☎ 2465472), south of the Victory Monument circle at 3/8 Soi Victory Monument, Phayathai Rd, has become a Bangkok institution for musicians of several genres. On the ground floor is a bar/restaurant with jazz from 9 pm to 1.30 am; the next floor up has a billiards hall with recorded music; the top floor has live bands playing reggae, R&B, jazz or blues from 10.30 pm to 4 am, and on Sunday there's an open jam session. There's no cover charge at Saxophone and you don't need to dress up.

Another very casual spot to hear music is the open-air bar operated by *Ruang Pung Art Community* next to Chatuchak Market. Thai rock, folk, blues and jam sessions attract an arty Thai crowd.

Bars with regular live jazz include *Why Art?* in the Royal City Avenue complex, off New Phetburi Rd (nightly 10 pm to 2 am), *Blues/Jazz* (☎ 258-7747) at Soi 53 Sukhumvit Rd and the strangely-named *Imageries by the Glass* on Soi 24 Sukhumvit Rd (Monday and Tuesday nights only). Imageries by the Glass is owned by Thai composer-musician Jirapan Ansvananada, and it boasts a huge sound board, closed circuit TV for its stage shows and good local as well as foreign bands of all genres. It also hosts pop, rock, funk and R&B bands – basically a different style each night of the week.

The Oriental's famous *Bamboo Bar* has live jazz nightly from 5 to 8.30 pm in an elegant but relaxed atmosphere; other hotel jazz bars include *Entrepreneur* at the Asia Hotel (Saturday night only), the Grand Hyatt's *Garden Lounge* (Tuesday through to Sunday), the Beaufort Sukhothai Hotel's *Colonnade* (Tuesday through to Sunday) and the Hilton's *The Lounge* (Friday night only).

The imaginatively named *Rock Pub*, opposite the Asia Hotel on Phayathai Rd, has Thai heavy metal – with plenty of hair-throwing and lip-jutting – nightly. Regulars include Kaleidoscope, Wizard, Uranium and the Olarn Project. The *Hollywood Rock Place* on Phayathai Rd near the MacKenna cinema is similar.

Bangkok's better-than-average *Hard Rock Cafe* (Map 7) has live rock music most evenings from around 10 pm to 12.30 am, including the occasional big name act (Chris Isaak's incendiary 1994 performance left boot-nail dents in the bar top).

Not to be overlooked on Sarasin Rd, the *Old West* (Thailand's original old-west-style pub) books good Thai folk and blues groups – look for a rockin' outfit called D-Train here. Down the road a bit, *Blue's Bar* is similar. The *Magic Mushroom* at 212/33 Sukhumvit Rd (next to Soi 12) hires a variety of rock and blues acts nightly, including some of Bangkok's biggest names. The *Front Page* (Soi Sala Daeng, off Rama IV Rd) hosts journeyman folk and blues groups on Monday, Tuesday and Saturday nights.

Elegant *Spasso* in the Grand Hyatt Erawan has imported pop/dance bands from Europe, America and Australia.

Bars

Bangkok has definitely outgrown the days when the only bars around catered to male go-go oglers. Trendy among Bangkok Thais these days are bars which strive for a more sophisticated atmosphere, with good service and choice music. The Thais call them pubs, but they bear little resemblance to any traditional English pub. Some are 'theme' bars, conceived around a particular aesthetic. All the city's major hotels feature Western-style bars as well.

One of the main hot spots in town for young Thais is a huge bar and dance club complex called *Royal City Avenue* (Soi Sunwichai, north off New Phetburi Rd). Originally designed a few years back as a shopping centre, RCA has been taken over by a 2.5 km strip of high-tech bars with names like *Absolute Zero, Baby Hand Pub, Bar Code, Chit, Cool Tango, Exit, Fahrenheit, Jigsaw, Radio Underground, Relax, Route 66, Shit Happens, Why Art?* and *X Symbol*. Most have recorded music – everything from soul to techno to Thai pop – but a few also feature local bands. *Cool Tango*, operated by the original owners of the now-defunct Brown Sugar on Sarasin Rd, has the best live music and most international ambience; bands from overseas play here regularly. Three-storey *Casper's Palace*, which features live as well as recorded music and has somehow been able to sidestep the national 2 am closing law (staying open as late as 5 am), is overall the most happening place at the moment, but the scene at RCA changes almost week to week.

RCA was immensely popular in 1995 and early 1996 until a police crackdown on under-18 drinkers stifled things a bit. Such enforcement is a first for Thailand, a country where any six-year-old child can walk into a market and buy a beer. Most of the RCA clientele are in their teens and early 20s; some bars are owned by loose collectives of 20 or more university students who just want a place to hang out with their friends and possibly make a little extra money, while others are serious high-roller clubs.

A similarly youthful scene can be found at another new complex called *Premier*. Aesthetically this one has a more interesting layout, as the bars and restaurants are centred around a fountain pool. Post-modern pubs here include *Pool Side, Talk of the Town, Zeal, Tied Up, Vintage Special, Sanggasi, Le Mans* and *La Dee Da*, each with an arty decor. The *Nude Bar* sports Robert Mapplethorpe prints, while the *Seri Art Gallery* doubles as a pub and Thai art gallery. Premier's *One Dollar Music Room* is a sans-bar disco where you dance to recorded music as long as you like for a 25B cover. There's also a *Beer Garden* open during the cool season only, and nearly a dozen restaurants serving Thai, American and French food. Premier is east of the city on New Rama IX Rd, near the Si Nakarin intersection, past Ramkhamhaeng Rd, near Soi 24 (Soi Seri).

Bangkok is a little short on plain neighbourhood bars without up-market pretensions or down-market sleaze. One that's close to fitting the bill is the *Front Page*, a one-time journalists' hang-out (before the nearby *Bangkok Post* offices moved to Khlong Toey) on Soi 1, Sala Daeng (off Silom and Rama IV Rds). Two low-key, Brit-style taverns include *Jool's* on Soi 4 near Nana Plaza, *Bull's Head* on the ground floor of Angus Steak House, Soi 33/1, Sukhumvit Rd and the *Witch's Tavern* at 306/1 Soi 55, Sukhumvit Rd. The latter features live music on weekends.

Delaney's Irish Pub (☎ 266-7160), a new place at 1-4 Sivadon Bldg, Convent Rd in the Silom Rd district, is so far the only place in Bangkok that serves Guinness on tap; the interior wood panels, glass mirrors and bench seating were all custom-made and imported from Ireland. Delaney's features a daily happy hour and live Irish music from Tuesday through to Saturday.

Henry J Bean's Bar & Grill, in the basement of the Amari Watergate Hotel (Map 7) on Phetburi Rd in Pratunam is a relaxed spot with an American-style 50s and 60s decor. Performing bartenders flip bottles and glasses while serving and there's an early evening happy hour daily. A house band called the Nighthawks plays roots rock and reggae most nights; other live bands occasionally appear. There's a separate entrance for the bar so that you don't have to walk through the hotel.

Wong's Place at 27/3 Soi Si Bamphen is a low-key hangout for residents and visitors staying in the Soi Ngam Duphli area and sports a good collection of music videos.

The guitar-shaped bar at Bangkok's *Hard Rock Cafe* (Map 7) (☎ 251-0792), Siam Square, Soi 11, features a full line of cocktails and a small assortment of local and imported beers. The crowd is an ever-changing assortment of Thais, expats and tourists. From 10 pm on there's also live music.

For slick aerial city views, the place to go is the *Sky Lounge*, in the Baiyoke Tower (Map 7) on Ratchaprarop Rd in Pratunam. It's 43 floors above the city and open 24 hours. The *Compass Rose*, a new bar on the 59th floor of the Westin Banyan Tree on Sathon Tai Rd, is even higher but is only open 10 am to 1 am.

TV jocks can keep up with their favourite teams via big-screen satellite TV at *Champs* (☎ 252-7651), a huge

American-style sports bar in the Nai Lert Building on Sukhumvit Road, near Soi 5.

Wireheads can check their email or skim the Net at the new *CyberPub* (☎ 236-0450 ext 2971) in the Dusit Thani Hotel (Map 8) at the corner of Silom and Rama IV Rds. Booze and food are available, along with a bank of 10 up-to-date computer stations. Charges are 5B per online minute; you pay for food, beverages and online time using a 'smart card' issued by CyberPub. This is surely only the first of many such cyber-cafes Bangkok will see over the next few years.

CM², a new complex attached to the Novotel at Siam Square (Map 7), contains a number of ultra-modern bars, including one where 'virtual reality machines' will soon be installed.

Discos & Dance Clubs

All the major hotels in the city have discotheques, but only a small number of them – those at the Dusit Thani, the Shangri-La, the Grand Hyatt and The Regent – can really be recommended. Cover charges are pretty uniform: around 150 to 200B on weeknights, including one drink, and around 300 to 350B on weekends, including two drinks. Most places don't begin filling up till after 11 pm.

Bangkok is famous for its huge high-tech discos that hold up to 5000 people and feature mega-watt sound systems, giant-screen video and the latest in light-show technology. The clientele for these dance palaces is mostly an aggro crowd of young, moneyed Thais experimenting with lifestyles of conspicuous affluence, plus the occasional Bangkok celebrity. The most 'in' disco of this nature at the moment is *Phoebus Amphitheatre Complex* on Ratchadapisek Rd. Other biggies include *Paradise* on Arun Amarin Rd in Thonburi and the *Palace* on Vibhavadi Rangsit Highway, towards the airport. A mega-disco that attracts older as well as younger Thais is the *Galaxy* on Rama IV Rd, from which WBA world boxing champions Khaosai Galaxy and his brother Khaokor have taken their surname. The Galaxy is also popular with visiting Japanese who patronise the 'no-hands' section of the club, where hostesses feed the customers so they never have to lift their hands.

Well-heeled Thais and Thai celebrities frequent the more exclusive, high-tech *Narcissus* (☎ 258-2549) at 112 Soi 23 Sukhumvit Rd. *FM 228* (☎ 231-1228), in the United Center Building, 323 Silom Rd, tries to cover all bases with rooms featuring videotheque dancing, live music, and karaoke, plus an American restaurant and bar.

Dance clubs sprinkled through the Royal City Avenue and premier entertainment complexes have become very popular very quickly, especially among young Thais in their late teens and early 20s – see Bars above for details.

A string of small dance clubs on Soi 2 and Soi 4 (Soi Jaruwan) off Silom Rd, both parallel to Patpong 1 and 2, attracts a more mixed crowd in terms of age, gender, nationality and sexual orientation than either the hotel discos or the RCA/Premier entertainment complexes. The norm for recorded music here includes techno, trance, hip-hop and other current dance trends. Main venues – some of which are small and narrow – include on Soi 2 *Disco Disco (DD)* and *DJ Station*, and on Soi 4 *Hyper, Divine, Deeper, Rome Club* and *Sphinx.* The larger places collect cover charges of 100 to 300B depending on the night of the week; the smaller ones are free. The clientele at these clubs was once predominantly gay but has become more mixed as word got around about the great dance scene. Things don't get started here till relatively late, around midnight; in fact on most nights the Soi 2/Soi 4 dance clubs serve more as 'after hours' hang-outs since they usually stay open past the official 2 am closing time.

Star Bar, on the rooftop of the building opposite the police station at the intersection of Khao San and Chakraphong Rds, is a casual dance scene that attracts the tie-dyed world travellers who frequent the area. In spite of its proximity to the police, Star Bar often manages to stay open past official closing times. Near the end of a dead-end soi on the north side of Khao San Rd (Map 6), the *Paradise* offers a similar ambience with a touch of 60s black-light retro-ism.

Temptations, at the Novotel Bangkok in Siam Square (Map 7), provides big band music for *lii-lâat*, or ballroom dancing. Every night of the week a dressed-to-the-nines crowd cha-chas, foxtrots, tangos and rumbas across the glazed dance floor. In addition to serving drinks, waiters and waitresses will lead novices through the steps. The cover charge of 400B includes one drink and all the instruction necessary to turn you into a *nák lii-lâat*.

Go-Go Bars

These are concentrated along Sukhumvit Rd between Sois 21 and 23, off Sukhumvit Rd on Soi Nana Tai and in the world-famous Patpong Rd area (Map 8), between Silom and Surawong Rds.

Patpong's neon-lit buildings cover roughly four acres of what was once a banana plantation owned by the

Bank of Indochina, which sold the land to the Hainan-ese-Thai Patpongphanit family for 60,000B (US$2400) just before WWII. The typical bar measures four by 12m; the Patpongphanit family collects 10 million baht (US$400,000) rent per month from Patpong tenants. According to the Patpongphanit patriarch himself, recently interviewed in *Bangkok Metro* magazine, it wasn't American GIs who originally supported the Patpong bar business but rather airline staff from some 15 airline offices established in the area after WWII. Bangkok's first massage parlour, Bangkok Onsen, was established here in 1956 to serve Japanese expats and senior Thai police officers. By the 60s Patpong Rd had a flourishing local nightclub scene that was further boosted by the arrival of American GIs in the early 70s.

Patpong has calmed down a bit over the years. These days it has more of an open-air market feel as several of the newer bars are literally on the street, and vendors set up shop in the evening hawking everything from roast squid to fake designer watches. On Patpong's two parallel lanes there are around 38 go-go bars, plus a sprinkling of restaurants and cocktail bars. The downstairs clubs with names like *King's Castle* and *Pussy Galore* feature go-go dancing, while upstairs the real raunch is kept behind closed doors. Don't believe the touts on the street who say the upstairs shows – featuring amazing anatomical feats – are free: after the show, a huge bill usually arrives. *Lipstick* and *Suzie Wong's* are the only 'sexotic' bars that don't add surprise charges to your bill. The 1 am closing law is strictly enforced on Patpong 1 and 2.

Another holdover from the R&R days is *Soi Cowboy*, a single-lane strip of 25 to 30 bars off Sukhumvit Rd between sois 21 and 23. *Nana Entertainment Plaza*, off Soi 4 (Soi Nana Tai) Sukhumvit Rd, is a three-storey complex which has surged in popularity among resident and visiting oglers. Nana Plaza comes complete with its own guesthouses in the same complex – almost exclusively used by Nana Plaza's female bar workers for illicit assignations. There are only 18 bars in the whole complex.

Soi Tantawan and Thaniya Rd, on either side of and parallel to Patpong Rds 1 and 2, feature expensive Japanese-style hostess bars (which non-Japanese are usually barred from entering) as well as a handful of gay bars that feature male go-go dancers and 'bar boys'.

Transvestite cabarets are big in Bangkok and several are found in the Patpong area. *Calypso Cabaret* (☎ 261-6355), in the Ambassador Hotel at Soi 11, has the largest regularly performing transvestite troupe in town, with nightly shows at 8.30 and 10 pm. Some of the gay bars on sois 2 and 4 off Silom Rd also feature short drag shows during intermissions between dance sets.

Gay/Lesbian Scene

See the comments on the Soi 2 and Soi 4 Silom Rd dance club scene under Discos & Dance Clubs for places that attract a gay/straight/bi clientele. In general, the Soi 2 clubs are more gay than the Soi 4 bars, though Soi 4's *Telephone* is more exclusively gay than other bars on this street. The hottest gay dance scene on Soi 2 is currently *DJ Station*. *Khrua Silom*, in Silom Alley off Soi 2, attracts a young Thai gay and lesbian crowd. There's a cluster of seedier gay bars off Soi Anuman Ratchathon, off Silom Rd opposite the Tawana Ramada Hotel – more or less the gay equivalent of Patpong.

Utopia (☎ 259-9619), at 116/1 Soi 23 Sukhumvit Rd, is a combination bar, gallery, cafe and information clearing house for the local gay and lesbian community – the only such facility in South-East Asia. Friday nights are designated women's night, and there are regular film nights as well as Thai language lessons. Special events – such as Valentine's Day candlelight dinners – are held from time to time. Utopia is open daily from noon to 2 am.

Other lesbian venues include *By Heart Pub* (☎ 570-1841) at 117/697, Soi Sainanikhom 1, Bang Kapi, *Be My Guest*, around the corner from Utopia on Soi 31 Sukhumvit Rd and *Obsession* in the Royal City Avenue Complex.

Babylon Bangkok (☎ 213-2108), at 50 Soi Atakanprasit, off Sathon Tai Rd, is a four-storey gay sauna, which *Thai Scene* called one of the top ten gay saunas in the world. Facilities include a bar, roof garden, gym, massage room, steam and dry saunas, and jacuzzi baths. It's open from 5 to 11 pm daily. Other gay-oriented saunas include *The Obelisks* (☎ 662-4377) at 39/3 Soi 53, Sukhumvit Rd, *The Colony* (☎ 391-4393), at 117 Soi Charoensuk (off Soi 55, Sukhumvit Rd) and *V Club* (☎ 279-3322), at 541 Soi Aree (Soi 7), Phahonyothin Rd. All of these facilities charge a cover of around 150B on weekdays and 250 to 300B on weekends.

Jet Set at 32/19 Soi 21, Sukhumvit Rd is a karaoke lounge patronised by young gay Thais.

The *Long Yang Club* (☎ 679-7727), PO Box 1077, Silom, Bangkok 10504, organises members-only activities for gay men in Bangkok on a regular basis.

THAI DANCE-DRAMA

Thailand's most traditional *lakhon* and *khon* performances are held at the *National Theatre* (☎ 224-1342) on

Ratchini Rd near Phra Pinklao Bridge (Map 5). The theatre's regular public roster schedules six or seven performances per month, usually on weekends. Admission is reasonable – around 20 to 200B depending on the seat. Khŏn performances (masked dance-drama based on stories from the *Ramakian)* are highly recommended.

Occasionally, classical dance performances are also held at the Thailand Cultural Centre (☎ 245-7711), on Ratchadaphisek Rd, and at the *College of Dramatic Arts* (☎ 224-1391), near the National Theatre.

Chalermkrung Royal Theatre (Map 5)

The 1993 renovation of this Thai Deco building at the edge of the Chinatown-Pahurat district provides a striking new venue for khŏn performance in Thailand. When originally opened in 1933, the royally funded Chalermkrung was the largest and most modern theatre in Asia, with state-of-the-art motion picture projection technology and the first chilled-water air-con system in the region. Prince Samaichaloem, a former student of the École des Beaux-Arts in Paris, designed the hexagonal building.

The reborn theatre's 80,000-watt audio system, combined with computer-generated laser graphics, enable the 170-member dance troupe to present a technologically enhanced version of traditional khŏn. Although the special effects are reasonably impressive, the excellent costuming, set design, dancing and music are reason enough to attend.

The khŏn performance lasts about two hours with intermission; performances are generally held twice a week (Tuesday and Thursday at 8 pm), but this schedule changes from time to time as the theatre feels its way through the Bangkok cultural market. Other Thai performing arts may also be scheduled at the theatre.

Khon tickets cost a steep 500, 700, 800, and 1000B. Theatre members can obtain a 200 to 300B discount on these rates; only Bangkok residents are eligible, although for once this includes foreigners as well as Thais. For reservations, call ☎ 222-0434 or visit the box office. The theatre requests that patrons dress respectfully, which means no shorts or thongs. Bring a wrap or long-sleeved shirt in case the air-con is running full blast.

The Chalermkrung Royal Theatre stands on the corner of Charoen Krung and Triphet Rds, adjacent to the Old Siam Plaza complex and only a block from the Pahurat fabric market. Air-con bus Nos 8, 48 and 73 pass the theatre (going west on Charoen Krung). You can also comfortably walk to the theatre from the western terminus of the Saen Saep canal ferry. Taxi drivers may know the theatre by its original name, Sala Chalerm Krung, which is in Thai script on the lighted sign surmounting the front of the building.

Dinner Theatres

Most tourists view performances put on solely for their benefit at one of the several Thai classical dance/dinner theatres in the city (see list). Admission prices at these evening venues average 200 to 500B per person and include a 'typical' Thai dinner (often toned down for farang palates), a couple of selected dance performances and a martial arts display.

The historic Oriental Hotel has its own dinner theatre, the *Sala Rim Nam*, on the Thonburi side of the Chao Phraya River opposite the hotel. The cost is well above average, but so is the food and the performance; the river ferry between the hotel and restaurant is free. The much less expensive dinner performance at Silom Village's *Ruen Thep* restaurant on Silom Rd is recommended because of the relaxed, semi-outdoor setting.

Baan Thai Restaurant
    7 Soi 32, Sukhumvit Rd (☎ 258-5403)
Maneeya Lotus Room
    518/5 Ploenchit Rd (☎ 251-0382)
Phiman Restaurant
    46 Soi 49, Sukhumvit Rd (☎ 258-7866)
Ruen Thep
    Silom Village, Silom Rd (☎ 233-9447)
Sala Norasing
    Soi 4, Sukhumvit Rd (☎ 251-5797)
Sala Rim Nam
    opposite Oriental Hotel, Charoen Nakhon Rd
    (☎ 437-6221/3080)
Suwannahong Restaurant
    Si Ayuthaya Rd (☎ 245-4448/3747)
Tum-Nak-Thai Restaurant
    131 Ratchadaphisek Rd (☎ 277-3828)

Shrine Dancing

Free performances of traditional *lakhon chatrii* dance can be seen daily at the Lak Meuang and Erawan shrines if you happen to arrive when a performance troupe has been commissioned by a worshipper. Although many of the dance movements are the same as those seen in classical lakhon, these relatively crude performances are specially choreographed for ritual purposes and don't represent true classical dance forms. But the dancing is colourful – the dancers wear full costume and are accompanied by live music – so it's worth stopping by to watch if you're in the vicinity. For more information on Thai classical dance, see the Arts section in the Facts about Bangkok chapter.

MASSAGE

Traditional Massage

Traditional Thai massage, also called 'ancient' massage, is widely available in Bangkok. One of the best places for one is *Wat Pho*, Bangkok's oldest temple. Massage here costs 180B per hour or 100B for half an hour. For those interested in studying massage, the temple also offers two 30-hour courses – one on general Thai massage, the other on massage therapy – which you can attend three hours per day for 10 days, or two hours per day for 15 days. Tuition is 4500B. You must also pay the regular 10B per day admission fee for Wat Pho whether you are a student or massagee.

Next to Wat Mahathat (toward Thammasat University at the south-east corner of Maharat and Phra Chan Rds) is a strip of Thai herbal medicine shops offering good massage for a mere 80B an hour.

A more commercial area for Thai massage as well as Thai herbal saunas is Surawong Rd. Here you'll find *Marble House* (☎ 235-3519) at 37/18-19 Soi Surawong Plaza; *SL* (☎ 237-5690) on the 10th floor of Silom-Surawong Condos,

BERNARD NAPTHINE

A sleeping Thai displays a tattoo of Buddha.

Prostitution

Thais generally blame 19th-century Chinese immigrants for bringing prostitution to Thailand, but in reality Thailand was fertile ground because of its long-standing concubinary tradition. The first known literary references to this tradition were recorded by Chinese visitors in the early 1400s. Dutch merchants visiting Pattani in 1604 commented that 'when foreigners come there from other lands to do their business … men come and ask them whether they do not desire a woman' and that in Ayuthaya most of their peers 'had concubines or mistresses, in order (so they said) to avoid the common whores'. Seventeenth century Ayuthaya, in fact, had an official Thai government office in charge of operating a corps of 600 concubines.

Until 1934 Siam had no laws forbidding polygamy – or even a word for this Judaeo-Christian concept. Most men of wealth counted among their retinue at least one *sŏhphenii* (from the Sanskrit term for a woman trained in the *kama sutra* and other amorous arts), a word often translated as 'prostitute' in English today, but which might better be translated as 'courtesan'. In addition, the traditional Thai *mia yài mia nói* (major wife, minor wife) system made it socially permissible for a man to keep several mistresses – all Thai kings up to Rama IV had mia nói, as did virtually any Thai male who could afford them until recent times. Even today talk of mia nóis hardly raises an eyebrow anywhere in Thailand as the tradition lives on among wealthy businessmen, *jâo phâw* (organised crime 'godfathers') and politicians.

The first bona-fide brothel district in Thailand was established by Chinese immigrants in Bangkok's Sampeng Lane area in the mid-19th century. In the beginning, only Chinese women worked as prostitutes there; when Thai women became involved at the turn of the century, they usually took Chinese names. Prostitution eventually spread from Sampeng's 'green-lantern district' to Chinese neighbourhoods throughout Thailand and is now found in virtually every village, town and city in the kingdom. Ethnic Chinese still control most of the trade, although the prostitutes themselves now come from almost every ethnic background. In the last few years Bangkok has even seen an influx of Russian women – most on tourist visas – participating in the sex trade through escort services. Women from nearby countries, particularly Myanmar (Burma) and China, have also found their way – both willingly and unwillingly – into the trade.

The first true prostitutes – non-cohabiting women who accepted cash for sex services – to work outside the Chinese districts appeared soon after King Rama VII's 1934 decree banning polygamy. During WWII the Thai government stationed large numbers of Thai troops in the north to prevent Bangkok from becoming a military target. At the beginning of the war, Chiang Mai had only two known prostitutes, but by 1945 there were hundreds servicing the soldiers. Prostitution wasn't declared illegal until the 1950s when Field Marshal Phibun bullied his way into the PM's seat. In the 1960s and 1970s the Vietnam War brought unprecedented numbers of foreign soldiers to Bangkok and Pattaya on 'Rest & Recreation' (R&R) tours, creating a new class of prostitutes who catered to foreigners rather than Thais.

Current estimates of the number of Thai citizens directly involved in offering sex services vary from the Ministry of Public Health's conservative 100,000 to wild bar-stool estimates of 500,000. After an intensive two-year study into prostitution, Chulalongkorn University's Population Institute came up with a reasoned estimate of 200,000 to 210,000, a figure now widely considered the most realistic. This number is thought to include around 10,000 male and child prostitutes. Although often portrayed as Asia's sex capital, Thailand actually ranks third (behind Taiwan and the Philippines) in per-capita numbers of sex workers, according to international human rights reports.

An East-West Center study noted that 'As throughout most of South and South-East Asia, men in Thailand have greater freedom in their sexual activities than women, who are expected to arrive at the marriage altar as virgins and to refrain from extramarital affairs.' The Center concluded that this attitude 'creates a sexual imbalance in which large numbers of males are seeking casual sexual contact, but few females are available. The resulting active and well-attended commercial sex industry, catering largely to indigenous demand, has created a reservoir of … sex workers and clients'. Sociologists estimate that as many as 75% of single Thai males engage the services of a prostitute on an average of twice a month. In highly urban Bangkok, attitudes are changing steadily as unpaid extramarital sex is becoming increasingly common and hence the percentage of Thai clients is significantly lower than elsewhere in the country.

Most of the country's sex industry is invisible to the visiting farang. A typical mid-level coffee house/brothel will offer girls ranked in price according to their beauty

or supposed skills; prices are denoted by coloured tags the women wear on their dresses. Back-alley places service low-wage earners for as little as 40B. At the other end of the spectrum, Thai businessmen and government officials entertain in private brothels and clubs where services average 1000 to 5000B.

Unlike Western prostitution, there are few 'pimps' (people who manage one or more prostitutes) in Thailand. Instead, a network of procurers/suppliers and brothel owners control the trade, taking a high proportion (or all) of the sex service fees. At its worst, the industry takes girls sold or indentured by their families, sometimes even kidnapped, and forces them to work in conditions of virtual slavery. A few years ago a Phuket brothel of the type rarely patronised by farangs caught fire; several young women who were chained to their beds by the management died in the fire.

In the Patpong-style bars catering to foreigners, most bar girls and go-go dancers are freelance agents; they earn their income from taking a percentage of drinks bought on their behalf and from sex liaisons arranged outside the premises – usually after closing (if they leave during working hours, a customer usually pays a 'bar fine' on their behalf). The average Patpong-type bar girl earns 6000 to 7000B per month directly from the bar she works in; fees for extracurricular services are negotiated between customer and prostitute and can cost anything from 800 to 2000B.

Most prostitutes – male and female – are young, uneducated and from village areas. Researchers estimate they have a maximum working life of 10 to 12 years – if they haven't saved up enough money to retire by then (few do), they're often unemployable due to mental and physical disabilities acquired during their short working life. Various Thai volunteer groups are engaged in counselling the country's sex workers – helping them escape the industry or educating them on the dangers of STDs, particularly AIDS.

In 1992 the Thai cabinet introduced a bill to decriminalise prostitution in the hope that it would make it easier for prostitutes to seek counselling or STD testing without fear of prosecution. So far no such bill has been enacted, but in June 1993 then-Prime Minister Chuan Leekpai ordered a crackdown on prostitutes under 18, an act which has had quantifiable results but has by no means completely banished under-18s from the trade. A recent US State Department human rights report of the same year found that the percentage of prostitutes in Thailand under 18 fell well below numbers

in India, Bangladesh, Sri Lanka or the Philippines. According to End Child Prostitution in Asian Tourism (ECPAT), as of 1996 the main centres for child prostitution are now India, Cambodia and the Philippines.

In July 1994 the government strengthened child prostitution laws by making clients of under-age sex workers subject to fines and jail terms. A Prostitution Prevention and Suppression Bill introduced in 1996 expands that to include procurers and brothel operators; under the latest law, a jail term of two to 20 years and/or a fine of 200,000 to 400,000B can be imposed on anyone caught having sex with prostitutes under 15 years of age (the age of consent in Thailand). Parents or patrons who conspire with others to supply underage prostitutes face similar punishment. Experts suggest these laws will have little effect on the indigenous market, though they may frighten away potential foreign clients and procurers. Thai men visit prostitutes an estimated aggregate of 18-million times each year, hence the economics of the industry are far-reaching and difficult to regulate. Realists point out that if Thailand has 200,000 prostitutes, each of whom works 25 days a month and earns an average 1000B a day for themselves and their employers, the resultant revenue is about 50% higher than the national budget. ■

176 Soi Anuman Ratchathon off Soi 6, Silom Rd; *Vejakorn* (☎ 237-5576), 37/25 Soi Surawong Plaza, Surawong Rd; and *Eve House* (☎ 266-3846), 18/1 Surawong Rd, opposite Thaniya Plaza. Eve House charges 150B per hour and accepts women only. The rest of these charge 200 to 300B per hour and offer Thai herbal sauna as well as massage. *Arima Onsen* (☎ 235-2142) at 37/10-11 Soi Surawong Plaza specialises in Japanese-style massage and reflexology.

Out on Sukhumvit Rd you can find traditional Thai massage at *Buathip Thai Massage* (☎ 255-1045) at 4/13 Soi 5, Sukhumvit Rd; and *Winwan* (☎ 251-7467) between sois 1 and 3, Sukhumvit Rd.

Fees for traditional Thai massage should be no more than 300B per hour, though some places have a 1½-hour minimum. Be aware that not every place advertising traditional or ancient massage offers a really good one; sometimes the only thing 'ancient' about the pummelling is the age of the masseuse or masseur. Thai massage aficionados say that the best massages are given by blind masseurs (available at Marble House).

Most hotels also provide legitimate massage services either through their health clubs or as part of room service. The highly praised *Oriental Hotel Spa* offers a 40 minute 'jet lag massage' designed to alleviate body-clock time differences.

Massage Parlours

Massage parlours have been a Bangkok attraction for many years now, though the Tourism Authority of Thailand (TAT) tries to discourage the city's reputation in this respect. Massage as a healing art is a centuries-old tradition in Thailand, and it is possible to get a really legitimate massage in Bangkok – despite the commercialisation of recent years. That many of the city's modern massage parlours (*àap òp nûat* or 'bathe-steam-massage') also deal in prostitution is well known; less well known is the fact that many (but by no means all) of the girls working in the parlours are bonded labour – they are not necessarily there by choice.

All but the most insensitive males will be saddened by the sight of 50 girls/women behind a glass wall with numbers pinned to their dresses. Often the bank of masseuses is divided into sections according to skill and/or appearance. Most expensive is the 'superstar' section, in which the women try to approximate the look of fashion models or actresses. A smaller section is reserved for women who are actually good at giving massages, with no hanky-panky on the side.

Before contemplating anything more than a massage at a modern massage parlour, be sure to read the Health section in the Facts for the Visitor chapter for information on sexually transmitted diseases. There is a definite AIDS presence in Thailand; condom use lowers the risk considerably, but remember that an estimated 11% of commercial Thai condoms are defective.

CINEMA & VIDEOS

Dozens of movie theatres around town show Thai, Chinese, Indian and Western movies. The majority of films shown are comedies and shoot-em-ups, with the occasional drama slipping through. These theatres are air-con and quite comfortable, with reasonable rates (40 to 80B). All movies are preceded by the Thai royal anthem along with projected pictures of King Bhumibol and other members of the royal family. Everyone in the theatre stands quietly and respectfully for the duration of the anthem (which was written by the king).

The main theatres showing commercial English-language films are *Scala* (Map 7), *Lido 1, 2 & 3* and *Siam* at Siam Square; *Major 1 & 2* at Mahboonkrong (Map 7); *Hollywood* at Hollywood Street Center, Phetburi Rd; *Metro*, Phetburi Rd; *World Trade Center 1, 2 & 3*, Ratchadamri Rd (Map 7); *Century 1 & 2* and *Mackenna* on Phayathai Rd; and the *Washington 1 & 2* at Soi 24 Sukhumvit Rd. Movie ads appear daily in both the *Nation* and the *Bangkok Post*; listings in the *Nation* include addresses and program times.

Foreign films are often altered before distribution by Thailand's board of censors; usually this involves obscuring nude sequences with Vaseline 'screens'. Some distributors also edit films they consider to be too long; occasionally Thai narration is added to explain the storyline (when *The Omen* was released in Thailand, distributors chopped off the ambiguous ending and added a voice-over, giving the film a 'new' ending).

Film snobs may prefer the weekly or twice-weekly offerings at Bangkok's foreign cultural clubs. French and German films screened at the cultural clubs are almost always subtitled in English. Admission is sometimes free, sometimes 30 to 40B. For addresses and phone numbers, see the Cultural Centres section in the Facts for the Visitor chapter.

Video

Video rentals are very popular in Bangkok; not only are videos cheaper than film admission, but many films are available on video that aren't approved for theatre distribution by Thailand's board of censors. For those with access to a TV and VCR, rental is around 20 to 50B. Sukhumvit Rd has the highest concentration of video shops; the better ones are found in the residential area between sois 39 and 55. Blockbuster, the world's largest video chain, has opened a branch on Soi 33/1, Sukhumvit Rd, and plans to open many more branches throughout the capital in coming years.

TVs and VCRs (both PAL and NTSC) can be rented at Silver Bell (☎ 236-2845), 113/1-2 Surawong Centre, Surawong Rd.

SPECTATOR SPORT

Thai Boxing

Muay thai (Thai boxing) can be seen at two boxing stadiums, *Lumphini* (on Rama IV Rd near Sathon Tai (South) Rd (Map 8) and *Ratchadamnoen* (on Ratchadamnoen Nok

Rd, next to the TAT office - Map 5). Admission fees vary: the cheapest seats are around 170B and ringside seats cost 500B or more. On Monday, Wednesday, Thursday and Sunday, the boxing is at Ratchadamnoen, while on Tuesday, Friday and Saturday it's at Lumphini. The Ratchadamnoen matches begin at 6 pm (except for Sunday shows which start at 5 pm) and the Lumphini matches all begin at 6.20 pm. Aficionados say the best-matched bouts are reserved for Tuesday nights at Lumphini and Thursday nights at Ratchadamnoen.

The restaurants on the north side of Ratchadamnoen stadium are well known for their delicious kài yâang and other north-eastern dishes. (For information on learning Thai boxing see the Courses section of the Things to See & Do chapter. For more on the sport itself, see the special aside in the same chapter).

Tàkrâw

Sometimes called Siamese football in old English texts, *tàkrâw* refers to a game in which a woven rattan ball about 12 cm in diameter is kicked around. The rattan (or sometimes plastic) ball itself is called a *lûuk tàkrâw*. Tàkrâw is also popular in several neighbouring countries; it was originally introduced to the SEA Games by Thailand and international championships tend to alternate between the Thais and Malays. The traditional way to play tàkrâw in Thailand is for players to stand in a circle (the size of the circle depends on the number of players) and simply try to keep the ball airborne by kicking it soccer-style. Points are scored for style, difficulty and variety of kicking manoeuvres. A popular variation on tàkrâw – and the one used in intramural or international competitions – is played with a volleyball net, using all the same rules as in volleyball except that only the feet and head are permitted to touch the ball. It's amazing to see the players perform aerial pirouettes, spiking the ball over the net with their feet. Another variation has players kicking the ball into a hoop 4.5 above the ground – basketball with feet, but without a backboard! Tàkrâw is most easily seen on the athletic fields at school grounds and university campuses around the city.

Shopping

Regular visitors to Asia know that, in many ways, Bangkok beats Hong Kong and Singapore for deals on handicrafts, textiles, gems, jewellery, art and antiques – nowhere else will you find the same selection, quality and prices. The trouble is finding the good spots, as the city's intense urban tangle sometimes makes orientation difficult. Nancy Chandler's *Map of Bangkok*, which was originally intended as a guide to the city's markets and shopping venues (but includes much more these days), makes a very good buying companion, with annotations on all sorts of small, out-of-the-way shopping venues.

For information on packaging and shipping goods, see the Facts for the Visitor chapter, under Post & Communications.

PRICES

Prices for items sold by street vendors in markets or in most shops are entirely negotiable (this includes hotel souvenir shops). The only places you'll see fixed prices in Bangkok is in department stores. If the same kind of merchandise is offered in a department store and a small shop or market, it would be a good idea to check the department store price for a point of reference. Sometimes the department store price will be lower than the market price, sometimes it won't – but it will almost always be a fairly realistic figure. For items that aren't available in department stores, eg antiques, your best research is accomplished by shopping around. Unless you already know the fair price on a certain item, you needn't take the first opportunity to purchase – not only because you might find a better price, but because better quality or selection may be just around the corner.

One sure way to keep prices down is to avoid shopping in the company of touts, tour guides or 'friendly strangers' as they will inevitably – no matter what they say – take a commission on anything you buy, thus driving prices up.

BARGAINING

Good bargaining is almost an art and Thais respect a good haggler. Always let the vendor make the first offer then ask 'Is that your best price?' or 'Can you lower the price?'. This usually results is an immediate discount from the first price. Now it's your turn to make a counter-offer; always start low but don't bargain at all unless you're serious about buying. Negotiations continue back and forth until a price is agreed upon – there's no set discount from the asking price as some vendors start ridiculously high, others closer to the 'real' price.

Most vendors will offer a set of excuses for why they can go no lower, but since you have no way to assess the validity of such excuses you can only go with your instincts as to what the merchandise is really worth. It helps if you have done your homework by shopping around, and the whole process becomes easier with practice. It helps immeasurably to keep the negotiations relaxed and friendly, and to speak slowly and clearly (but not in a condescending manner). Vendors will almost always give a better price to someone they like.

GUARANTEES

Guarantees are an important consideration if you're buying expensive items like gems or electronic goods. Make sure the guarantee is international – usually this is no problem but check it out before you start haggling. A national guarantee is next to useless – are you going to return a gem to Bangkok if you discover it's fake? Finally, make sure that the guarantee is filled out correctly with the shop's name and, if appropriate, the serial number of the item. For electronic goods, check the item's compatibility back home. You don't want a brand or model that has never found its way to your home country.

Particularly when buying gems or jewellery, be wary of special 'deals' that are offered for 'one day only' or which set you up as a 'courier' in which you're promised big money. Many travellers end up losing big time. Shop around and don't be hasty. Remember: there's no such thing as a 'government sale' or a 'factory price' at a gem or jewellery shop; the Thai government does not own or manage any gem or jewellery shops. See the special Scams aside in the Facts for the Visitor chapter for a detailed warning on gem fraud.

Also, make sure you have exactly what you wanted before you leave the shop. Check your receipts and guarantees – make sure they are dated and include serial numbers and the shop's stamp.

WHERE TO SHOP

Chatuchak (Weekend) Market (Map 3)

This is the Disneyland of Thai markets; on weekends 8672 vendor stalls cater to an estimated 200,000 visitors a day, and they sell everything from live chickens and snakes to opium pipes and herbal remedies. Thai clothing such as the *phâakhamāa* (sarong for men) and the *phâasîn* (sarong for women), *kaang keng jiin* (Chinese pants) and *sêua mâw hâwm* (blue cotton farmer's shirt) are good buys. You'll also find musical instruments, hill-tribe crafts, religious amulets, antiques, flowers, clothes imported from India and Nepal, camping gear and military surplus. The best bargains are household goods like pots and pans, dishes, drinking glasses, etc. If you're moving to Thailand for an extended period, this is the place to pick up stuff for your kitchen. Don't forget to bargain. There's plenty of interesting and tasty food if you're hungry, and live music in the early evening in Thai folk music cafes. And if you need some cash, a couple of banks have ATMs and foreign exchange booths at the Chatuchak Park offices, near the north end of the market's sois 1, 2 and 3. Plan to spend a full day, as there's plenty to see, eat, and listen to. And leave time for getting lost!

An unfortunate footnote is that Chatuchak Park remains an important hub of Thailand's illegal exotic wildlife trade – in spite of occasional police raids – as well as a conduit for endangered species from surrounding countries. Some species are sold for their exotic food value, eg barking deer, wild boar, crocodiles and pangolins, while some are sold for their supposed medicinal value, eg rare leaf-monkeys. Thai law protects most of these species, but many Thais flout these restrictions. Not all wildlife trade here is illicit though; many of the birds sold, including the hill mynah and zebra dove, have been legally raised for sale as pets.

The main part of Chatuchak Market is open on Saturday and Sunday from around 8 am to 8 pm. There are a few vendors out on weekday mornings and a daily vegetable/plant/flower market opposite the market's south side. One section of the latter, known as the Aw Taw Kaw Market, sells organically grown (no chemical sprays or fertilisers) fruits and vegetables.

Chatuchak Market lies at the southern end of Chatuchak Park, off Phahonyothin Rd and across from the Northern (Maw Chit) bus terminal (Map 11). Air-con bus Nos 2, 3, 9, 10 and 13, and a dozen other ordinary city buses (No 3 from Phra Athit Rd in Banglamphu), all pass the market – just get off before the Northern bus terminal. The air-con bus No 12 and ordinary bus No 77 conveniently terminate right next to the market.

The market's directors are considering constructing a huge three storey building with parking lots and modern vendor stalls on the existing 70-rai plot of land,

Chatuchak (Weekend) Market

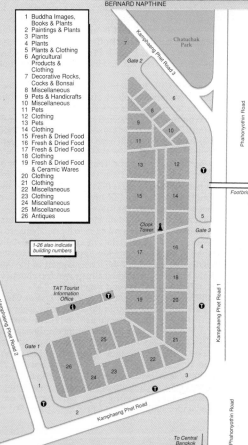

MAP 3

0   100   200 m

1 Buddha Images,
   Books & Plants
2 Paintings & Plants
3 Plants
4 Plants
5 Plants & Clothing
6 Agricultural
   Products &
   Clothing
7 Decorative Rocks,
   Cocks & Bonsai
8 Miscellaneous
9 Pets & Handicrafts
10 Miscellaneous
11 Pets
12 Clothing
13 Pets
14 Clothing
15 Fresh & Dried Food
16 Fresh & Dried Food
17 Fresh & Dried Food
18 Clothing
19 Fresh & Dried Food
   & Ceramic Wares
20 Clothing
21 Clothing
22 Miscellaneous
23 Clothing
24 Miscellaneous
25 Miscellaneous
26 Antiques

1-26 also indicate
building numbers

BERNARD NAPTHINE

Kamphaeng Phet Road 3

Chatuchak Park

Gate 2

Phahonyothin Road

Footbridge

Clock Tower

Gate 3

Kamphaeng Phet Road 1

TAT Tourist
Information
Office

Gate 1

Kamphaeng Phet Road 2

Kamphaeng Phet Road

To Central
Bangkok

Phahonyothin Road

which is leased from the Railway Authority of Thailand. Opponents of the plan point out that around 75% of Chatuchak market-goers currently arrive by public transport, hence the construction of a huge parking facility will worsen traffic and change the character of the market by catering to the more affluent.

Flower Markets & Nurseries

A good selection of tropical flowers and plants is available at the Thewet Market near the Tha Thewet pier (Map 1) on Krung Kasem Rd to the north-west of Banglamphu. The city's largest wholesale flower source is Pak Khlong Market on the right bank of the Chao Phraya River at the mouth of Khlong Lawt, between Atsadang Rd and Memorial Bridge (Map 5). Pak Khlong is also good for vegetables. The newest and largest plant market is opposite the south side of Chatuchak Market (Map 3), near the Northern bus terminal off Phahonyothin Rd; unlike Chatuchak Market it's open all week long. It's sometimes called Talaat Phahonyothin or Phahonyothin Market.

The best area for nursery plants, including Thailand's world-famous orchid varieties, is Thonburi's Phasi Charoen district, which is accessible via the Phetkasem Hwy north of Khlong Phasi Charoen. The latter is linked to the Chao Phraya River via Khlong Bangkok Yai. Two places with good selections are Eima Orchid Co (☎ 454-0366; fax 454-1156) at 999/9 Mu 2, Bang Khae, Phasi Charoen, and Botanical Gardens Bangkok (☎ 467-4955) at 6871 Kuhasawan, Phasi Charoen. Bus Nos 7 and 80 plus air-con bus No 9 stop in the Phasi Charoen district.

JOANNA O'BRIEN

Frangipani is a common sight and scent during festivities.

Other Markets

Under the expressway at the intersection of Rama IV and Narong Rds in the Khlong Toey district, the **Khlong Toey Market** is possibly the cheapest all-purpose market in Bangkok (best on Wednesday). South of the Khlong Toey Market, closer to the port, is the similar **Penang Market**, so called because a lot of the goods 'drop off' cargo boats from Penang (and Singapore, Hong Kong, etc). Both markets are in danger of being demolished under current urban renewal plans.

Pratunam Market (Map 7), at the intersection of Phetburi and Ratchaprarop Rds, runs every day and is very crowded, but it has great deals in new, cheap clothing. You won't see it from the street; you must look for one of the unmarked entrances that lead back behind the main store fronts.

The huge **Banglamphu Market** spreads several blocks over Chakraphong, Phra Sumen, Tanao and Rambutri Rds – a short walk from the Khao San Rd guesthouse area. The Banglamphu market area is probably the most comprehensive shopping district in the city as it encompasses everything from street vendors to up-market department stores.

The **Pahurat** and **Chinatown** districts (Map 5) have interconnected markets selling tons of well-priced fabrics, clothes and household wares, as well as a few places selling gems and jewellery. The **Wong Wian Yai Market** in Thonburi, next to the large traffic circle (*wong wian yài* means 'big circle') directly south-west of Memorial Bridge (Saphaan Phut), is another all-purpose market – but this one rarely gets tourists.

Shopping Centres & Department Stores

The growth of large and small shopping centres has accelerated over the last few years into a virtual boom. Central and Robinson department stores, the original stand-bys, have branches in the Sukhumvit and Silom Rds areas with all the usual stuff – designer clothes, Western cosmetics – plus supermarkets and Thai delis, cassette tapes, fabrics and other local products. Typical opening hours are 10 am to 8 pm. The Central branch on Ploenchit Rd (Map 7) suffered a major fire in 1995 and is under reconstruction.

Oriental Plaza (Soi Oriental, Charoen Krung Rd) and River City Shopping Complex (near the Royal Orchid Sheraton, off Charoen Krung and Si Phraya Rds, Map 8) are centres for high-end consumer goods. They're expensive but do have some unique merchandise; River City has two floors specialising in art and antiques.

The much smaller Silom Village Trade Centre on Silom Rd (Map 8) has a few antique and handicraft shops with merchandise several rungs lower in price. Anchored by Central Department Store, the six storey Silom Complex nearby (Map 8) remains one of the city's busiest shopping centres. Also on Silom Rd is the posh Thaniya Plaza (Map 8), a newer arcade housing clothing boutiques, bookshops, jewellery shops and more.

Along Ploenchit and Sukhumvit Rds you'll find many newer department stores and shopping centres, including Sogo, Landmark Plaza and Times Square (Map 4), but these Tokyo clones tend to be expensive and not that exciting. Peninsula Plaza on Ratchadamri Rd (named after the Bangkok Peninsula Hotel, which has since changed its name to the Regent Bangkok) has a more exclusive selection of shops – many of which have branches at River City and Oriental Plaza – and a good-sized branch of Asia Books. The Promenade, in front of the Hilton International on Withayu Rd, is a very posh mall containing jewellery shops, cafes, antiques, art galleries and modern Thai art of very high quality.

The eight floors of the World Trade Center (WTC), near the intersection of Ploenchit and Phayathai Rds, seem to go on, wing after wing, with no end in sight. The main focus is the Zen department store, which has clothing shops reminiscent of Hong Kong's high-end boutiques. On the 8th floor is Bangkok's premier antidote to the tropics, the World Ice Skating Center. If you're looking for clothing or toys for kids, ABC Babyland on WTC's 2nd floor has just about everything. Asia Books has a branch in the WTC and more shops are opening as a new wing is being added, including a new Thailand Duty Free Shop on the 7th floor (passport and airline ticket required for purchases).

Siam Square, on Rama I Rd near Phayathai Rd (Map 7), is a network of some 12 sois lined with shops selling mid-priced designer clothes, books, sporting goods and antiques. On the opposite side of Rama I stands Thailand's first shopping centre, the four storey, 20-year-old Siam Center. Before a 1995 fire (four Bangkok department stores suffered fires that year) it was big on designer clothing shops – Benetton, Chaps, Esprit, Chanel, Jaspal, Anne Cole, Guy Laroche and Paul Smith to name a few – as well as coffee shops, travel agencies, banks and airline offices. At the time of writing Siam Center was still closed for repairs.

One of the most varied shopping centres is Mahboonkrong (MBK), near Siam Square (Map 7). All air-con,

MBK has many small, inexpensive shops in addition to the flashy Tokyu Department Store. Bargains can be found if you look. The Travel Mart on MBK's 3rd floor stocks a reasonable supply of travel camping equipment – not the highest quality but useful in a pinch.

North of Siam Square on Phetburi Rd, Phanthip Plaza (Map 7) specialises in computer equipment and software shops. Until 1992 or so, bootleg software was abundant here; some of the shops still knock off a few pirated programs under the counter.

Old Siam Plaza (Map 5), bounded by Charoen Krung, Burapha, Pahurat and Triphet Rds, is the first new development of any significance in the Chinatown-Pahurat area in over a decade. Along with the renovation and reopening of the adjacent Chalermkrung Royal Theatre, the old Bangkok-style shopping centre represents a minor renaissance for an otherwise shabby and congested district. Most of the shops purvey Thai-style goods or services; one whole side is devoted to gun dealers, another to gem and jewellery stores, the rest to Thai handicrafts, furniture, restaurants and coffee shops. The only establishments without a Thai theme are McDonald's and Furama, a Japanese restaurant.

South-East Asia's largest shopping centre/mall is Seacon Square (Map 11), east out on Si Nakarin Rd. It has practically every type of shop mentioned in this section, including huge branches of DK Books and Asia Books, a cinema multiplex and a number of cafes.

WHAT TO BUY

Antiques & Decorative Items

Real Thai antiques are rare and costly. Most Bangkok antique shops keep a few antiques around for collectors, along with lots of pseudo-antiques or traditionally crafted items that look like antiques. The majority of shop operators are quite candid about what's really old and what isn't. As Thai design becomes more popular abroad, many shops are now specialising in Thai home decorative items.

Reliable antique shops (using the word 'antiques' loosely) include Elephant House (☎ 286-2780) at 67/12 Soi Phra Phinit, Soi Suan Phlu; Peng Seng, on the corner of Rama IV and Surawong Rds; Asian Heritage (☎ 258-4157), at 57 Soi 23, Sukhumvit Rd; Thai House (☎ 258-6287), 720/6 Sukhumvit Rd, near Soi 28; and Artisan's in the Silom Village Trade Centre, Silom Rd (Map 8). The River City and Oriental Plaza shopping complexes also have several good, if pricey, antique shops.

Gems & Jewellery

Thailand is one of the world's largest exporters of gems and ornaments, rivalled only by India and Sri Lanka. The biggest importers of Thai jewellery are the USA, Japan and Switzerland. One of the results of the remarkable growth of the gem industry – in Thailand the gem trade has increased nearly 10% every year for the last decade – is that the prices are rising rapidly.

If you know what you are doing you can make some really good buys in both unset gems and finished jewellery. Gold ornaments are sold at a good rate as labour costs are low. The best bargains in gems are jade, rubies and sapphires. Buy from reputable dealers only, unless you're a gemologist. Be wary of special 'deals' that are 'one day only' or which set you up as a 'courier' in which you're promised big money. Many travellers end up losing big. Shop around and don't be hasty.

Recommending specific shops is tricky since, to the average eye, one coloured stone looks as good as another, so the risk of a rip-off is much greater than for most other goods. One shop that's been a long-time favourite with expats for service and value in set jewellery is Johnny's Gems (☎ 222-1756) at 199 Feuang Nakhon Rd (off Charoen Krung Rd). Another reputable jewellery place is Merlin et Delauney (☎ 234-3884), with a large showroom and lapidary at 1 Soi Pradit (Soi 20), Surawong Rd and a smaller shop at the Novotel hotel, Soi 6, Siam Square. Both have unset stones as well as jewellery. Three dependable places that specialise in unset stones are Lambert International (☎ 236-4343) at 807 Silom Rd, Gemexpert (☎ 236-2638) at 50/29 Pan Rd and Thai Lapidary (☎ 214-2641), at 277/122 Rama I Rd.

BERNARD NAPTHINE

Buddha amulets come in all shapes and sizes.

The Asian Institute of Gemological Sciences (☎ 513-2112; fax 236-7803) 484 Ratchadaphisek Rd (off Lat Phrao Rd in the Huay Khwang district, north-east Bangkok) offers short-term courses in gemology as well as tours of gem mines. You can bring gems here for inspection but they don't assess value, only authenticity and grading. John Hoskin's book *Buyer's Guide to Thai Gems & Jewellery*, available at most Bangkok bookshops, is a useful introduction.

Bronzeware

Thailand has the oldest bronze-working tradition in the world and there are several factories in Bangkok producing bronze sculpture and cutlery. Two factories which sell direct to the public (and where you may also be able to observe the bronze-working process) are: Siam Bronze Factory (☎ 234-9436), at 1250 Charoen Krung Rd; and SN Thai Bronze Factory (☎ 215-7743), at 157/33 Phetburi Rd. Make sure the items you buy are silicon-coated, otherwise they'll tarnish. To see Buddha images being cast, go to the Buddha-Casting Foundry next to Wat Wiset Khan on Phrannok Rd, Thonburi (take a river ferry from Tha Phra Chan or Tha Maharat on the Bangkok side to reach the foot of Phrannok Rd).

Many vendors at Wat Mahathat's Sunday market and at the Chatuchak (Weekend) Market sell old and new bronzeware – haggling is imperative.

Handicrafts

Bangkok has excellent buys in Thai handicrafts, though for northern hill-tribe materials you might do better in Chiang Mai. Narayana Phand (☎ 252-4670) on Ratchadamri Rd (Map 7), is a bit touristy but has a large selection and good marked prices – no haggling is necessary. Central Department Store on Ploenchit Rd (Map 7) has a Thai handicrafts section with marked prices.

International School Bangkok (ISB) (☎ 583-5401/5428) puts on a large charity sale of Thai handicrafts every sixth Saturday or so (except during ISB's summer holiday from June to August). Sometimes you can find pieces at the ISB craft sales that are practically unavailable elsewhere. At other times it's not very interesting; it all depends on what the sale managers are able to collect during the year. Call the school for the latest sale schedule. ISB is north of the city proper, towards the airport, off Route 304 (Chaeng Wattana Rd) on the way to the Pak Kret district. It's inside the Nichada Thani condo/townhouse complex; the address is 39/7 Soi Nichadathani Samakhi (see Map 11).

Perhaps the most interesting places to shop for handicrafts are the smaller, independent shops – each has its own style and character. Rasi Sayam (☎ 258-4195), 32 Soi 23, Sukhumvit Rd, carries many items made for them – including wall-hangings and pottery. Another good one for pottery as well as lacquerware and fabrics (especially the latter) is Vilai's (☎ 391-6106) at 731/1 Soi 55 (Thong Lor), Sukhumvit Rd.

Nandakwang (☎ 258-1962), 108/3 Soi 23 (Soi Prasanmit), is a branch of a factory shop of the same name in Pasang, northern Thailand; high-quality woven cotton clothing and household wares (tablecloths, napkins, etc) are their speciality. Prayer Textile Gallery (☎ 251-7549), a small shop on the edge of Siam Square facing Phayathai Rd, stocks a nice selection of new and antique textiles – in both ready-to-wear original fashions or in traditional rectangular lengths – from Thailand, Laos, and Cambodia.

Lao Song Handicrafts (☎ 261-6627) at 2/56 Soi 41, Sukhumvit Rd, is a non-profit shop which sells village handicrafts to promote rural cottage industries.

Khon (Thai classical dance-drama) masks of intricately formed wire and papier-mâché can be purchased at Padung Chiip (no English sign) on Chakraphong Rd just south of the Khao San Rd intersection.

For quality Thai celadon (porcelain with a distinctive greyish-green glaze), check Thai Celadon (☎ 229-4383) at 8/6-8 New Ratchadaphisek Rd. For new Thai pottery of all shapes and sizes at wholesale prices there are two places on Soi On Nut, off Soi 77, Sukhumvit Rd: United Siam Overseas (☎ 721-6320) and Siamese Merchandise (☎ 333-0680). Shipping can be arranged.

Tailor-Made Clothes

Bangkok abounds in places where you can have shirts, trousers, suits and just about any other article of clothing designed, cut and sewn by hand. Workmanship ranges from shoddy to excellent, so it pays to ask around before committing yourself. Shirts and trousers can be turned around in 48 hours or less with only one fitting. But no matter what a tailor may tell you, it takes more than one or two fittings to create a good suit – most reputable tailors will ask for three to five. A custom-made suit, no matter what the material, should cost less than US$200. An all-cashmere suit can be had for as little as US$160 to US$180 with a little bargaining; bring your own fabric and it will cost even less.

TAT

Colourful, comfortable Thai cushions.

Bangkok tailors can be particularly good at copying your favourite piece of clothing. Designer-made shirts costing upward of US$100 at home can be knocked off for not much more than a tenth of the price. But be very careful in fabric selection. If possible, bring your own fabric from home, especially if you want 100% cotton. Most of the so-called 'cotton' offered by Bangkok tailors is actually a blend of cotton and a synthetic; more than a few tailors will actually try to pass off full polyester or dacron as cotton. Good-quality silk, on the other hand, is plentiful. Tailor-made silk shirts should cost no more than US$12 to US$20, depending on the type (Chinese silk is cheaper than Thai).

Virtually every tailor working in Bangkok is of either Indian or Chinese descent. Generally speaking, the best shops are those found along the outer reaches of Sukhumvit Rd (out beyond Soi 20 or so) and on or off Charoen Krung (New) Rd. Silom Rd also has some good tailors. The worst tailor shops tend to be found in tourist-oriented shopping areas such as inner Sukhumvit Rd, Khao San Rd, the River City Shopping Complex and other shopping malls. 'Great deals', like four shirts, two suits, a kimono and a safari suit all in one package almost always turn out to be of inferior materials and workmanship.

Recommended tailors include Marzotto (3 Soi Wat Suan Phlu, off Charoen Krung Rd), Julie (1279 Charoen Rd, near Silom Center), Marco Tailor (at Amarin Plaza, Silom Complex and Siam Square) and Macway's Exporters (248/3-4 Silom Rd, near the Narai Hotel). If Siam Center re-opens, Siam Emporium (3rd floor) can also be recommended.

Bookshops

Bangkok probably has the largest selection of English-language books and bookshops in South-East Asia. The principal chains are Asia Books (headquarters on Sukhumvit Rd near Soi 15) and DK Book House (Siam Square); each has branch shops in half a dozen street locations around Bangkok as well as in well-touristed cities like Chiang Mai, Hat Yai and Phuket. Asia and DK offer a wide variety of fiction and periodicals as well as books on Asia. Some of Thailand's larger tourist hotels also have bookshops with English-language books and periodicals.

Suksit Siam, opposite Wat Ratchabophit on Feuang Nakhon Rd, specialises in books on Thai politics, especially those representing the views of Sulak Sivaraksa and the progressive Santi Pracha Dhamma Institute (which has offices next door). The shop also has a number of mainstream titles on Thailand and Asia, both in English and Thai.

Elite Used Books, 593/5 Sukhumvit Rd near Villa supermarket, carries a good selection of used foreign-language titles (English, Chinese, French, German, Swedish). The Chatuchak (Weekend) Market, in Chatuchak Park (Map 3), is also a source of used, often out-of-print books in several languages.

Cameras & Film

For a wide range of camera models and brands, two of the best shops are Sunny Camera (three store branches: ☎ 233-8378 at 1267/1 Charoen Krung Rd; ☎ 237-2054 at 134/5-6 Soi 8 Silom Rd; and ☎ 217-9293, 3rd floor, Mahboonkrong Centre) and Niks (☎ 235-2929) at 166 Silom Rd.

Film is generally cheaper in Bangkok than anywhere else in Asia, including Hong Kong. Slide and print film is widely available, although the highest concentration of photo shops can be found along Silom and Surawong Rds. In Mahboonkrong Centre, FotoFile on the ground floor has the best selection of slide film, including refrigerated pro film.

Quick, professional processing of most film types is available at E6 Processing Centre (☎ 259-9573) at 59/10 Soi 31 Sukhumvit Rd; IQ Lab (☎ 238-4001) at 60 Silom Rd or (☎ 391-4163) at 9/34 Thana Arcade, Soi 63, Sukhumvit Rd; Eastbourne Professional Color Laboratories (☎ 236-1156) at 173/4-5 Surawong Rd; and Supertouch (☎ 235-4711, 235-6415) at 35/12 Soi Yommarat, Sala Daeng Rd.

Furniture

Rattan and hardwood furniture are often good buys and can be made to order. Teak furniture has become relatively scarce and expensive; rosewood is a more reasonable buy. Star House (☎ 392-0865) at 746-52 Sukhumvit Rd (near Soi 34) stocks both rosewood and teak furniture, as does Prinya Decoration (☎ 318-1824) at New Phetburi Rd and Phetburi Soi 63.

Several rattan shops can be found along Sukhumvit Rd between Sois 35 and 43, including Corner 43, Hawaii, Pattaya, Pacific Design, Thai Home and Thai Pattana. Siam Krung Wai Furniture (☎ 213-4529), at 1567 Phahonyothin Rd, opposite Soi 35, specialises in made-to-order rattan furniture.

Fake or Pirated Goods

In all the various tourist centres, eg Patpong, Sukhumvit and Silom Rds, there is black-market street trade in fake designer goods; particularly Benneton pants and sweaters, Lacoste (crocodile logo) and Ralph Lauren polo shirts, Levi's jeans, and Rolex, Dunhill and Cartier watches. No-one pretends they're the real thing, not even the vendors. Western manufacturers are applying heavy pressure on Asian governments to get this stuff off the street, so it may not be around for much longer.

In some cases foreign name brands are legally produced and are good value. A pair of Levi's 501s made under licence can cost US$10 from a Thai vendor, and US$30 to US$40 in Levi's home town of San Francisco! Careful examination of the product usually reveals telltale characteristics that confirm or deny the item's legality. Pre-recorded cassette tapes are another illegal bargain in Thailand. The tapes are 'pirated', that is, no royalties are paid to the copyright owners. Average prices are 25 to 35B per cassette for amazingly up-to-date music. These too may disappear from the streets since a 1991 concession from four major piraters under pressure from the US music industry. Nowadays it is becoming quite difficult to find pirated tapes except on Khao San Rd. Licensed tapes, when available, cost 70 to 110B each (average price 90B); Thai music tapes cost the same.

Excursions

When you've had enough of Bangkok's intensity, there are several spots outside the city you can escape to for day visits or overnight trips. Within a 150-km radius you have a choice of 16th to 18th-century temple ruins (Ayuthaya), the two tallest Buddhist monuments in the world (Phutthamonthon, Nakhon Pathom) and the most famous railway bridge in the world (the 'Bridge Over the River Kwai' in Kanchanaburi).

OUTSKIRTS OF BANGKOK

Just outside Bangkok a host of artificial tourist attractions provide either the 'see the whole country in an hour' theme or the standard Western-style amusement park. If these attractions appeal to you, it's often worth booking tickets through travel agencies if such a booking includes round-trip transport from your lodgings.

West

Thirty-two km west of Bangkok, on the way to Nakhon Pathom, the **Rose Garden Country Resort** (☎ 253-0295), is a canned Thai 'cultural village' (with demos of handicrafts, dancing, traditional ceremonies and martial arts). There's also a resort hotel, swimming pools, tennis courts, a three-hectare lake, elephant rides and a golf course. Admission to the 24-hectare garden – which boasts 20,000 rose bushes – is 10B; it's another 220B for the 11 am and 2.45 pm performances in the cultural village. The resort and rose garden are open from 8 am to 6 pm daily, the cultural village from 10.30 to 5 pm. Shuttle buses run between the resort and major Bangkok hotels.

Just one km north of the Rose Garden, at the nine hectare **Samphran Elephant Ground & Zoo** (☎ 284-1873), you can see elephant 'roundups' and crocodile shows; a number of other animals can also be observed in zoo-like conditions. Kids generally like this place. It's open daily from 8.30 am to 6 pm, with crocodile wrestling shows at 12.45, 2.20 and 4.30 pm and elephant shows at 1.45 and 3.30 pm weekdays, plus additional shows on weekends and holidays at 11.30 am. Admission is 220B for adults, 120B children.

North

On the east bank of the Chao Phraya River in Pathum Thani Province is Wat Phailom. This old, wooden Mon wat is noted for the tens of thousands of open-billed storks *(Anastomus oscitans)* that nest in bamboo groves opposite the temple area from December to June. The temple is 51 km from the centre of Bangkok in Pathum Thani's Sam Kok district. Take a Pathum Thani-bound bus (8B) from Bangkok's Northern bus terminal and cross the river by ferry to the wat grounds.

Bus No 33 from Sanam Luang goes all the way to Phailom and back. The Chao Phraya Express tours from Tha Maharat to Bang Pa-In each Sunday also make a stop at Wat Phailom.

North-East

In Minburi, 10 km north-east of Bangkok, **Siam Park** (☎ 517-0075) at 101 Sukhaphiban 2 is a huge recreational park with pools, water slides, a wave pool and the like. It's highly recommended for a splash. Admission is 200B for adults, 100B for children. Saturday is less crowded than Sunday. Get there on bus No 26 or 27 from the Victory Monument or bus No 60 from the Democracy Monument.

Also in Minburi is **Safari World** (☎ 518-1000), at 99 Ramindra 1, a 69 hectare wildlife park said to be the largest 'open zoo' in the world. It's divided into two portions, the drive-through Safari Park and walk-through Marine Park. The five-km drive-through Safari Park (aboard air-con coaches or your own vehicle) intersects eight habitats featuring giraffes, lions, zebras, elephants, orang-utans and other African and Asian animals (75 mammal and 300 bird species in all). A panda house displays rare white pandas. The Marine Park focuses on trained animal performances by dolphins and the like. Safari World is open daily from 10 am to 6 pm; admission is 250B for adults, 150B for children three to 12 and free for under threes. It's 45 km east of central Bangkok; catch a No 26 bus from the Victory Monument to Minburi, then a *songthaew* (small pickup truck) to the park.

South

Billed as the largest open-air museum in the world, **Ancient City (Meuang Boran)** covers more than 80 hectares and presents scaled-down facsimiles of many of the kingdom's most famous monuments. The grounds follow Thailand's general geographical outline,

with the monuments placed accordingly. The main
entrance places visitors at the country's southern tip,
from where you work your way to the 'northernmost'
monuments. A sculpture garden focuses on episodes
from the Ramakian, the Thai version of India's Ramayana. Although the entire facility is in dire need of a
facelift, for students of Thai architecture it's worth a
day's visit (it takes an entire day to cover the area). It's
also a good place for long, undistracted walks, as it's
usually quiet and uncrowded.

The Ancient City Co also puts out a lavish bilingual
periodical devoted to Thai art and architecture called
Meuang Boran. The journal is edited by some of Thailand's leading art historians. The owner of both journal
and park is Bangkok's largest Mercedes Benz dealer,
who has an avid interest in Thai art.

Ancient City (☎ 323-9252) is in Samut Prakan, 33 km
from Bangkok along the Old Sukhumvit Hwy. Hours are
8 am to 5 pm; admission is 50B for adults and 25B for
children. The public bus trip (ordinary bus No 25 for 3.5B
or air-con bus No 7, 8 or 11 for 12 to 16B) to the Samut
Prakan terminal can take up to two hours depending on
traffic; from the terminal get a 10 minute songthaew to
Meuang Boran for another 5B. Transport can also be
arranged through Ancient City Co's Bangkok office
(☎ 226-1936/7, 224-1057, 222-8143), at 78 Democracy
Monument circle, Ratchadamnoen Klang Rd.

In the same area there is a **Samut Prakan Crocodile
Farm & Zoo** (☎ 387-0020), where you can even see crocodile wrestling! There are over 30,000 crocs here, as well
as elephants, monkeys and snakes. The farm is open
from 7 am to 6 pm daily with trained animal shows –
including croc wrestling – every hour between 9 and 11
am and 1 and 4 pm daily. Elephant shows take place at
9.30 and 11.30 am, while the reptiles usually get their
dinner between 4 and 5 pm. Admission is a steep 300B
for adults, 200B for children (50B/30B for Thais). CITES-
certified items – handbags, belts, shoes – made from
crocodile hide are available from the farm's gift shop.
You can reach the croc farm on air-con bus No 7, 8 or 11,
changing to songthaew No S1 or S80.

AYUTHAYA

Approximately 86 km north of Bangkok, Ayuthaya
(population 60,300) was the Thai capital from 1350 to
1767 and by all accounts it was a splendid city. Prior to
1350, when the capital was moved there from U Thong,
it was a Khmer outpost. The city was named for Ayodhya
(Sanskrit for 'unassailable' or 'undefeatable'), the home

of Rama in the Indian epic *Ramayana*. Its full Thai name is Phra Nakhon Si Ayuthaya (Sacred City of Ayodhya).

Although the Sukhothai period is often referred to as Thailand's 'golden age', in many ways the Ayuthaya era was the kingdom's true historical apex – at least this was so in terms of geographic rule (sovereignty extended well into present-day Laos, Cambodia and Myanmar), dynastic endurance (over 400 years) and world recognition. Thirty-three kings of various Siamese dynasties reigned in Ayuthaya until it was conquered by the Burmese. During its heyday, Thai culture and international commerce flourished in the kingdom and Ayuthaya was courted by Dutch, Portuguese, French, English, Chinese and Japanese merchants. By the end of the 17th century Ayuthaya's population had reached one million – virtually all foreign visitors claimed it to be the most illustrious city they had ever seen.

Orientation

The present-day city is located at the confluence of three rivers, the Chao Phraya, the Pa Sak and the smaller Lopburi. A wide canal joins them and makes a complete circle around the town.

At many of the city's ruins a 10 to 20B admission fee is collected during civil-service hours (8 am to 4.30 pm). The ruins are most inundated with visitors on weekends – go during the week to avoid the crowds. Ayuthaya's area code is ☎ 35.

Information

The Tourism Authority of Thailand (TAT) has a temporary information office (☎ 246-076) next to the Chao Sam Phraya National Museum. The office is open daily from 8.30 am to 4.30 pm. Eventually the TAT plans to open a permanent office across the street next to the tourist police office on Si Sanphet Rd.

National Museums

There are two museums, the main one being the **Chao Sam Phraya National Museum**, which is near the intersection of Rotchana Rd (Ayuthaya's main street, connecting with the highway to Bangkok) and Si Sanphet Rd, near the centre of town. It features your basic roundup of Thai Buddhist sculpture with an emphasis, naturally, on Ayuthaya pieces. A selection of books on Thai art and archaeology can be bought at the ticket kiosk. The museum is open daily from 9 am to 4 pm; entry is 10B.

The second museum, **Chan Kasem Palace** (Phra Ratch-awong Chan Kasem), is a museum piece itself, built by the 17th king of Ayuthaya – Maha Thammarat – for his son Prince Naresuan. Among the exhibits is a collection of gold treasures from Wat Phra Mahathat and Wat Ratburana. Chan Kasem Palace is in the north-east corner of town, near the river. Hours are the same as at the other museum. Entry here is also 10B.

Temples & Ruins

Recently declared a UNESCO World Heritage Site, Ayuthaya's historic temples are scattered throughout the city and along the encircling rivers. Several of the more central ruins – Wat Phra Si Sanphet, Wat Mong-khon Bophit, Wat Phra Ram, Wat Thammikarat, Wat Ratburana and Wat Mahathat – can easily be visited on foot if you avoid the hottest part of the day from 11 am to 4 pm. Or you could add more temples and ruins to your itinerary by touring the city on rented bicycle. For visitors who want to 'do it all', you can bicycle around the central temples and charter a long-tail boat for the outlying ruins along the river. See Ayuthaya's Getting Around section for details on different modes and rates of transport.

Wat Phra Si Sanphet This was the largest temple in Ayuthaya in its time, and was used as the royal temple/palace by several Ayuthaya kings. Built in the 14th century, the compound once contained a 16m standing Buddha covered with 250 kg of gold, which was melted down by the Burmese conquerors. It is mainly known for the *chedis* (stupas) erected in the quint-essential Ayuthaya style, which has come to be identified with Thai art more than any other single style. Admission is 20B.

Wat Mongkhon Bophit This monastery near Si San-phet contains one of Thailand's largest Buddha images, a blackened 15th-century bronze casting. The present *wihāan* (Buddhist image house) was built in 1956.

Wat Phra Mahathat This wat, at the corner of Chee Kun and Naresuan Rds, dates back to the 14th century, to the reign of King Ramesuan. Despite extensive damage – not much was left standing by the Burmese hordes – the *prang* (Khmer-style tower) is still impressive. Admission is 20B.

RICHARD I'ANSON

The grand Khmer-style prang of Ayuthaya's Wat Phra Mahathat stands over an expanse of spires and crumbling pillars, once a magnificent temple compound.

JOE CUMMINGS

On the banks of the Chao Phraya River, Wat Phanan Choeng is one of the best sited of Ayuthaya's temples.

JOE CUMMINGS

Wat Na Phra Meru, built in 1546.

JOE CUMMINGS

The people of modern-day Ayuthaya show their reverence
for the Buddha images in the compound of Wat Chai
Mongkhon by swathing them in sacred cloth.

Wat Ratburana The Ratburana ruins are the counterpart to Mahathat across the road; the chedis, however, contain murals and are not quite as dilapidated. Admission is 20B.

Wat Thammikarat To the east of the old palace grounds, inside the river loop, Thammikarat features overgrown chedi ruins and lion sculptures.

Wat Phra Chao Phanan Choeng South-east of town on the Chao Phraya River, this wat was built before Ayuthaya became a Siamese capital. It's not known who built the temple, but it appears to have been constructed in the early 14th century so it's possibly Khmer. The main wihãan contains a highly revered 19m sitting Buddha image from which the wat derives its name.

The easiest way to get to Wat Phanan Choeng is by ferry from the pier near Phom Phet fortress, inside the south-east corner of the city centre. For a few extra baht you can take a bicycle with you on the boat.

Wat Na Phra Meru (Phra Mehn/Mane) Across from the old royal palace (*wang lŭang*) grounds is a bridge which can be crossed to arrive at Wat Phra Meru. This temple is notable because it escaped destruction in the 1767 Burmese capture, though it has required restoration over the years. The main *bòt* (central chapel) was built in 1546 and features fortress-like walls and pillars. During the 18th-century Burmese invasion, Burma's Chao Along Phaya chose this site from which to fire cannon at the palace; the cannon exploded and the king was fatally injured, thus ending the sacking of Ayuthaya.

The bòt interior contains an impressive carved wooden ceiling and a splendid Ayuthaya-era crowned sitting Buddha, six-metres high. Inside a smaller wihãan behind the bòt is a green-stone, European-pose (sitting in a chair) Buddha from Ceylon, said to be 1300 years old. The walls of the wihãan show traces of 18th or 19th century murals.

Admission to Wat Phra Meru is 10B.

Wat Yai Chai Mongkhon Wat Yai, as the locals call it, is south-east of the town proper, but can be reached by minibus for 4B. It's a quiet old place that was once a famous meditation wat, built in 1357 by King U Thong. The compound contains a very large chedi from which the wat takes its popular name (*yài* means big), and there is a community of *mâe chii*, or Buddhist nuns, residing here. Admission is 10B.

Boat Trips

Long-tail boats can be rented from the boat landing across from Chan Kasem (Chandra Kasem) Palace for a tour around the river/canal; several of the old wat ruins (Wat Phanan Choeng, Wat Phutthaisawan, Wat Kasatthirat and Wat Chai Wattanaram) may be glimpsed from the canal, along with picturesque views of river life.

Festivals

Ayuthaya holds one of the country's largest **Loi Krathong** festivals on the full moon of the 12th lunar month, usually November. The festival, held on full moon night, is peculiarly Thai and probably originated in the northern city of Sukhothai. Celebrations are held at several spots in Ayuthaya; the largest spectacle takes place at Beung Phra Ram, the large lake in the centre of the city between Wat Phra Ram and Wat Mahathat. Thousands of people, many of them from Bangkok, flock to the Beung Phra Ram event to crowd around four or five outdoor stages offering *li-khe* (often bawdy folk plays with dancing and music), Thai pop, cinema and *lakhon chatrii* (dance-drama) – all at the same time (the din can be deafening)! Fireworks are a big part of the show, and there are lots of food vendors on the site.

More low-key and traditional is the celebration at the **Chan Kasem pier**, where families launch their *krathongs* (small lotus-shaped floats made from banana leaves and topped with incense, flowers, coins and candles) onto the Lopburi-Pa Sak river junction. Although kids throw fireworks here, the overall atmosphere is much closer to the heart of Loi Krathong than at Beung Phra Ram. Krathongs can be purchased at the pier (or you can make your own from materials for sale); for a few baht you can board one of the many waiting canoes at the pier and be paddled out to launch your krathong in the middle of the river. Thai tradition says that the any couple who launch a krathong together are destined to be lovers – if not in this lifetime then the next.

Another large Loi Krathong festival takes place at the Royal Folk Arts & Crafts Centre in Bang Sai, about 24 km west of Ayuthaya. At this one the emphasis is on traditional costumes and hand-made krathongs. If you can put together a small group, any of the hotels or guesthouses in Ayuthaya can arrange a trip to the Bang Sai Loi Krathong for around 250B or less per person.

During the 10 days leading to the **Songkran Festival**, the lunar New Year celebration held in mid-April, there is a sound & light show with fireworks over the ruins.

Places to Stay – bottom end

Guesthouses & Hostels For budgeteers, there are five guesthouses and one hostel in Ayuthaya to choose from. Four of them are located on or off Naresuan Rd, not far from the bus terminal. As elsewhere in Thailand, tuk-tuk and samlor drivers will tell you anything to steer you toward guesthouses that pay commissions (up to 35B per head in this city).

Near the end of a soi off Naresuan Rd (not far from the Sri Smai Hotel), *Ayuthaya Guest House* charges 100B for singles/doubles in an old house. Next door, a branch of the same family runs the *Old BJ Guest House* (☎ 251526) at 80/100B for a single/double, or 60B per bed in a dorm; the Ayuthaya Guest House is cleaner. Both offer minimal food service.

Yet another BJ relative operates the *New BJ Guest House* (☎ 244046) at 19/29 Naresuan Rd. Rooms cost 100B per single/double, dorm beds 60B and there's a simple dining area in front. One drawback is that it's right on Naresuan Rd, a main Ayuthaya thoroughfare, so it could be noisy.

Thongchai Guest House (☎ 245210), on a back road parallel to Naresuan Rd and off Chee Kun Rd, has a choice of rooms in bungalows or in a row house for 120B without bath, 200 to 250B with fan and bath, or 300 to 350B for air-con and bath. The staff tends to be a bit unruly; a woman friend who stayed here said she was hassled.

Almost directly across the river from the train station in an old teak house is the *Ayuthaya Hostel* (☎ 241978), also known as Reuan Derm, at 48/2 U Thong Rd. Plain, small rooms with ceiling fans and shared bath cost 200B, or it's 250B for larger ones. A very good floating restaurant extends from the river side of the house; it is open from 10 am till 11 pm. If you can put up with some ambient noise from the restaurant and traffic on busy U Thong Rd, it's not a bad choice. No one seems to care whether you show a Hostelling International card or not – if you have one, it wouldn't hurt to ask for a discount.

Pai Thong Guest House, right on the river within walking distance of the train station, has recently been torn down to allow a total reconstruction to take place.

Hotels Two standard Thai/Chinese-style hotels at the junction of the Lopburi and Pa Sak rivers have been accommodating Ayuthaya visitors for two decades now. The *U Thong Hotel* (☎ 251136), on U Thong Rd near Hua Raw Market and Chan Kasem Palace, has adequate one-bed/two-bed rooms with fan for 180/250B and air-con for 300/400B. TV can be added for 30B extra. A little

south-east of the U Thong Hotel, the *Cathay Hotel*
(☎ 251562), at 36/5-6 U Thong Rd costs 150/270B for a
one-bed/two-bed room with fan, 300B for a single/
double with air-conditioning. Both hotels back up to the
river.

The *Thai Thai Bungalow* (☎ 244702), at 13/1 Naresuan
Rd is set well off the road between the bus terminal and
the road to Wat Phra Meru. It has large, semi-clean but
run-down rooms from 120 to 300B with air-con. It's
obviously the type of place to rely on short-time traffic
but is otherwise OK.

Sri Smai (Si Samai) Hotel (☎ 252249), 12 Thetsaban Soi
2, just off Naresuan Rd, is a more up-market place that
charges 400B for rooms with fan and bath, 550B with
air-con, 600B with air-con and hot water.

Places to Stay – middle & top end

The *Wieng Fa Hotel* (☎ 241353) at 1/8 Rotchana Rd
(between the river and the Chao Sam Phraya National
Museum) is a friendly, cosy spot with clean, relatively
quiet rooms around a garden courtyard for 400B. All
rooms come with TV and air-conditioning; English is
spoken.

Suan Luang (Royal Garden) (☎/fax 245537) is a new
five-storey hotel training facility next to the Ayuthaya
Historical Study Centre. Decent air-con rooms with
fridge and TV cost a moderate 500B; a couple of six-bed
air-con rooms are available for 600B.

My House (☎ 335493), on Rotchana Rd out toward
Ratchathani Hospital, has decent rooms for 500B; the
isolated location is a definite drawback.

Moving towards the top end, the *U-Thong Inn*
(☎ 242618) offers comfortable air-con rooms for 950 to
1400B. Facilities include a pool, sauna and massage
room. It's out on Rotchana Rd past the turn-off for the
train station. The newer six storey *Ayuthaya Grand Hotel*
(☎ 335483, fax 335492), out towards U-Thong Inn and
Wat Yai Chai Mongkhon at 75/5 Rotchana Rd, features
rooms with all the mod cons for 1100 to 1500B. There's a
large swimming pool on the premises.

Ayuthaya's flashiest digs are the 202 room, eight
storey *Krungsri River Hotel* (☎ 244333, fax 243777) at 27/2
Rotchana Rd, where decked-out lodgings cost 1600 to
2000B. Facilities include a pub/coffeehouse, fitness
centre, pool, bowling alley and snooker club.

Next door to the Krungsri, the 102 room *Tevaraj Tanrin
Hotel* (☎/fax 244139) has similar rooms in the 1000 to
2500B range (including breakfast), a floating restaurant
and beer garden.

Places to Eat

The most dependable and least expensive places to eat are at the Hua Raw market, on the river near Chan Kasem Palace, and the Chao Phrom market, opposite the ferry piers along the east side of the island. The *Chainam*, opposite Chan Kasem Palace next to the Cathay Hotel, has tables on the river, a bilingual menu and friendly service; it's also open for breakfast.

The arty *Moon Cafe*, a tiny spot on the same soi as Ayuthaya Guest House, serves Thai and farang food for 30 to 50B per dish, also beer and espresso. *Duangporn*, on Naresuan Rd near the main bus terminal, is an indoor air-con place with Thai and Chinese food in the 40 to 80B range. There's also a *KFC* on this street near the Sri Smai Hotel.

Quite a few restaurants are on the main road into Ayuthaya, Rotchana Rd. There are four floating restaurants on the Pa Sak River, three on either side of the Pridi Damrong bridge on the west bank, and one on the east bank north of the bridge. Of these, the *Phae Krung Kao* – on the south side of the bridge on the west bank – has the better reputation. There's no English sign – look for Thai flags and topiary at the entrance. North of the bridge on the west bank, *Ruenpae* is similar. The floating *Reuan Doem*, in front of the Ayuthaya Youth Hostel, is also quite good and has the most intimate atmosphere of the riverside places.

Off Chee Khun Rd near the Thongchai Guest House, *Ruay Jaroen* is a huge wooden place specialising in seafood and duck dishes – it has medium to moderately high prices. It's open from 11 am to 11 pm.

In the evenings a very choice night market comes to life near the pier opposite Chan Kasem Palace.

For something a little fancier, try the air-con *Rodeo Saloon* on U Thong Rd. Despite the name and 'old-west' decor, the food is mostly Thai (English menu available); it's only open at night, when a small band plays Thai and international folk music.

Getting There & Away

Bus Ordinary buses run between Bangkok's Northern bus terminal and Naresuan Rd every 20 minutes between 5 am and 7 pm. The trip costs 22B and takes around two hours. Air-con buses operate along the same route every half hour from 6 am to 6.30 pm and cost 36B; the trip takes 1½ hours when traffic north of Bangkok is light, two hours otherwise. There is also a 30B minivan service every 20 minutes from 5 am to 5 pm.

If you're arriving in Ayuthaya by bus from some place other than Bangkok or other nearby cities, you may be dropped off at the long-distance bus station, five-km east of the Pridi Damrong bridge at the Highway 32 junction.

Songthaews to/from Bang Pa-In leave from the same area on Naresuan Rd and cost 8B; it's about half an hour away.

Train Trains to Ayuthaya leave Bangkok's Hualamphong station every hour or so between 4.20 am and 10 pm. The 3rd class fare is 15B for the 1½ hour trip; it's hardly worth taking a more expensive class, rapid or express for this short trip. Train schedules are available from the information booth at Hualamphong station.

After getting off at the Ayuthaya train station, the quickest way to reach the old city is to walk west to the river, where you can catch a short ferry ride across to the Chao Phrom pier for 1B.

Upon arrival at Bangkok International airport, savvy repeat visitors to Thailand sometimes choose to board a northbound train direct to Ayuthaya rather than head south into the Bangkok maelstrom. This only works if you arrive by air during the day or early evening, as local trains to Ayuthaya quit running around 9 pm. There are frequent 3rd class trains throughout the day between Don Meuang train station (opposite Bangkok International) and Ayuthaya.

Boat There are no longer any scheduled or chartered boat services between Bangkok and Ayuthaya. Several companies in Bangkok operate luxury cruises to Bang Pa-In with side trips by bus to Ayuthaya for around 1000 to 1200B per person, including a lavish luncheon. Longer two-day trips in converted rice barges start at 3000B. See the River & Canal Trips section of the Things to See & Do chapter for more details.

Getting Around

Songthaews and shared tuk-tuks ply the main city roads for 3 to 5B per person depending on distance. A tuk-tuk from the train station to any point in old Ayuthaya should be around 30B; on the island itself figure no more than 20B per trip.

For touring the ruins, the most economical and eco-logical option is to rent a bicycle from one of the guesthouses (40 to 50B a day) or walk. You can hire a samlor, tuk-tuk or songthaew by the hour or by the day to explore the ruins, but the prices are quite high by Thai standards (150B per hour for anything with a motor in it, 400B all day when things are slow).

It's also interesting to hire a boat from the palace pier to do a semi-circular tour of the island and see some of the less accessible ruins. A long-tail boat taking up to eight people can be hired for 300B for a three hour trip with stops at Wat Phutthaisawan, Wat Phanan Choeng and Wat Chai Wattanaram.

BANG PA-IN

Twenty km south of Ayuthaya is Bang Pa-In, which has a curious collection of palace buildings in a wide variety of architectural styles. It's a nice boat trip from Ayuthaya, although in itself it's not particularly noteworthy. The palace is open from 8.30 am to 3.30 pm daily. Admission is 50B.

Palace Buildings

The postcard stereotype here is a pretty little Thai pavilion in the centre of a small lake by the palace entrance. Inside the palace grounds, the Chinese-style **Wehat Chamrun Palace** is the only building open to visitors. The **Withun Thatsana** building looks like a lighthouse with balconies. It was built to give a fine view over gardens and lakes. There are various other buildings, towers and memorials in the grounds plus an interesting example of topiary: the bushes have been trimmed into the shape of a small herd of elephants.

Wat Niwet Thamaprawat

Across the river and south from the palace grounds, this unusual wat looks much more like a gothic Christian church than anything from Thailand. It was built by Rama V (Chulalongkorn). You get to the wat by crossing the river in a small trolley-like cable car. The crossing is free.

Getting There & Away

Bang Pa-In can be reached by minibus (it's really a large songthaew truck rather than a bus) from Ayuthaya's Chao Phrom Market, Naresuan (Chao Phrom) Rd, for 8B. From Bangkok there are buses every half hour or so from the Northern bus terminal and the fare is 17B ordinary, 25B air-con. You can also reach Bang Pa-In by train from Bangkok for 12B in 3rd class.

The Chao Phraya River Express Boat Company does a tour every Sunday from the Maharat pier in Bangkok that goes to Wat Phailom in Pathum Thani (November to June) or Wat Chaloem Phrakiat (July to October) as well as Bang Pa-In and Bang Sai's Royal Folk Arts & Crafts Centre. The trip leaves from Bangkok at 8 am and returns at 5.30 pm. The price is 180B not including lunch, which you arrange on your own in Bang Pa-In. For more expensive, all-inclusive river cruises to Bang Pa-In, which include tours of old Ayuthaya, see the River & Canal Trips section of the Things to See & Do chapter.

NAKHON PATHOM

Only 56 km west of Bangkok, Nakhon Pathom (population 48,000) is regarded as the oldest city in Thailand – the name is derived from the Pali 'Nagara Pathama', meaning 'First City'. It was the centre of the Dvaravati Kingdom, a loose collection of city states that flourished between the 6th and 11th century in the Chao Phraya

JOE CUMMINGS

The enormous Phra Pathom Chedi, Nakhon Pathom.

River valley. The area may have been inhabited before India's Ashokan period (3rd century BC), as it is theorised that Buddhist missionaries from India visited Nakhon Pathom at that time.

Nakhon Pathom's area code is ☎ 34.

Phra Pathom Chedi

The central attraction in Nakhon Pathom is the famous Phra Pathom Chedi, the tallest Buddhist monument in the world, rising to 127m. The original monument, buried within the massive orange-glazed dome, was erected in the early 6th century by Theravada Buddhists of Dvaravati, but in the early 11th century the Khmer King Suryavarman I of Angkor conquered the city and built a Brahman prang over the sanctuary. The Pagan Burmese, under King Anuruddha, sacked the city in 1057 and the prang was in ruins until King Mongkut had it restored in 1860. The king had a larger chedi built over the remains according to Buddhist tradition, adding four wihãans, a bòt, a replica of the original chedi and assorted salas, prangs and other embellishments. There is even a Chinese temple attached to the outer walls of the Phra Pathom Chedi, next to which outdoor lakhon (classical Thai dance-drama) is sometimes performed.

On the eastern side of the monument, in the bòt, is a Dvaravati-style Buddha seated in 'European pose' (in a chair) similar to the one in Wat Phra Meru in Ayuthaya. It may, in fact, have come from Phra Meru.

Opposite the bòt is a museum, open Wednesday to Sunday from 9 am to 4 pm, which contains some interesting Dvaravati sculpture.

Other Attractions

Beside the chedi, the other features of the town are **Silpakorn University**, west of the chedi off Phetkasem Hwy, and **Sanam Chan**, adjacent to the university. Sanam Chan, formerly the grounds for Rama VI's palace, is a pleasant park with a canal passing through it. The somewhat run-down palace still stands in the park but entry is not permitted.

South-east of the city toward Bangkok, between the districts of Nakhon Chaisi and Sam Phran, is the recently completed **Phra Phutthamonthon** (from the Pali 'Buddhamandala'). This 40.7m Sukhothai-style standing Buddha is reportedly the world's tallest; it's surrounded by a 400-hectare landscaped park containing replicas of important Buddhist pilgrimage spots in India and Nepal. Any Bangkok to Nakhon Pathom bus passes the access road to the park (signed in English as well as Thai); from there you can walk, hitch or flag one of the frequent songthaews into the park itself.

Places to Stay – bottom end

Budget accommodation in Nakhon Pathom can be a bit on the dreary side. Some visitors prefer passing through to spending the night, while others may find the town of interest for its typical provincialism. The *Mitrthaworn Hotel* or Mitthawon (☎ 243115) is on the right as you walk towards the chedi from the train station. It costs 200/220B for one/two-bed rooms with fan and bath, 300B with air-con. The *Mitphaisan Hotel* (☎ 242422) – the English sign reads 'Mitr Paisal' – is farther down the alley to the right from Mitthawon. Rooms here are 250B for fan and bath, 350B with air-con.

Near the west side of Phra Pathom Chedi, next to a furniture store on Lang Phra Rd, the *Mitsamphan* (☎ 242422) offers clean rooms with fan and bath for 150B. All three 'Mit' hotels are owned by the same family. Price differences reflect cleanliness and service. My budget vote again stays with Mitphaisan.

West of the chedi a few blocks from Mitsamphan on Thetsaban Rd is the *Siam Hotel* (☎ 241754). The staff here remain curt at best and rooms cost 140/180B for one/two beds with fan and bath or up to 250/280B with air-con. A bit farther south at 24/22 to 44/1 Thetsaban Rd is the *Suthathip Hotel* (☎ 242242), with a boisterous Chinese restaurant downstairs. Rooms seem like an afterthought and cost 150/200B for one/two beds with fan and bath, 300B for air-con.

Places to Stay – top end

The *Nakhon Inn* (☎ 242265, 251152) at 55 Ratwithi Rd is a pleasant 70 room air-con hotel where Thai guests are charged 400B per room, and farangs double that for the same accommodation! Since this is a private establishment (not government-subsidised), this is simple racial discrimination. If you speak Thai well enough, you might be able to get the Thai price.

The newer *Whale Hotel* (☎ 251020, fax 253864), 151/79 Ratwithi Rd (south-west of the monument) offers good air-con rooms in four separate buildings starting at 480B. Facilities and services include a coffee shop, restaurant, karaoke, disco, snooker club, golf driving range, sauna and massage.

Places to Eat

Nakhon Pathom has an excellent fruit market along the road between the train station and the Phra Pathom Chedi; the khâo lãam (sticky rice and coconut steamed in a bamboo joint) is reputed to be the best in Thailand. There are many good, inexpensive food vendors and restaurants in this area.

Song Saen, on Ratchadamnoen Rd a few blocks directly west of Phra Pathom Chedi, offers a pleasant Thai sala (open-air) setting with good, medium-priced Thai food.

Getting There & Away

Bus Buses for Nakhon Pathom leave the Southern bus terminal in Bangkok every 10 minutes from 5.45 am to 9.10 pm; the fare is 16B for the one hour trip. Air-con buses are 28B and leave about every 20 minutes between 6 am and 10.30 pm. There are two bus routes; be sure to take the *sãi mài* or 'new route' buses; the 'old route' buses take half an hour longer.

Buses from Nakhon Pathom to Kanchanaburi leave throughout the day from the west side of the Phra Pathom Chedi – get bus No 81. Buses to Damnoen Saduak floating market leave from the south side of the chedi.

Train Ordinary trains (3rd class only) leave Bangkok Noi (Thonburi) train station daily at 7.20 and 7.50 am and 12.35, 1.45, 5.40, 7.15 and 8.20 pm, arriving in Nakhon Pathom in about an hour and 10 minutes. The fare is 14B.

There are also rapid and express trains to Nakhon Pathom from Hualamphong station roughly hourly between 1.30 and 9.55 pm. The 2nd class fare is 28B, 1st class 54B (add 20B and 30B respectively for rapid and express service); rapid trains from Hualamphong take 1½ hours, the express is only 10 minutes faster. There are no longer any ordinary trains to Nakhon Pathom from Hualamphong station.

AROUND NAKHON PATHOM

Floating Markets

If the commercialisation of Bangkok's floating markets puts you off, there is a much more lively floating market (*talàat náam*) on Khlong Damnoen Saduak in Ratchaburi Province, 104 km south-west of Bangkok, between Nakhon Pathom and Samut Songkhram.

Talaat Ton Khem is the main market on Khlong Damnoen Saduak Canal, while **Talaat Hia Kui**, just south on the parallel Khlong Hia Kui, gets the most tourists – one area in fact has been set aside especially for tourists now, with a large open shop with souvenirs for bus tours as well as souvenir-laden boats. There is a third, less crowded, market on a smaller canal, a bit south of Damnoen Saduak, called **Talaat Khun Phitak**. To get there, take a water taxi going south from the pier on the south side of Thong Lang Canal, which intersects Damnoen Saduak near the larger floating market and ask for Talaat Khun Phitak. You can rent a boat to tour the canals and all three markets for 150 to 200B per hour (300B if you stay till the markets close around 11 am) – depending on your bargaining skills. Try to arrive by 8 am – by 9 am the package tours are in full swing.

One sure way to beat the tour buses from Bangkok is to spend the night in Damnoen Saduak and get up before the hordes of tourists arrive. Try the *Noknoi (Little Bird)* (☎ (32) 251382), where rooms cost 100 to 140B with fan, 170 to 250B air-con. *Ban Sukchoke Resort* (☎ (32) 253044, fax 254301) offers comfortable bungalows set over the canal for 250B and up. Ban Sukchoke is 1.5 km north-west of Damnoen's market area.

Getting There & Away Bus No 78 goes direct from Bangkok's Southern bus terminal to Damnoen Saduak every 20 minutes, beginning at 6.20 am, but you'll have to get one of the first few buses to arrive in Damnoen Saduak by 8 or 9 am when the market's at its best. The fare is 49B for air-con or 30B for an ordinary bus. Once there, take a 20B water taxi to the talàat náam from the pier nearest the bus station, or simply walk east from the station along the canal until you come to the market area.

Some people spend the night in Nakhon Pathom and catch an early morning bus out of Nakhon Pathom headed for Samut Songkhram, asking to be let out at Damnoen Saduak. It is also possible to get to Damnoen Saduak by bus (6B) from Samut Songkhram, a trip of around 25 minutes. A minibus to/from Ratchaburi costs 20B.

One interesting way to get there is by boat from Samut Sakhon. From Samut Sakhon, take a local bus to Kratum Baen and then take a songthaew a few km north to the Tha Angton pier on the right bank of the Tha Chin River. From the pier, catch a ferry boat across the river to Khlong Damnoen Saduak, which runs west off the Tha Chin. From the Bang Yang lock, where ferry passengers disembark, take a 30 km trip by *reua haang yao* (long-tail boat) to the floating market. The fare is 16B and includes a boat change halfway at Ban Phaew – it's worth it for what is one of Thailand's most beautiful stretches of waterway.

Less touristed floating markets can be reached by boating south from Damnoen Saduak to Amphawa district in Samut Songkhram Province.

KANCHANABURI

Kanchanaburi (population 33,000) lies 130 km west of Bangkok in the slightly elevated valley of the Mae Klong River amidst hills and sugar cane plantations. It was originally established by Rama I as a first line of defence against the Burmese who might use the old invasion route through the Three Pagodas Pass on the Thai-Burmese border. It's still a popular smuggling route into Burma today.

During WWII, the Japanese used Allied prisoners of war to build the infamous Death Railway along this same invasion route, in reverse, along the Khwae Noi River to the pass. Thousands and thousands of prisoners died as a result of brutal treatment by their captors, a story chronicled by Pierre Boulle's book *The Bridge over the River Kwai* and popularised by a movie based on the same. The bridge is still there (still in use, in fact) and so are the graves of the Allied soldiers. The river is actually spelled and pronounced Khwae, like 'quack' without the '-ck'.

The town itself has a certain atmosphere and is a fine place to hang out for a while. The weather is slightly cooler than in Bangkok and the evenings are especially pleasant. Although Kan (as the locals call it; also Kan'buri) gets enough tourists to warrant its own tourist office, not many Western visitors make it here – most are Thai, Japanese, or Hong Kong and Singapore Chinese, who blaze through on air-con buses, hitting the River Khwae Bridge, the cemetery on Saengchuto Rd, the Rama River Kwai Hotel, and then hurrying off to the nearby sapphire mines or one of the big waterfalls before heading north to Chiang Mai or back to Bangkok.

Information

The TAT office (☎ (34) 511200) is on Saengchuto Rd, on the right as you enter town before the police station. A free map of the town and province is available, as well as comprehensive information on accommodation and transport. Hours are 8.30 am to 4.30 pm daily. The office has a contingent of tourist police – any problems with theft or other criminal occurrences should be reported both to them and the regular provincial police.

Kanchanaburi's telephone area code is ☎ 34.

Death Railway Bridge

The so-called Bridge over the River Kwai may be of interest to war historians but really looks quite ordinary. It spans the Khwae Yai River, a tributary of the Mae Klong River, a couple of km north of town – Khwae Yai literally translates as 'large tributary'. It is the story behind the bridge that is dramatic. The materials for the bridge were brought from Java by the Imperial Japanese Army during their occupation of Thailand. In 1945 the bridge was bombed several times and was only rebuilt after the war – the curved portions of the bridge are original. The first version of the bridge, completed in February 1943, was all wood. In April of the same year a second bridge of steel was constructed.

It is estimated that 16,000 POWs died while building the Death Railway to Burma, of which the bridge was only a small part. The strategic objective of the railway was to secure an alternative supply route for the Japanese conquest of Burma and other Asian countries to the west. Construction on the railway began on 16 September 1942 at existing terminals in Thanbyuzayat, Burma and Nong Pladuk, Thailand. Japanese engineers at the time estimated that it would take five years to link Thailand and Burma by rail, but the Japanese army forced the POWs to complete the 415 km railway, roughly two-thirds of which ran through Thailand, in 16 months. The rails were finally joined 37 km south of Three Pagodas Pass. Much of the railway was built in difficult terrain that required high bridges and deep mountain cuttings. The Death Railway Bridge was in use for 20 months before the Allies bombed it in 1945. Only one POW is known to have escaped, a Briton who took refuge among pro-British Karen guerrillas.

Although the number of POWs who died during the Japanese occupation is horrifying, the fatality rate of the labourers, many from Thailand, Burma (Myanmar), Malaysia and Indonesia, was even worse. It is thought 90,000 to 100,000 coolies died in the area.

Train nuts may enjoy the **railway museum** in front of the bridge, with engines used during WWII on display. During the first week of December there is a nightly sound & light show at the bridge, commemorating the Allied attack on the Death Railway in 1945. It's a pretty big scene, with the sounds of bombers and explosions, fantastic bursts of light, etc. The town gets a lot of Thai tourists during this week, so book early if you want to witness the spectacle.

There are a couple of large outdoor restaurants near the bridge, on the river, but these are for tour groups that

TOM SMALLMAN

Bridge over the River Kwai.

arrive en masse throughout the day. If you're hungry, better to eat with the songthaew and tour bus drivers in the little noodle places at the northern end of Pak Phraek Rd.

Getting There & Away The best way to get to the bridge from town is to catch a songthaew along Mae Nam Khwae Rd (parallel to Saengchuto Rd towards the river) heading north. If you're standing at the River Kwai Hotel, just cross Saengchuto Rd, walk to the right, turn left at the first street and walk until you come to Mae Nam Khwae Rd. Regular songthaews are 5B and stop at the bridge. It's about four km from the centre of town. You can also take a train from the Kanchanaburi railway station to the bridge for 2B.

Allied War Cemeteries

There are two cemeteries containing the remains of Allied POWs who died in captivity during WWII; one is north of town off Saengchuto Rd, just before the railway station, and the other is across the Mae Klong River west of town, a few km down the Khwae Noi (Little Tributary) River.

The **Kanchanaburi War Cemetery** is better cared for, with green lawns and healthy flowers. It's usually a cool spot on a hot day. To get there, catch a songthaew anywhere along Saengchuto Rd going north – the fare is 5B. Jump off at the English sign in front of the cemetery on the left, or ask to be let off at the *susăan* (cemetery). Just before it on the same side of the road is a very colourful Chinese cemetery with burial mounds and inscribed tombstones.

To get to the other cemetery, the **Chung Kai Allied War Cemetery**, take a 2B ferry boat from the pier at the west end of Lak Meuang Rd across the Mae Klong, then follow the curving road through picturesque corn and sugarcane fields until you reach the cemetery on your left. This is a fairly long walk, but the scenery along the way is pleasant. You can also easily take a bicycle along on the ferry. A new bridge may be going in between Sam's Place and Nitaya Raft House to a large island in the river, with a second bridge to the river's west bank – if this happens the ferry service may be discontinued.

Like the more visited cemetery north of town, the Chung Kai burial plaques carry names, military insignia and short epitaphs for Dutch, British, French and Australian soldiers.

About one km south-west of the Chung Kai Cemetery is a dirt path that leads to **Wat Tham Khao Pun**, one of Kanchanaburi's many cave temples. The path is approximately one km long and passes through thick forest with a few wooden houses along the way.

JEATH War Museum

This odd museum at Wat Chaichumphon is worth visiting just to sit on the cool banks of the Mae Klong. Phra Maha Tomson Tongproh, a Thai monk who devotes much energy to promoting the museum, speaks some English and can answer questions about the exhibits, as well as supply information about what to see around Kanchanaburi and how best to get there. If you show him this book, he'll give you a 5B discount off the 20B admission. The museum itself is a replica of the bamboo-atap huts used to house Allied POWs in the Kanchanaburi area during the Japanese occupation. The long huts contain photographs taken during the war, drawings and paintings by POWs, maps, weapons and other war memorabilia. According to Phra Tomson, the acronym

JEATH represents the fated meeting of Japan, England, Australia/America, Thailand and Holland at Kanchanaburi during WWII.

The War Museum is at the end of Visutrangsi (Wisuttharangsi) Rd, near the TAT office, next to the main compound of Wat Chaichumphon. It's open daily from 8.30 am to 4.30 pm.

Lak Meuang Shrine

Like many other older Thai cities, Kanchanaburi has a *làk meuang*, or town pillar/phallus, enclosed in a shrine at what was originally the town centre. Kanchanaburi's Lak Meuang shrine is appropriately located on Lak Meuang Rd, which intersects Saengchuto Rd two blocks north of the TAT office.

The bulbous-tipped pillar is covered with gold leaf and is much worshipped. Unlike Bangkok's Lak Meuang you can get as close to this pillar as you like – there's no curtain.

Within sight of the pillar, towards the river, stands Kanchanaburi's original city gate.

WWII Museum

Also called 'Art Gallery & War Museum', this new, somewhat garish structure just south of the famous bridge on the river looks like a Chinese temple on the outside. The larger, more lavishly built of the two buildings has nothing to do with WWII and little to do with art unless you can count the tacky murals throughout. The bottom floor contains Burmese-style alabaster Buddhas and a *phra khreuang* (sacred amulets) display. Upper floors exhibit Thai weaponry from the Ayuthaya period and a fair collection of historic and modern ceramics. Brightly painted portraits of all the kings in Thai history fill the 4th floor. Finally on the 5th and uppermost floor – above the royal portraits – is the history of the Chinese family who built the museum, complete with a huge portrait of the family's patriarch in China.

A smaller building opposite contains WWII relics, including photos and sketches made during the POW period and a display of Japanese and Allied weapons. Along the front of this building stand life-size sculptures of historical figures associated with the war, including Churchill, MacArthur, Hitler, Einstein, de Gaulle and Hirohito. The English-language captions are sometimes unintentionally amusing – a reference to the atomic bomb dropped on Hiroshima, for example, reads 'Almost the entire city was destroyed in a jiffy'. Inside a glass case are 106 skeletons unearthed in a mass grave of Asian labourers. The gossip around town says these remains were stolen from municipal excavations. The museum is open from 9 am to 4.30 pm daily. Entry is 30B.

Wat Tham Mongkon Thong

The 'Cave Temple of the Golden Dragon' is well known because of the 'Floating Nun' – a *mâe chii* who meditates while floating on her back in a pool of water. Sunday's the best day to try to see her because she seems to be doing it less frequently nowadays. Another nun, now in her late 70s, began the floating tradition and has passed it on to this younger disciple. Thais come from all over the country to see the younger nun float and to receive her blessings, which she bestows by whistling onto the top of a devotee's head or by stuffing a cluster of burning candles into her mouth, then exhaling the smoke over a devotee's hands or head. A sizeable contingent of young Thai nuns stay here under the old nun's tutelage.

A long and steep series of steps with dragon-sculpted handrails lead up the craggy mountainside behind the main bòt to a complex of limestone caves. Follow the string of light bulbs through the front cave and you'll come out above the wat with a view of the valley and mountains below. One section of the cave requires crawling or duck-walking, so wear appropriate clothing. Bats squeak away above your head and the smell of guano permeates the air.

Another cave wat is off this same road about one or two km from Wat Tham Mongkon Thong towards the pier. **Wat Tham Khao Laem** can be seen on a limestone outcropping back from the road some 500m or so. The cave is less impressive than that at Wat Tham Mongkon Thong, but there are some interesting old temple buildings on the grounds.

Getting There & Away Heading south-east down Saengchuto Rd from the TAT office, turn right on Chukkadon Rd (marked in English – about halfway between the TAT and GPO), or take a songthaew (3B) from the town centre to the end of Chukkadon Rd. A bridge has replaced the river ferry that used to cross here; wait for any songthaew crossing the bridge and you can be dropped off in front of the temple for 5B.

The road to the wat passes sugar cane fields, karst formations, wooden houses, cattle and rock quarries. Alternatively you could ride a bicycle here from town – the road can be dusty in the dry season but at least it's flat.

Wat Tham Seua & Wat Tham Khao Noi

These large hilltop monasteries about 15 km south-east of Kanchanaburi are important local pilgrimage spots, especially for Chinese Buddhists. Wat Tham Khao Noi (Little Hill Cave Monastery) is a Chinese temple and monastery similar in size and style to Penang's Kek Lok Si. Adjacent is the half-Thai, half-Chinese style Wat Tham Seua (Tiger Cave Monastery). Both are built on a ridge over a series of small caves. Wat Tham Khao Noi isn't much of a climb, since it's built onto the side of the slope. Seeing Wat Tham Seua, however, means climbing either a steep set of *naga* (snake) stairs or a meandering set of steps past the cave entrance.

A climb to the top is rewarded with views of the Khwae River on one side, rice fields on the other. Wat Tham Seua features a huge sitting Buddha facing the river, with a conveyor belt that carries money offerings to a huge alms bowl in the image's lap. The easier set of steps to the right of the temple's naga stairs leads to a cave and passes an aviary with peacocks and other exotic birds. The cave itself has the usual assortment of Buddha images.

Getting There & Away By public transport, you can take a bus to Tha Meuang (12 km south-east of Kan), then a motorcycle taxi (30B) from near Tha Meuang hospital directly to the temples.

If you're travelling by motorcycle or bicycle, take the right fork of the highway when you reach Tha Meuang, turn right past the hospital onto a road along the canal and then across the dam (Meuang Dam). From here to Wat Tham Seua and Khao Noi is another four km. Once you cross the dam, turn right down the other side of the river and follow this unpaved road 1.4 km, then turn left toward the pagodas, which can easily be seen in the distance at this point. The network of roads leading to the base of the hill offers several route possibilities – just keep an eye on the pagodas and you'll be able to make the appropriate turns.

By bicycle, you can avoid taking the highway by using back roads along the river. Follow Pak Phraek Rd in Kan south-east and cross the bridge toward Wat Mongkhon Thong, then turn left on the other side and follow the gravel road parallel to the river. Eventually (after about 14 km) you'll see the Meuang Dam up ahead – at this point you should start looking for the hilltop pagodas on your right. This makes a good day trip by bicycle –

the road is flat all the way and avoids the high-speed traffic on the highway. You can break your journey at Ban Tham, a village along the way with its own minor cave wat.

Boat Trips

Rafts Several small-time enterprises offer raft trips up and down the Mae Klong River and its various tributaries. The typical raft is a large affair with a two storey shelter that will carry 15 to 20 people. The average rental cost per raft is 2000B for one day and one night, divided among as many people as you can fit on the boat. Such a trip would include stops at Hat Tha Aw, Wat Tham Mongkon Thong, Khao Pun Cave and the Chung Kai Allied War Cemetery, plus all meals and one night's accommodation on the raft. Alcoholic beverages are usually extra. A day trip only typically costs 300 to 400B per person including lunch. Add more nights and/or go farther afield and the cost can escalate quite a bit. Bargaining can be fruitful as there are said to be over 500 rafts available in the city. A more elaborate trip that includes hiking and elephant-riding components are available for around 1100 to 1400B per person. It is even possible to arrange trips all the way to Sai Yok Falls.

Enquire at any guesthouse, the TAT office, or at the main pier at the end of Lak Meuang Rd about raft trips. Perhaps the best trips are arranged by groups of travellers who get together and plan their own raft excursions.

Long-Tail Boats One way to see the same river sights at a lower cost is to hire a long-tail boat instead of a raft. Long-tails cost around 175B per hour and can take up to six passengers. For 350B a group could take a two hour long-tail trip to the JEATH Museum, Wat Tham Khao Pun, Chung Kai Allied War Cemetery and the Death Railway Bridge. Such craft can be hired from the boat pier off Song Khwae Rd or at the JEATH Museum.

Aerial Tours

Sam's Place can arrange a 30 minute small plane tour over the river, bridge, and so on for 750B per person.

Places to Stay – bottom end

Kanchanaburi has numerous places to stay in every price range but especially in the guesthouse category. The ones along the river can be quite noisy on weekends and holidays due to the floating disco traffic (the worst offender is a multi-raft monstrosity called 'Disco Duck'), so choose your accommodation carefully if an all-night beat keeps you awake. Inevitably, there are even karaoke rafts now! A local commission of guesthouse owners is attempting to enact a ban on the floating discos, so perhaps they will soon disappear.

Samlor drivers get a 25B commission for each farang they bring to guesthouses from the bus or train station (on top of what they charge you for the ride), so don't believe everything they say with regard to 'full', 'dirty' or 'closed' – see for yourself. Most guesthouses will provide free transport from the bus or train station if you call.

On the River At the junction of the Khwae and Khwae Noi rivers, is the *Nita Raft House* (☎ 514521), where older singles/doubles with mosquito net are 40/60B, doubles with fan are 100B, or with private shower 150B. It's basic but quite well run, though you should heed the warning about floating discos on weekends and holidays. The manager speaks English and has good info on local sights and activities.

Spanning the bottom end to middle range is *Sam's Place* (☎ 513971, fax 512023), near the floating restaurants. The owner is a local called Sam who spent 10 years in the USA and speaks excellent English. His raft complex is tastefully designed and reasonably priced for what you get. A room with fan and private bath is 150B for a single or double, 100B with shared bath; all rooms come with mosquito nets. For 250 to 300B you can get a room with air-con, plus an extra sitting room. The raft has a small coffee shop. The only drawback to Sam's is that it's within range of the floating discos.

If you want to stay out near the River Khwae Bridge (and away from the floating discos), the *Bamboo House* (☎ 512532) at 3-5 Soi Vietnam, on the river about a km before the Japanese war memorial off Pak Phraek Rd (continuation of Mae Nam Khwae Rd), costs 100B per room with shared bath, 200B with fan and private bath, 450B with air-con. The owners are very friendly and the setting is peaceful.

Two popular places a little closer to the city centre (but also distant from Disco Duck) are the *River Guest House* (☎ 512491) and the *VN Guest House* (☎ 514082) where small, basic rooms in bamboo raft houses are 50 to 70B, 100 to 130B with bath. Both are in the same vicinity on the river, not far from the train station. They tend to get booked out in the high travel season. A bit farther north on the river is the similar *PS Guest House*, also a good choice at the same rates.

North of the VN, River and PS is the *Jolly Frog Backpacker's* (☎ 514579), a comparatively huge, 45 room 'bamboo motel' with a popular but nothing-special restaurant. Singles/doubles with shared bath are 50/90B; doubles with private bath are 130B. For samlor transport to any guesthouse in this vicinity, you shouldn't pay more than 10B from the train station, or 20 to 25B from the bus station.

A bit farther north-west along the river, at the end of Laos Rd on the river, is *Mr Tee* (☎ (01) 948-2163), another two storey thatched-bamboo place. Rooms upstairs are 100B without bath, while downstairs rooms are 150B with private bath.

The latest additions to the riverside guesthouse scene are just south of Mr Tee. *C & C River Kwai Guest House* (☎ 624547), 265/2 Mae Nam Khwae Rd, Soi Angkrit (Soi England) offers clean rooms on quiet, semi-landscaped grounds for 100 to 150B with fan and private bath. You can also rent tents for 30 to 50B a night. The restaurant serves fish farmed in adjacent ponds. A bit farther south, below the bridge that crosses over to Sutjai Restaurant, *Sam's Paradise* is under construction. When finished it will have 16 rooms in six bungalows built over the water for 100B shared bath, 200B private bath, 350B air-con. As at the original Sam's Place, a terrace restaurant will be attached.

In Town On Pak Phraek Rd, in the oldest section of town just a block off the river, stands the ageing *Kanchanaburi Hotel*. With a little fixing up this classic could be turned into a real gem. For now, quite plain one/two bed rooms cost 60/80B, with shared bath only.

Happy Guest House (☎ 620848) sits next to Punnee Cafe & Bar and Valentine's Bar on Ban Neua Rd. Small but clean rooms cost 100 to 120B single, 150B double with fan or 250 to 350B with air-con; some rooms come with attached bath, while some don't. Happy could be a bit noisy due to street and bar traffic.

Places to Stay – middle

Rick's Lodge (☎ 514831) is along the river between the cheaper VN and PS guesthouses. Tastefully decorated bamboo accommodation with fan and private bath cost 280B on the river and 250B back from the river. Very near Sam's Place is *Supakornchai Guest House*, which is similar in scope to Rick's but not quite as nice. Rooms with fan and bath are 150 to 200B for a large bed, or 300 to 350B for two beds.

One of the better places in this price range is the three storey *VL Guest House*, across from the River Kwai Hotel. A clean, spacious room with fan and hot-water bath is 150B single/double. Larger rooms sleeping four to eight go for 50B per person. A double with air-con and hot water is 300B. The VL has a dining area downstairs, and bicycles (20B a day) and motorcycles (200B and up) are for rent. There's also a generous 2 pm checkout time.

South of the River Kwai Hotel on Saengchuto Rd, on the site of what once held an earlier version of the same hotel, the *River Inn* (☎ 511184) has decent air-con rooms for 450/700B single/double.

The family that owns Sam's Place on the river has recently opened a good-value mid-range place called *Sam's Village* just east of the city centre, next to a large lotus pond in a quiet housing development. Rooms in sturdy modern houses rent for 150B with two beds, ceiling fan and attached shower, 250B with air-con and hot-water shower, or 350B with air-con, hot-water bath and shower, and fridge. Bicycles and motorcycles are available for rent. To reach Sam's Village, head east on U Thong Rd over the train tracks and turn right just before the power station. Continue alongside the lotus pond till you see Sam's ahead.

Other hotels in town include the *Si Muang Kan* (☎ 511609), at 313/1-3 Saengchuto Rd (the north end), with clean singles/doubles with fan and bath for 100 to 170B, 350B with air-con, and the *Thai Seri Hotel* at the southern end of the same road, near the Visutrangsi Rd intersection and the TAT office, with somewhat dilapidated but adequate rooms for 120B and up.

Wang Thong Bungalows (☎ 511046) at 60/3 Saengchuto Rd, and *Boon Yang Bungalows* (☎ 512598) at 139/9 Saengchuto Rd, offer OK rooms in sturdy bungalows for 160 to 240B. In case you haven't figured this out on your own, 'bungalows' (not the beach kind) are the upcountry equivalent of Bangkok's 'short-time' hotels. They're off the road for the same reason their Bangkok counterparts have heavy curtains over the carports: so that it will be difficult to spot licence plate numbers. Still, they function well as tourist hotels, too.

The bungalow-style *Luxury Hotel* (☎ 511168) at 284/1-5 Saengchuto Rd is a couple of blocks north of the River Kwai Hotel, and not as centrally located, but good value. Clean one/two-bed rooms with fan and bath start at 100/150B, 200 to 300B with air-con. Similarly, *Si Rung Rung Bungalows* (☎ 511087) has fan rooms with bath for 150B and air-con for 250B. *Don Rung* (☎ 513755), up the street toward the bridge, has more of the same in buildings on both sides of the road.

Places to Stay – top end

Kanchanaburi's original 1st class hotel, the *River Kwai Hotel* (☎ 511184/269) at 284/3-16 Saengchuto Rd offers semi-deluxe rooms with air-con, hot water, telephone and TV for 1400B and up. Facilities include a coffee shop, disco and swimming pool. Next door is the huge River Paradise massage parlour, bearing a sign on the door which reads: 'No women allowed' (working masseuses are exempted of course).

Farther north along Saengchuto Rd, past the train station, is the new four storey *Mittaphan Hotel* (☎ 514498; (2) 291-9953 in Bangkok). Standard rooms with all the amenities cost 700 to 2000B. A large massage parlour and snooker club are next door.

The luxurious *Felix Kanchanaburi Swissotel River Kwai* (☎ 515061, fax 515095; (2) 255-3410, fax 255-5769 in Bangkok) sits on the west bank of the river, about two km north of the one-lane bridge. The very nicely landscaped grounds include two swimming pools. Spacious rooms with IDD phones, cable TV, minibar and personal safe cost 2300 to 3500B.

River Resorts The *Kasem Island Resort* (☎ 513359; (2) 255-3604 in Bangkok) sits on an island in the middle of the Mae Klong River just a couple of hundred metres from Tha Chukkadon. The tastefully designed thatched cottages and house rafts are cool, clean and quiet and range in price from 700 to 2000B. There are facilities for swimming, fishing and rafting as well as an outdoor bar and restaurant. The resort has an office near Tha Chukkadon where you can arrange for a free shuttle boat out to the island. But don't get caught out – the shuttle service stops at 10 pm.

In the vicinity of the bridge are several river resorts of varying quality, most featuring standard wooden bungalows in the 800B range. Just above the bridge, two km before the turn-off for Highway 323, is the *Prasopsuk Garden Resort* (☎ 513215) with air-con town-house doubles for 800B, air-con bungalows with two bedrooms at 1200B, and large bungalows for 10 people at 2400B per night. *River Kwai Lodge* (☎ 513657; (2) 251-4377 in Bangkok), has a large room for two at 600B with fan and bath or 800B with air-con. Just beyond it is *River Kwai Honeywell Resort* (☎ 515413), where bungalows with private bath on the river bank cost 800B.

On the river, opposite Wat Tham Mongkon Thong to the south, the *Boon Sri River Kwai Resort* (☎ (01) 939-4185) offers more of the same for 400 to 800B a night.

Places to Eat

The greatest proliferation of inexpensive restaurants in
Kanchanaburi is along the northern end of Saengchuto
Rd near the River Kwai Hotel. South from here, to where
U Thong Rd crosses Saengchuto Rd, are many good
Chinese, Thai and Isaan-style restaurants. As elsewhere
in Thailand, the best are generally the most crowded.

For years, one of the most popular has been the *Isaan*,
on Saengchuto Rd between Hiran Prasat and Kratai
Thong Rds. The Isaan still serves great kài yâang (whole
spicy grilled chicken), khâo niãw (sticky rice), sôm-tam
(spicy green papaya salad), as well as other Thai and
local specialities and inexpensive, ice-cold beer. The kài
yâang is grilled right out front and served with two
sauces – the usual sweet and sour (náam jîm kài) and a
roast red pepper sauce (náam phrík phão).

Good, inexpensive food can be found in the markets
along Prasit Rd and between U Thong and Lak Meuang
Rds east of Saengchuto Rd. In the evenings, a sizeable
night market convenes along Saengchuto Rd near the
Lak Meuang Rd intersection.

The *Sabai-jit* restaurant, north of the River Kwai Hotel
on Saengchuto Rd, has an English menu. Beer and
Maekhong whisky are competitively priced and the
food is consistently good. Other Thai and Chinese dishes
are served apart from those listed on the English menu.
If you see someone eating something not listed, point.

Punnee Cafe & Bar (☎ 513503) on Ban Neua Rd serves
Thai and European food for expat tastes and advertises
the coldest beer in town. Lots of info on Kanchanaburi
is available here; there are also used paperback books for
sale or trade.

On the river several large floating restaurants have
fine atmosphere, but don't expect Western food or large
portions. Recommended are the *Thongnatee* and the *Mae
Nam*. Across from the floating restaurants, along the
road, are several restaurants that are just as good but less
expensive; the best on this row is *Jukkru* (no English sign
– look for blue tables and chairs). A little out of the way,
one of the better riverside restaurants in town is *Sutjai*,
a garden-style place on the west bank of the river next
to the one-lane bridge.

There are also food vendors on both sides of Song
Khwae Rd along the river near the new waterfront park
where you can buy inexpensive takeaways and picnic
on mats along the riverbank. This is a festive and pros-
perous town and people seem to eat out a lot.

Most of the pastry and bread business in Kan is done
by *Srifa Bakery*, on the north side of the bus terminal, and

Aree Bakery, on Pak Phraek Rd. Srifa has everything from French-style pastries to Singapore-style curry puffs, while the less fancy Aree has coffee, tea, breakfast, ice cream and sandwiches, as well as great chicken curry puffs and a very tasty young coconut pie.

Getting There & Away

Bus Buses leave Bangkok daily for Kanchanaburi from the Southern bus terminal on Charan Sanitwong Rd, Thonburi, every 20 minutes (first at 5 am, last at 10 pm). The trip is about three hours and costs 34B. Buses to Bangkok leave Kanchanaburi between the same hours.

Air-con buses leave Bangkok's Southern air-con terminal every 15 minutes from 5.30 am to 10 pm for 62B. These same buses depart Kanchanaburi for Bangkok from opposite the police station on Saengchuto Rd, not from the bus station. Air-con buses only take about two hours to reach Bangkok. The first bus out is at 5 am; the last one to Bangkok leaves at 7 pm.

There are frequent buses throughout the day from nearby Nakhon Pathom. Bus No 81 leaves from the east side of the Phra Pathom Chedi, costs 20B, and takes about 1½ hours. For travellers heading south, Nakhon Pathom makes a good connecting point – this way you avoid having to go back to Bangkok. Other frequent direct bus services are available to/from Ratchaburi (No 461, 26B, 2½ hours) and Suphanburi (No 411, 25B, 2½ to three hours).

Train Ordinary trains leave Bangkok Noi (Thonburi) station at 7.50 am and 1.45 pm, arriving at 10.55 am and 4.26 pm. Only 3rd-class seats are available and the fare is 25B. Trains return to Bangkok from Kanchanaburi at 7.31 am and 3.21 pm, arriving at 10.35 am and 6.10 pm. Ordinary train tickets to Kanchanaburi can be booked on the day of departure only. There are no trains – ordinary or otherwise – between Bangkok's Hualamphong station and Kanchanaburi.

You can also take the train from the Kanchanaburi station out to the River Khwae Bridge – a three minute ride for 2B. There are two trains per day at 6.10 am (No 353) and 10.55 am (No 171).

The same trains go on to the end of the train line at Nam Tok, which is near Sai Yok Falls. You can catch the train in Kanchanaburi at 6.10 am or 10.55 am or at the River Khwae Bridge at 6.16 or 11 am; the fare is the same, 17B. Nam Tok is eight km from Khao Pang Falls and 18 km from Hellfire Pass and the River Khwae Village. A third train (No 197) makes the trip to Nam Tok daily, leaving Kanchanaburi at 4.26 pm. The trip to Nam Tok takes about two hours. Coming back from Nam Tok, there are trains at 5.25 am, 1.15 and 3.10 pm. The early morning trains between Kanchanaburi and Nam Tok (6.10 am) do not run on weekends and holidays.

Tourist Train The State Railway of Thailand (SRT) has a special tourist train from Hualamphong station on weekends and holidays which departs Bangkok at around 6.30 am and returns at 7.30 pm. The return fare is 250B for adults, 120B for children. It includes an hour-long stop in Nakhon Pathom to see the Phra Pathom Chedi, an hour at the River Khwae Bridge, a minibus to Prasat Meuang Singh Historical Park for a short tour, a walk along an elevated 'Death Railway' bridge (no longer in use), a three hour stop at the river for lunch and a bat-cave visit before returning to Bangkok with a one hour stopover at the Allied War Cemetery. Also on weekends and holidays there's a direct train to Nam Tok, no stops, for 100B each way. These tickets should be booked in advance, although it's worth trying on the day even if you're told it's full. The SRT changes the tour itinerary and price from time to time.

Share Taxi & Minivan You can also take a share taxi from Saengchuto Rd to Bangkok for 50B per person. Taxis leave throughout the day whenever five passengers accumulate at the taxi stand. These taxis will make drops at Khao San Rd or in the Pahurat district. Kanchanaburi guesthouses also arrange daily minivans to Bangkok for 80B per person. Passengers are dropped at Khao San Rd.

Getting Around

Prices are very reasonable in Kanchanaburi, especially for food and accommodation. If you prefer to be your own tour guide don't even consider letting a samlor driver show you around, they want big money. The town is not very big, so getting around on foot or bicycle is easy. A samlor to anywhere in Kanchanaburi should be 10 to 15B for one person. Songthaews run up and down Saengchuto Rd for 3B per passenger.

Bicycles and motorcycles can be rented at some guesthouses, at the Suzuki dealer near the bus station, at the Punnee Cafe & Bar and at a motorcycle repair shop near Sam's Place. Expect to pay about 200B per day for a motorbike (more for a dirt bike), 30 to 40B a day for bicycles. Punnee Cafe & Bar also rents mountain bikes for 80B per 24 hours.

Glossary

ao – bay or gulf

baht – units of gold/Thai currency
bòt – central chapel or sanctuary in temple

chedi – stupa

farang – foreigner of European descent

hang yao – long-tailed boat
hat – beach

isãan – general term for North-Eastern Thailand, from the Sanskrit name for the medieval kingdom Isana, which encompassed parts of Cambodia and North-Eastern Thailand.

jataka – life stories of the Buddha

khlong – canal

lákhon – classical Thai dance-drama
làk meuang – city pillar/phallus

muay thai – Thai boxing

prang – Khmer-style tower
prasada – blessed food offerings

soi – lane, small street
songthaew – small pickup truck literally meaning 'two rows' for the wooden benches in the back. Common form of public transport outside Bangkok.

thanon – road
trok – alleyway
tuk-tuk – motorised pedicab

wát – temple, monastery
wihãan – counterpart to bòt in Thai temple which contains Buddha images

Index

Boxed Asides
Bangkok Traffic 136
Bangkok Primacy 15
Eastern & Oriental
    Express 117
Emerald Buddha 154
Muay Thai 192

Prostitution 274
Rama V Cult 148
Scams 99
The Original Siamese
    Twins 182
Tuk-Tuk Wars 139

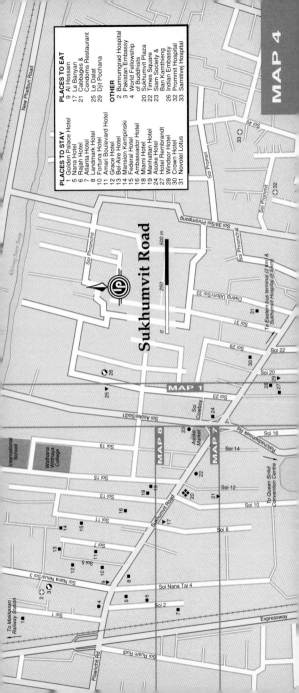

MAP 4

PLACES TO STAY
1 Golden Palace Hotel
5 Nana Hotel
6 Rajah Hotel
7 Atlanta Hotel
8 Landmark Hotel
10 Fortuna Hotel
11 Amari Boulevard Hotel
12 Grace Hotel
13 Bel-Aire Hotel
14 Mansion Kempinski
15 Federal Hotel
16 Ambassador Hotel
18 Miami Hotel
19 Manhattan Hotel
24 Asoke Hotel
27 Hotel Rembrandt
28 Windsor Hotel
30 Promri Hotel
31 Novotel Lotus

PLACES TO EAT
9 Al Hossain
17 Le Banyan
21 Cabbages &
   Condoms Restaurant
25 Le Dalat
29 Djit Pochana

OTHER
2 Bumungrad Hospital
3 Pakistan Embassy
4 World Fellowship
   of Buddhists
20 Sukhumvit Plaza
22 Times Square
23 Siam Society &
   Ban Kamthieng
26 Indian Embassy
32 Promri Hospital
33 Samitivej Hospital

Sukhumvit Road

500 m

250

0

New Phetburi Road

Khlong Saen Saep

Soi Phromchit

Soi Phromri

Soi 49

Soi 39/Soi Phrompong

Soi Phrompong

Soi Phromchai

Soi Promri

Soi 32

Daeng Udom/Soi 33

Soi 31

Soi 29

Soi 22

Soi 20

MAP 1

Soi 23

Soi Cowboy

Soi Asoke/Soi21

Ratchadaphisek Rd

Soi 16

Asoke Market

MAP 8

Soi 19

Soi 14

Soi 15

Soi 12

Soi 10

Soi 11

Soi 8

Soi 7

Sukhumvit Road

MAP 7

To Queen Sirikit
Convention Centre

International
School

Wattana
Witthaya College

Soi 5

Soi 3

Soi Nana Nua/Soi 3

Soi Nana Tai 4

Soi 2

Soi 1

Pleenchit Rd

Soi Ruam Rudi

Expressway

To Makkasan
Railway Station

To Eastern bus terminal (2 km) &
Sukhumvit Hospital (2.5 km)

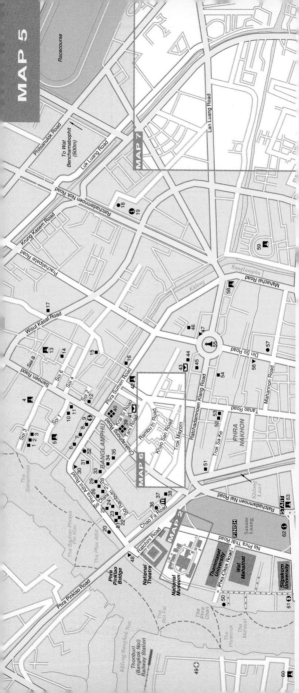

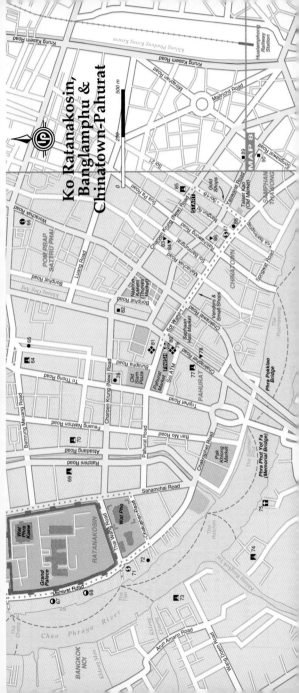

Ko Ratanakosin, Banglamphu & Chinatown-Pahurat

MAP 3

0   250   500 m

Krung Kasem Road

Khlong Phadung Krung Kasem

Krung Kasem Road

Hualamphong Railway Station

Maitrichit Road

Mittaphan Road

Soi 21

85

START

Gold Shops

Sua Pa Road

Charoen Krung (New) Road

Yaowarat Road

Soi 16

Luang Road

Boriphat Road

POM PRAP SATTRU PHAI

66

Worachak Road

Khlong Ong Ang

Maitrichit Road

89

Songsawat Road

SAMPHAN THAWONG

Talaat Kao (Old Market)

Yaowarat Road

90

87

Soi Itsaranuphap

Ratchawong Road

43

85

Plaeng Nam Road

CHINATOWN

Maha Chak Road

Soi Bamrung Rat

Charoen Krung (New) Road

83

84

Songwat Road

Boriphat Road

Nakhon Kasem (Thieves' Market)

82

Burapha Road

81

Soi Wanit 1

Chakkrawat Road

Vendors & Small Shops

Saphaan Han Market

Tha Ratchawong

80

78

Phra Pokklao Bridge

Old Siam Plaza

76

Pahurat Market

Soi ATM

FINISH

77

PAHURAT

Chakraphet Road

Charoen Krung (New) Road

65

64

Tri Thong Road

Feuang Nakhon Road

Triphet Road

Ban Mo Road

Pak Khlong Market

Chakraphet Road

Bamrung Meuang Road

70

Atsadang Road

Ratchini Road

Pahurat Road

Sanamchai Road

Phra Phut Yot Fa (Memorial Bridge)

The Saphan Phut

75

69

Wat Phra Kaew

Grand Palace

RATANAKOSIN

Wat Pho

Thai Wang Road

Chetuphon Road

72

71

67

68

Maharat Road

Tha Tien

Tha Ratchini

Khlong Bangkok Yai

74

73

Ann Amarin Road

Wang Doem Road

Chao Phraya River

BANGKOK NOI

Khlong Mon

MAP 5

PLACES TO STAY
1 Home & Garden Guest House
2 Clean & Calm Guest House
3 River House
6 PS Guest House
7 Gipsy Guest House
8 Banglamphu Square Guest House
10 Villa Guest House
11 Truly Yours Guest House
12 New World House Apartment
   & Guest House
14 AP Guest House
15 Vimol Guest House
16 Canalside Guest House
17 Trang Hotel
21 Beer & Peachy Guesthouses
22 Apple Guest House
23 Rose Garden Guest House
24 Mango Guest House

25 New Merry V Guest House
26 New Siam Guest House
27 Green Guest House
28 Merry V Guest House
29 My House
31 Apple II Guest House
32 KC Guest House
33 Super Siam Guest House
34 Chusri Guest House
35 Sawasdee House/Terrace Guest
   House
36 Chai's House
38 Charlie's House
44 Nat II Guest House
45 Sweety Guest House
46 Prasuri Guest House
51 Royal Hotel
52 P Guest House
53 Palace Hotel
54 Hotel 90
82 Burapha Hotel

89 White Orchid
90 Chinatown Hotel

PLACES TO EAT
30 Roti Mataba
47 Vijit Restaurant
48 Wang Ngar Restaurant
56 Arawy Restaurant
78 Royal India Restaurant
83 Lie Kee Restaurant
84 Laem Thong
86 Yau Wah Yuen

OTHER
4 Wat Samphraya
5 Wat Sangwet
9 Siam Commercial Bank
13 Wat Mai Amararot
18 Ratchadamnoen Boxing Stadium
19 TAT Office

Map 5 key continues next page

Map 5 key continued (from previous page)

OTHER		58	Wat Rajanadda (Ratchanatda	73	Wat Arun
20	UNICEF	59	Wat Saket	74	Wat Kalayanimit
37	National Gallery	60	Wat Rakhang	75	Santa Cruz Church
39	Banglamphu Department Store	61	Khositaram Siam City Bank	76	Chalermkrung Royal Theatre
40	New World Shopping Centre	62	TAT Office	77	Chinese Temple
		63	Lak Meuang (City Pillar)	79	ATM Department Store
41	Post Office	64	Wat Suthat & Giant Swing	80	Sikh Temple
42	Wat Bovornives (Bowonniwet)	65	Monk's Bowl Village	81	Central Department Store
43	Post Office	66	TAT Office		
49	Siriraj Hospital (Department of Forensic Medicine)	67	No 8 Bus Stop	85	Wat Mangkon Kamalawat
		68	No 12 Bus Stop	87	Bangkok Bank
		69	Wat Ratchapradit	88	Tang To Kang Gold Shop
50	Amulet Market	70	Wat Ratcha-bophit		
55	Democracy Monument	71	Bangkok Bank		
57	City Hall	72	Market		

MICHAEL CLARK

Flower vendor.

MAP 6

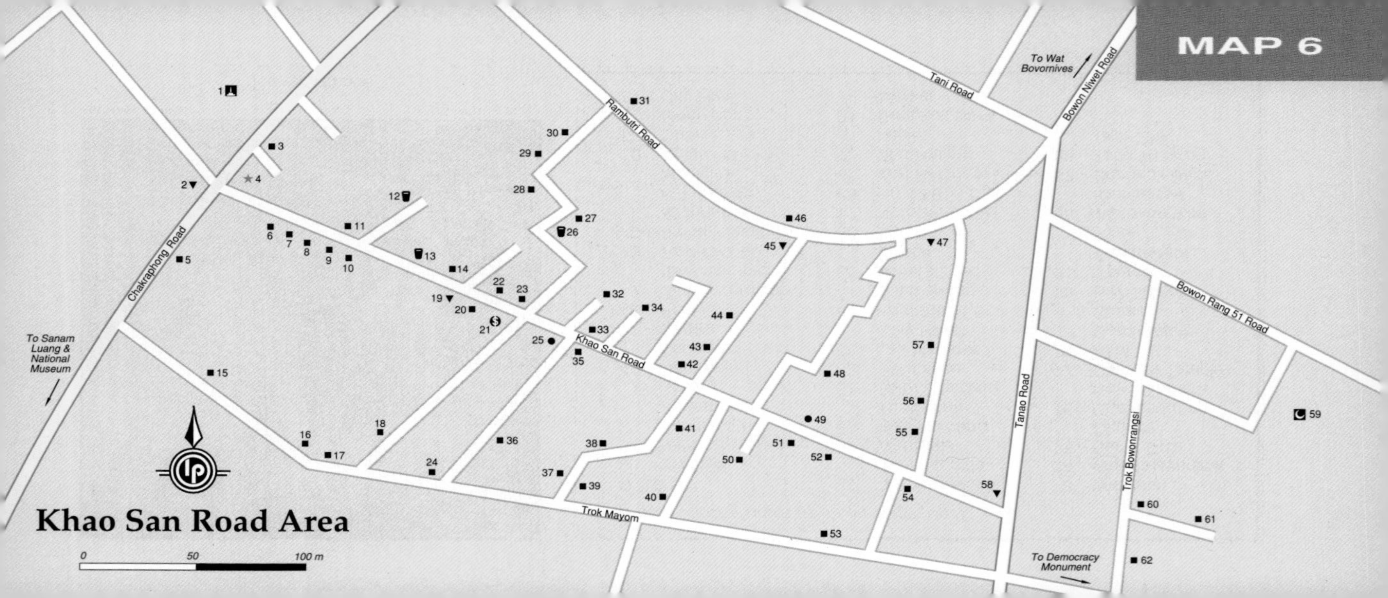
Khao San Road Area
0
50
100 m
To Sanam Luang & National Museum
To Wat Bovornives
To Democracy Monument
Chakraphong Road
Rambutri Road
Tani Road
Bowon Niwet Road
Khao San Road
Trok Mayom
Tanao Road
Bowon Rang 51 Road
Trok Bowonrangsi
1
2
3
4
5
6
7
8
9
10
11
12
13
14
15
16
17
18
19
20
21
22
23
24
25
26
27
28
29
30
31
32
33
34
35
36
37
38
39
40
41
42
43
44
45
46
47
48
49
50
51
52
53
54
55
56
57
58
59
60
61
62

MAP 6

PLACES TO STAY

3 Siam Guest House
5 Ploy Guest House
6 Thai Guest House
7 NS Guest House
8 Prakorp's House & Restaurant
9 Hello Guest House
10 Chart Guest House
11 Sitdhi Guest House
14 Mam's Guest House
15 J & Joe Guest House
16 Ranee Guest House
17 New Joe Guest House
18 Kaosarn Privacy Guest House
20 PB Guest House
22 Lek Guest House
23 Buddy Guest House
24 Thai Massage Guest House
27 Doll Guest House & Others
28 Suneeporn Guest House
29 AT, Leed & Jim's Guesthouses
30 Green House
31 Viengtai Hotel
32 Khaosan Palace Hotel
33 Grand Guest House
34 New Nith Jaroen Hotel
35 Dior Guest House
36 Bonny & Top Guesthouses
37 Marco Polo (160 Guest House)
38 Good Luck Guest House
39 Tong Guest House
40 Neo Guest House
41 VIP Guest House
42 Nat Guest House
43 Best Guest House, Best Aladdin Guest House & Restaurant
44 Marco Polo Hostel
46 Orchid House
48 New Royal Guest House
50 Nana Plaza Inn
51 Siri Guest House
52 CH Guest House
53 7-Holder Guest House
54 Chada Guest House
55 Harn Guest House
56 Nisa Guest House
57 VS Guest House
60 Central Guest House
61 PC Guest House
62 Srinthip Guest House

PLACES TO EAT

2 Gaylord Indian Restaurant
13 Hello Pub
19 Royal India Restaurant
45 Chabad House
47 Pizza Hut
58 Arawy Det

OTHER

1 Wat Chana Songkhram
4 Chana Songkhram Police Station
12 Paradise, No-Name & Hole in the Wall
21 Krung Thai Bank
25 Shops
26 Artsy Fartsy Bar & Art Gallery
49 Central Minimart
59 Mosque

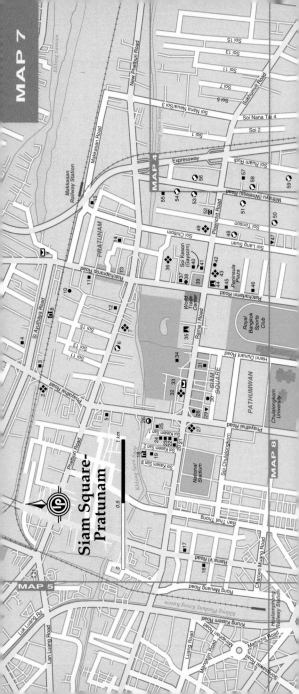

MAP 7

PLACES TO STAY
3 Florida Hotel
4 Siam City Hotel
5 Asia Hotel
11 Indra Regent Hotel
12 Amari Watergate Hotel
14 Boram House
15 Mercure Hotel Bangkok
16 Sol Twin Tower Hotel
17 Tong Poon Hotel
19 MP Villa
20 Krit Thai Mansion
21 Pranee Building & Muangphol Mansion
22 Reno Hotel
23 White Lodge & Wendy House
24 Star Hotel & Bed Breakfast Inn
25 A-One Inn
31 Novotel Bangkok
34 Siam Intercontinental Hotel
37 Felix Arnoma Swissotel
40 Siam Orchid Inn
41 Le Meridien President Hotel
45 Grand Hyatt Erawan
46 Regent Bangkok
55 Hilton International Bangkok
57 Imperial Hotel

PLACES TO EAT
29 Hard Rock Cafe
47 Whole Earth Restaurant

OTHER
1 Bangkok Adventist Hospital
2 Payathai Plaza
6 Indonesian Embassy
7 Phanthip Plaza
8 Wang Suan Phakkard
9 Post Office
10 Baiyoke Towe (Sky Lounge)
13 Pratunam Market
18 Jim Thompson's House
26 Tha Ratchathewi (Canal Taxis)
27 Mahboonkrong Shopping Centre
28 Scala Cinema
30 British Council
32 Siam Center
33 Post Office
35 Wat Patum
36 Robinson Department Store
38 Narayana Phand
39 Gaysom Plaza
42 Maneeya Building
43 Sogo Department Store
44 Erawan Shrine (Saan Phra Phrom)
48 Israeli Embassy
49 Central Department Store
50 Netherlands Embassy
51 Spanish Embassy
52 TOT Office
53 UK Embassy
54 Norwegian Embassy
56 Swiss Embassy
58 Vietnamese Embassy
59 New Zealand Embassy

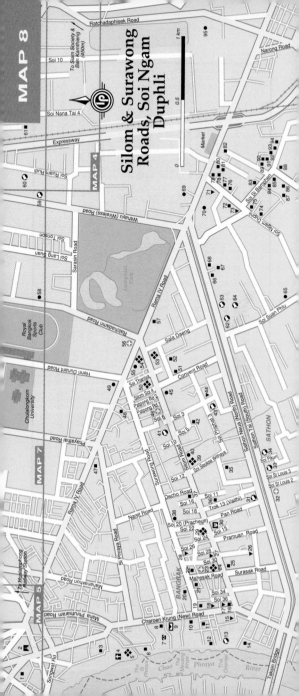

MAP 8

Silom & Surawong
Roads, Soi Ngam
Duphli

Ratchadaphisek Road

Soi 10

To Siam Society &
Ban Kamthieng (450m)

Soi Nana Tai 4

Expressway

Narong Road

1 km

0.5

0

95

Market

92

80
90
81
79
78
77
76
71
72
73
74
70
69

91 93 94
89
82
83
88
85 86 87
84
75

Soi Si Bamphen

Soi Ngam Duphli

68
67
66
65
64
63
62

57

58

59

60

61

Royal
Bangkok
Sports
Club

Henri Dunant Road

Sarasin Road

Soi Lang Suan

Soi Tonson

Witthayu (Wireless) Road

Rama IV Road

Ratchadamri Road

Soi Ruam Rudi

Lumphini
Park

Sala Daeng

Soi Suan Phlu

56
53
55
54
52
51
50
49
48
47
46
45
44
43
42
41
40
39

Convent Road

Soi Thaniya

Silom Soi 1
Patpong Rd 2
Patpong Rd

Soi 6

Soi 3

Soi 5

Soi 10

Silom Road

Surawong Road

Soi Phiphat 2

Soi Phiphat

Soi Seuksa Witthaya

Soi 12

Sathon Neua (North) Road

Sathon Tai (South) Road

SATHON

34

Soi Pikun

Soi St Louis 3

Soi St Louis 2

35

38
37
36
33
32
31
30
29
28
27
26
25
24
23
22
21
20
19
18
17
16
15
14
13
12
11
10
9
8
7
6
5
4
3
2
1

Decho Road

Soi 16

Soi 18

Soi 20 (Pracheun)

Soi 22

Soi 24

Soi 26

Soi 28

Soi 30

Naret Road

Soi 11

Trok 13 (Vaithi)

Pan Road

Soi 15

Pramuan Road

Surasak Road

Mahesak Road

Soi 34

Soi 36

Charoen Krung (New) Road

Si Phraya Road

Mahanakhon Road

Maha Phruttharam Road

To Hualamphong
Railway Station

Chulalongkorn
University

Phayathai Road

Rama IV Road

MAP 4

MAP 7

MAP 5

Soi Ruam Rudi

BANGRAK

Chao
Phraya
The Mae Nam Khrong

The
Si Phraya

Tha Oriental

Taksin Bridge

MAP 8

PLACES TO STAY

1 New Empire Hotel
3 River View Guest House
6 Royal Orchid Sheraton
8 Woodlands In & Cholas
10 Newrotel
11 Swan Hotel
12 Oriental Hotel
14 Shangri-La Hotel
16 Victory Hotel
19 New Trocadero
20 Manohra Hotel
21 New Fuji Hotel
22 New Peninsula
25 Holiday Inn Crowne Plaza
35 Niagara Hotel
36 Madras Lodge & Cafe
37 Narai Hotel & Rabianthong
  Restaurant

42 Clarion Trinity
47 Mandarin Hotel
48 Montien Hotel
51 Swiss Lodge
52 Bangkok Christian
  Guest House
57 Dusit Thani Hotel
61 Atlanta Hotel
66 YMCA Collin International
  House
67 Beaufort Sukhothai Hotel
68 YWCA
72 Malaysia Hotel
74 Honey Guest House
75 Tungmahamek Privacy Hotel
76 Anna Guest House
77 Tokyo Guest House
78 Quality Hotel Lumphini
79 ETC Guest House
80 Four Brothers Best House
81 Charlie House

82 Lumphini Tower
83 Home Sweet Home
  Guest House
84 Boston Inn
85 Kenny Guest House
86 Freddy 3 Guest House
87 TTO Guest House
88 Turkh Guest House
89 Lee 4 Guest House
90 Madam Guest House
91 Lee 3 Guest House
92 Sala Thai Daily Mansion
93 Lee 1 Guest House
94 Freddy 2 Guest House

PLACES TO EAT

15 Muslim Restaurant
17 Simla Cafe
18 Himali Cha-Chaè
26 Ban Chiang Restaurant

Map 8 key continues next page

Map 8 key continued (from previous page)

27 Chaai Karr Thai Cusine
28 Maria Bakery & Restaurant
44 Bussaracum
71 Mai Mawn
73 Hua Hin Restaurant

OTHER
2   Wat Traimit
4   Holy Rosary Church
5   River City Shopping
    Complex
7   CAT Office
9   GPO
13 Danish Embassy
23 Mahesak Hospital
24 Central Department Store
29 Silom Village Trade Centre

30 Maha Uma Devi Temple
31 Myanmar Embassy
32 St Louis Hospital
33 Lao Embassy
34 Singaporean Embassy
38 Neilson Hays Library
39 Silom Plaza
40 THAI Office
41 Canadian Embassy
43 Belgian Embassy
45 CP Tower
46 Bangkok Christian
    Hospital
49 Queen Saovabha Memorial
    Institute (Snake Farm)
50 Thaniya Plaza
53 Silom Complex

54 Silom Center/Robinson
    Department Store
55 Cham Issara Tower
56 Chulalongkorn Hospital
58 AUA Language Center
59 US Embassy
60 New Zealand Embassy
62 Australian Embassy
63 Alliance Française &
    French Embassy
64 Malaysian Embassy
65 Immigration Office
69 Lumphini Boxing Stadium
70 Goethe Institute
95 Queen Sirikit Convention
    Centre

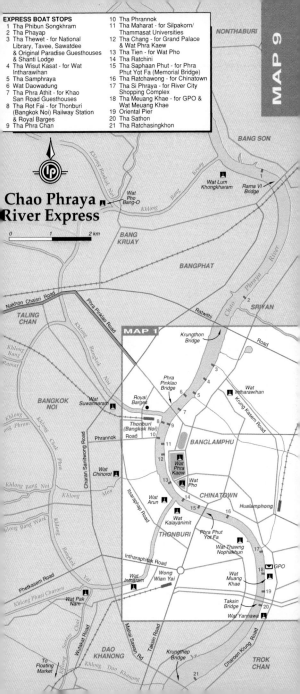

MAP 9

EXPRESS BOAT STOPS

1 Tha Phibun Songkhram
2 Tha Phayap
3 Tha Thewet - for National Library, Tavee, Sawatdee & Original Paradise Guesthouses & Shanti Lodge
4 Tha Wisut Kasat - for Wat Intharawihan
5 Tha Samphraya
6 Wat Daowadung
7 Tha Phra Athit - for Khao San Road Guesthouses
8 Tha Rot Fai - for Thonburi (Bangkok Noi) Railway Station & Royal Barges
9 Tha Phra Chan
10 Tha Phrannok
11 Tha Maharat - for Silpakorn/ Thammasat Universities
12 Tha Chang - for Grand Palace & Wat Phra Kaew
13 Tha Tien - for Wat Pho
14 Tha Ratchini
15 Tha Saphaan Phut - for Phra Phut Yot Fa (Memorial Bridge)
16 Tha Ratchawong - for Chinatown
17 Tha Si Phraya - for River City Shopping Complex
18 Tha Meuang Khae - for GPO & Wat Meuang Khae
19 Oriental Pier
20 Tha Sathon
21 Tha Ratchasingkhon

Chao Phraya River Express

NONTHABURI

BANG SON

Wat Lum Khongkharam

Rama VI Bridge

Wat Pho Bang-O

BANG KRUAY

BANGPHAT

SRIYAN

TALING CHAN

Nakhon Chaisri Road

Phra Pinklao Road

Khlong Bang Ramat

Khlong Bangkok Noi

BANGKOK NOI

Wat Suwannaram

Ratwithi

MAP 1

Krungthon Bridge

Phra Pinklao Bridge

Royal Barges

Wat Intharawihan

Thonburi (Bangkok Noi) Road

Phrannok Road

BANGLAMPHU

Charan Sanithwong Road

Wat Chinorot

Wat Phra Kaew

Wat Pho

CHINATOWN

Hualamphong

Itsaraphap Road

Wat Arun

Wat Kalayanimit

Phra Phut Yot Fa

THONBURI

Intharaphitak Road

Wong Wian Yai

Wat Intharam

Wat Thawng Nophakhun

GPO

Wat Muang Khae

Phetkasem Road

Khlong Phasi Charoen

Taksin Bridge

Wat Yannawa

Wat Pak Nam

Sathon Road

Witthkat Road

Maha Setawat Rd

Taksin Road

DAO KHANONG

Krungthep Bridge

Charoen Krung Road

TROK CHAN

To Floating Market

Kung Kasem Road

Khlong Dao Khanong

0   1   2 km

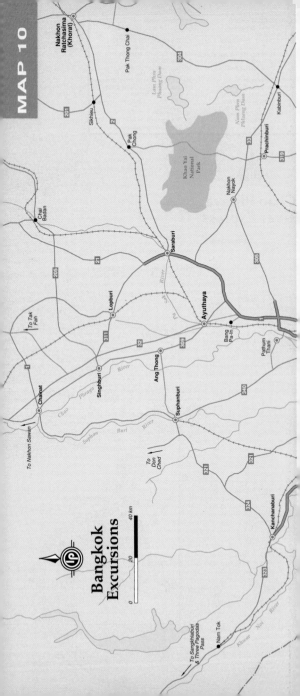

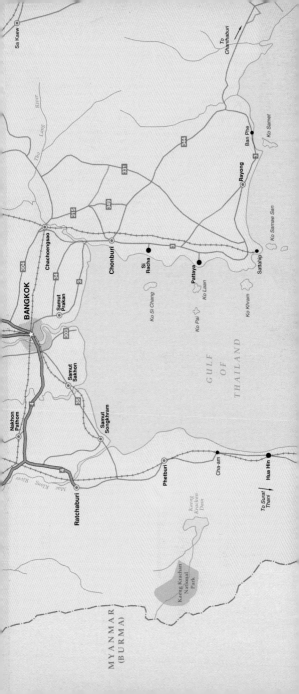

MAP 11

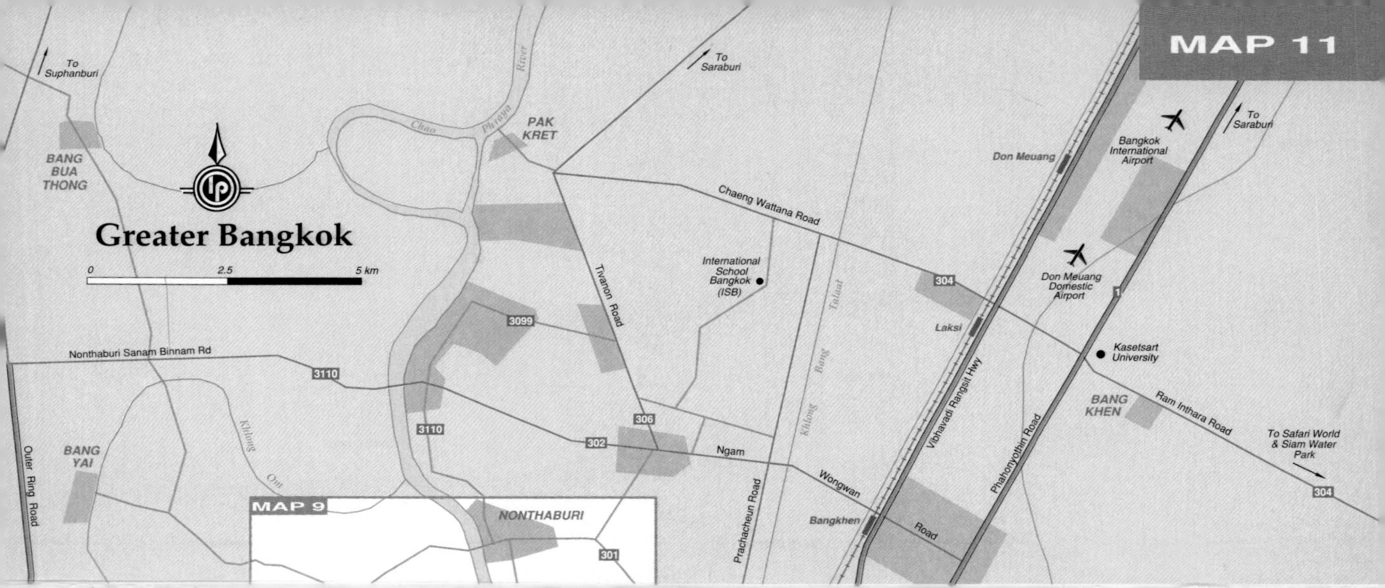

Greater Bangkok

To Suphanburi

To Saraburi

BANG BUA THONG

Chao Phraya River

PAK KRET

Tivanon Road

Chaeng Wattana Road

International School Bangkok (ISB)

To Saraburi

Nonthaburi Sanaeb Biinam Rd

BANG YAI

Outer Ring Road

Khlong Chit

3110

3110

3009

S02

305

Ngam

NONTHABURI

301

MAP 9

0   2.5   5 km

Prachacheun Road

Bangkhen

Wongwan

Khlong Bang Talaat

Vibhavadi Rangsit Hwy

304

Laksi

Don Meuiang

Bangkok International Airport

Don Meuiang Domestic Airport

To Saraburi

Phahonyothin Road

Kasetsart University

BANG KHEN

Ram Intara Road

To Safari World & Siam Water Park

304

Road